MW01620358

Seeing and Not Believing

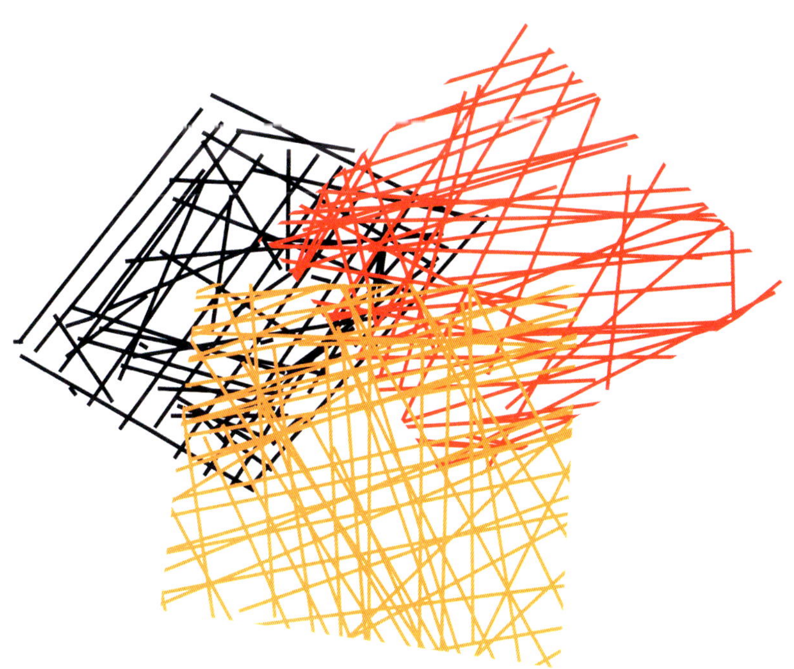

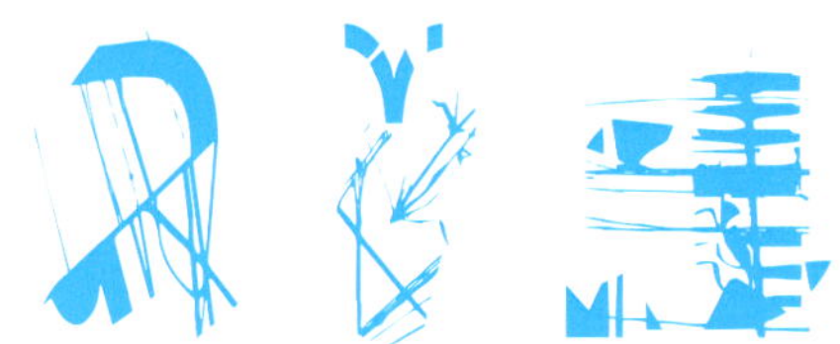

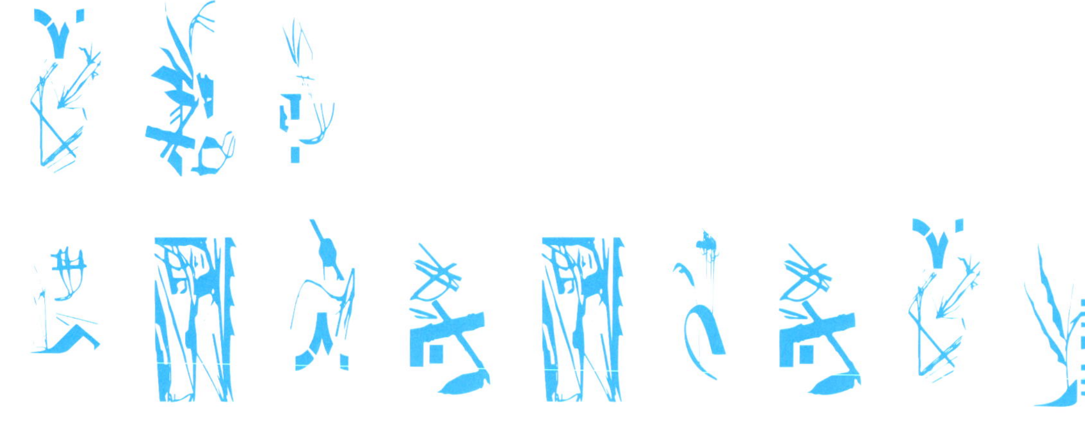

Seeing and Not Believing

The Photography of Allan Chasanoff

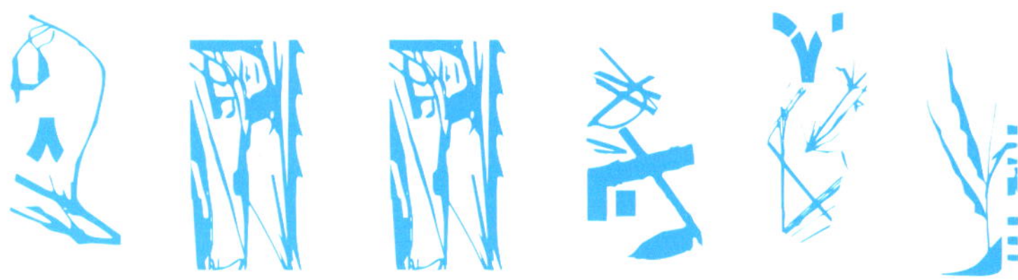

Mónika Sziládi

With a preface
by Richard Ovenden

Yale University Art Gallery
New Haven

Distributed by
Yale University Press
New Haven and London

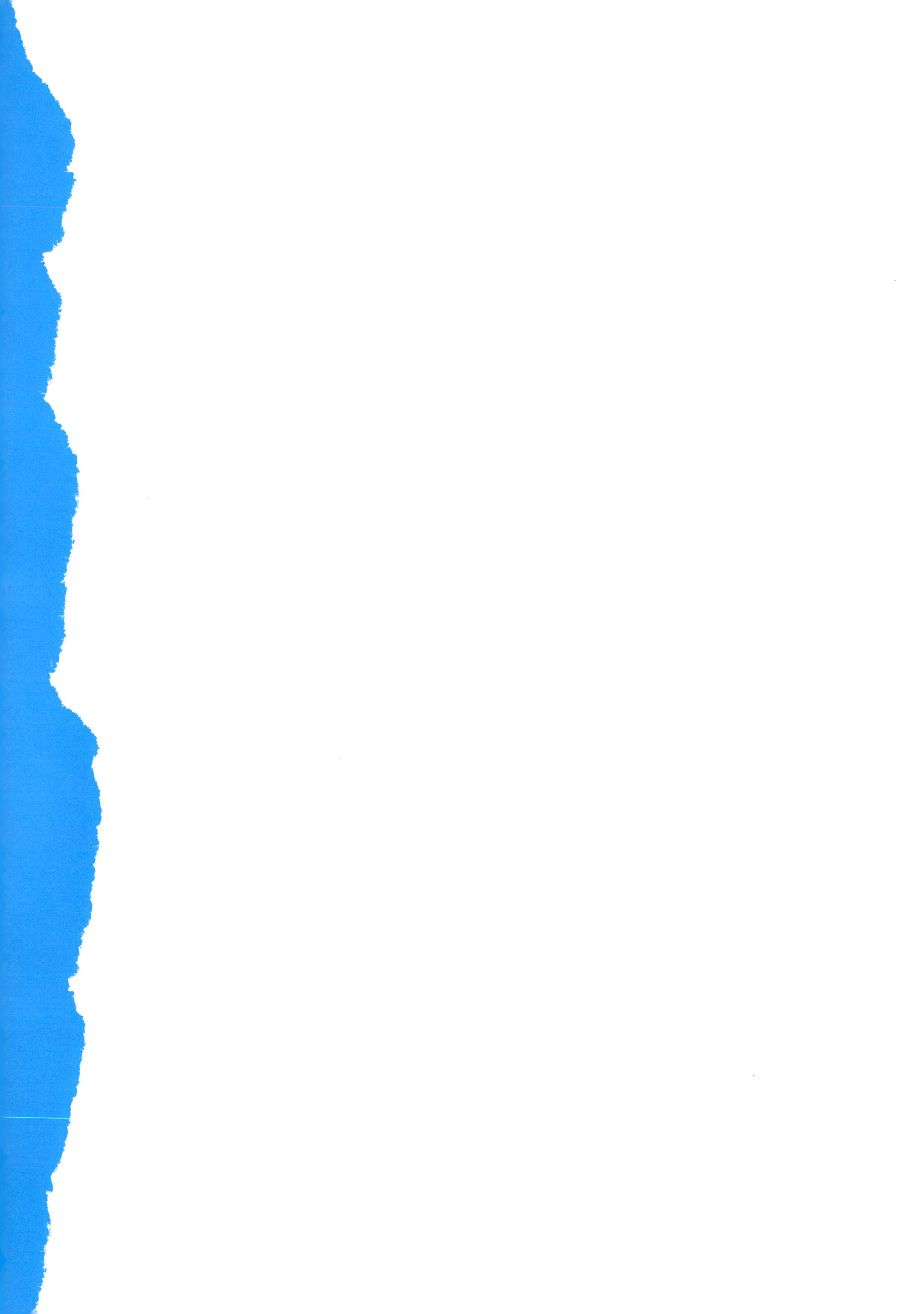

Seeing is complicated, and don't trust it. . . . And then using it as a metaphor—don't trust anything . . . which is what I want to put inside the museum, in order for you to doubt the museum . . . a little bit.

— Allan Chasanoff

I hope that the visual dislocations in my work cause the viewer to blink in the first instance—causing a rupture prior to immediate interpretation and imagination—surprising anticipation. I am reaching for an ahistorical, aprivileged, basic visceral doubt.

— Allan Chasanoff

Contents

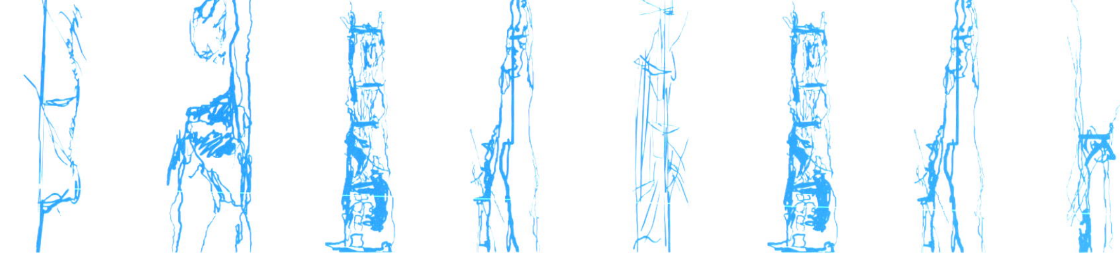

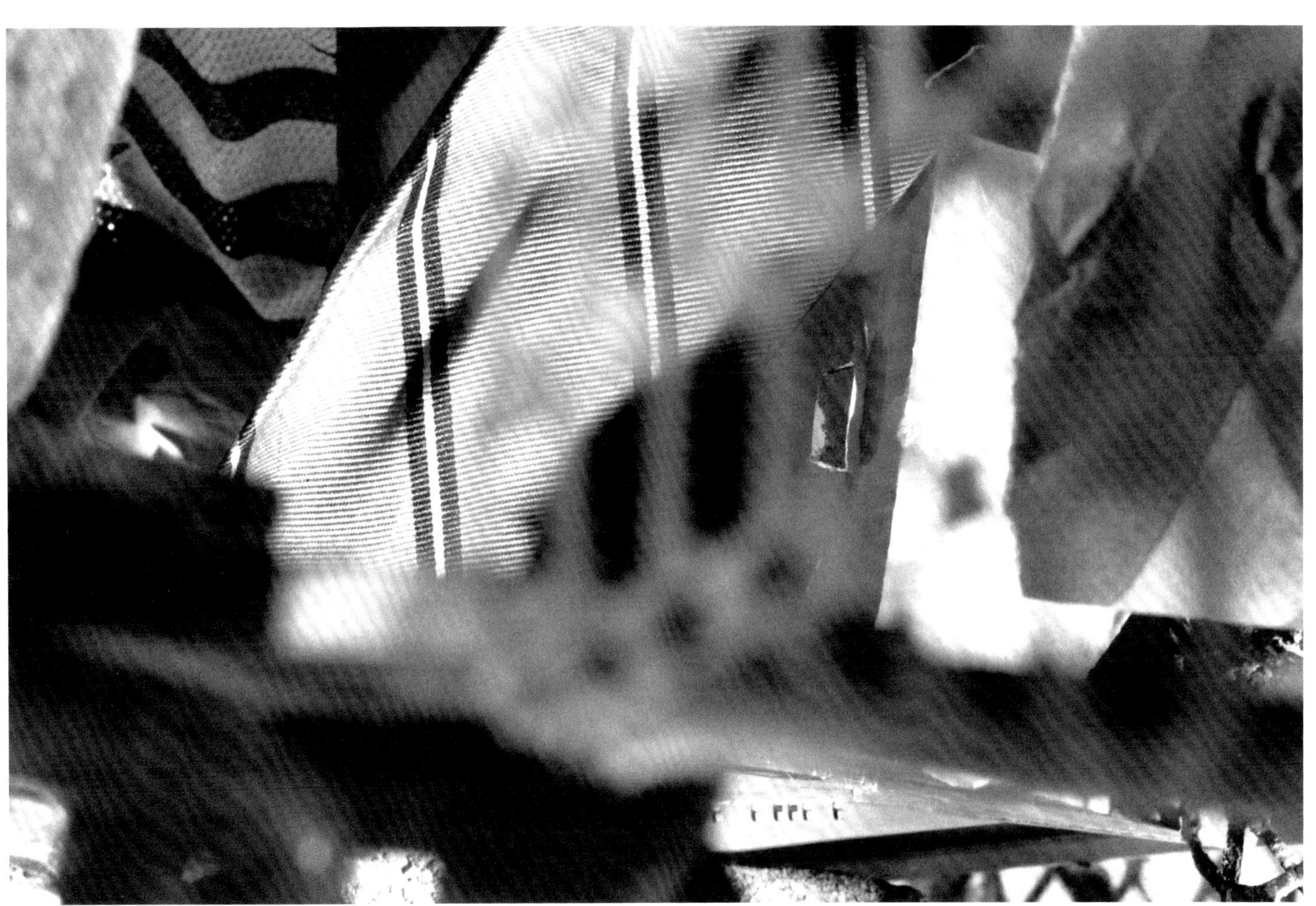

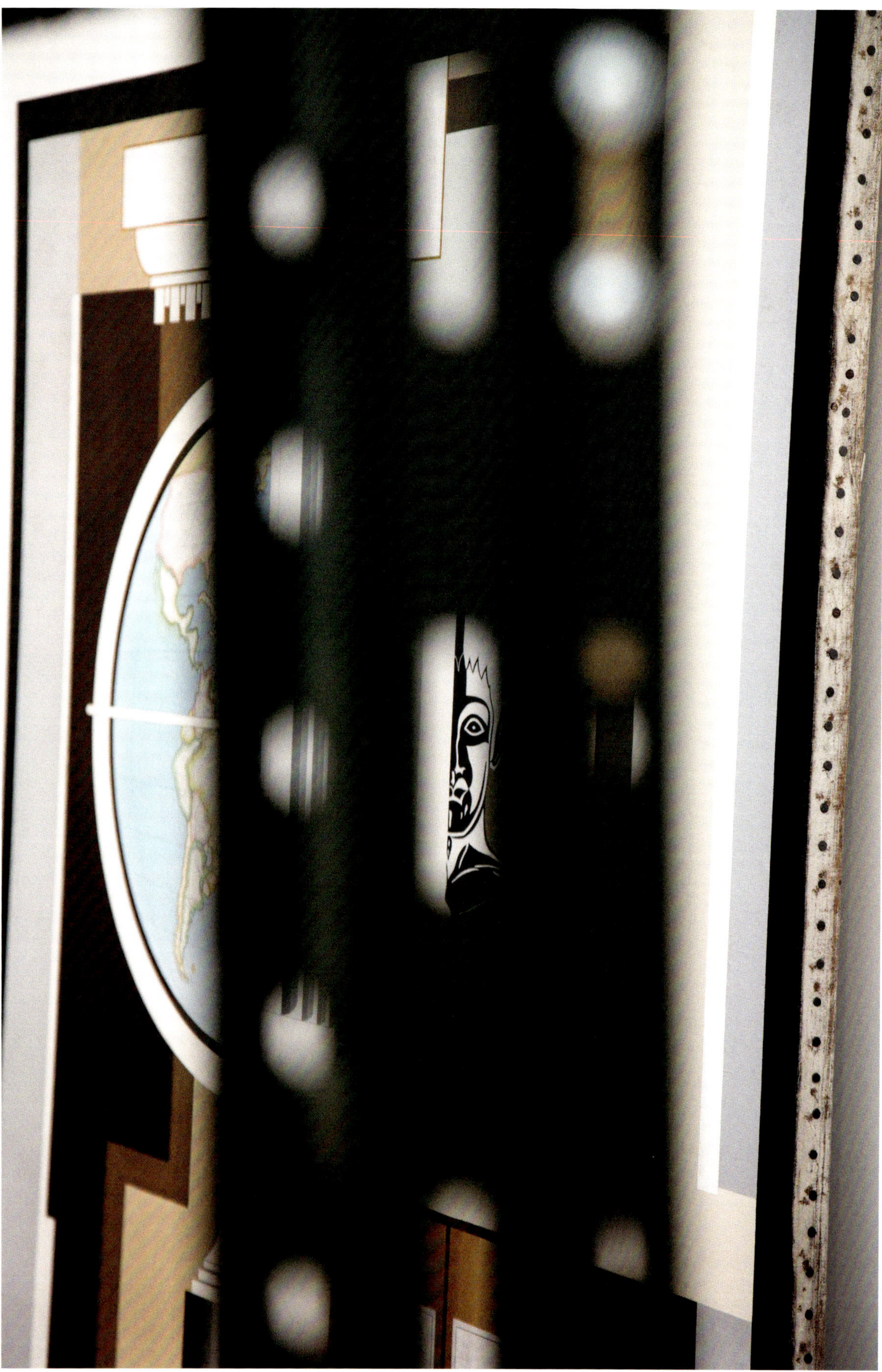

Director's Foreword

It is a great pleasure for the Yale University Art Gallery to publish the present monograph, *Seeing and Not Believing*, on the photography of Allan Chasanoff. This is the first book to present Chasanoff's highly diverse and often cutting-edge Postmodern experiments in photography, with images selected from a life's work of thousands now preserved at the Gallery.

Allan Chasanoff (1936–2020) received his B.A. from Yale College in 1961. After graduation, he worked with his father and brother in commercial real estate development, became an avid collector, and pursued a daily practice of making photographs, first using analog equipment and later employing a sophisticated array of digital tools. Throughout his life, Allan's fascination with the photographic process and desire to challenge our instinctive belief in the photograph as "truth teller" never wavered. The intellectual curiosity, technical inventiveness, and sheer joy he brought to his explorations in the medium are brilliantly described here in Mónika Sziládi's comprehensive presentation of his work.

By his own choice, Chasanoff's innovative work in photography was largely a personal journey. He focused on the pleasures of engaging with the medium and exploring its newest iterations, such as 3-D scanning and printing, rather than on participation in the art world. He was, however, a widely read and generous thinker who gathered a "salon" of creative and highly intellectual voices around him. The close friendships that ensued generated exciting conversations that reflected and informed Chasanoff's explorations of photography and the world.

To assist him in organizing his photographic output, Chasanoff enlisted several talented studio collaborators, including Sziládi. A Yale-educated photographer herself, Sziládi worked with Chasanoff from 2013 until his death to edit and preserve his vast and experimental photographic legacy. Her selection of nearly two hundred works shown here explores Chasanoff's main avenues of inquiry, some technical (montages of layered images that took advantage of digital photography and editing tools), others formal (light and shadow), and even, perhaps especially, those that confronted the philosophical (the veracity of photography in all its psychological, political, and social dimensions). This book would not have been possible without her expertise in the medium and their professional collaboration.

Chasanoff's long and close friendship with the late Richard Benson, master printer, photographer, teacher, and former Dean of the Yale School of Art, was a decisive link in his consideration of Yale as a repository for his collections and for his own creative output. Additionally, Chasanoff's inclination and temperament as a natural visual thinker was profoundly appreciated by my predecessor, Jock Reynolds, the former Henry J. Heinz II Director of the Gallery and himself an artist. Over time, these ongoing Yale connections led to a mutual understanding that Chasanoff's collections of book art, Japanese seals, and other objects would benefit from being housed in a university museum, where students and artists could use them as inspiration to create new work.

Today, the Allan Chasanoff Classroom and its contents, housed at the Margaret and Angus Wurtele Study Center at Yale West Campus, present a composite of resources and ideas for students, scholars, artists, and visitors. Some ten thousand images made by Chasanoff are recorded and searchable in databases in the Chasanoff Classroom. In addition, Yale houses Chasanoff's library of photography books, a significant asset for research that amplifies and is intended to be used in combination with the collections.

Sziládi's book provides captivating insight into Chasanoff's approach to photography and his strategy to respond to the image-rich culture of his time by "speak[ing] with the words in which one has been spoken to." Another window on Chasanoff's devotion to image making and interpretation is provided by distinguished writer and personal friend of the photographer Richard Ovenden. Together, their contributions celebrate Chasanoff's lifelong intellectual and artistic pursuits.

The Gallery is particularly grateful to Robert Chasanoff, whose close personal relationship with his uncle was critical in understanding how best to support the Gallery in organizing, presenting, and making accessible a unique legacy. We thank Robert for his generosity and unwavering support for this book and the collection, which seamlessly integrate Allan Chasanoff's inimitable curiosity and artistic output in ways that will generate creative new pathways for future generations of Yale students and visitors.

Stephanie Wiles
The Henry J. Heinz II Director
Yale University Art Gallery

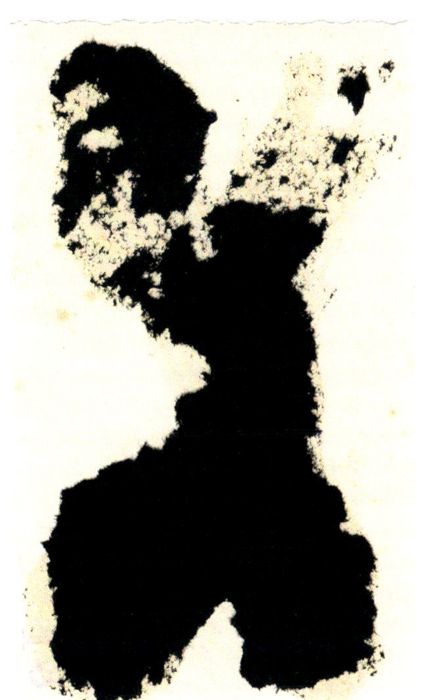

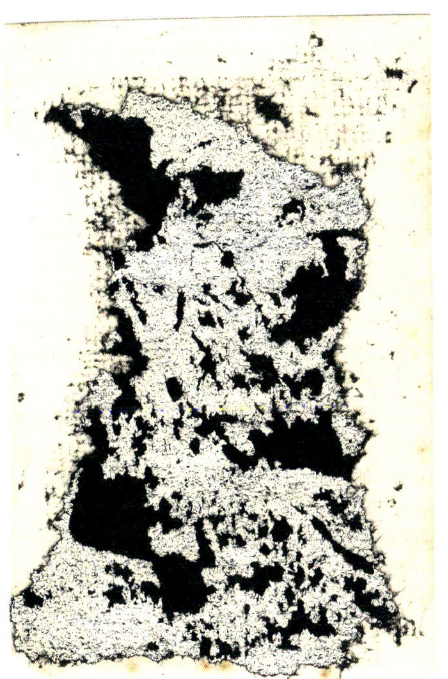

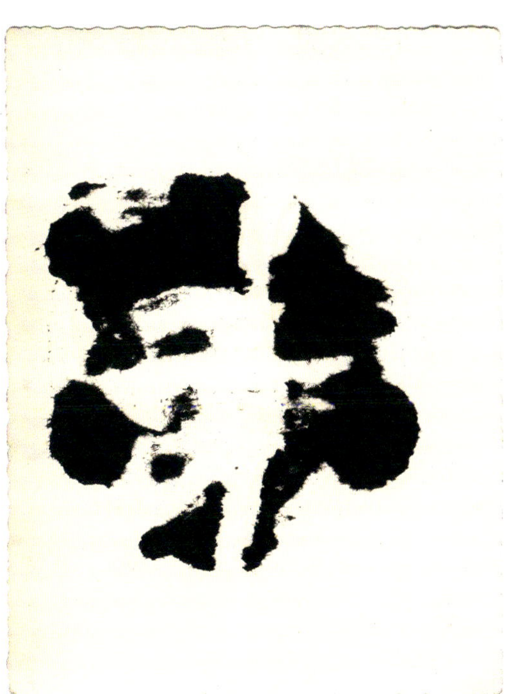

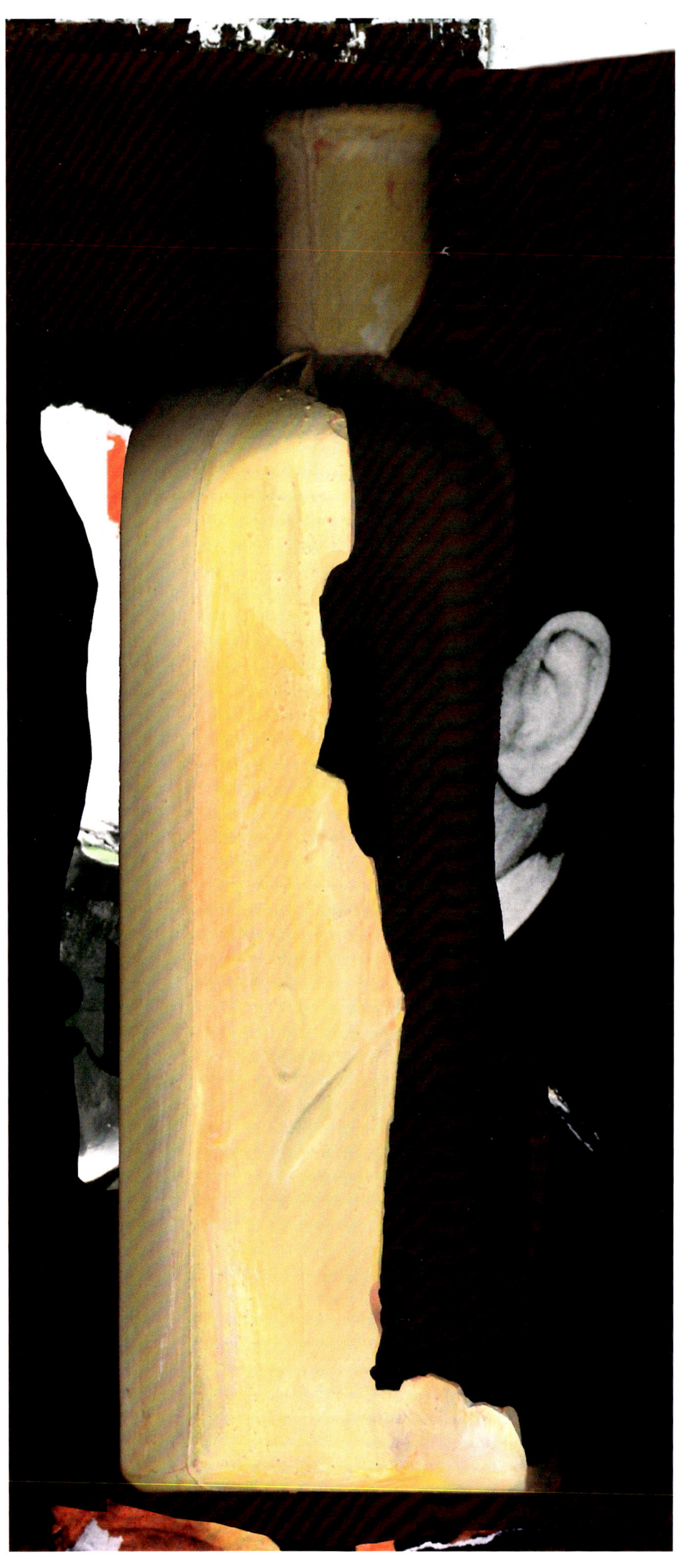

Acknowledgments

As a new student at the Yale School of Art, the first exhibition I saw at the Yale University Art Gallery was *First Doubt: Optical Confusion in Modern Photography, Selections from the Allan Chasanoff Collection* (2008). The pictures, although “straight,” or unmanipulated, challenged the reliability of the photograph as document. Spatial ambiguity and naturally occurring distortions made it difficult to decipher the images’ contents, at least at first glance, and forced the viewer to consider divergent realities that might underlie them. Both lesser- and well-known photographers were represented, sometimes by images that were anomalies rather than typical of their oeuvre. I was left wondering who would identify such a theme and, in turn, have the will to go about assembling a collection around it.

Several years and chance encounters later, I found myself working with Allan Chasanoff at his Manhattan studio as part of a small team of artists and creative thinkers. I related naturally to his sense of humor, which was similar to the one I had absorbed growing up in Budapest. He was quick, direct, and often played with double meanings and irony, and he could jump deftly from the funny to the serious. This sensibility might explain his habit of turning assumptions upside down—such as the everyday visceral trust in the veracity of photographic images. Conversations with him felt like mental workouts and also jam sessions: free, generative, and communal but with respect for soloing and the occasional reflective pause. I am grateful for having had this experience and honored that he entrusted me with the responsibility of conceiving this volume.

I wish to thank Robert Chasanoff, executor of the Estate of Allan Chasanoff, for extending that trust and for his unrelenting support of this project. I also thank him for confirming biographical details included here.

At the Gallery, I owe special thanks to Stephanie Wiles, the Henry J. Heinz II Director; Judy Ditner, the Richard Benson Associate Curator of Photography and Digital Media; and Tiffany Sprague, Director of Publications and Editorial Services. They drew on a wealth of experience to support the making of this book, including bringing together an outstanding production team.

I am deeply indebted to the editor and project manager of this book, Livia Tenzer, for her dedication, expertise, and kind and invaluable guidance; to Gabriella Svenningsen Omonte, Senior Museum Assistant, Department of Photography, at the Gallery, for her impeccable image research during this project and gracious attention during the years in which the Gallery established the Allan Chasanoff Archive; and to Christopher Sleboda, Associate Professor of Art, Graphic Design, at Boston University, and former Director of Graphic Design at the Gallery, for his creativity and skill, as well as his understanding of Allan’s world, gained in designing the catalogue for the exhibition mentioned above and the one accompanying the

Gallery's exhibition *Odd Volumes: Book Art from the Allan Chasanoff Collection* (2014).

In order to write this book and assemble a selection of Allan's photographic pictures, I relied on the Chasanoff Archive, much of which reflects the work of collaborators at his studio. I would like to thank my former colleagues there for the good times and for the resources I was able to reference: Nicole DeGeorge, Victoria Miguel, Mary Mormile, David Pattillo, and Miho Suzuki. I am especially grateful to Elizabeth Hansen, whom I have never met but whose database of Allan's photographs made between 1958 and 2008 was a primary source for this book. My citations of materials in the Chasanoff Archive, including writings, videotapes, and databases, are accurate to the full extent possible at this time; the archive continues to undergo cataloguing.

Among other associates of Allan, I thank Howard Greenberg, Chris Insinger, Francis Olschafskie, Zoë Sheehan Saldaña, and Suzanne Williamson for their help confirming details about his collecting, creative work, and exhibitions. And I thank Allan's friend, the artist Raymon Elozua, for introducing me to Allan in 2013.

For their support of this book, I must also thank Jock Reynolds, the former Henry J. Heinz II Director of the Gallery and the impetus behind preserving Allan's creative archive; and Richard Ovenden, Bodley's Librarian at the University of Oxford.

Always: thankful to Brian for his love and support. And to my family and friends on both sides of the Atlantic for their encouragement.

Mónika Sziládi

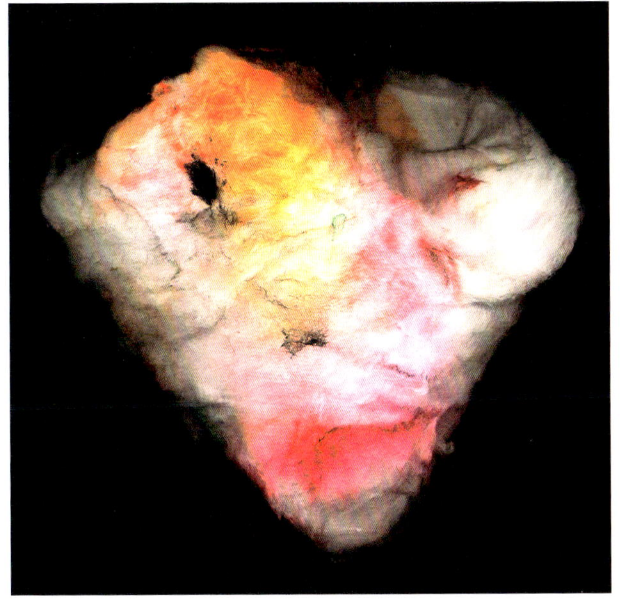

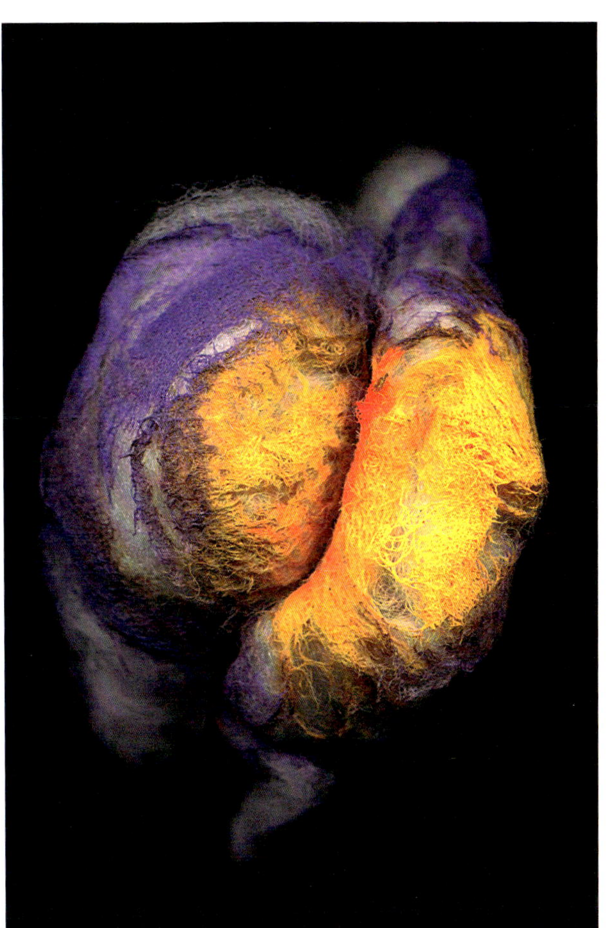

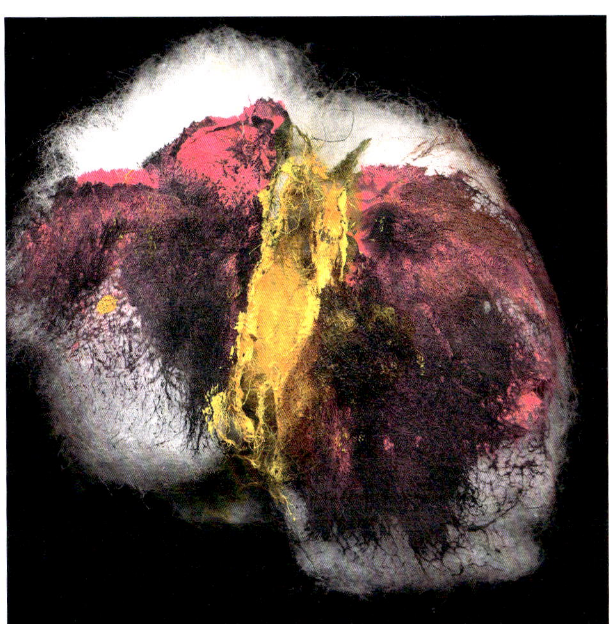

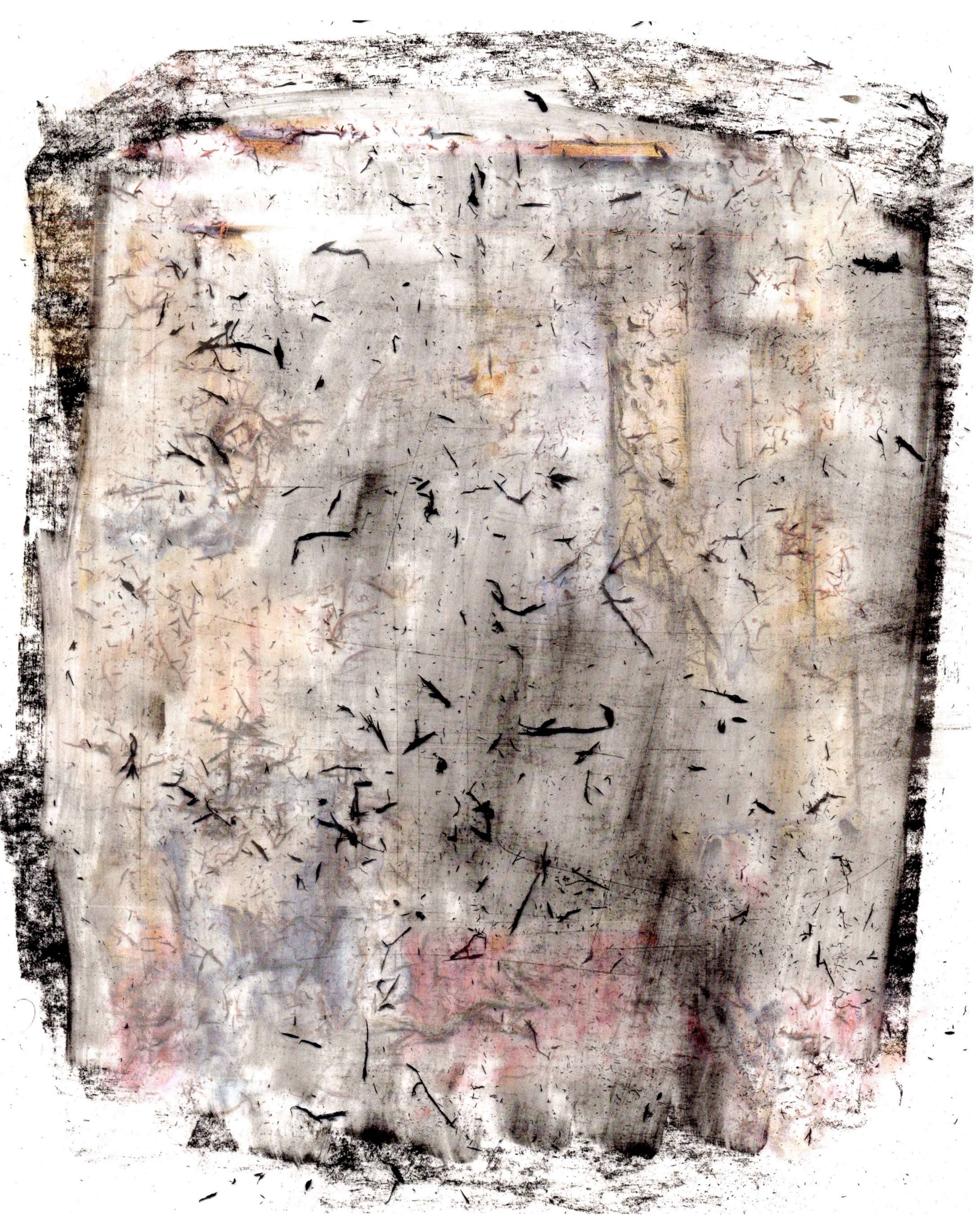

Preface: Unique Allan Chasanoff

In my line of work you meet a lot of interesting people. I have worked in universities for twenty-three years, and in arts and culture for thirty-five years. Among all the thousands of people I have encountered, Allan Chasanoff had the most original and interesting mind of them all.

I first met Allan in 2004, through his elder brother Micky, whom I met through an Oxford alum living in New York. Micky thought that Allan and I would get along. He was right. From that moment I would visit Allan in New York three or four times a year, and he even came to Oxford a few times, once I took up my role leading the Bodleian Libraries in 2014. We would speak on the phone and trade emails in the times in between. Our conversations began on our mutual interest in photography, but then expanded to cover art more generally. Allan was very keen to hear about my work and the state of the university, and would often compare these with what he knew was going on at Yale. He loved to hear about my family. A major topic throughout was the digital world: the opportunities that technology provided for creativity and innovation, but also the growing power of the tech industry. These issues would animate Allan the most—these, and the state of the roads in Manhattan.

On my visits, Allan was to be found in his brownstone in the city's Murray Hill neighborhood. It would be slightly misleading to say that it was the house that he lived in, as it seemed to me more a studio and workshop that happened to incorporate his bedroom. The place was unlike any other house I had visited. It contained his archive—or at least part of his archive—his workshop (where I did my first 3-D printing), and his study, which had the level of technology one would normally associate with the trading floor of a major investment house. Squirreled away in the rest of the building were various colleagues, a group of talented individuals who supported Allan's artistic creativity and would occasionally come down to fix things, set things up, or chat. Mary, Allan's faithful deputy, would preside over this unique institution—and most aspects of Allan's life—from the ground floor. But the entire property was really the domain of Allan's cats, Bit and Byte, who would boss him and everyone else around in a borderline tyrannical fashion.

The conversations I had with Allan were among the most enjoyable, and occasionally the most challenging, of my life. They were always

unpredictable, and I never failed to learn new things, or to gain a new, original, and unexpected perspective on life (often on my own). Many of those conversations were had in the brownstone, but often they were had walking around various museums, art fairs, or commercial art galleries (at least until his declining health prevented those visits). Allan had strong feelings—and often highly critical things to say—about the shows we visited. He loved the van Gogh drawings at the Met but was scathing about Marina Abramović at MoMA. He loved the early Rothkos at Pace/MacGill (then on 57th Street, now Pace Gallery on 25th), and delighted in taking me to see the Cai Guo-Qiang show at the Guggenheim and the Hiroshi Sugimoto show at the Japan Society.

Whenever we visited a show together, I would be focused on the objects on the wall or in the exhibition cases, but Allan's eye would lead him elsewhere. He would be entranced by the shadows formed by the exhibition lighting, by the angles and shapes cast by the museum objects, and by the cases themselves. These were what Allan alone, in a packed Met or MoMA, would notice and photograph. Similarly the painted lines on the roads outside the museums or galleries. It wasn't so much the paint, but the erosion, the wear and tear caused by the billions of car tires (and the vagaries of Manhattan's extreme weather) that forced the painted lines to crack, fade, and generally change their shape, revealing new lines and forms. All of these were at least of equal, if not superior, interest to the serious art in the institutions we had just visited. Allan would photograph the shadows as we walked around the shows, and the cracks in the road paint as we waited for a cab back to the brownstone. His artistic practice was always part of his consciousness.

Allan's eye was drawn to the mistakes and confusion that randomness brings to bear. It caused him repeated delight, and his collections of photographs—those given to the Museum of Fine Arts, Houston, and to the Yale University Art Gallery—held strong thematic principles of this kind. These concerns spread into other areas of Allan's creativity. One November afternoon Allan invited me on a stroll just a few blocks from the brownstone to the Collectors Club of New York, an organization with a fine library dedicated to philately. Was this a new broad collecting interest? Not exactly. Allan had become obsessed with examples of the famous nineteenth-century stamp of Andrew Jackson (the so-called Black Jack), particularly the marks made by the manual process of cancellation. This process involved applying a wooden hand stamp to Jackson's face, and the random, unexpected impressions on the presidential visage were what delighted Allan. He soon

started to amass as many examples as he could: digitizing them, enlarging them, and making art out of them.

As digital technology became increasingly advanced, Allan became schizophrenic about it. He loved that technology put sophisticated tools at his disposal (especially as he had the resources to buy the latest kit, and to have his team install, learn, and master it very quickly and skillfully). He delighted in the disruptive influence it brought to bear on so many aspects of our lives, forcing us out of complacency. But he hated the monopolistic control that the tech

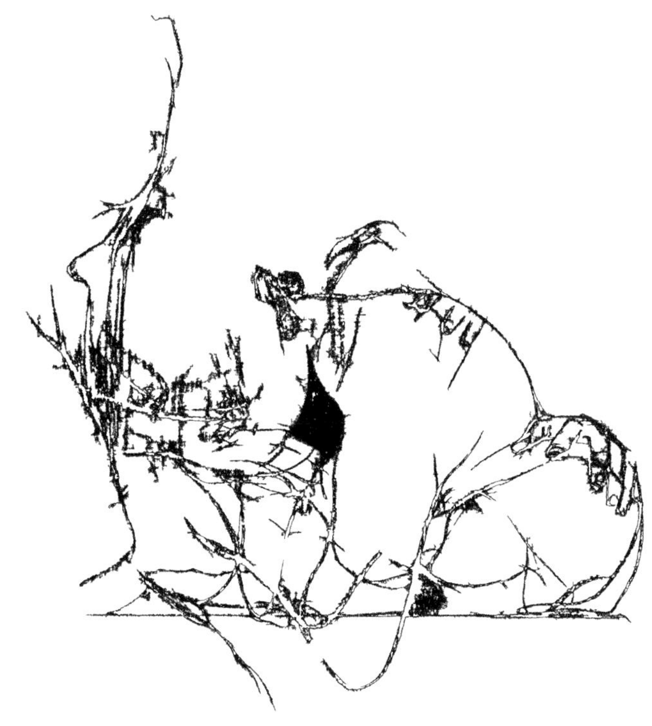

companies exert on users, and on society more generally. He loathed being tied down by regulations imposed on him (especially copyright). The format of the codex was a good example: he preferred to dismember an art book and reorder the images in the way he found interesting (and he built a whole collection of artists' books to explore this broad principle, now at Yale).

Allan's creativity was a mixture of seeing, manipulating, and combining. To say that he loved the interplay between text and image would be a dangerous understatement—to Allan, these two facets of human invention could and should not be separated—and you can see this in his experimentation with letterforms: turning the cracks in the painted lines on Manhattan's streets into fonts inspired by Asian calligraphy.

The creative aspect of Allan's life was also a facet of combination. He was a great collector but also a great maker. He had an original way of viewing the world, both visually and intellectually. He loved words and images, particularly when he had the freedom to arrange and change them according to his own instinct and inventiveness. He bounced ideas off his friends, but he held true to his own convictions. His art, as seen in these pages, displays all of these characteristics. It changed

as the means of making art evolved, but it retained throughout his love of confusion and the creativity of randomness. Allan rarely showed his work, but, fundamentally, he made it to satisfy his own curiosity. That is what has motivated the greatest artists.

Richard Ovenden, OBE
Bodley's Librarian, Bodleian Libraries
Head, Gardens, Libraries, and Museums
University of Oxford

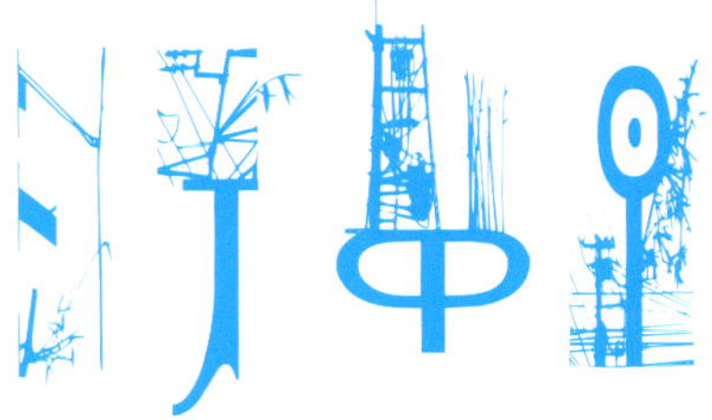

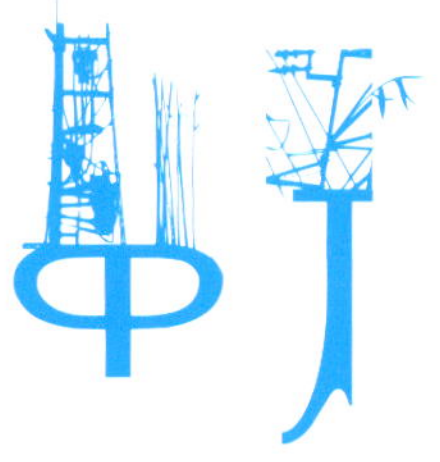

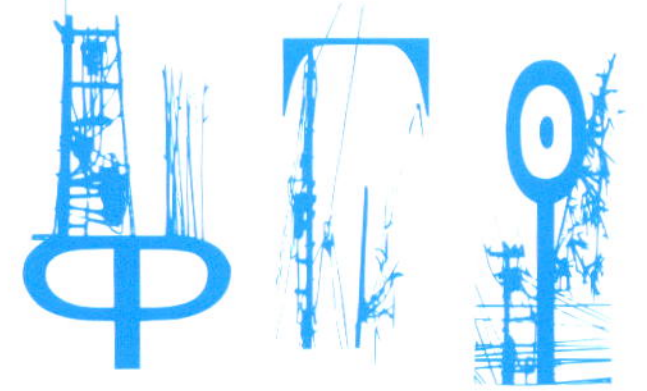

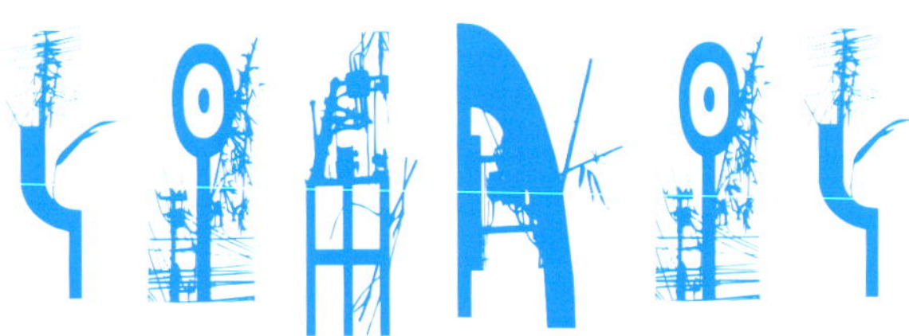

Allan Chasanoff (1936–2020) made analog and digital photographs, and he produced digital montages from a variety of sources, including his own photographs, graphic elements he created, and a range of appropriated images. These photographic works—negatives, transparencies, prints, and digital image files—are now preserved in the Allan Chasanoff Archive at the Yale University Art Gallery.

Other works by Chasanoff discussed in this volume, including his 3-D prints and digitally designed fonts, are also held in the archive. In addition, it houses his writings, interviews, video and audio projects, drawings, and ceramics, as well as objects he commissioned and collected.

An important resource at the archive—and a guide to other holdings—are the forty-odd databases that Chasanoff used to organize many of his projects and collections, two of which are devoted to his photography.

Titles

Chasanoff did not title his photographic works. In this volume, they are identified by their ID numbers in the two photography databases. These were maintained by Elizabeth Hansen and Mónika Sziládi, who performed editing, archival, and other work at Chasanoff's studio in 2002–8 and 2013–20, respectively. Together, the databases describe approximately ten thousand images selected by Chasanoff, Hansen, and Sziládi from his much-larger oeuvre. The first contains records of images created between 1958 and 2008 with ID numbers 1000 to 8560, and the second, images created between 2006 and 2020 with ID numbers 10001 to 12650.

Series

Chasanoff defined series loosely within his body of work; annotations and categorization in the photography databases reveal themes and motifs that he returned to repeatedly. In this volume, some of these are treated as titled series based on the terms used in the databases with occasional modifications for clarity.

Image Types and Media

Plate captions in this volume provide a guide to image type. The medium in a caption indicates whether the photograph is analog or digital, unmanipulated or manipulated (with digital tools). In the Chasanoff Archive, images often exist in more than one medium; the medium in the caption is the one used for purposes of reproduction in these pages.

Image Type	Medium
Analog photograph (unmanipulated)	black-and-white negative, color negative, color transparency; gelatin silver print, chromogenic print, silver dye-bleach print
Digital photograph (unmanipulated)	digital image file; pigmented inkjet print; digital scan
Digital photograph (manipulated)	digital montage, extraction from digital photograph, extraction from digital scan; pigmented inkjet print (from digital montage), chromogenic print (from digital montage)
Other digital images	digital drawing, font

Notes on Plates

Notes accompanying the plates provide details about Chasanoff's rich visual vocabulary and varied techniques. They are based on the author's memory of her conversations with Chasanoff, recorded conversations between Chasanoff and Hansen, information in the photography databases, other sources in the Chasanoff Archive, and, in the case of many digital montages, information stored in the layers of image files.

Sources

Several endnotes in this volume refer to unpublished texts held in the Chasanoff Archive at the Yale University Art Gallery. They exist as digital files as well as printed texts. The page numbers here refer to the printed texts available at the time of publication. Some quotations from these sources have been edited for clarity.

Fonts

Several of the fonts Chasanoff created, often incorporating elements stylized from his photographs, have been used in the design of this volume. See BAPHT, title page; Tpolesum, p. 6; FBT, p. 22; AMF, p. 28; Baseball (BB) Pitch, p. 114; Half Linotext, p. 128; Pole B, p. 158; Bamboo B, p. 182; Roots A, p. 206; and Half Didot, p. 228. This volume's spine is typeset with Erasure. Mónika Sziládi's essay, pp. 72–101, uses BAPHT, Baseball (BB) Hit, Baseball (BB) Pitch, Baseball (BB) Slide, FBT, Pole A, Roots A, Roots AB UC, Tpole-etc., and Tpolesum.

Some fonts were updated to OpenType format by Lauren Had, under the direction of Christopher Sleboda, the graphic designer of this catalogue, through an Undergraduate Research Opportunities Program grant from Boston University in fall 2022. Had researched the experimental font forms created by Allan Chasanoff and provided technical support for digitization.

Plates I

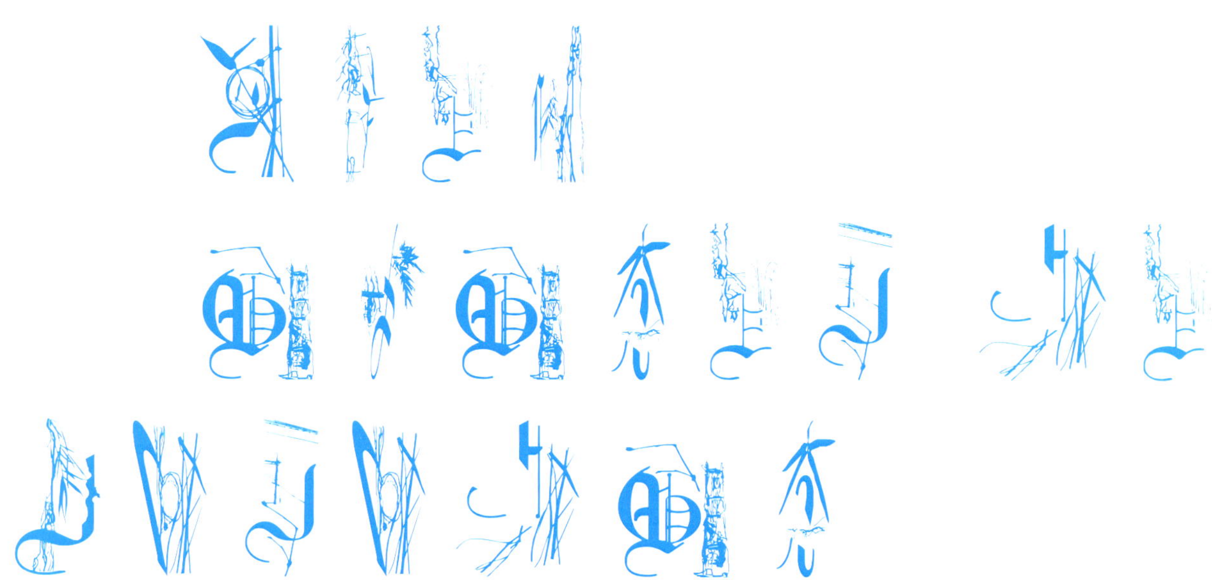

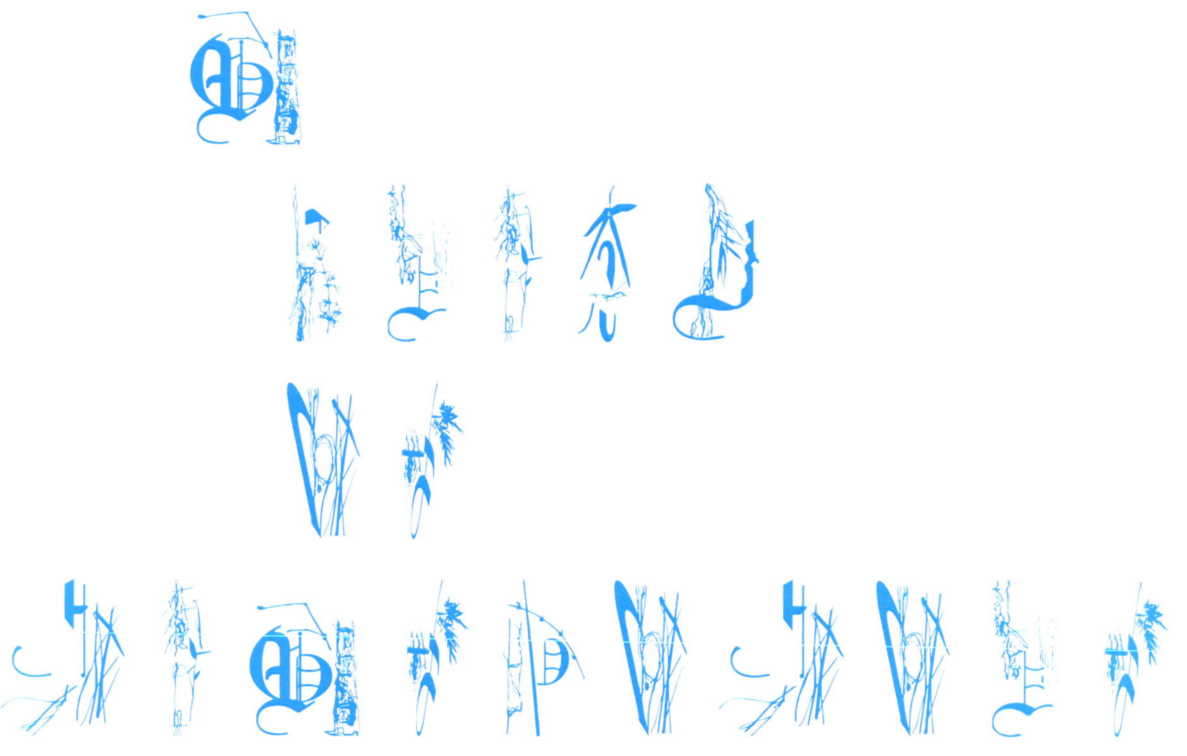

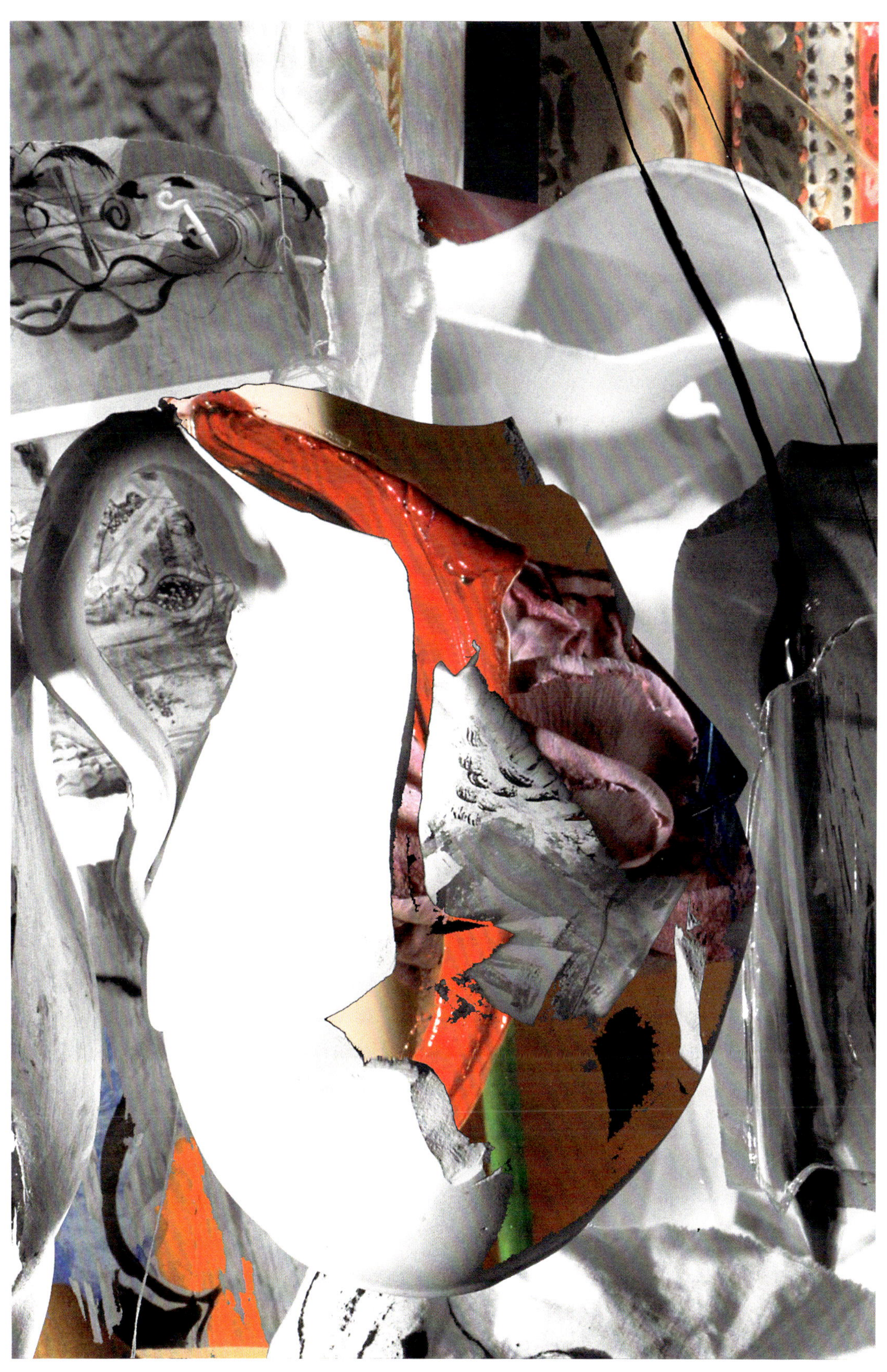

Plate 1
No. 1002, ca. 1997, digital montage.
Allan Chasanoff Archive, Yale University Art Gallery

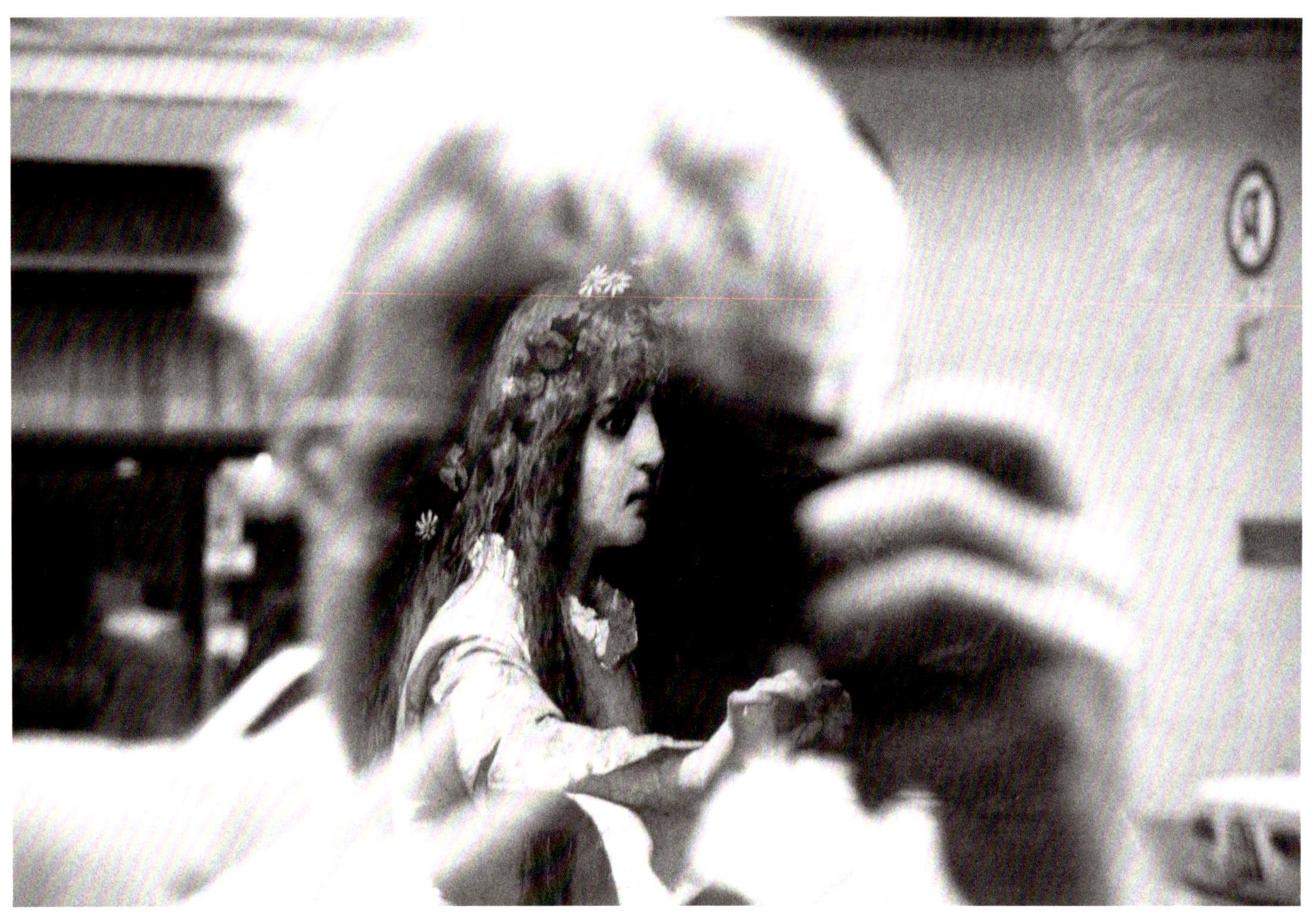

Plate 2
No. 3983 (self-portrait), 1985, gelatin silver print.
Allan Chasanoff Archive, Yale University Art Gallery

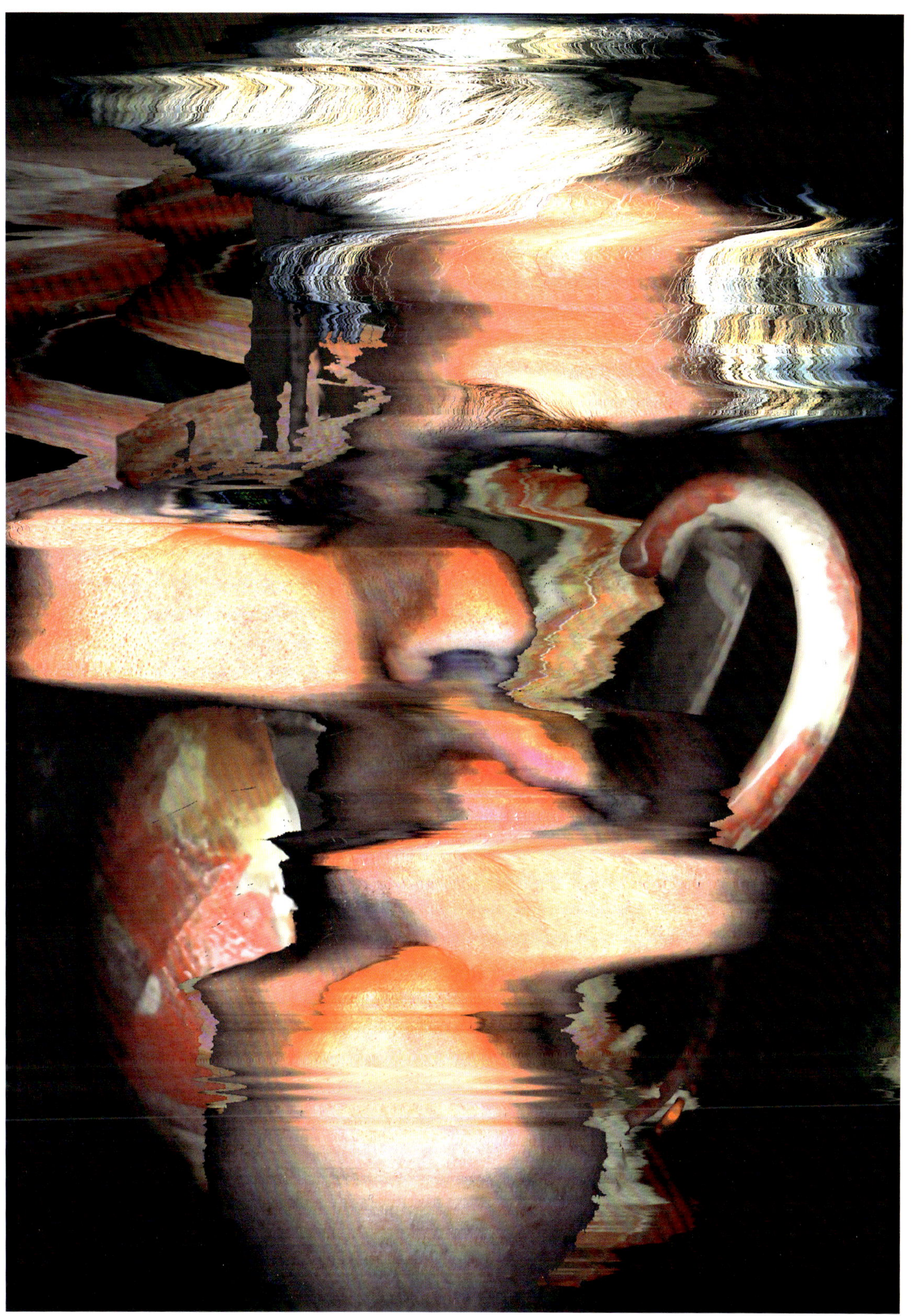

Plate 3
No. 1077 (self-portrait), ca. 1997, digital montage. Teapot series.
Allan Chasanoff Archive, Yale University Art Gallery

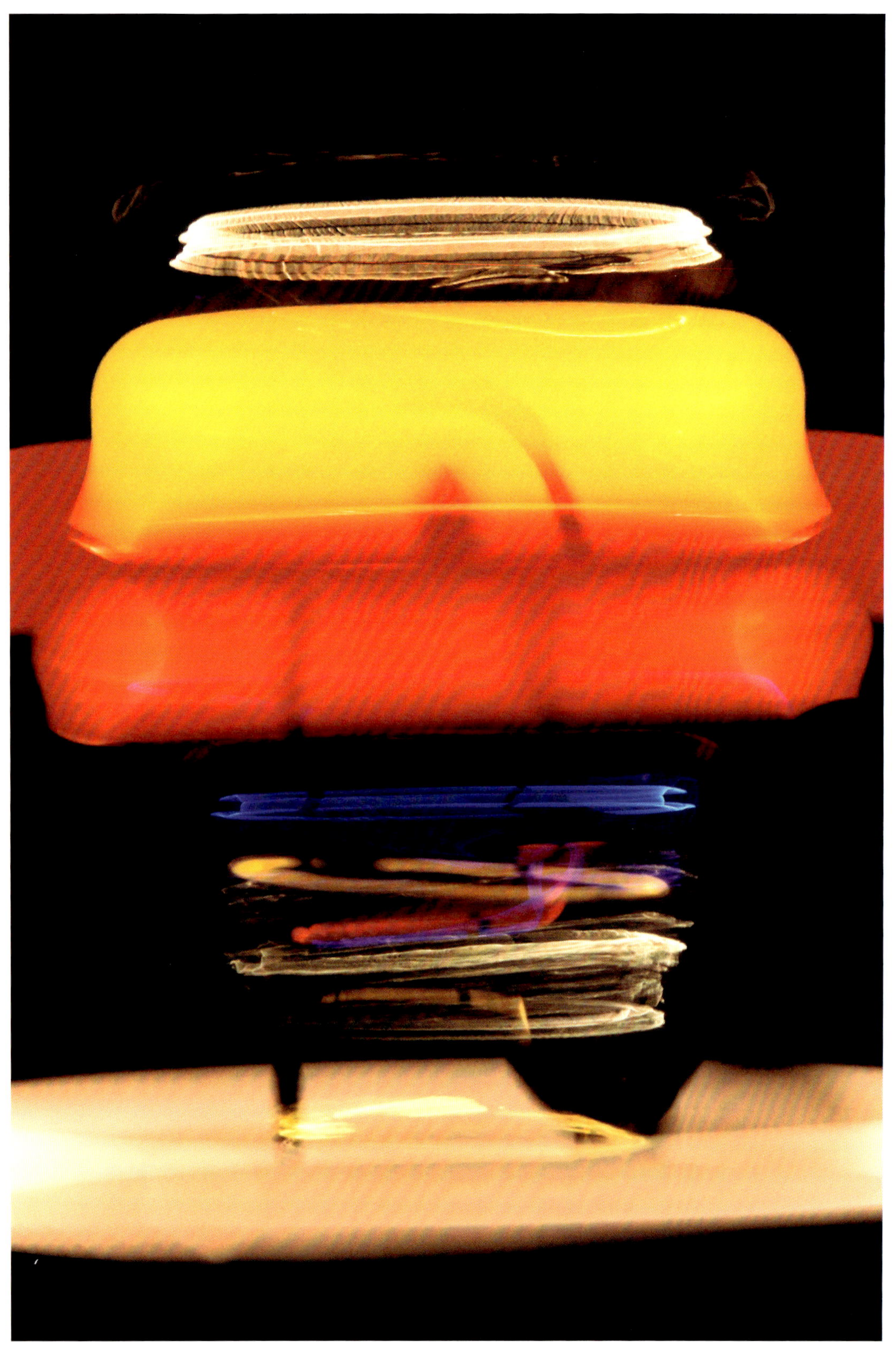

Note

To make this image, Chasanoff photographed light bulbs attached to a spinning element of his Light Table (see fig. 2).

Plate 4

No. 2431, 1972, color transparency. Light Bulb series.
Allan Chasanoff Archive, Yale University Art Gallery

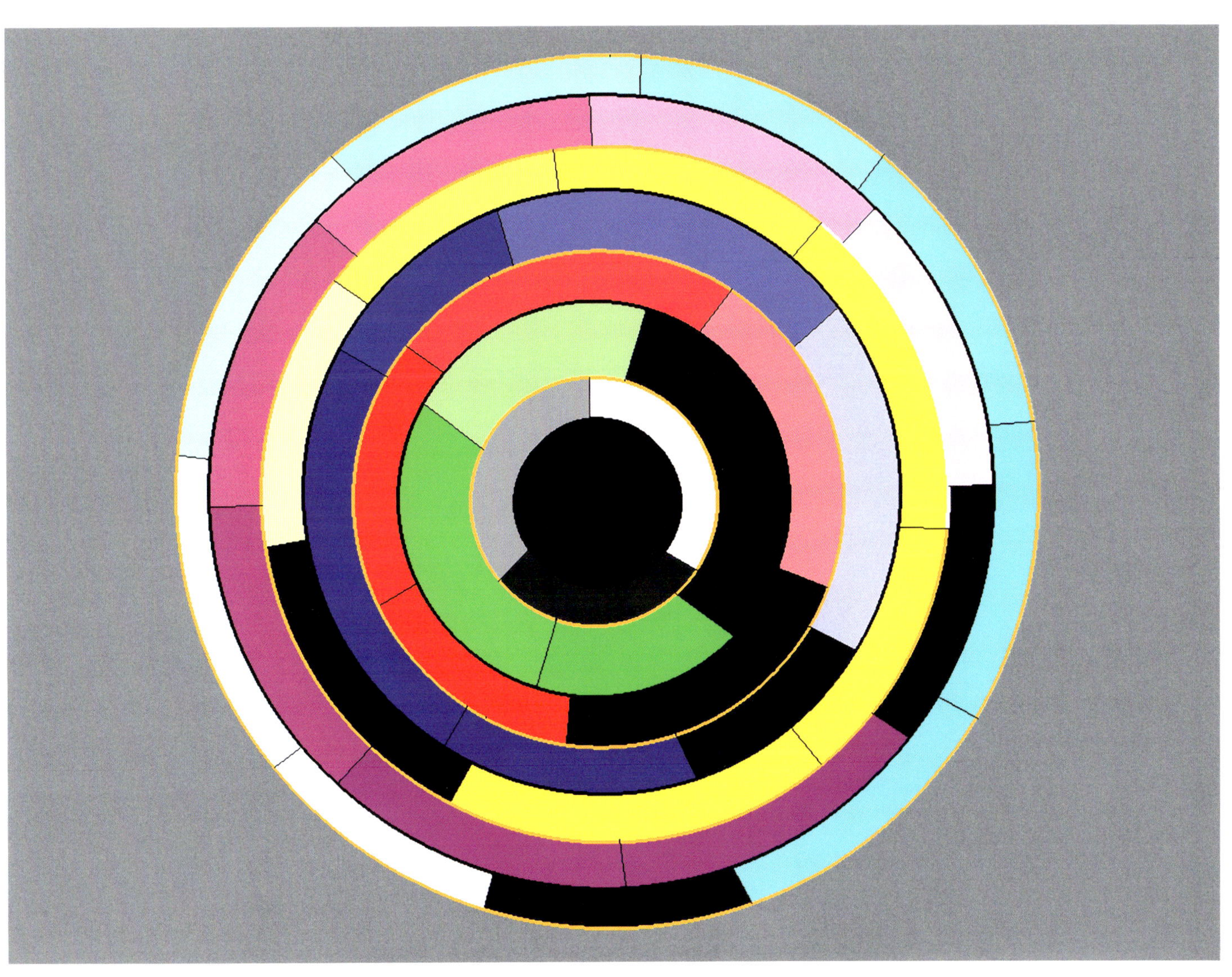

Plate 5
No. 4642, 1992, digital drawing.
Allan Chasanoff Archive, Yale University Art Gallery

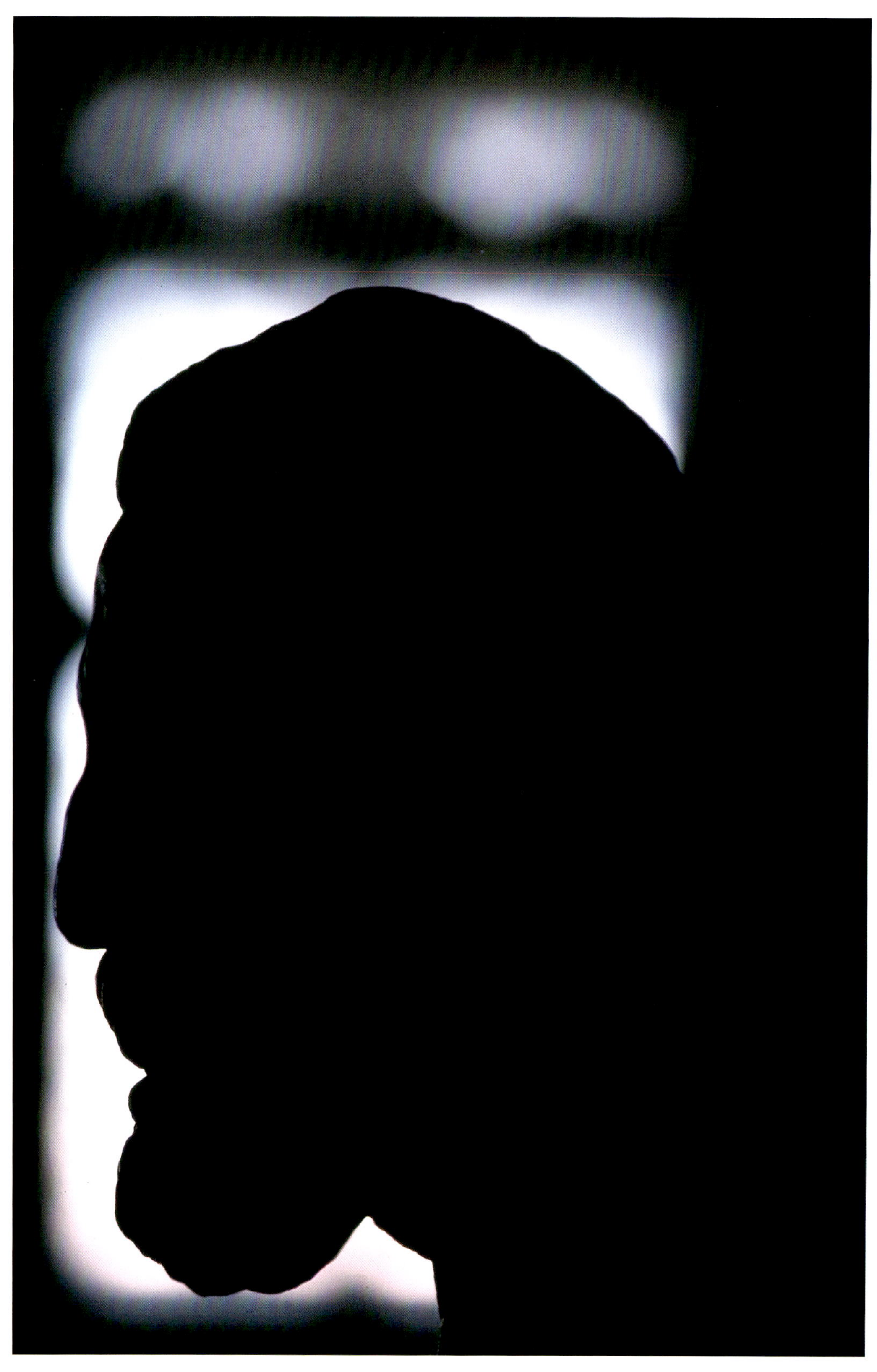

Plate 6
No. 2553, 1975, color transparency.
Allan Chasanoff Archive, Yale University Art Gallery

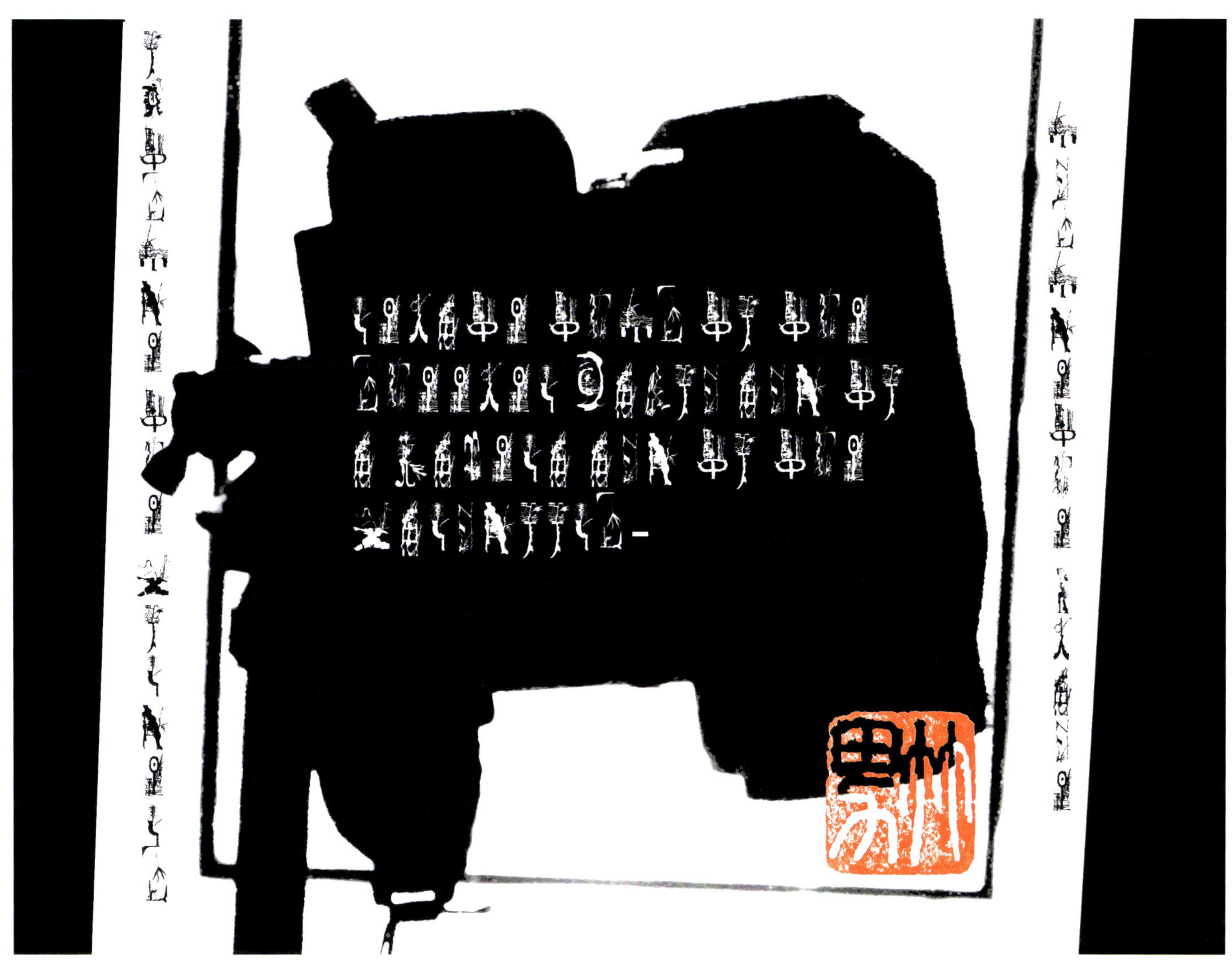

Note

At center is a silhouette of one of Chasanoff's video cameras; vertical and horizontal writing is in Chasanoff's FBT font; the stamp at bottom right comes from Chasanoff's signature Japanese seal, which he had created ca. 2006 to reflect the nickname "Bamboo Boy" given to him by Jock Reynolds, then director of the Yale University Art Gallery, because of his persistent interest in the multiuse plant (the kanji on the seal means "Bamboo Man").

In connection with this image, Chasanoff commented about writing in his specially designed fonts: "Sometimes I'll say yes, I know what it means, I'm just not going to tell you. Or it could mean absolutely nothing. It is the signifier alone."

Plate 7

No. 7502, 2006, digital montage. AC Fonts series.
Allan Chasanoff Archive, Yale University Art Gallery

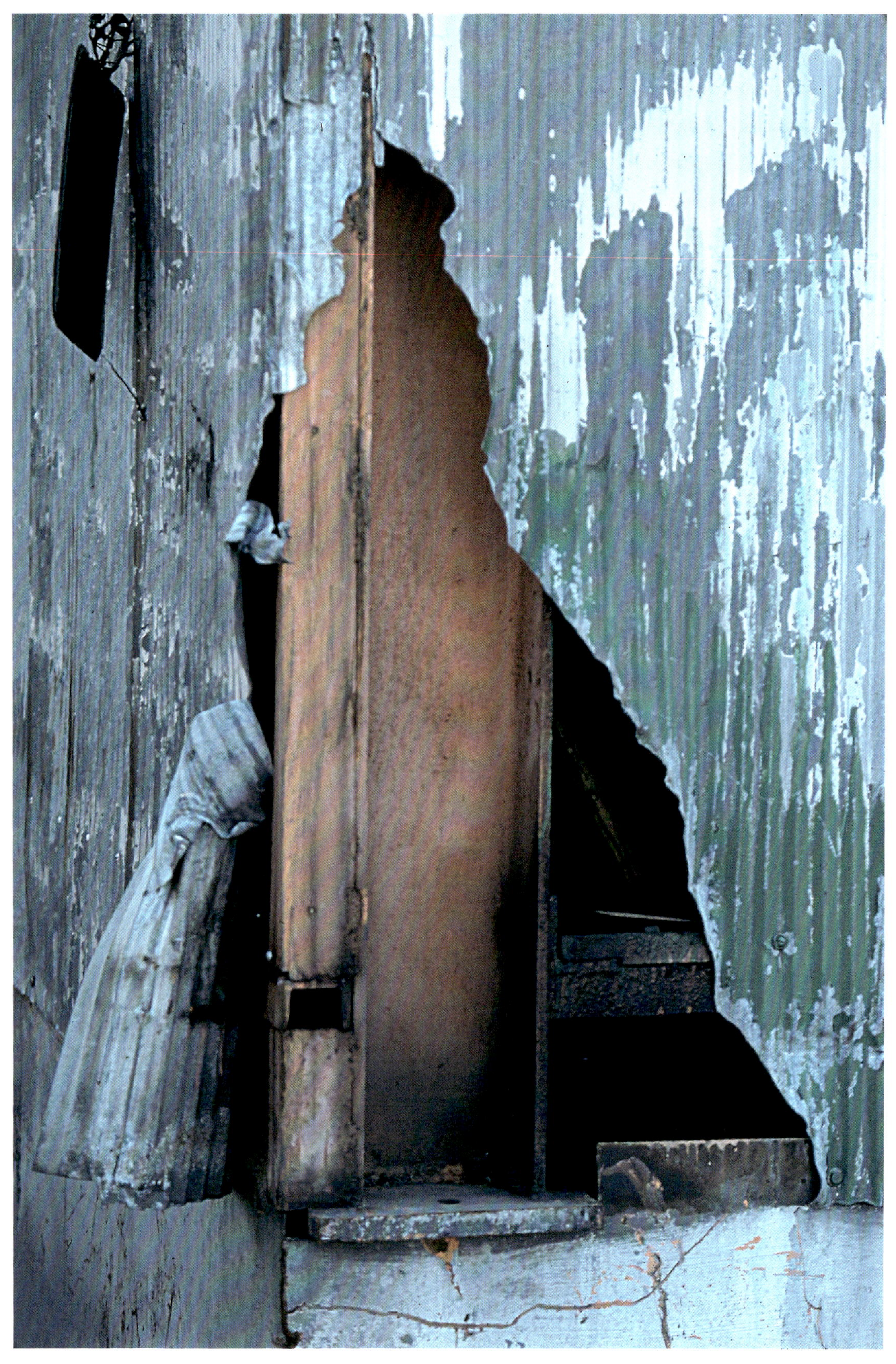

Plate 8
No. 2863, 1977, color transparency.
Allan Chasanoff Archive, Yale University Art Gallery

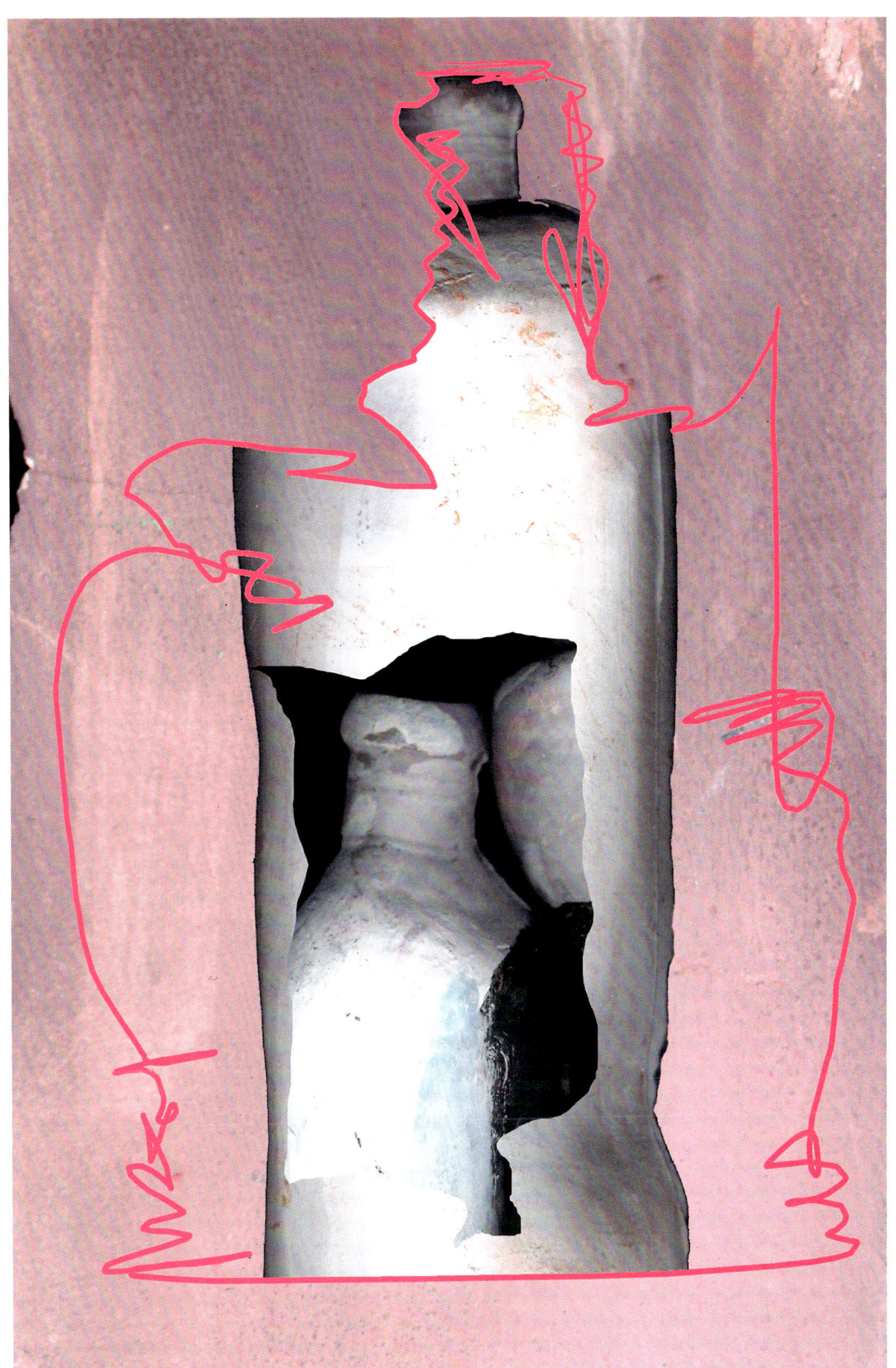

Plate 9
No. 1147, ca. 1998, digital montage.
Allan Chasanoff Archive, Yale University Art Gallery

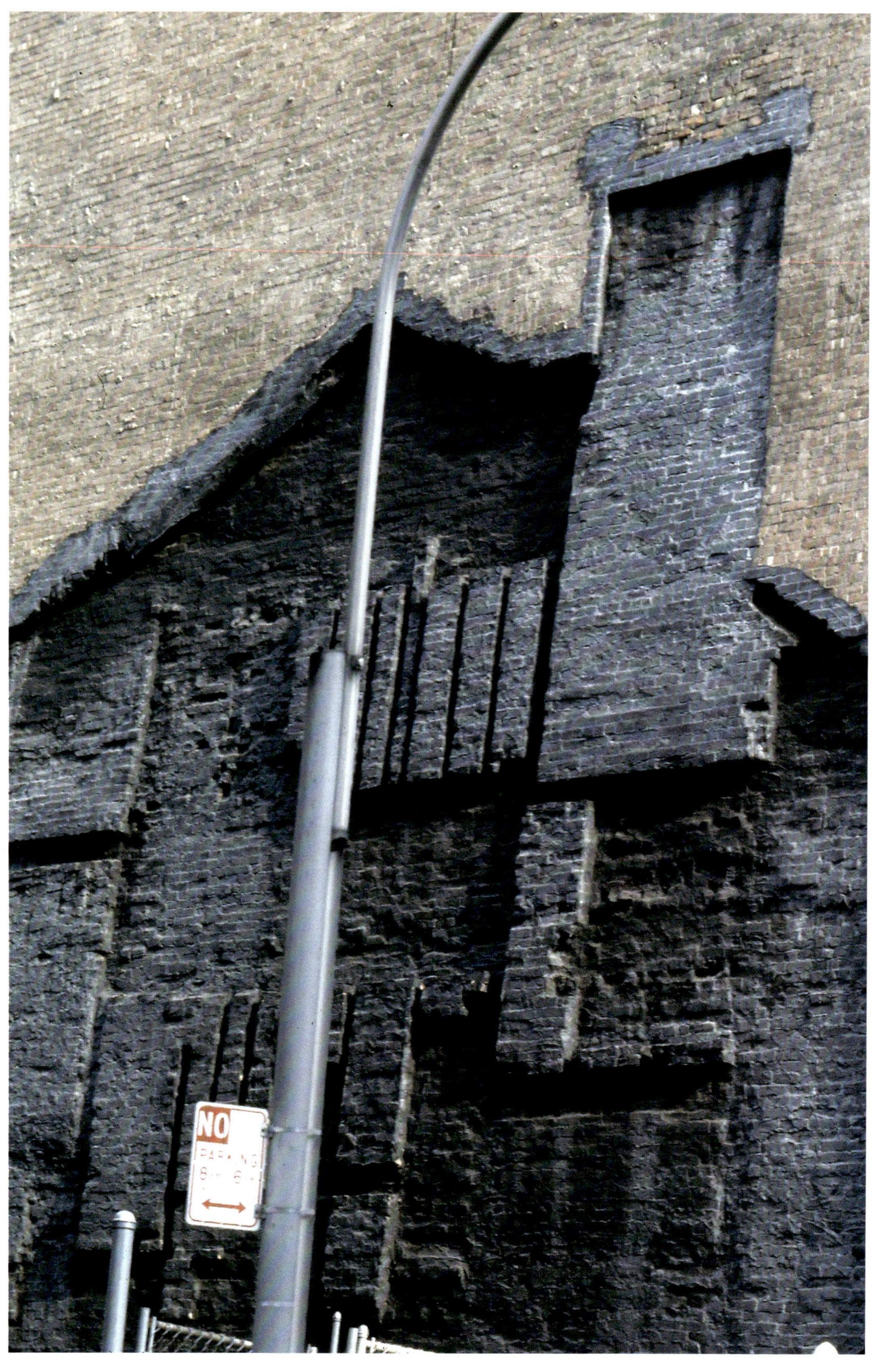

Plate 10
No. 2966, 1977, color transparency.
Allan Chasanoff Archive, Yale University Art Gallery

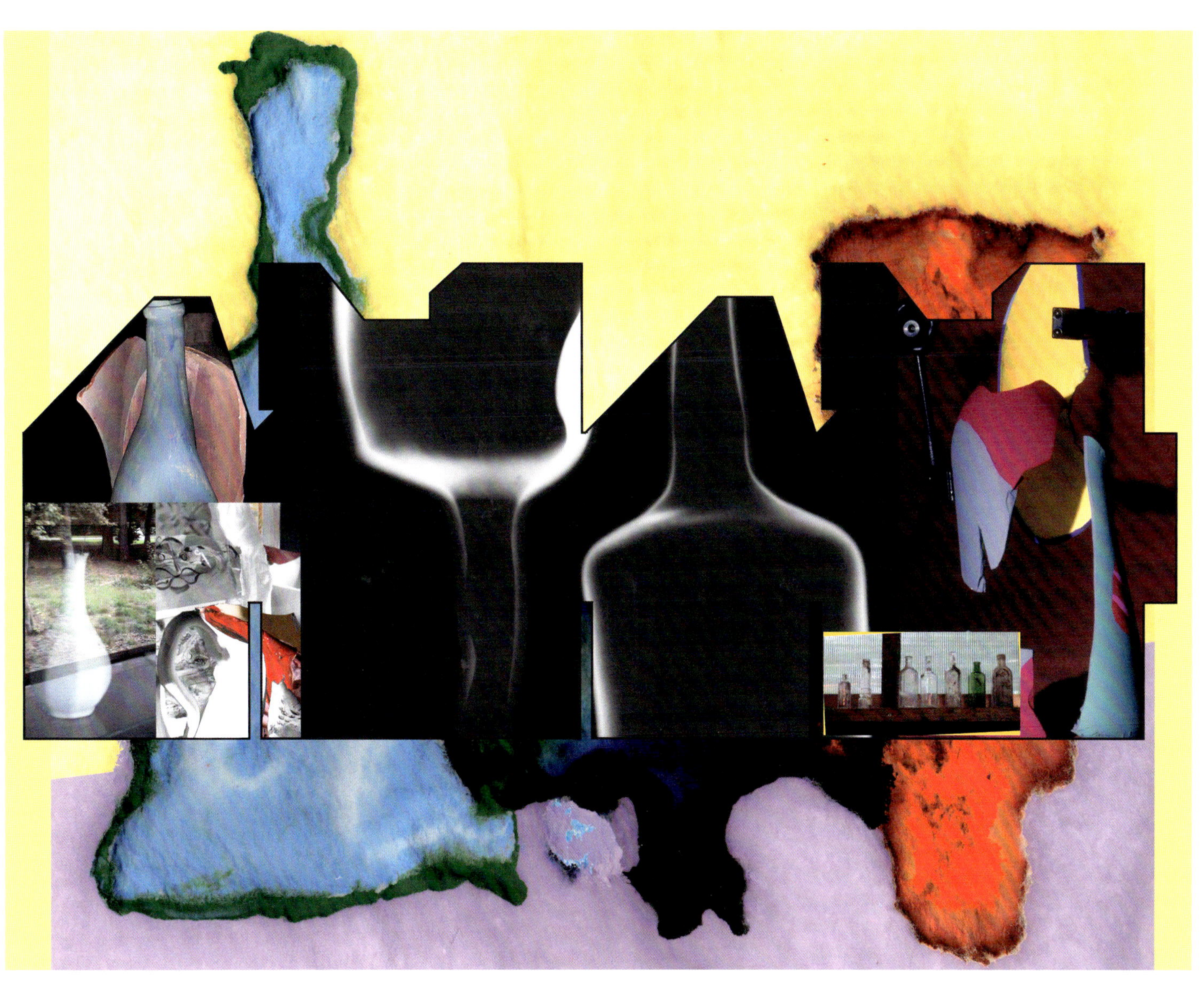

Plate 11
No. 7407, 2006, digital montage. Box (outline) series.
Allan Chasanoff Archive, Yale University Art Gallery

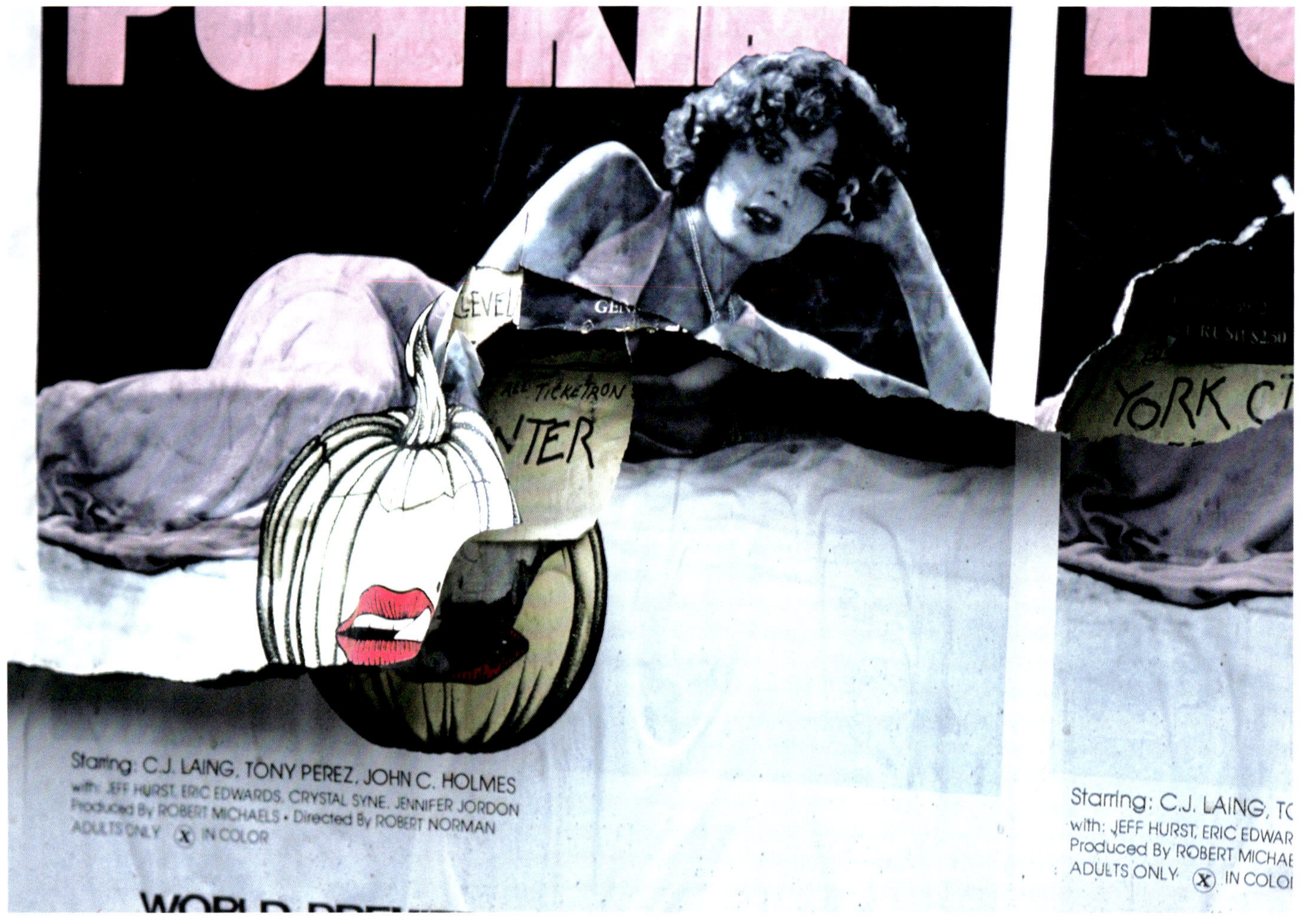

Plate 12
No. 2338, 1976, color transparency. Poster series.
Allan Chasanoff Archive, Yale University Art Gallery

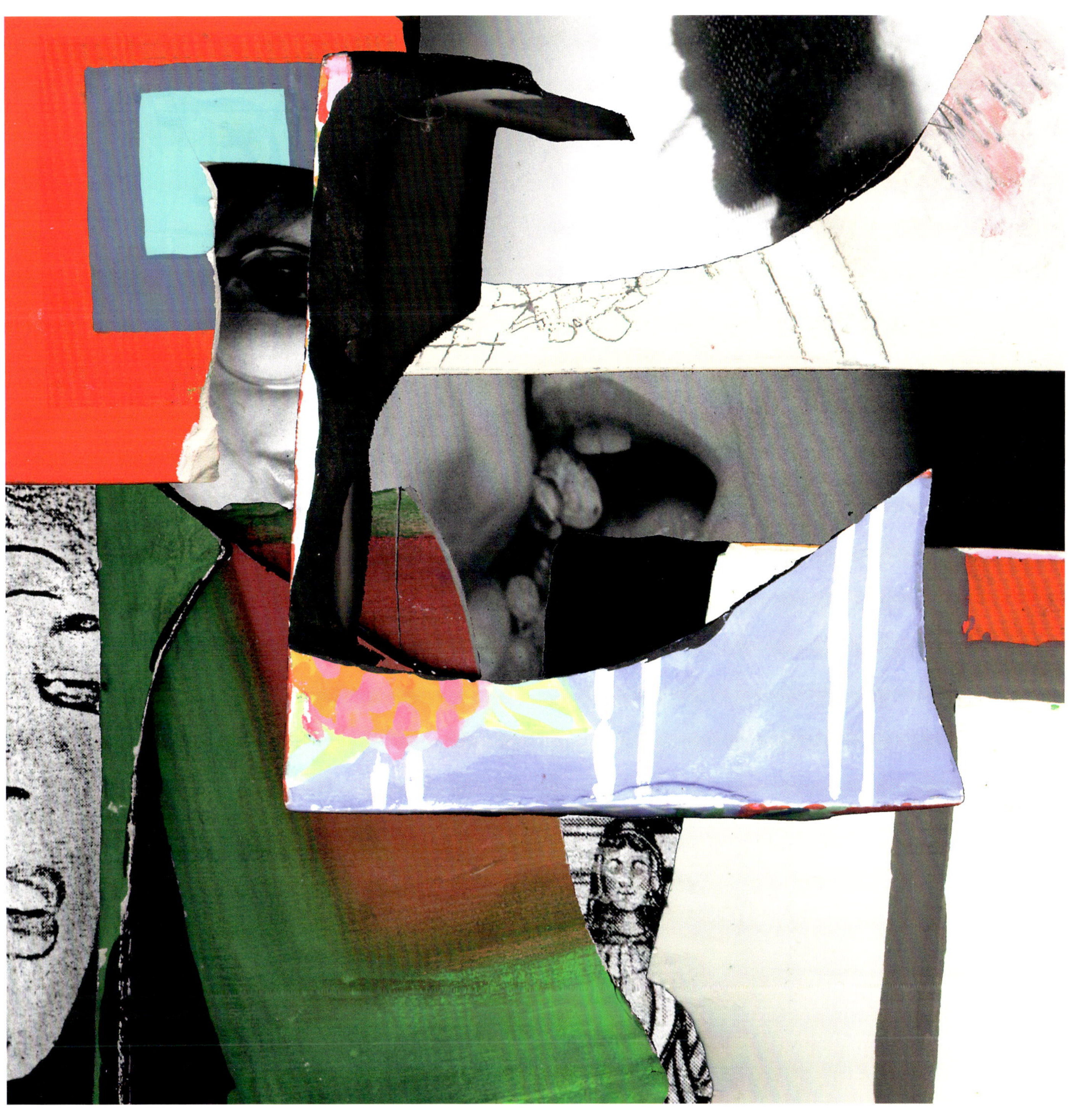

Note

Chasanoff enjoyed the fact that this digital montage looks like it could be a “straight” photograph of a still life setup, saying, “I know I could have done this either way.”

The ceramic shards in the image are painted in the styles of (clockwise from top left) Josef Albers, Cy Twombly, Piet Mondrian, Mark Rothko, and, most likely, Henri Matisse.

Plate 13

No. 1015, ca. 1998, digital montage.
Allan Chasanoff Archive, Yale University Art Gallery

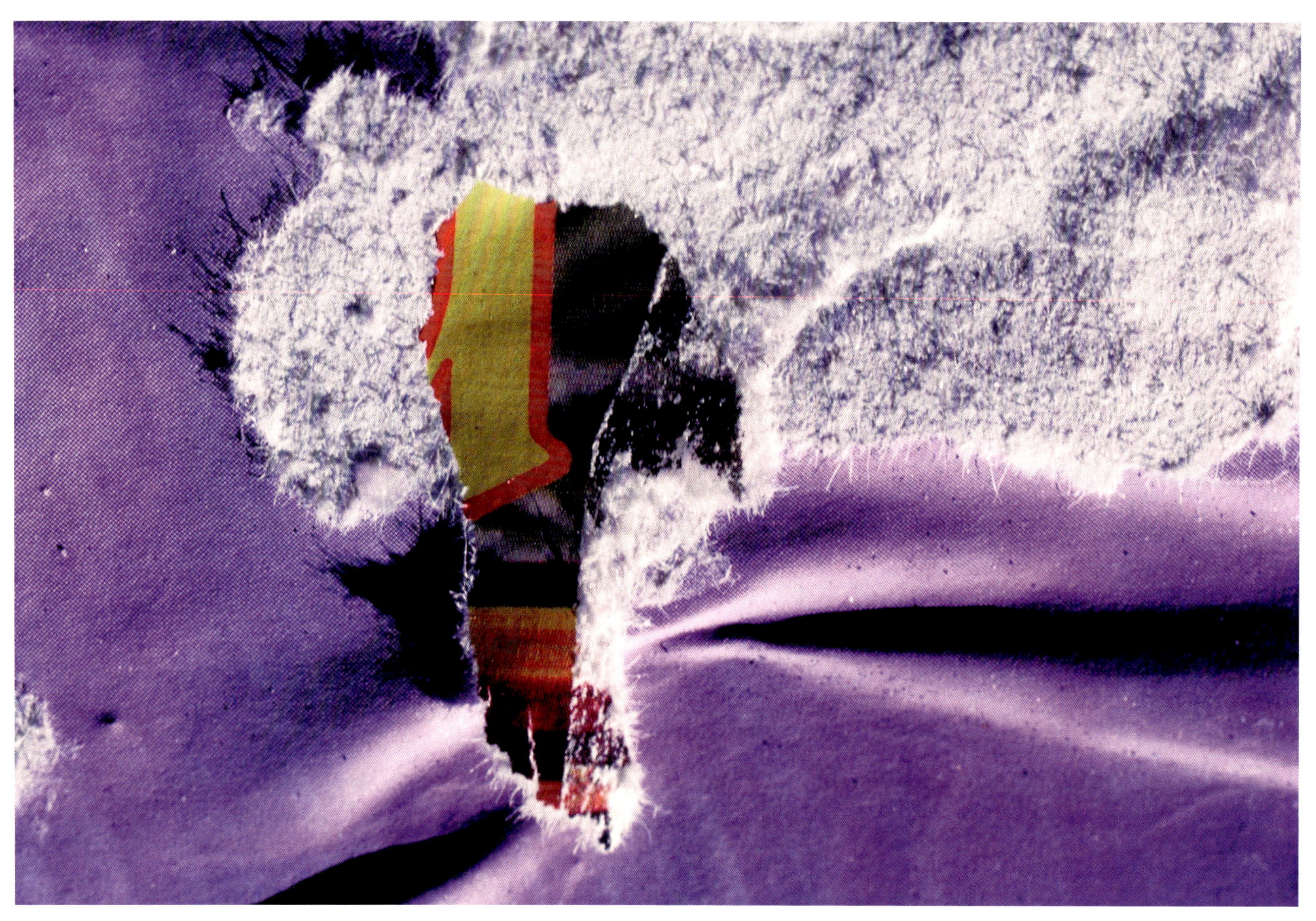

Plate 14
No. 1245, 1981, color transparency. Poster series.
Allan Chasanoff Archive, Yale University Art Gallery

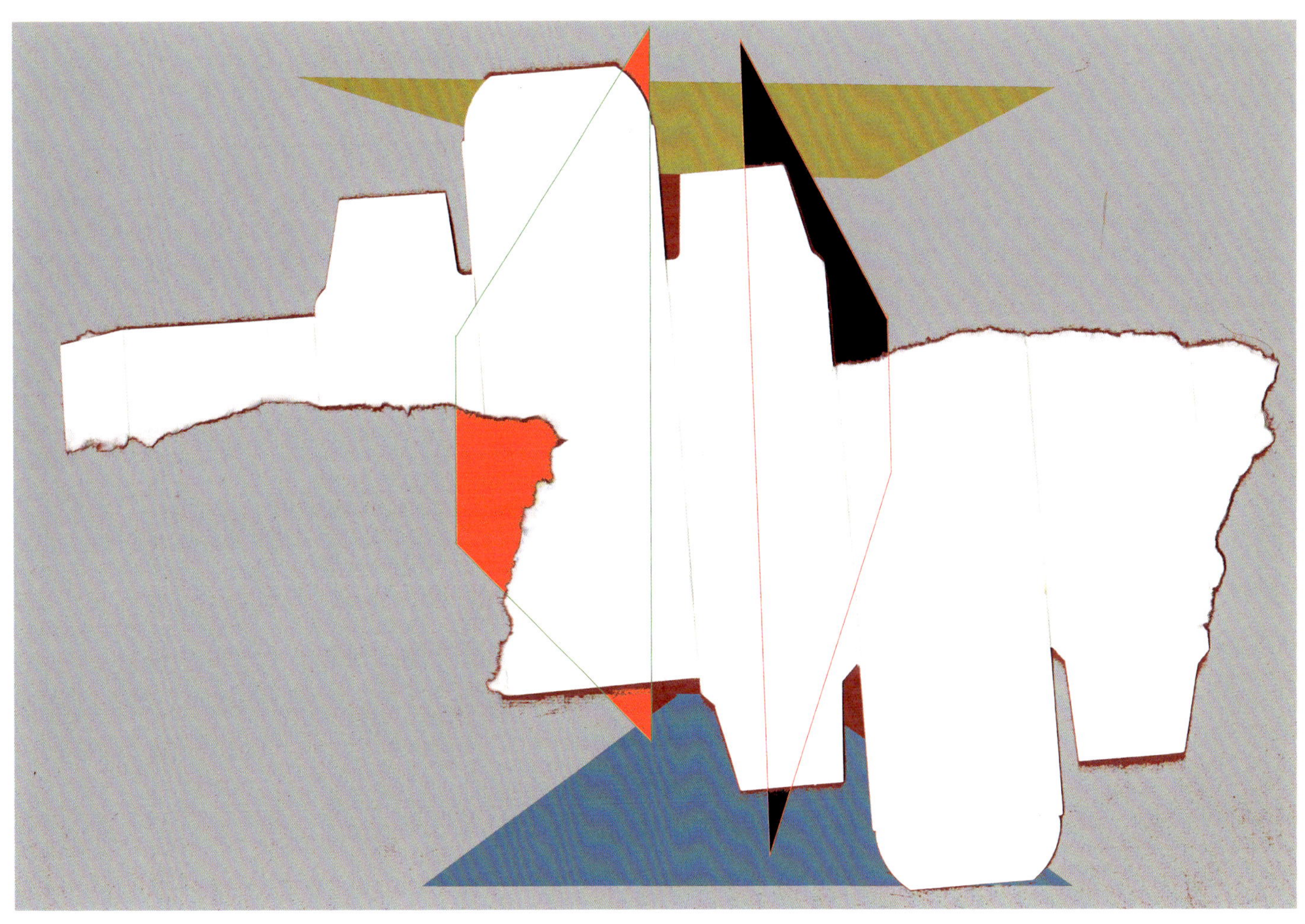

Note
The irregular white shape is a convertible box that was opened flat, torn, and scanned.

Plate 15
No. 7950, 2007, digital montage. Barn Door series.
Allan Chasanoff Archive, Yale University Art Gallery

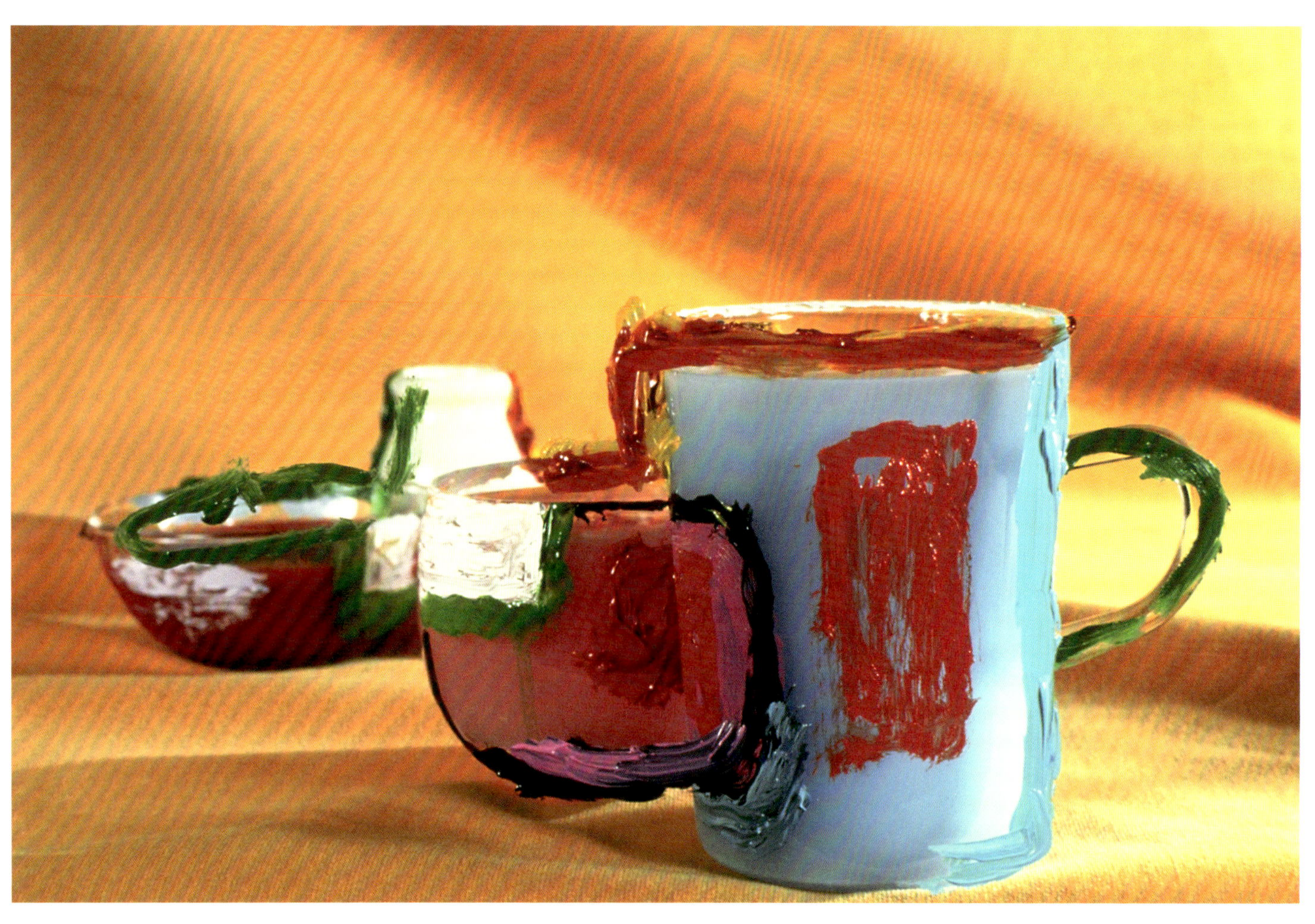

Plate 16
No. 3478, 1982, silver dye-bleach print.
Allan Chasanoff Archive, Yale University Art Gallery

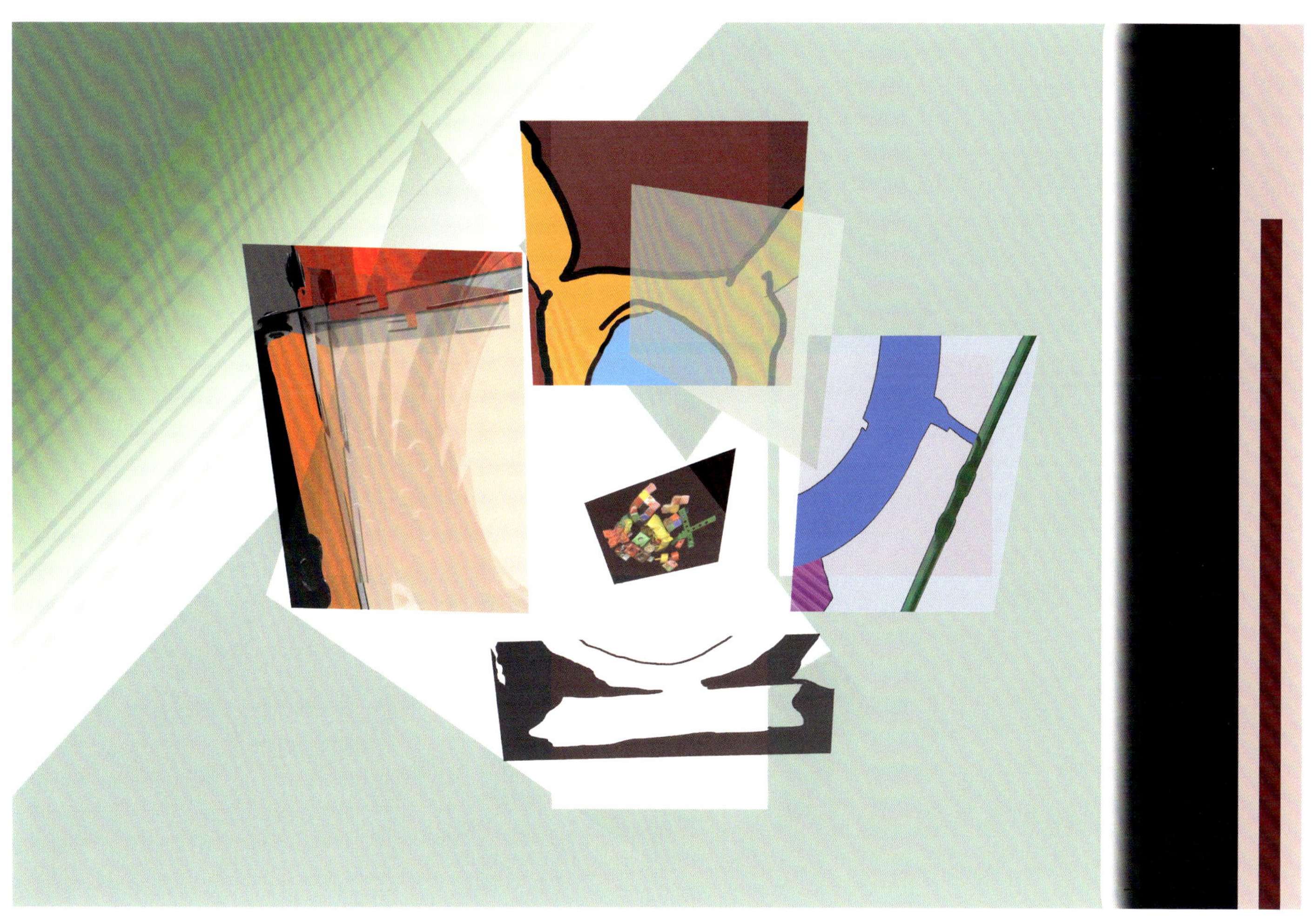

Plate 17
No. 7847, 2007, digital montage. Barn Door series.
Allan Chasanoff Archive, Yale University Art Gallery

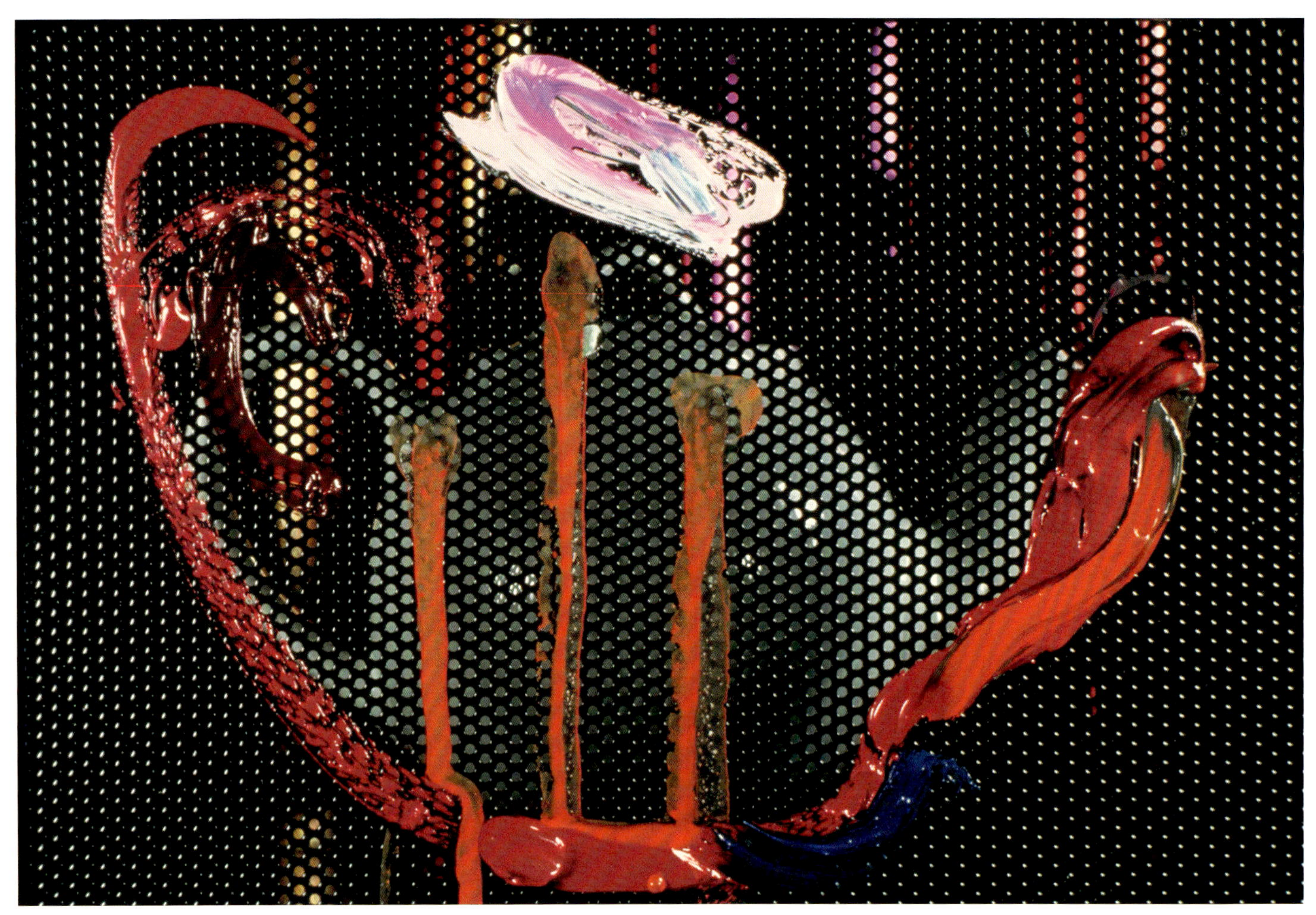

Plate 18
No. 1334, 1983, silver dye-bleach print. Teapot series.
Allan Chasanoff Archive, Yale University Art Gallery

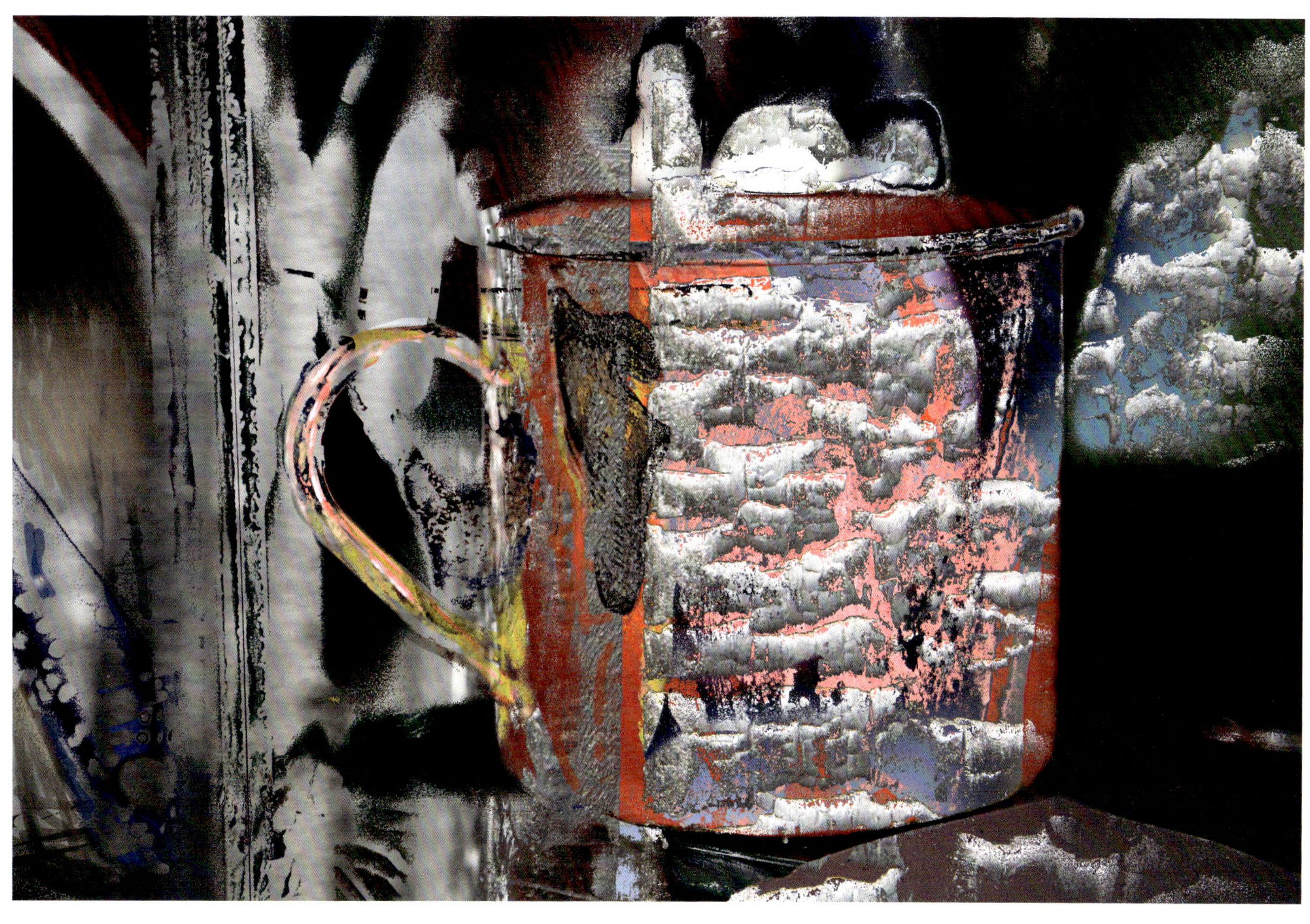

Plate 19
No. 10496, 2008, digital montage.
Allan Chasanoff Archive, Yale University Art Gallery

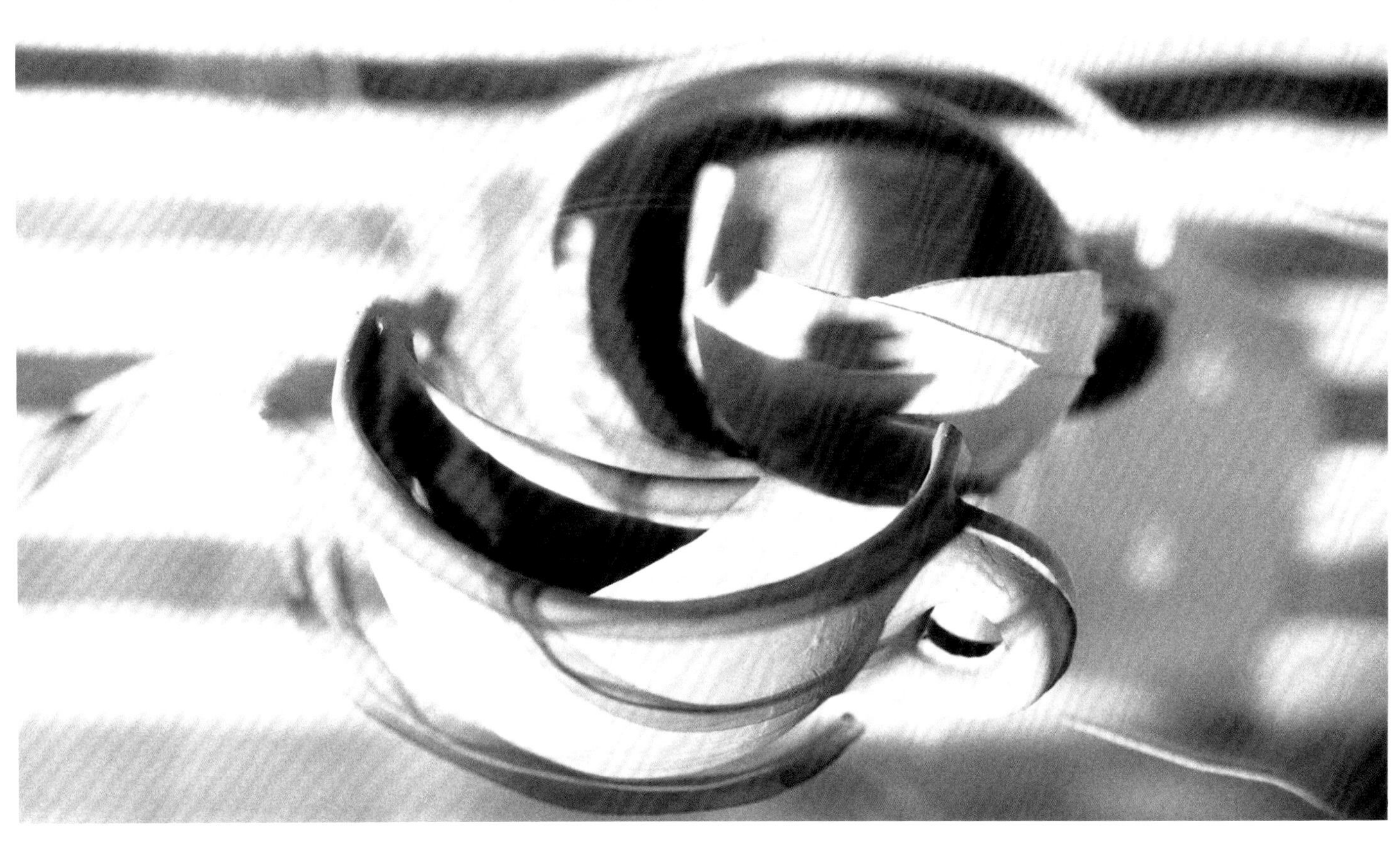

Plate 20
No. 3830, 1985, gelatin silver print. Cup series.
Allan Chasanoff Archive, Yale University Art Gallery

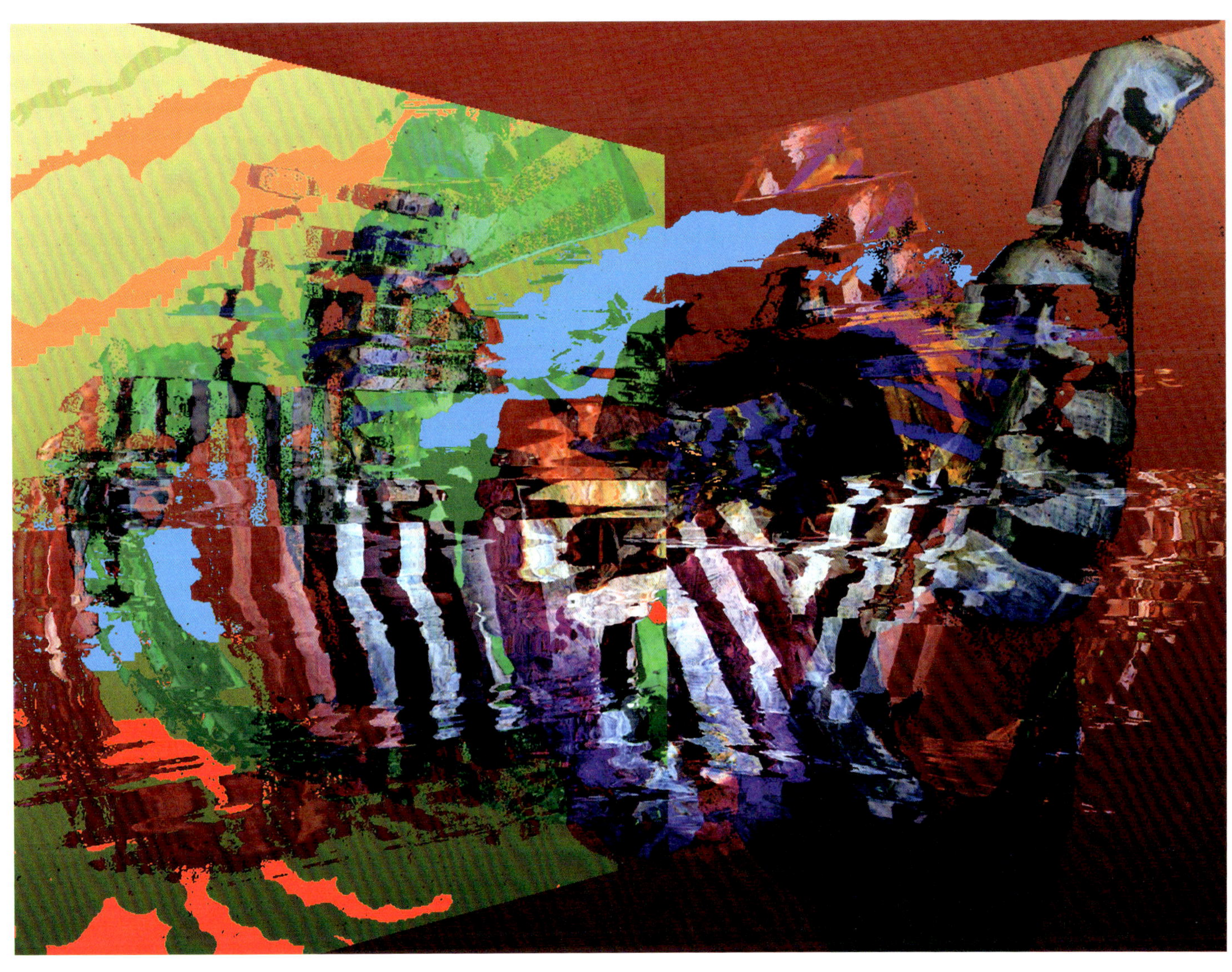

Plate 21
No. 4593, 1992, digital montage(?). Teapot series.
Allan Chasanoff Archive, Yale University Art Gallery

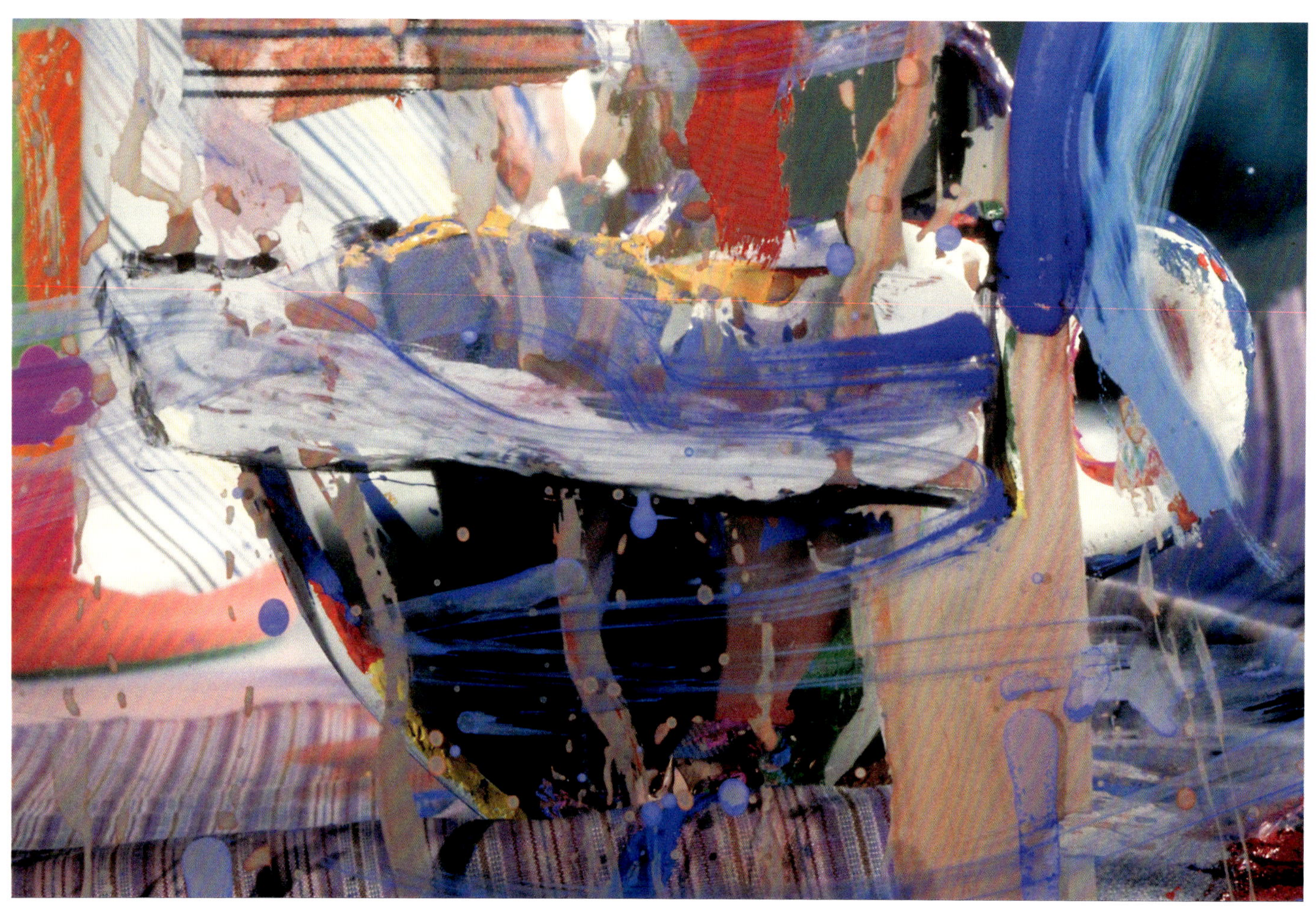

Plate 22
No. 1398, 1985, color transparency. Cup series.
Allan Chasanoff Archive, Yale University Art Gallery

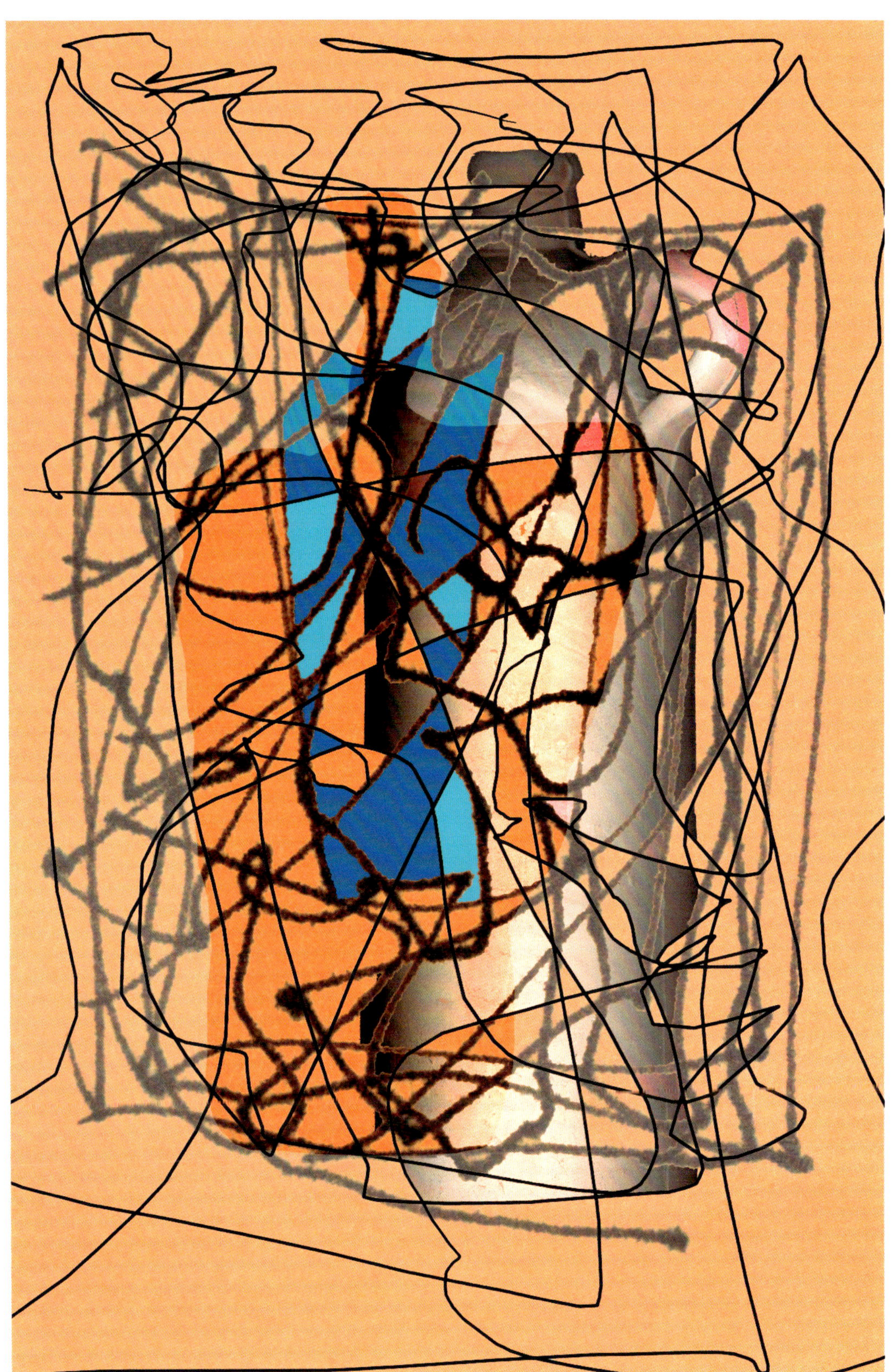

Plate 23
No. 1217, ca. 1998, digital montage.
Allan Chasanoff Archive, Yale University Art Gallery

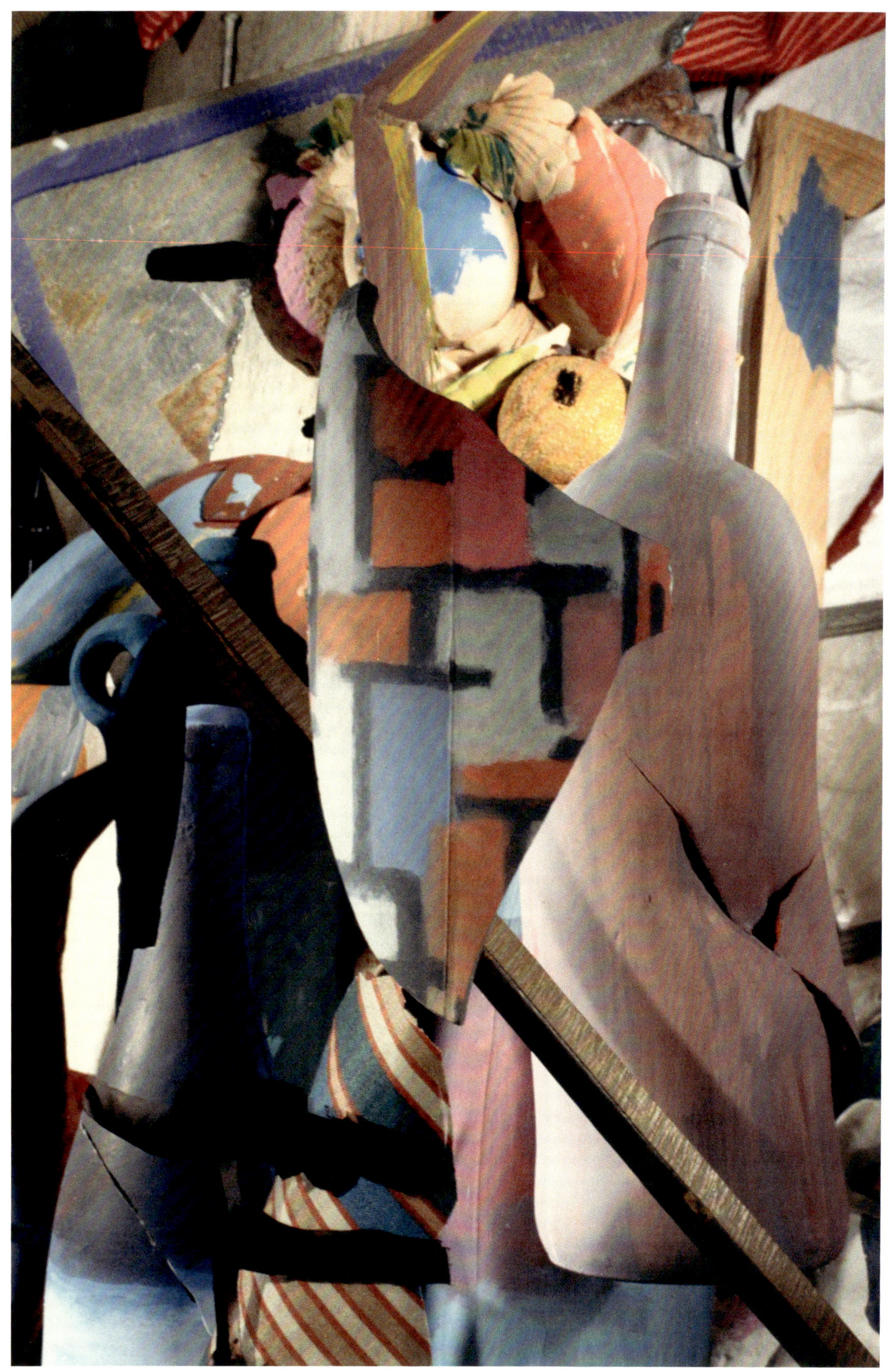

Note
The ceramic shard at center is painted in the style of Piet Mondrian. Chasanoff often had ceramics painted, then broken, for use in his still life setups.

Plate 24
No. 3747, 1986, chromogenic print.
Allan Chasanoff Archive, Yale University Art Gallery

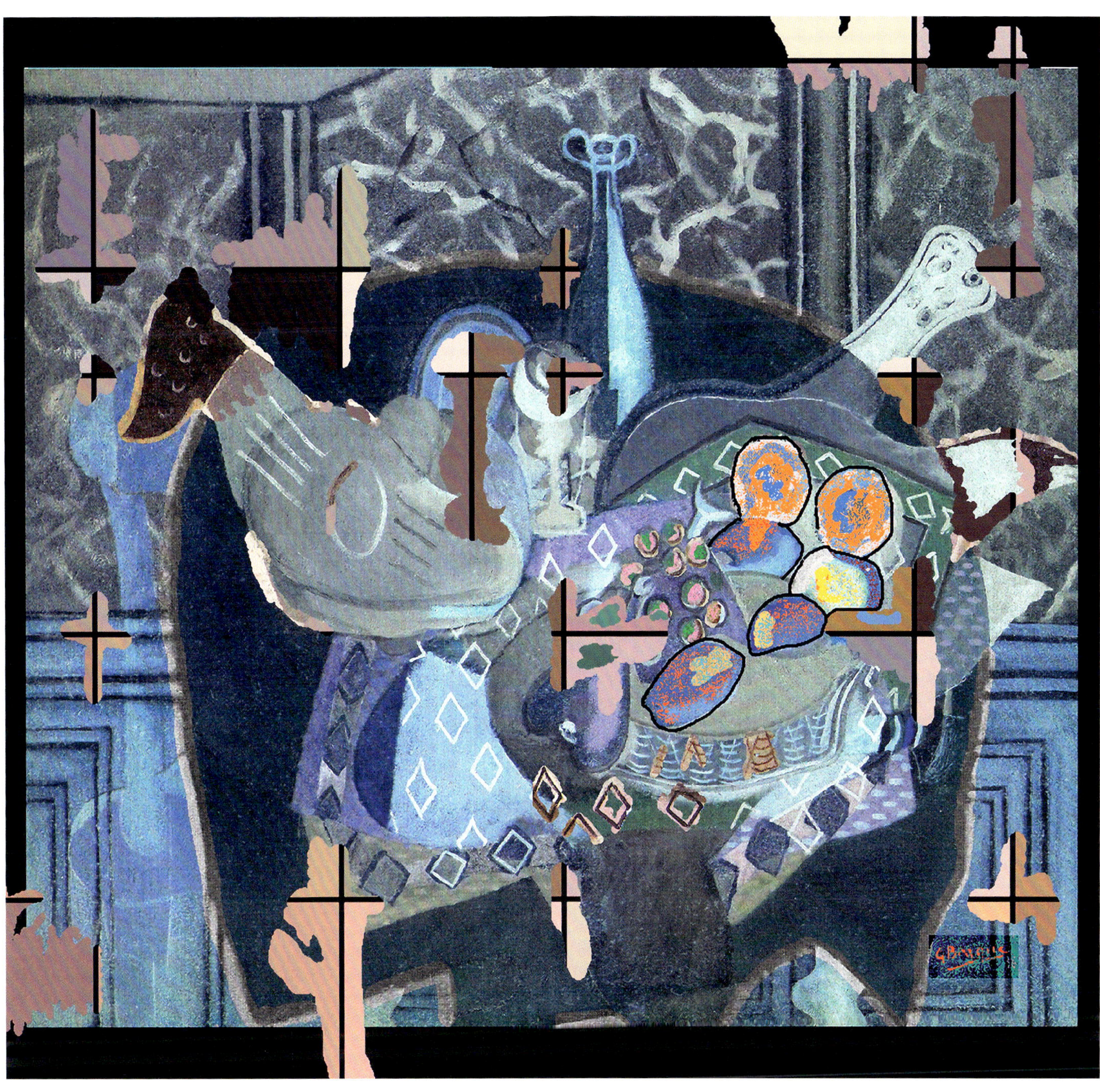

Plate 25
No. 4261, 1989, digital montage.
Allan Chasanoff Archive, Yale University Art Gallery

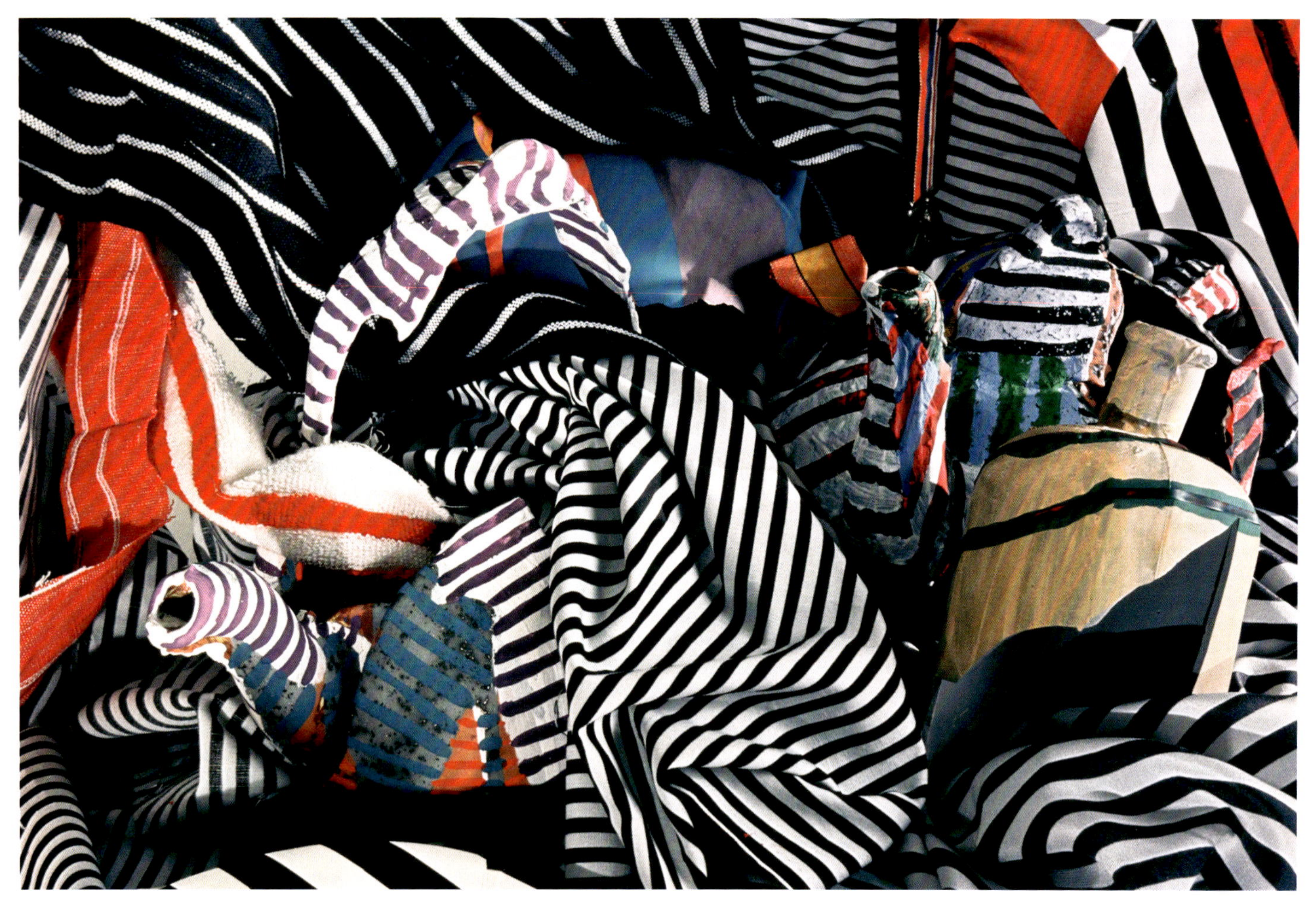

Plate 26
No. 1401, 1986, silver dye-bleach print. Teapot series.
Allan Chasanoff Archive, Yale University Art Gallery

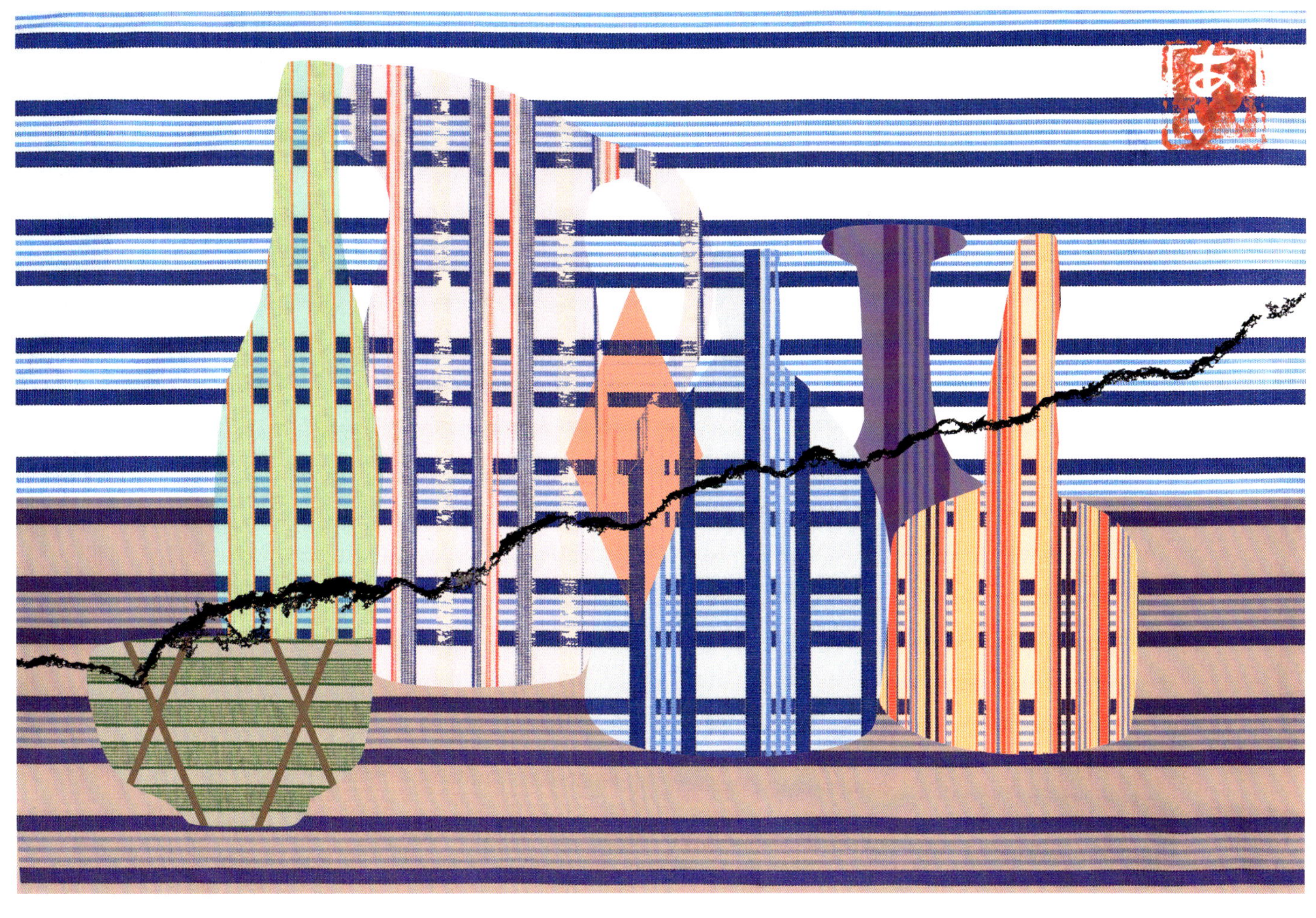

Note

The outline in this series is taken from a work by Giorgio Morandi that fascinated Chasanoff (see fig. 5). Striped patterns were scanned from Chasanoff's shirts. The black horizontal line is an early example of a pavement crack used as a montage element (see pls. 141–61).

The scanned seal impression at top right is an interpretation of Chasanoff's concepts of ember: charcoal remnant or ash powder, drawing and writing material, associated with erasure/erasing. Commissioned by Chasanoff from Dairin Arakane in Japan in 2008, it includes the kanji character for "love."

Plate 27

No. 11825, 2015, digital montage. Morandi (outline) series.
Allan Chasanoff Archive, Yale University Art Gallery

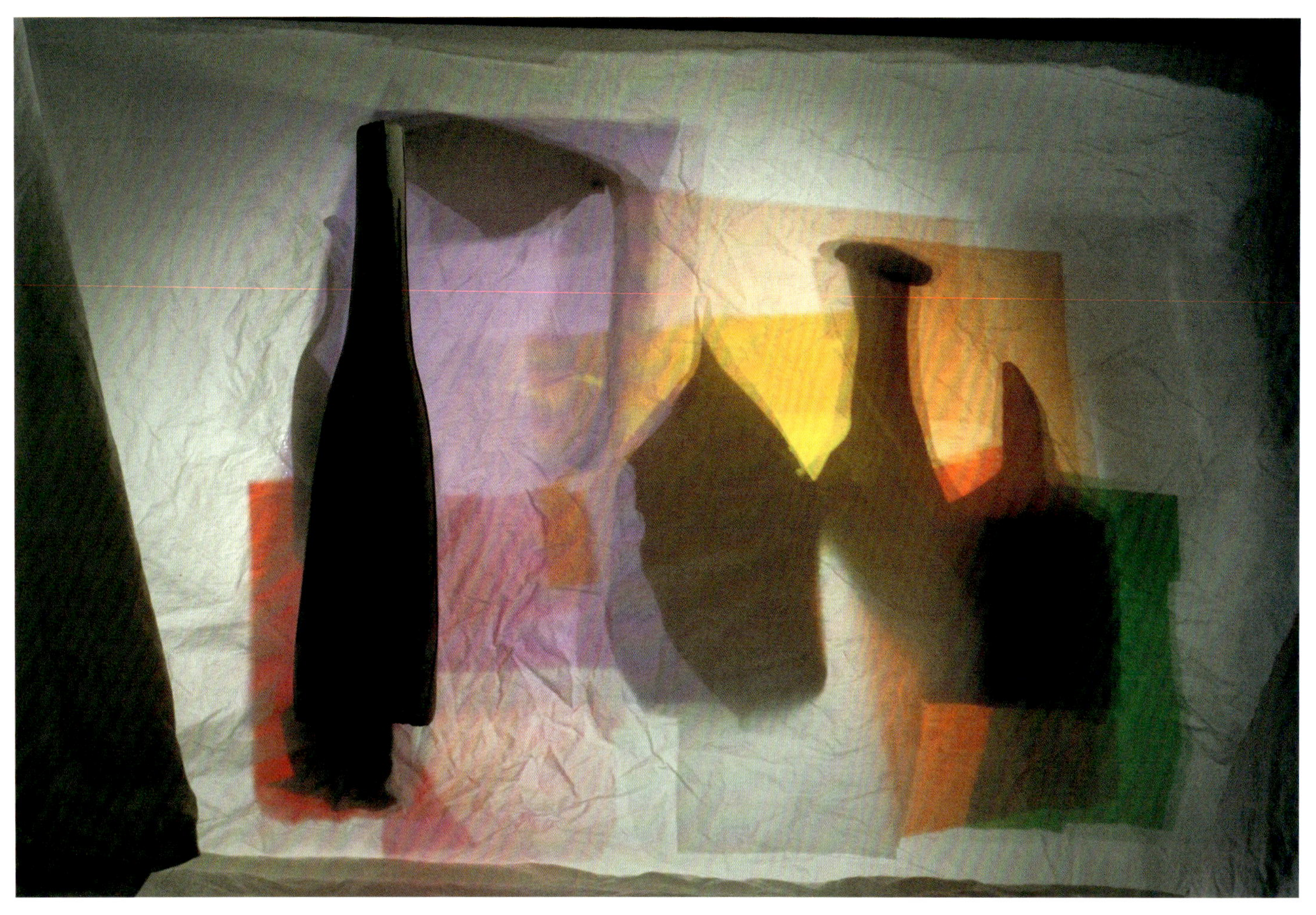

Note
Inspired by his preferred Giorgio Morandi work (see fig. 5), Chasanoff had objects made in ceramic, glass, and other materials, which he used in his still life setups, sometimes after breaking them. See also pls. 34, 39, 91, 166–67.

Plate 28
No. 1418, 1987, chromogenic print. Morandi series.
Allan Chasanoff Archive, Yale University Art Gallery

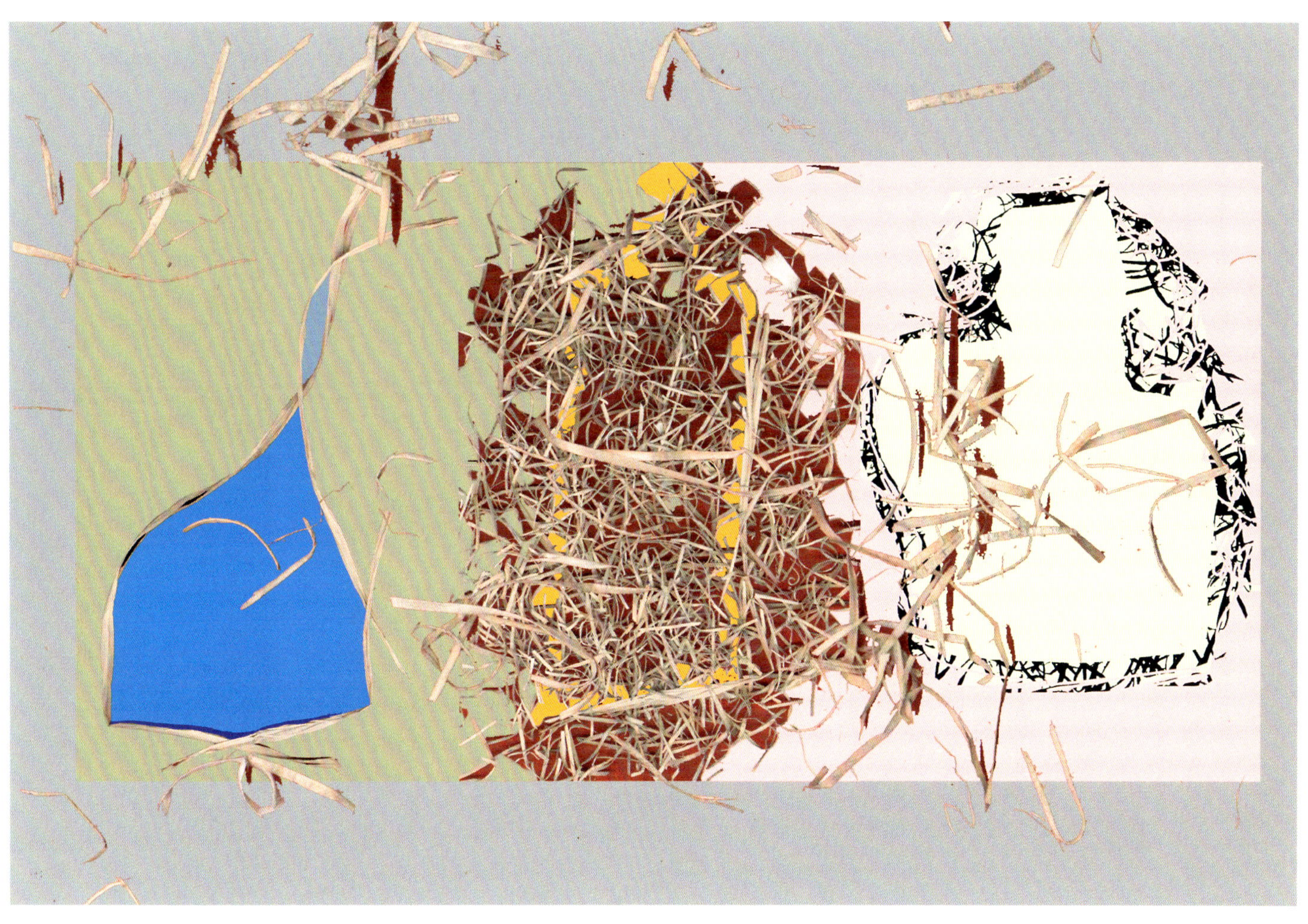

Note
This image incorporates scans of straw.

Plate 29
No. 1044, 1997, digital montage.
Allan Chasanoff Archive, Yale University Art Gallery

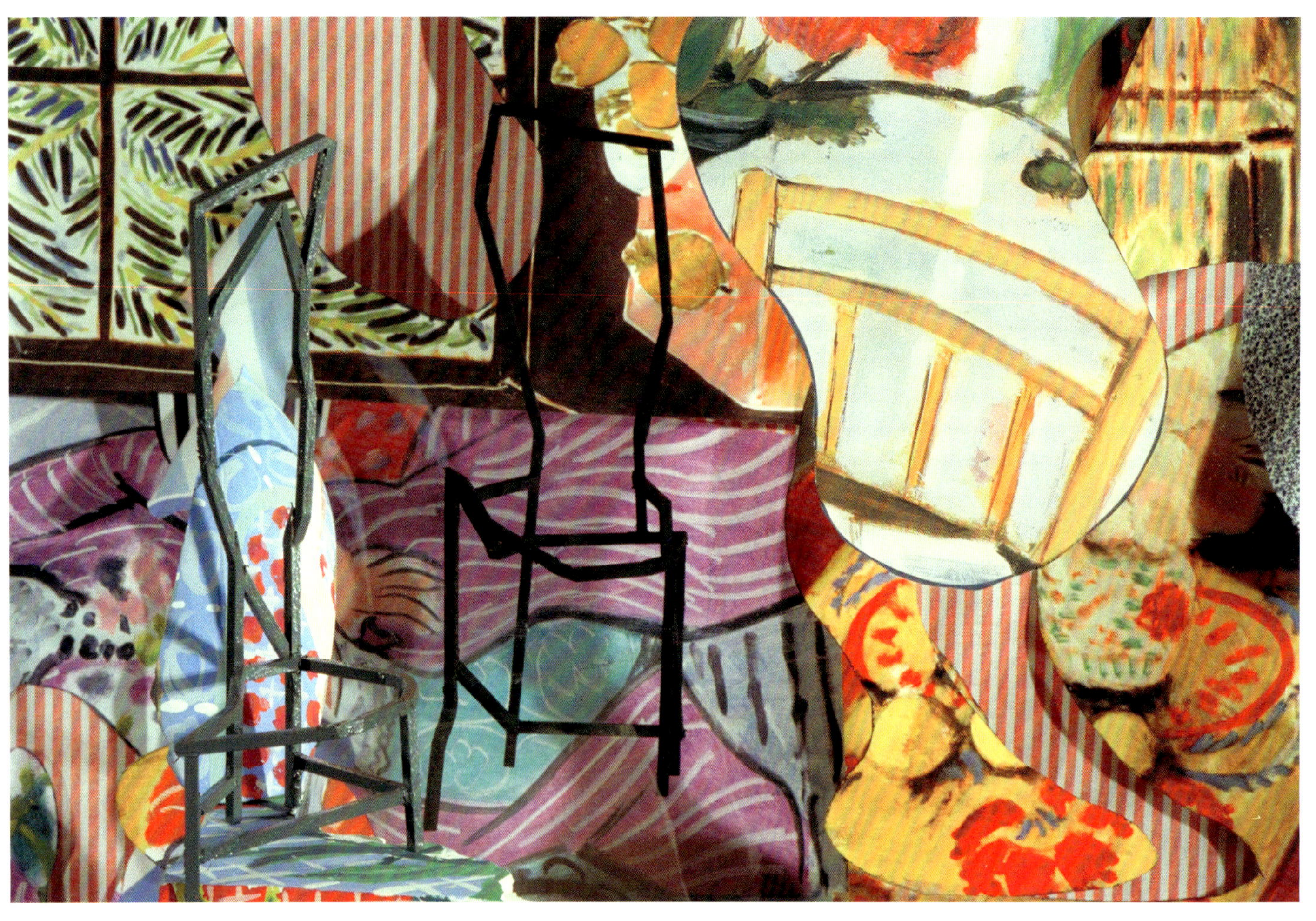

Note

The still life setup for this photograph included pieces of fabric, cutouts from reproductions of paintings by Henri Matisse, ceramic shards, and small chairs assembled from painted modeling wood.

Plate 30

No. 1408, 1987, color negative.

Allan Chasanoff Archive, Yale University Art Gallery

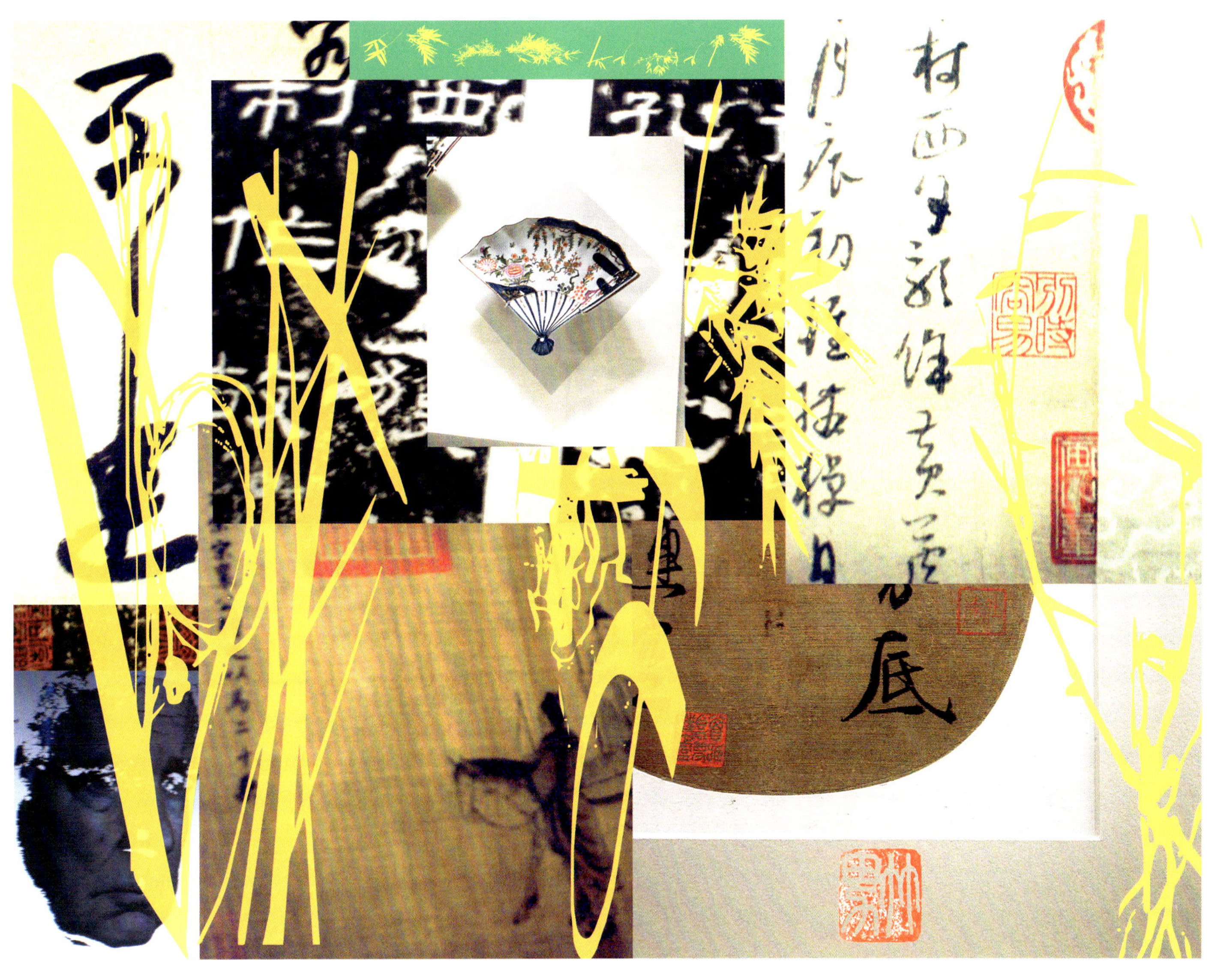

Note
The photographs combined here were taken by Chasanoff in New York on September 30, 2006, and present a visual diary of visits to the Metropolitan Museum of Art and a technology show at the Javits Center, where he made the self-portrait at bottom left. The image also includes his AMF and Bamboo A fonts (in yellow) and Bamboo Boy stamp (at bottom).

Plate 31
No. 7344, 2006, digital montage.
Allan Chasanoff Archive, Yale University Art Gallery

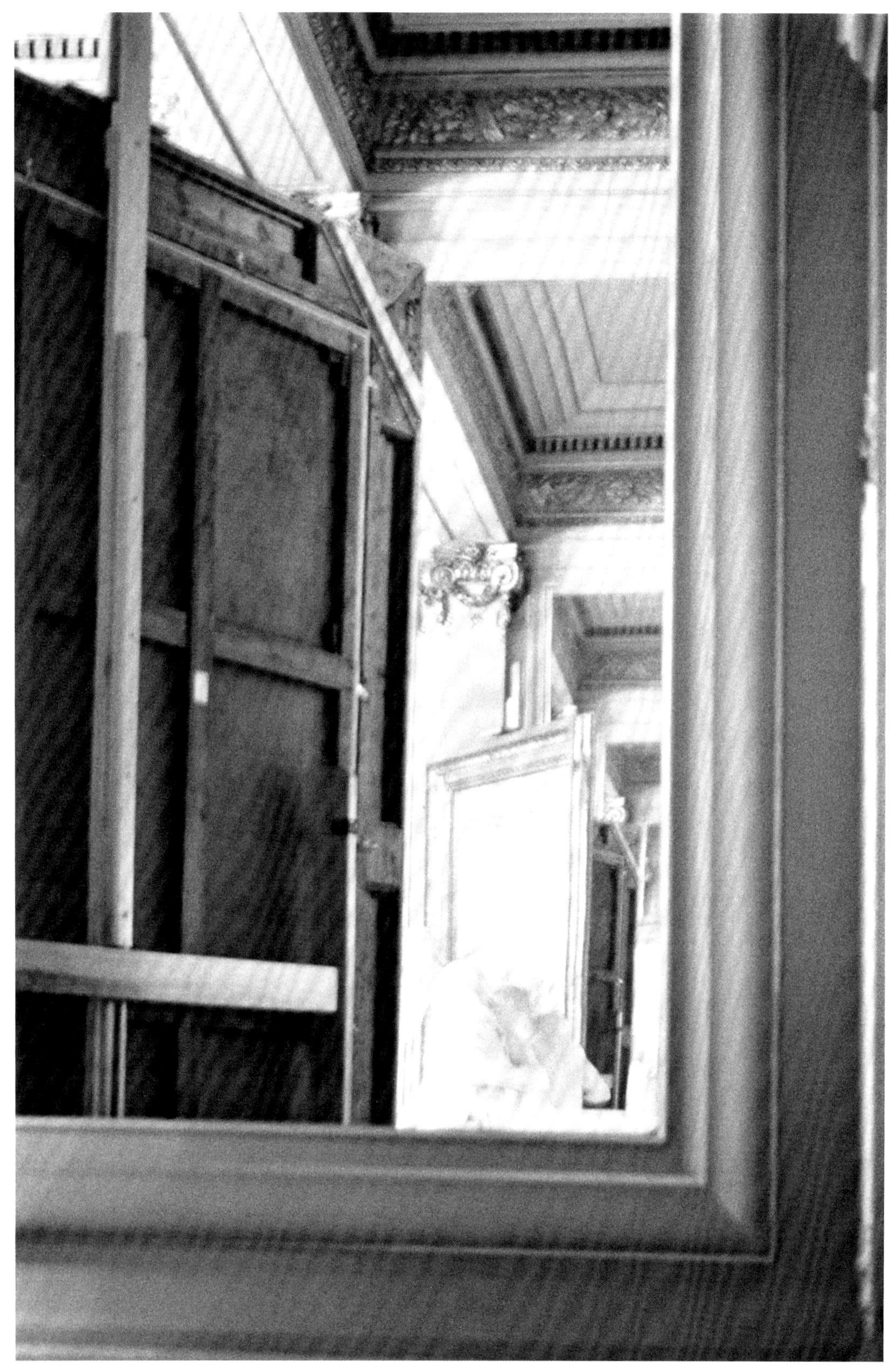

Plate 32
No. 4181, 1989, gelatin silver print.
Allan Chasanoff Archive, Yale University Art Gallery

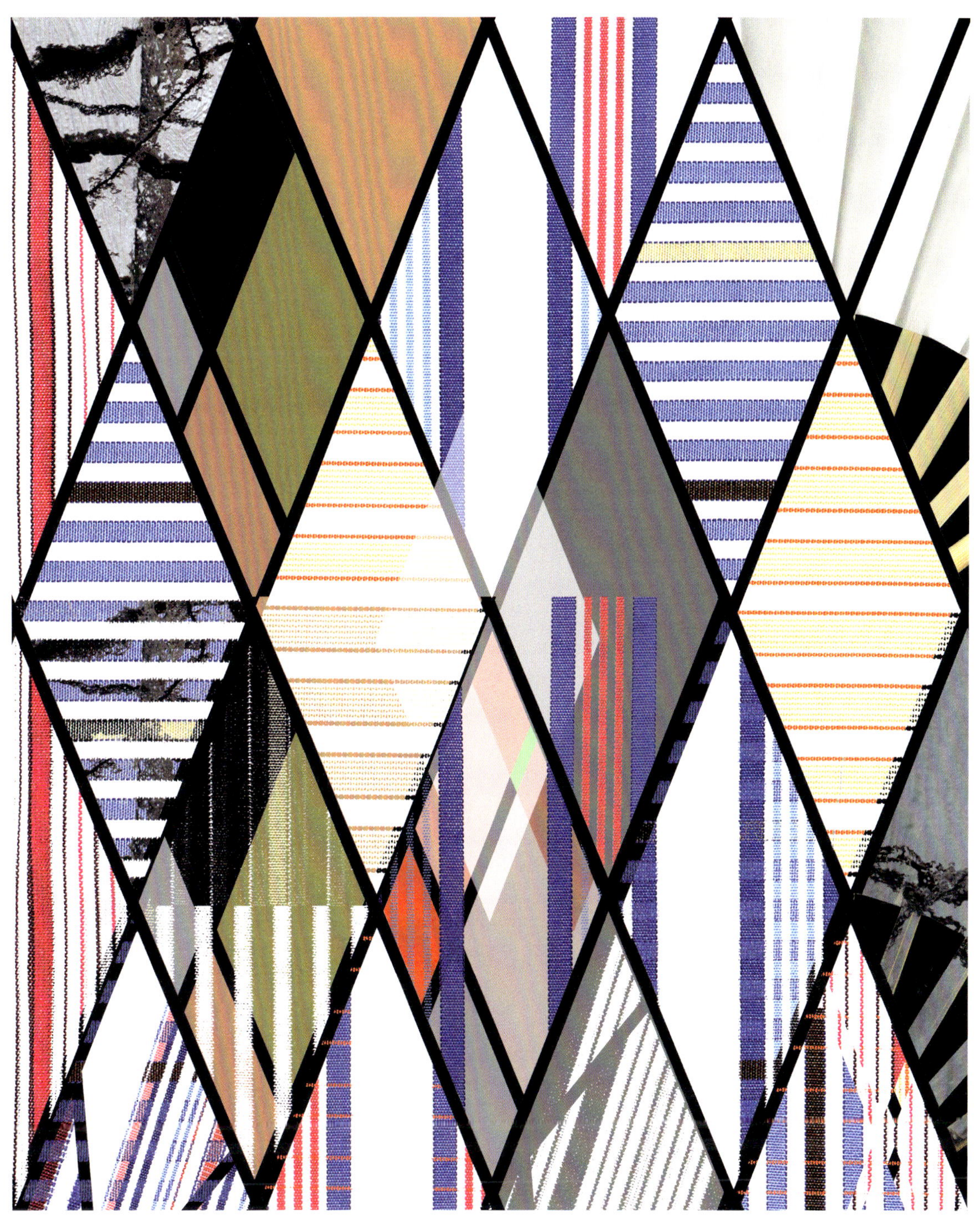

Note
Striped patterns were scanned from Chasanoff's shirts. The diamond (or *X* or harlequin) pattern had various symbolic meanings for him.

Plate 33
No. 12006, 2015, digital montage.
Allan Chasanoff Archive, Yale University Art Gallery

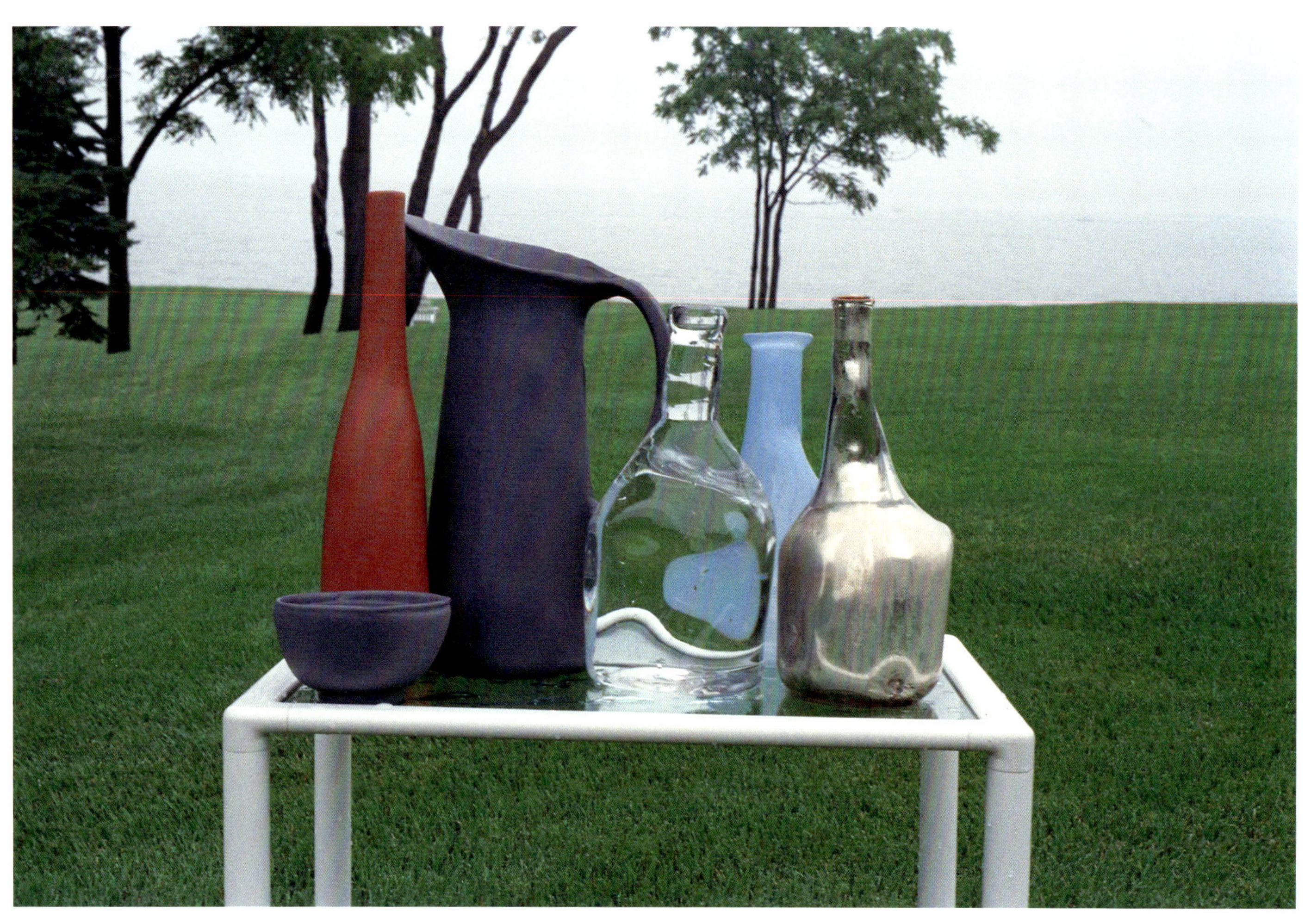

Plate 34
No. 1882, 1991, color negative. Morandi series.
Allan Chasanoff Archive, Yale University Art Gallery

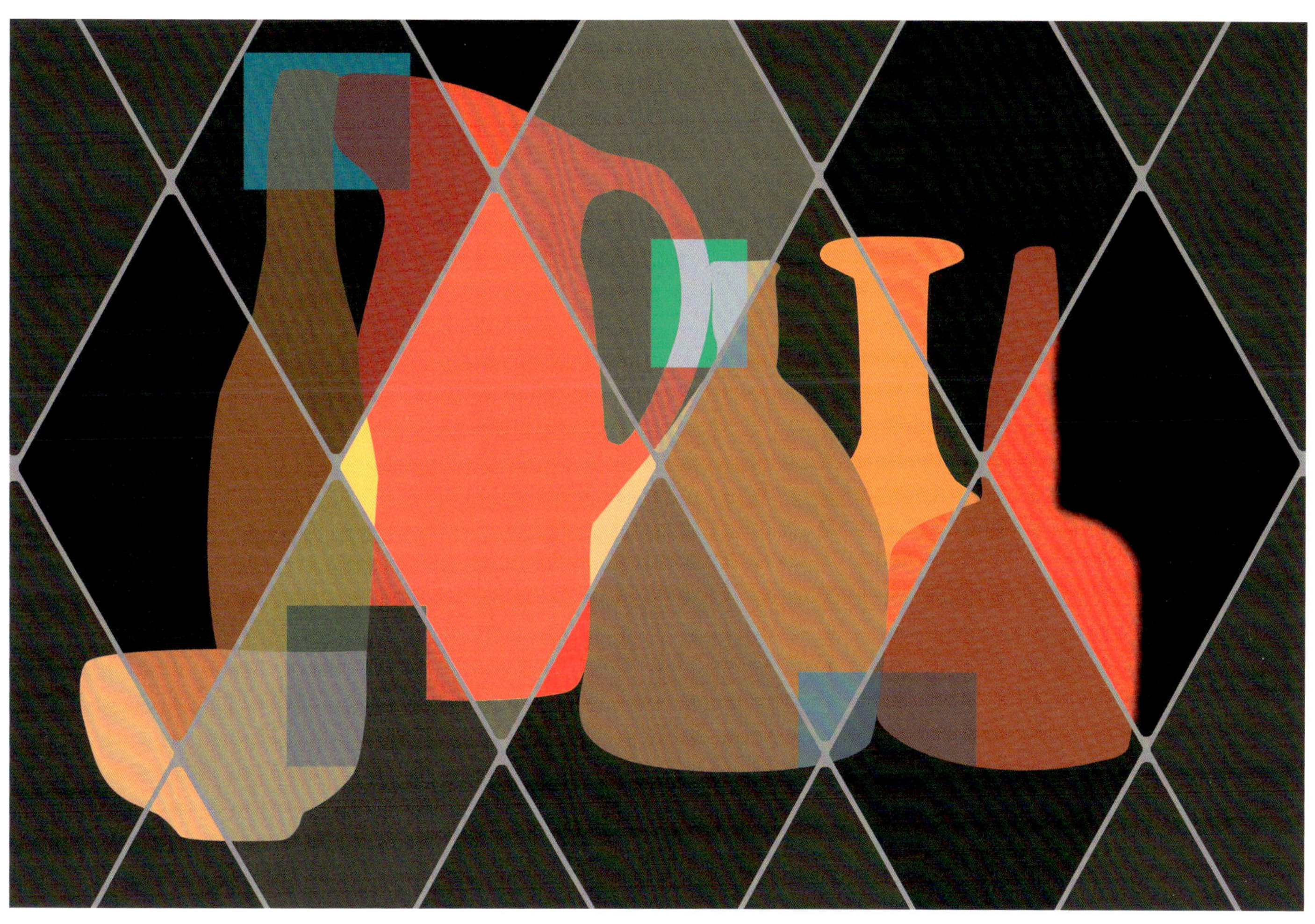

Plate 35
No. 11845, 2015, digital montage. Morandi (outline) series.
Allan Chasanoff Archive, Yale University Art Gallery

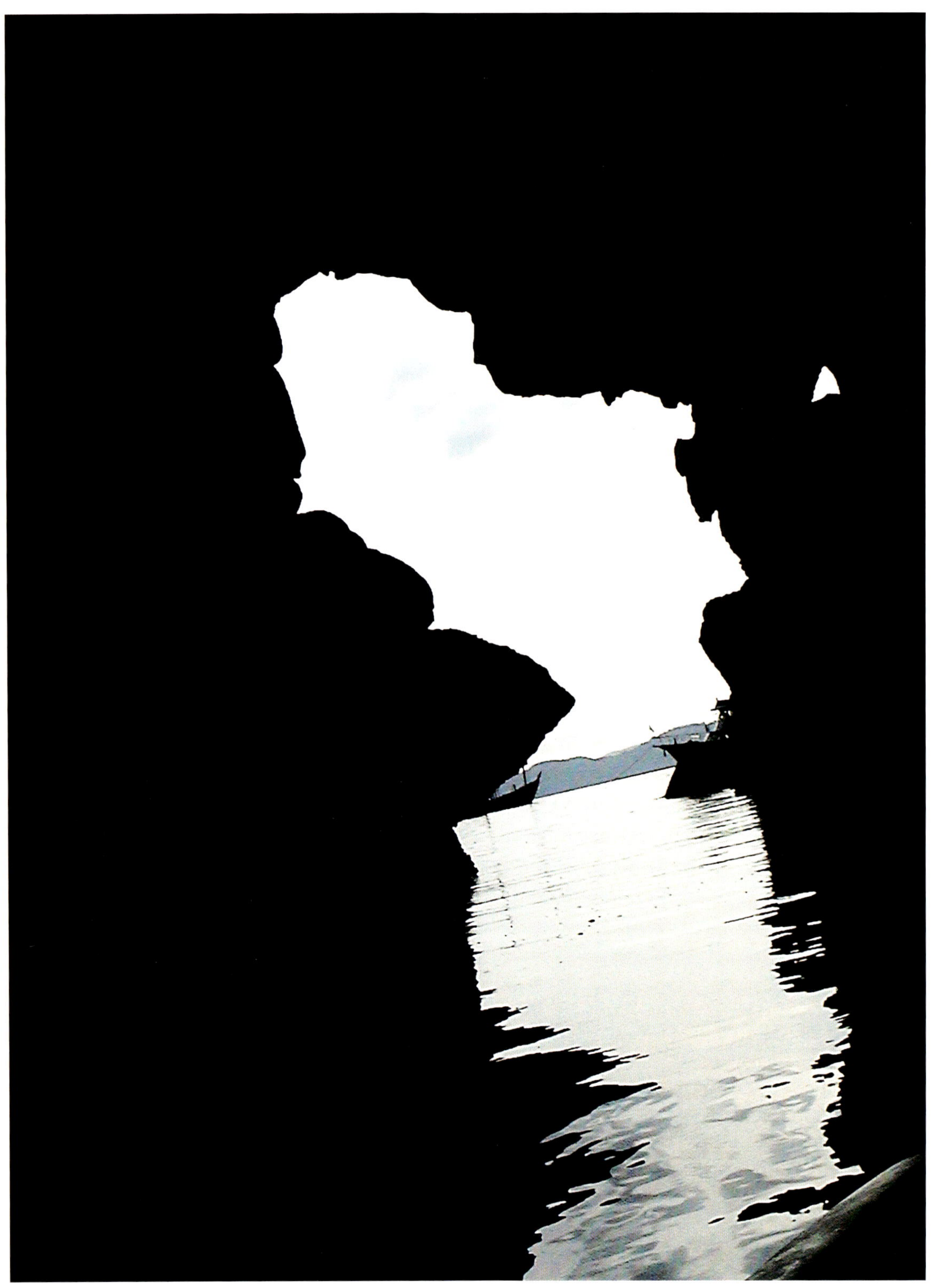

Plate 36
No. 5955, 2003, digital image file.
Allan Chasanoff Archive, Yale University Art Gallery

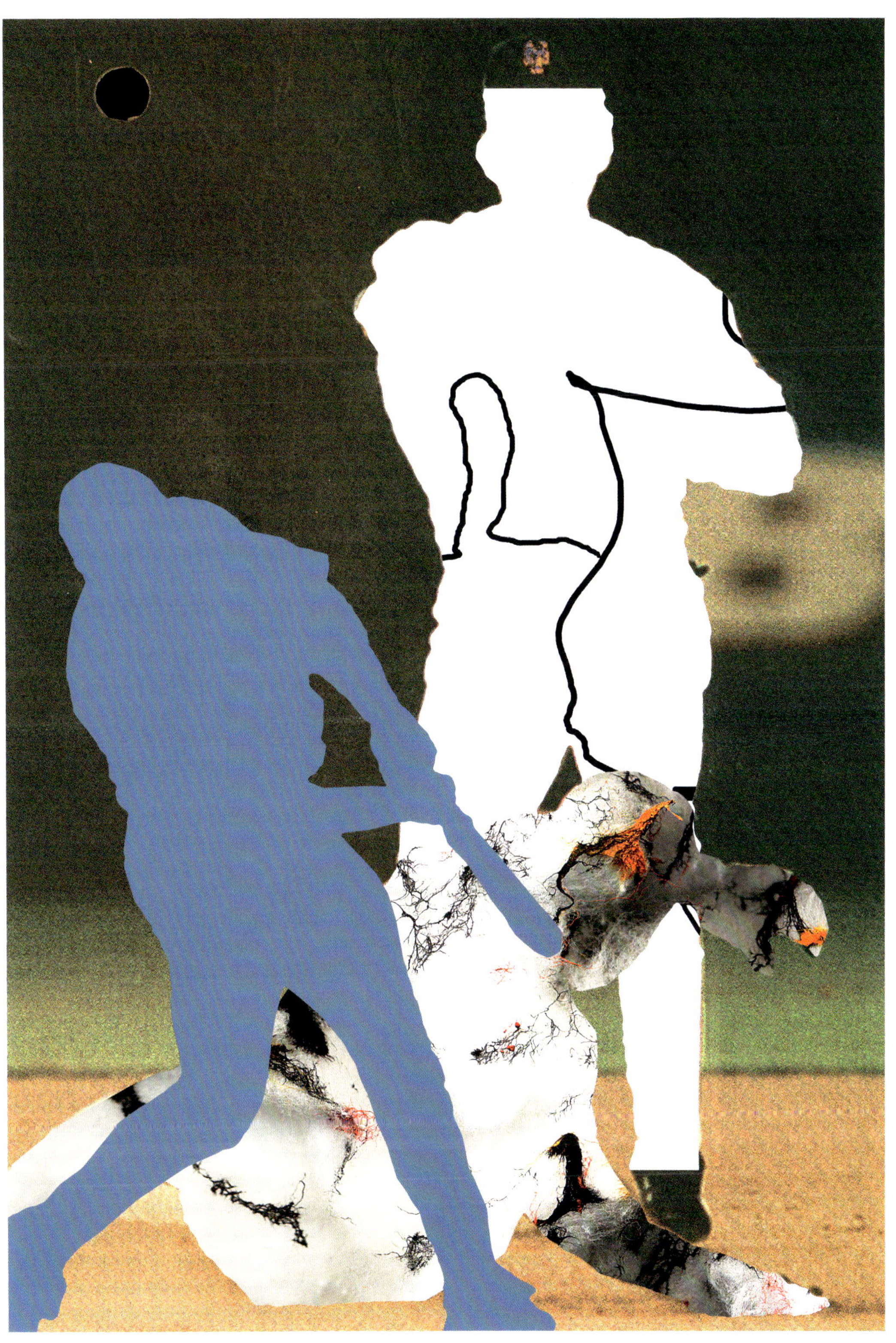

Note
The figure at bottom center contains a scan of painted cotton; the figure at top center, most likely a scan of a detail of a drawing by Chasanoff.

Plate 37
No. 6406, 2005, digital montage. Baseball (outline) series.
Allan Chasanoff Archive, Yale University Art Gallery

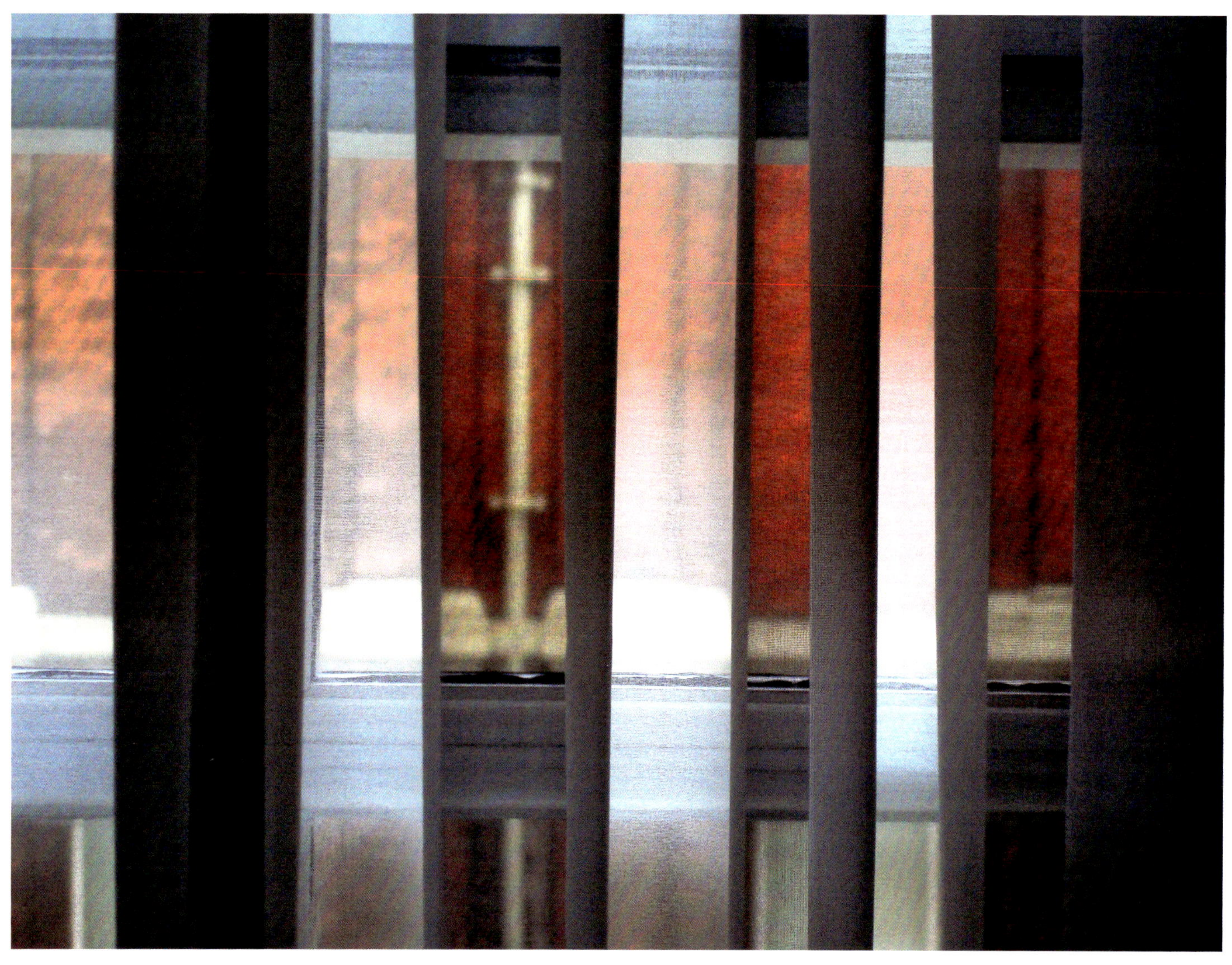

Plate 38
No. 7996, 2007, pigmented inkjet print.
Allan Chasanoff Archive, Yale University Art Gallery

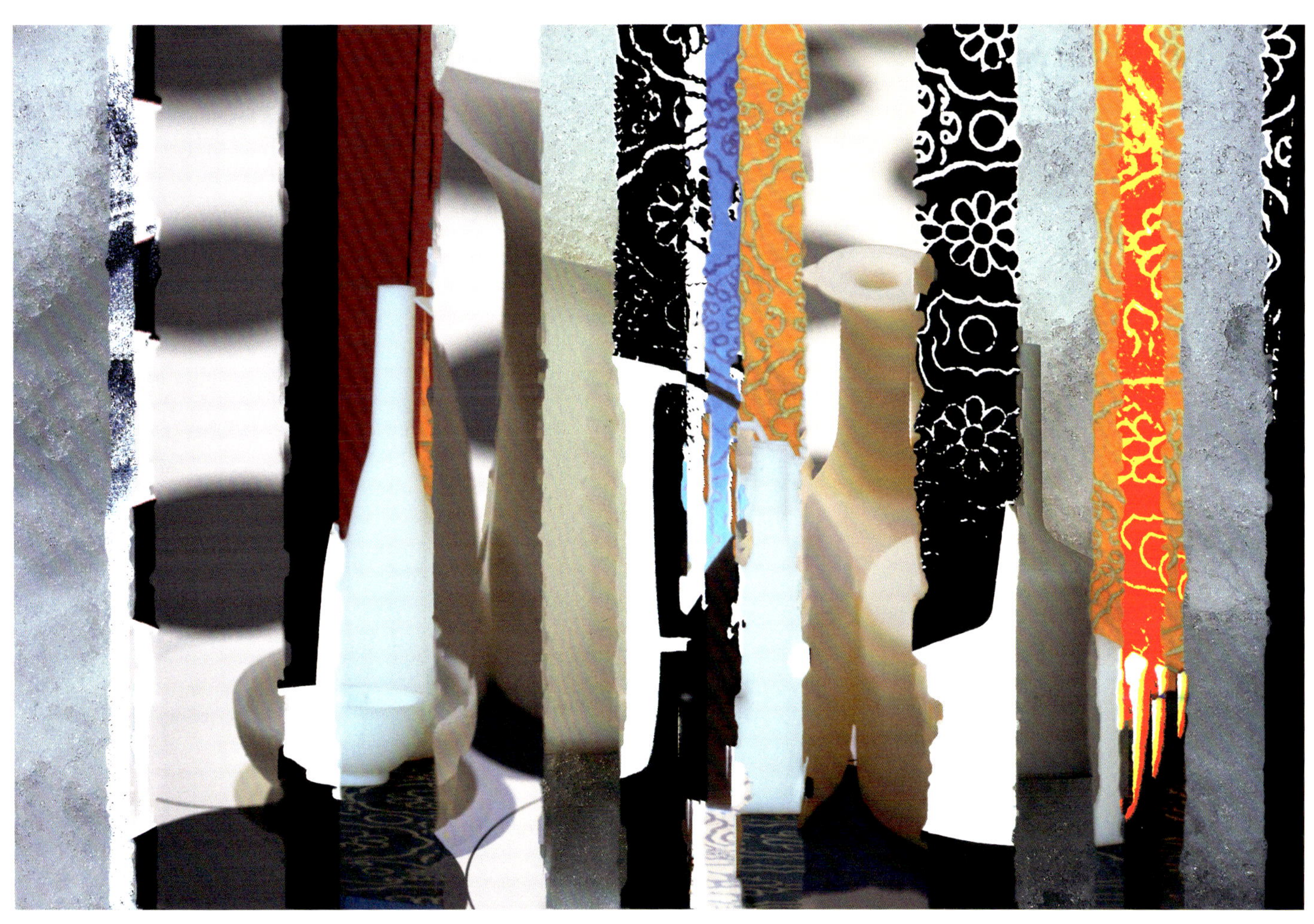

Plate 39
No. 10310, 2010, pigmented inkjet print (from digital montage). Morandi series.
Allan Chasanoff Archive, Yale University Art Gallery

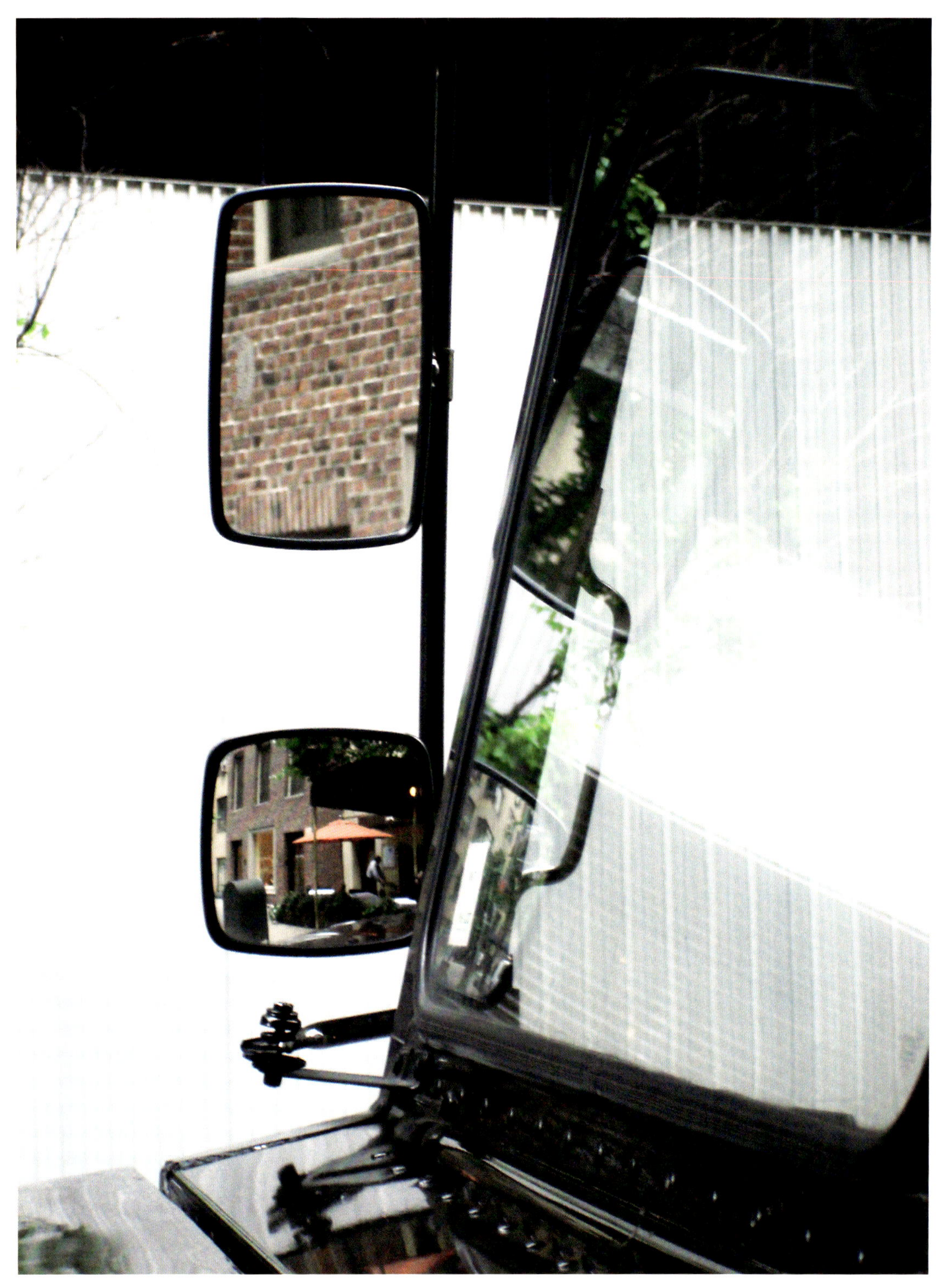

Plate 40
No. 7953, 2007, pigmented inkjet print.
Allan Chasanoff Archive, Yale University Art Gallery

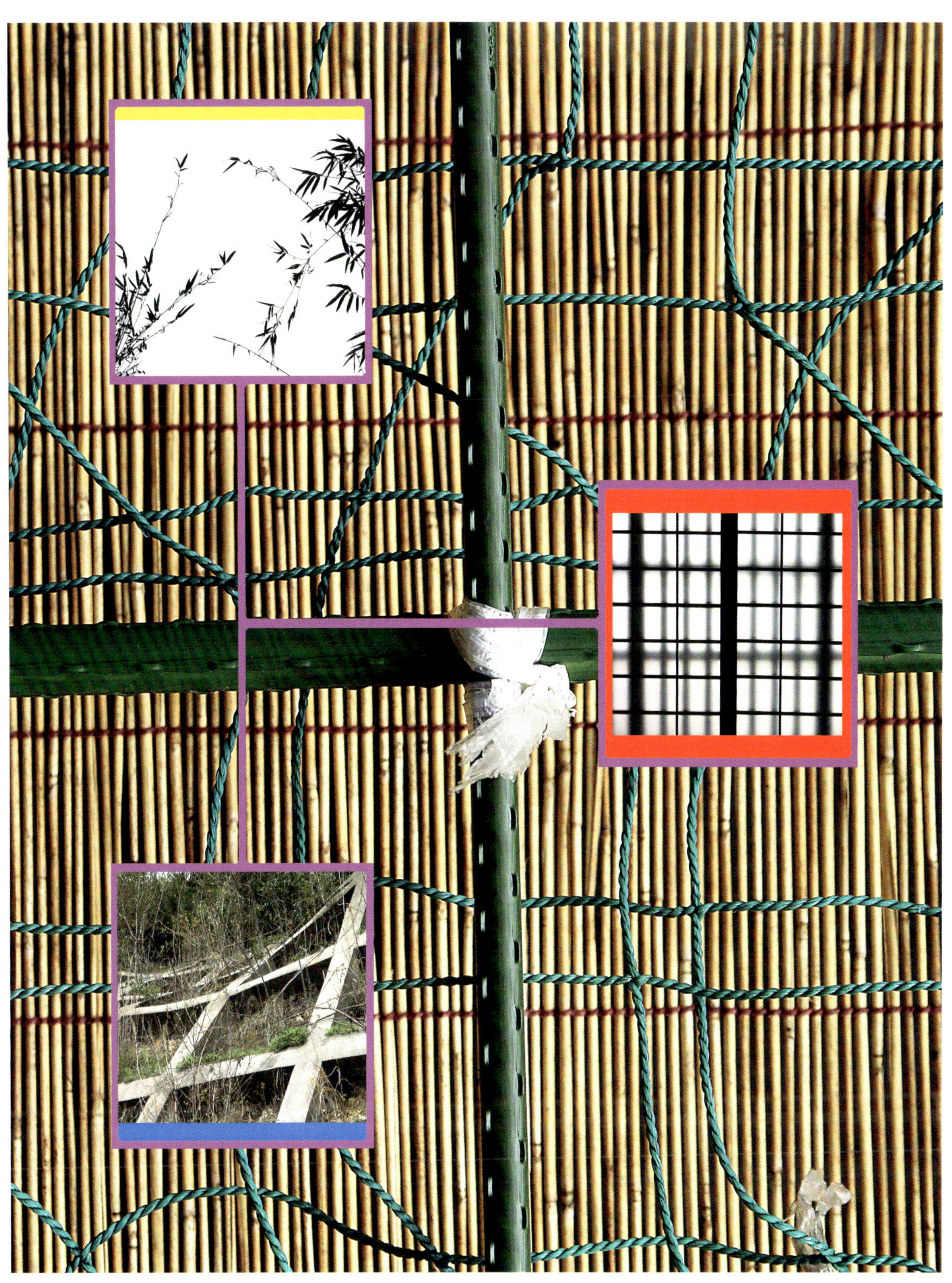

Note
In the series name, “Mean” is short for “meaningful.”

Plate 41
No. 7457, 2006, digital montage. Mean Images series.
Allan Chasanoff Archive, Yale University Art Gallery

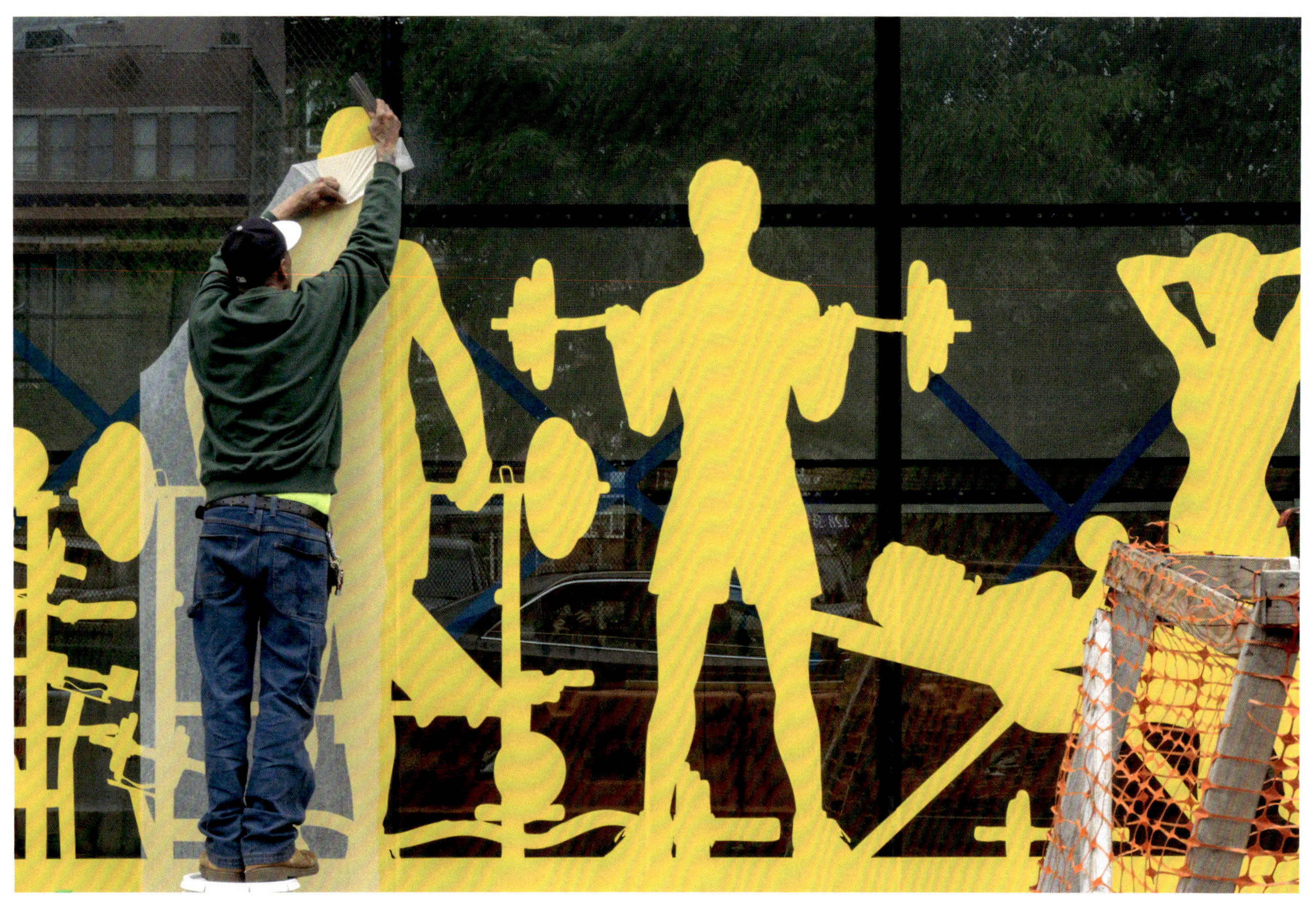

Plate 42
No. 12321, 2019, digital image file.
Allan Chasanoff Archive, Yale University Art Gallery

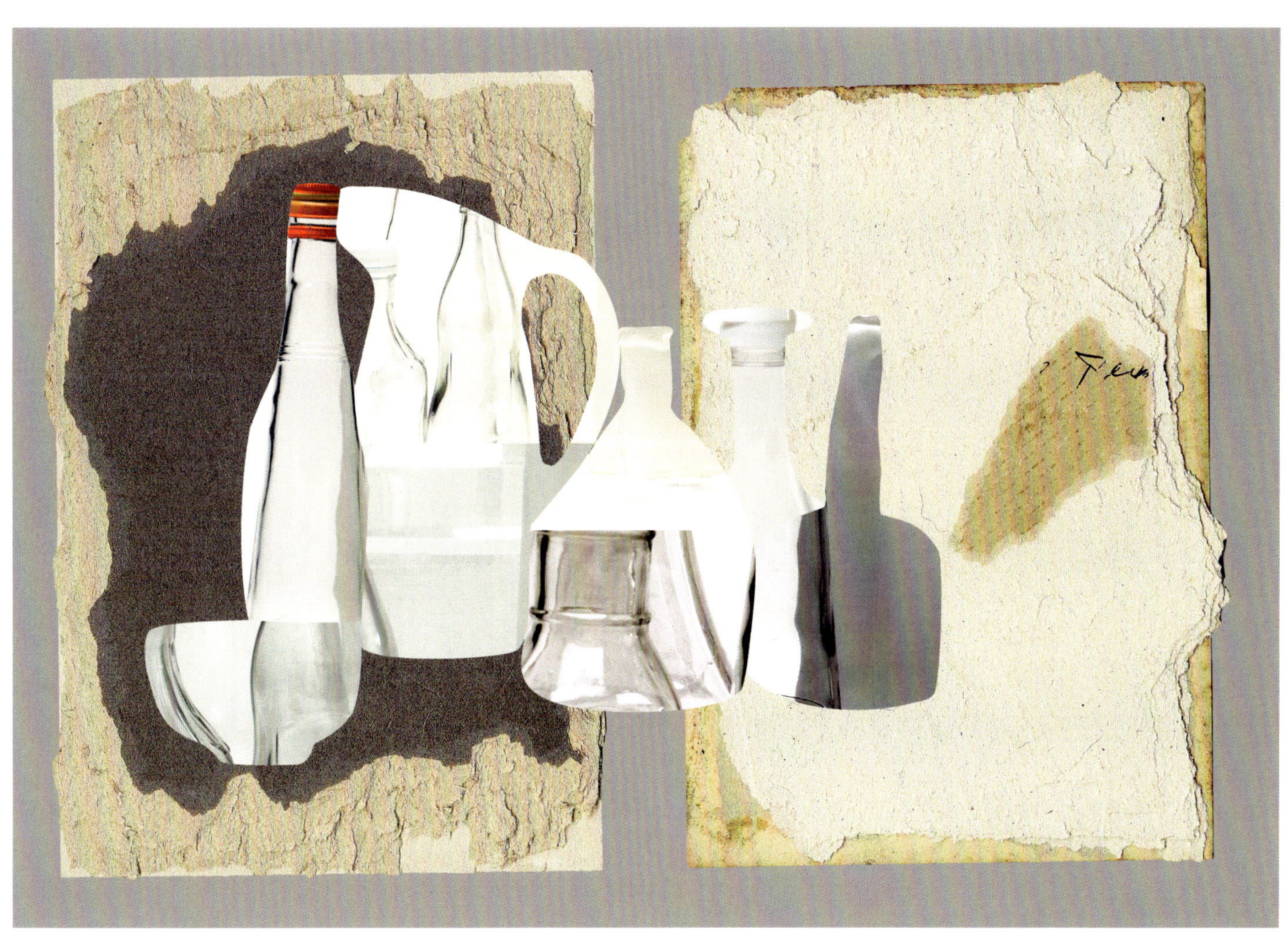

Plate 43
No. 11838, 2015, digital montage. Morandi (outline) series.
Allan Chasanoff Archive, Yale University Art Gallery

(a) pre•text
Mónika Sziládi

I touch the paper, make a font, play with the word, confuse the image and—what is a major issue—make an annotation.[1] —Allan Chasanoff

For Allan Chasanoff, the experience of seeing was both frustrating and gratifying, as he discovered early on that apprehending the world through sight often yields confusion and only rarely instances of clarity. The problems and revelations of sight fascinated him and were his entry point into the realm of creative action where all the human senses engage in making meaning. Exploring the ways our senses and creative abilities interconnect as we navigate society and culture would become his life's work: a multifaceted, open-ended endeavor he approached through projects that flowed freely among making and collecting images and objects; building databases to map his interests and holdings; developing software for reading and annotating texts; studying psychology and Postmodern thought; and writing treatises on mass media, consumer capitalism, and aesthetics. A successful businessman whose creative side was largely private, he is best known today for building significant collections of twentieth- and twenty-first-century photography, ceramics, and book art, now preserved in important museums.[2] The present volume is the first to address his own innovative work in photography, the medium in which he was engaged the longest—from the 1960s until his death in 2020—and proved to be extraordinarily prolific. While he also explored ideas in drawings, ceramics, video and audio projects, and font designs, most of his interconnected interests are manifested in his thousands of photographic works. These images reflect his complex understanding of seeing and believing, and they may also be considered an entryway into the labyrinth of his larger endeavor.

Chasanoff worked away from the public eye by choice, only exhibiting his photography on a few occasions in the 1980s.[3] He rejected being called an artist in part because his occupations were so varied, but also because making photographs was, for him, a habitual practice not always aimed at art.[4] However, he was far from isolated in his creative work, enjoying friendships and collaborations with artists, gallerists, and technologists, as well as key figures in the field of photography, such as Carole Kismaric, renowned editor of photography books and magazines.[5] Among his trusted associates in the museum world were Anne Wilkes Tucker, who placed the majority of his photography collection at the Museum of Fine Arts, Houston, in 1993, as its founding curator of photography; and Jock Reynolds, director of the Yale University Art Gallery from 1998 to 2018, who secured a home at the Gallery for later additions to the photography collection and for Chasanoff's entire archive. Reynolds also introduced Chasanoff to the photographer Richard Benson, dean of the Yale School of Art from 1996 to 2006, launching years of frequent meetings and daily phone and video conversations between two souls of contrasting sensibilities yet deep mutual fascination.[6]

Chasanoff's magnetism may be explained by the fact that he was an utterly engaging interlocutor. Continually pushing to expand his understanding of art, mass media, consumer capitalism, and the transition to the Digital Age, he was a voracious reader, diligent note taker, and incessant thinker. Not only a witty conversationalist, he was also an exceedingly free spirit as a maker. During the creative hours of the day, when social and business obligations let up, he improvised and enjoyed himself at what he viewed as forms of play:

> I always wanted to play and I still want to play. "Play" meaning a non-social and non-goal oriented activity which explores the self and its probes into the environment. This is "play" in its purest sense. As it transmogrifies, other strictures and rules and limitations "come into play."[7]

In his photographic practice, he chose to play extensively in an expanded understanding of the still life genre, including images made in the studio, in the world, and using the computer. In the studio his setups were unusual and his approach experimental. He arranged various props and objects (often broken), and frequently used plate glass, sometimes painted, to complicate the camera's view, at times overlaying the "actual" with its depiction (fig. 1). Employing analog equipment, he then made "straight" pictures of these assemblages—with no in-camera or other manipulation—that were deliberately confusing to the eye and quasi-abstract (see pl. 26 and p. 9; with glass, pls. 18, 20, 22, 63). When out and about, finding the right—most visually ambiguous—viewpoint in random "still" objects, buildings, and landscapes reminded him of his studio shooting process (see pls. 8, 32, 76–89, 94–97). The advent of digital cameras, scanners, and

editing tools, which he embraced early on, expanded and sped up the free experimentation of his studio play. He found that, on the computer screen, he could easily move around and layer whole images or fragmented pieces gathered from his photographs, scanned objects, and art reproductions. Further, digital extraction and drawing tools allowed him to generate motifs—lines, shapes, and fonts—and insert these into pictures. Some of his digital montages, while always rooted in the photographic image, ended up hardly looking like photographs (see pls. 9, 98, 111, 123, 135, 152).[8] As Chasanoff had pushed straight photographs away from clear verisimilar description, so he followed a similar process in the digital realm, pushing away from what commonly seems photographic.

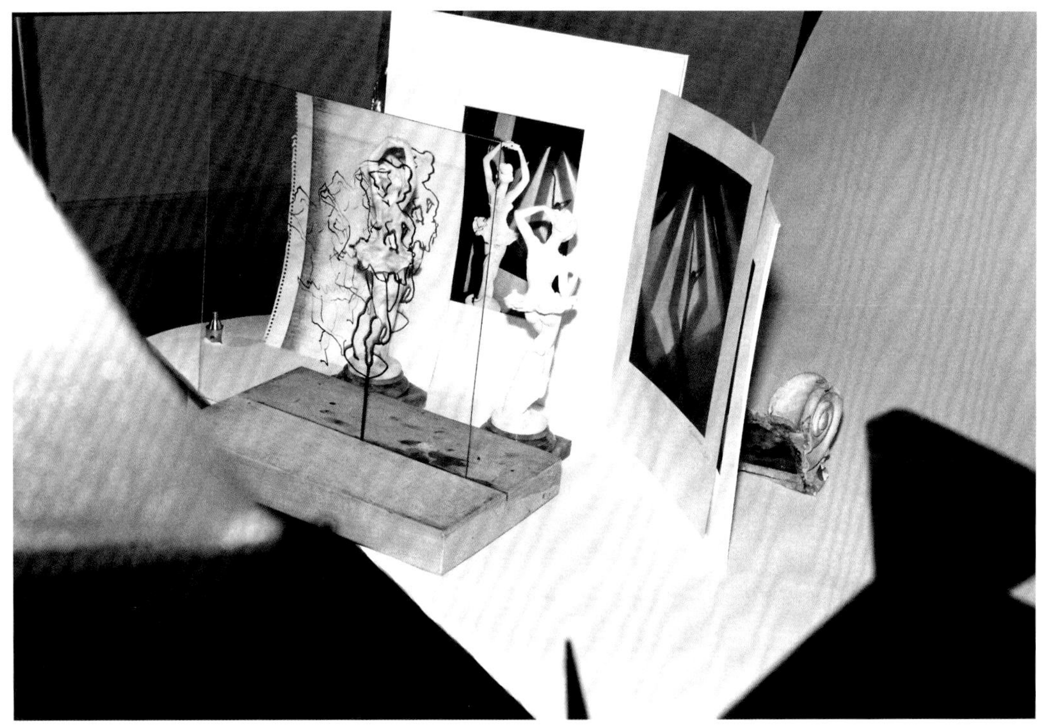

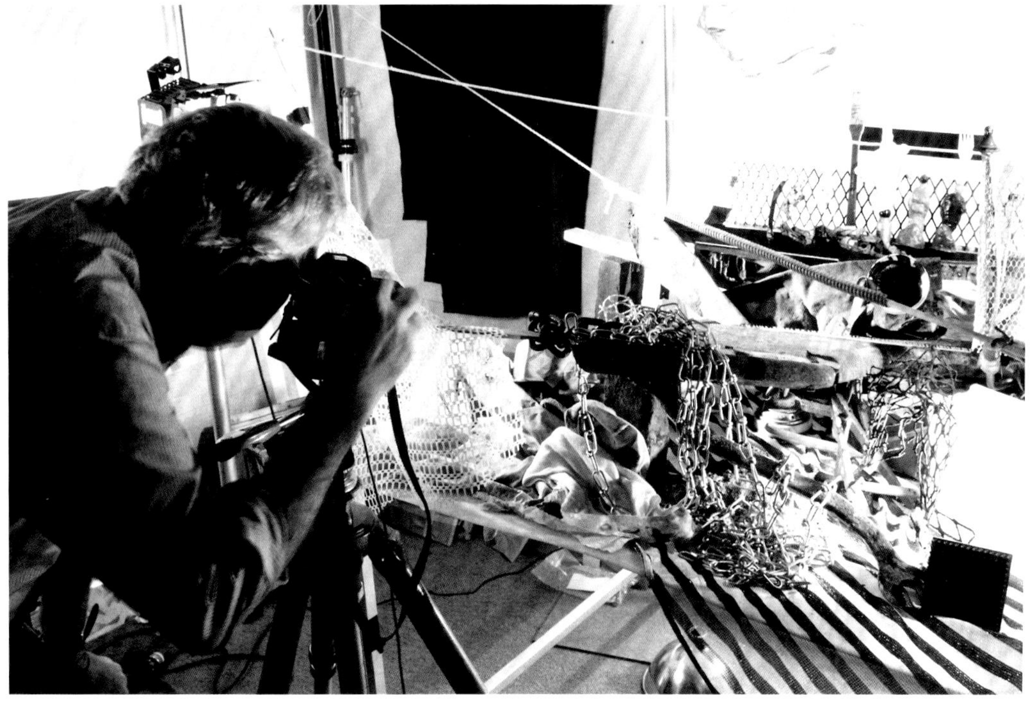

Fig. 1. (top) Still life arrangement with painted glass, 1986 (no. 3853); (bottom) Allan Chasanoff photographing a still life arrangement in his studio, 1986 (no. 3856). Yale University Art Gallery, Allan Chasanoff Archive

Khasanoff's wide-ranging photographic work explored issues of vision, language, and meaning, with a particular focus on how these relate to early childhood and psychological development, as well as to the uneven power dynamics permeating culture, media, and institutions. His intentionally ambiguous pictures question the truthfulness of photography and, more broadly, the validity of the images that surround us in late capitalism. These preoccupations, along with his frequent use of appropriation—borrowing images from high art as well as everyday sources—may place Khasanoff's oeuvre under the rubric of Postmodern art. He often described himself as a "Postmodern man," emphasizing the significance of his historical moment, which saw the transition from analog technologies to the Digital Age. Khasanoff considered this leap comparable to that from oral to written culture in ancient Greece and believed that the emergence of the computer may be of greater cultural consequence than that of Gutenberg's printing press.[9]

An early adopter of the personal computer as a powerful creative tool, Khasanoff also organized his multifarious projects, collections, and ideas in about forty databases of heavily annotated entries. The databases only partially reference the vast archive of his actual creations and collections, accumulated over a lifetime, of which his photography is but one part. Now preserved at the Yale University Art Gallery, the databases and archive may be understood as the intellectual biography of a Postmodern cultural explorer. Two databases are dedicated to photographs made by Khasanoff and contain entries on some ten thousand images, selected from his total output of thirty-five to forty thousand prints and countless transparencies, negatives, and digital image files (on these databases, see "Note to the Reader," p. 23). Khasanoff photographed nearly every day outside in the world, while also pursuing affiliated projects in the studio and on the computer, and, through database categorization, organized his broad output into a relational structure. Two collaborators—Elizabeth Hansen from 2002 to 2008 and myself from 2013 to 2020—were enlisted to help select pictures for inclusion in the databases, and to annotate and assign categories to each entry, with quite a bit of freedom in the process. The categories record recurring themes and motifs in his work, some of which are treated as series in this volume, though only loosely defined as such by Khasanoff. For the present introduction to Khasanoff's photography, I have drawn only on images recorded in the databases, considering these an "edit" of his larger oeuvre.

Presented in seven sections of plates, the selected images track technical, conceptual, and aesthetic developments in Khasanoff's work—largely the result of his transition from analog to digital photography and, late in life, his push into 3-D scanning and printing. An initial section, presented in Plates I, playfully pairs analog and digital works, sometimes created decades apart, to examine this transition and introduce select themes and motifs to which Khasanoff often returned. In Plates II, the first section examines Khasanoff's early analog work, revealing the beginnings of his engagement with light, shadow, color, and line—the rudimentary elements of seeing. A section on "the optical" follows, dedicated to his lifelong fascination with optical confusion and its implications for photographs' believability and meaning. These images, both analog and digital, are unmanipulated, reporting what the camera "sees," however difficult to interpret. The next two sections focus on Khasanoff's use of line and shape to form abstract compositions, often incorporating alphabetic characters from fonts he created. Some straight and some montage (manipulated on screen), the pictures explore Khasanoff's fluid interpretation of images and textual signs as he pushed the boundaries of photography. The final sections explore his last major project, Multi-Line, and his foray into 3-D print technology, a new form of photography, as he saw it. Throughout the plate sections, overarching themes are prioritized over strict chronology or the presentation of series. Some of these are represented by a few images—such as his 1970s Light Bulb, Paint Squeezing, and Lens series (pls. 52–60)—and others by more examples—such as his post-2000 engagement with outlines and fonts (see, among many others, pls. 99–113, 131–40).[10] Together, the sections and sequence take into consideration Khasanoff's propensity to relate things and ideas both systematically and freely, allowing room for unintended connections and meanings. They may be thought of as a cross section of a rhizome-like body of work born organically from daily practice, or a map offering multiple inroads into the network of his intermeshed interests.

Early Years: Seeing, Speaking, Connecting

Born in 1936 to first-generation Jewish American parents, Allan Khasanoff spent his childhood in Far Rockaway, Queens, and later in Nassau County on Long Island. There were also frequent trips to the Bronx to visit his paternal grandfather, an immigrant from Russia.[11] Some of Allan's cherished early memories

included playing basketball and baseball, two sports to which he paid attention his whole life (see pls. 37, 105).[12] The former he learned to play rather well, and the latter his older brother, Michael, played while a student at Yale University. During the brothers' youth, the family rose into the middle class thanks to the efforts of their father, whom Allan remembered as an "exceedingly competent" real estate attorney. He was closer to his mother, whom he would describe as especially kind though slightly melancholy, which he thought might have been due to her stay-at-home role, "living in a world where the female (mother) was not able to have a richer life of their own."[13] Following a couple of years at Woodmere Academy, Allan finished high school at the Riverdale Country School and went on to college at Yale. After graduating in 1961, he joined his father and brother as partner in developing commercial real estate. In the mid-1960s, Allan lived for a couple of years in Kew Gardens, Queens, likely to split the distance between his work and family on Long Island and his friends and interests in Manhattan, but eventually decided it was not an ideal solution. He then moved to Manhattan, where he spent the rest of his life: first, in a high-rise building on East 40th Street, where he rented one apartment to live in and another as a studio; and from 1984, after he withdrew from the family business, in a townhouse he bought on East 36th Street, where he lived and worked under one roof until his passing in 2020.

Chasanoff's early years coincided with the spread of psychoanalysis in the United States, and he often mentioned that he was in analysis during his adolescence, commuting into Manhattan for treatment. It is likely this formative experience is what later led him to an in-depth reading of Freud's *Complete Works*,[14] which left a significant mark on his thinking about how mental connections and meaning are made. He also felt that certain childhood experiences had established enduring questions for him, and one, in particular, involved a problem of seeing. He frequently referenced a memory from infancy (possibly imagined, he admitted) of being in his baby carriage, bundled up against the winter cold, unable to move as he tried to see past the rattle hanging down from the top of the carriage. "This deficiency of vision, this blockage was imprinted. I sensed the incompleteness of seeing a whole object or scene nice and clearly." The inability to see clearly, he concluded, impacted "the faculty of understanding" and was "more an issue of psychology than vision per se."[15] In his photographic work he would repeatedly use partially blocked or unclear images to explore the nature of vision and meaning (see pls. 2, 51, 61; pp. 9–10).

In the late 1960s and early 1970s, Chasanoff's reading took in the ideas of Marshall McLuhan, semiotics, and Postmodern philosophy.[16] Among the French theories of the time, he was especially drawn to Jacques Derrida's deconstruction, possibly due to his enduring interest in "Freud the interpreter"—the aspect of Freud the Postmoderns emphasized[17]—and what he quite openly and casually described as his inner "brokenness."

In interviews and conversations, Chasanoff would readily reveal various aspects of this "brokenness" if they were relevant to his creative ideas. One of them was a peculiar trouble "deeply engrained in my psyche" with reading.[18] He described lingering on the graphic shape of alphabet characters rather than letting his mind slip through them to words and meanings. Beyond this initial hurdle, he would manage to "grasp the word" and how it functioned in a sentence but would have trouble fathoming what connected one sentence to the next in a paragraph. There is no grammar that guides us beyond the sentence, he would complain: "I am sentenced to the sentence."[19] This malaise, which accompanied him through his school years, became so distressing that he had to interrupt his college education for two years. Paradoxically, through arduous work he became a highly intellectual adult. In the context of the family business, he was responsible for reviewing contracts and architectural documents, and became a self-taught master builder. He developed his own creative methods for aiding his memory and maintaining quality control well before personal computers.[20] In addition, on his own time he gradually amassed, read, and often annotated over three thousand volumes of nonfiction with a special focus on modern and Postmodern theory, philosophy, and psychology. This was alongside numerous art books.

The word as a unit, or building block, seems to have stayed with Chasanoff in the way he thought about his collecting and creative practices, which he considered related ways of exploring specific cultural issues extrapolated from memories of his personal, usually childhood, experiences. He saw an analogy between collecting and making art, on the one hand, and collecting words and connecting them to speak, on the other. His embrace of appropriation is connected to this concept of visual units as words. Chasanoff liked to deconstruct the iconic and reassemble it to make his own statement.[21] He would cut out details of reproductions of Henri Matisse's paintings (pls. 30, 73–74); have ceramics painted in the style of Piet Mondrian (pls. 13, 24, 71), Josef Albers (pl. 13), or Mark Rothko (pls. 13, 68, 93), and then break them; or extract selections out of digital scans and photographs of artworks (pls. 102, 141, 149–51, 161).[22] Then he would include these fragments in still life arrangements that he photographed or in digital montages. Through this process he built up a vocabulary, both from existing images and from things he photographed in the world around him, and used it to speak visually.[23]

For Chasanoff, then, an artwork assembled from pieces, or fragments, was like a sentence assembled

from words—but the analogy goes further. A collection assembled from artworks is another kind of sentence (rather than a paragraph), put together by connecting "artwork-words." A set of collections is yet another set of words to speak with, as much for him as for anyone interacting with them. In this manner, Chasanoff's photographic practice may be thought of as consisting of "image-fragment words" (cutouts, shards, digital extractions) that may build "image words" (pictures), which in turn may build "series words" (series of pictures with recurring themes). To build sentences, all of these may be connected to one another individually, within or outside of a picture or series, or to anything in the outside world, as one would play with a vast set of modular puzzle pieces, or with crossword puzzles or Scrabble, which were favorite games of his.[24] As Chasanoff put it,

> A collection is the same thing as a photograph for me, or anything else. It's an idea that has some form to it, that's all. . . . But it's very important for me . . . that . . . even the individual little parts of it have a life to [them] and can be related to [things] outside.[25]

Starting to Make Photographs: Primary Materials

Soon after graduating from college, and around the time he started to work in the family business, Chasanoff built a darkroom in the basement of his parents' home and taught himself how to print.[26] While he had enjoyed photographing earlier in his life, it was around this time, in the mid- to late 1960s, that he honed in on the medium. At first he mostly photographed out in the world and from his high-rise window in Manhattan (pls. 44–48, 50–51). Some of his pictures were layered and dealt with obstruction of vision. In a photograph of paintings and poster announcements, for example, borders overlap, hiding words and images (pl. 48). Some pictures were shot from viewpoints that force us to see the world through something (pls. 50–51). This is particularly poignant in a photograph where real-world traffic is seen through the window reflection of a newspaper photograph of traffic, the mass media image imposing a filter on direct experience (pl. 51).[27] Other pictures emphasize shadows rather than the objects that cast them (pls. 44–45), prompting questions about the role that light and shadow play in our perception of what is real.[28] Shadows are also silhouettes devoid of details—abstract projections literally, and open to projected meanings figuratively. Abstraction is present in these early pictures in varying degrees, in images of geometric industrial structures (pls. 46–47), of outlines and shapes of everyday objects (pl. 48), and of simple Euclidean shapes saturated with color in a photograph of color gels (pl. 49).

In the 1970s, while he continued to photograph out in the world, Chasanoff embarked on his first studio still lifes. His early subjects were not those traditionally associated with the genre, but instead the basic elements and tools of photography itself—light, light bulbs, and lenses. He also explored the raw material of painting, in particular, the intense colors and sensual materiality of paint squeezed directly from tubes. In his own words,

> The prominent underlying motivation for my photography . . . was to respond to the exaggerated authority of the Mass Media. One strategy I used to address this issue was to

make sculptural objects dealing with some "primary" materials (oil paint squeezings, lenses, etc.) used in the visual arts and then photograph those objects. It was a way in which to deconstruct the Mass Media's representation process by creating my own microreality and then photographing and manipulating that reality.[29]

The Light Bulb series (pls. 4, 52–54), in which light source and photographed object become practically inseparable, was created with the help of a "light table" (fig. 2), a motorized cabinet designed by Chasanoff in 1969, which is tool and storage system all in one.[30] Equipped with electrical sockets, modular extenders, and Plexiglass slides, it could store, hold, and rotate various light bulbs, many of them colored, and filter their light. The cabinet is a testament to its maker's inventive spirit, also manifested later in his forays into computer software and hardware projects. In visual terms, the motif of rotation (see especially pls. 4, 53) comes back when he is inspired by digital storage of information on spinning segmented circular disks (see pls. 5, 92).

The photographs in the Light Bulb series show Chasanoff playing with pure light and color, or elements of what we see. The resulting abstract images, some featuring geometric forms reminiscent of celestial bodies (pl. 54) and others, possibly shaped by glare, evoking calligraphic lines (pl. 52), signal how detached photographic description can be from material substance and the "real." In his Lens series, begun in the mid-1970s, he made images of what we see with, or through (pls. 58–60). Here he highlights the distorting effects of lenses, how they bend and fragment light, confuse rather than clarify.

The Paint Squeezing series, in contrast, shows us something with a distinctly material, tactile look

(pls. 55–57). Starting in the mid-1970s, Chasanoff shaped soft paint, direct from the tube, into small sculptures that were stacked, layered, squashed, and some of them cut, sewn, and spray painted. Sometimes he used pins as a support system—suggestive perhaps of scaffolding used in construction—against which the squeezings could lean (fig. 3). The sculptures and photographs may be seen as "indicative of a reaction to the austerity of conceptual art and represent a return to a visceral use of paint and pigment."[31] While the paint creations were a microreality

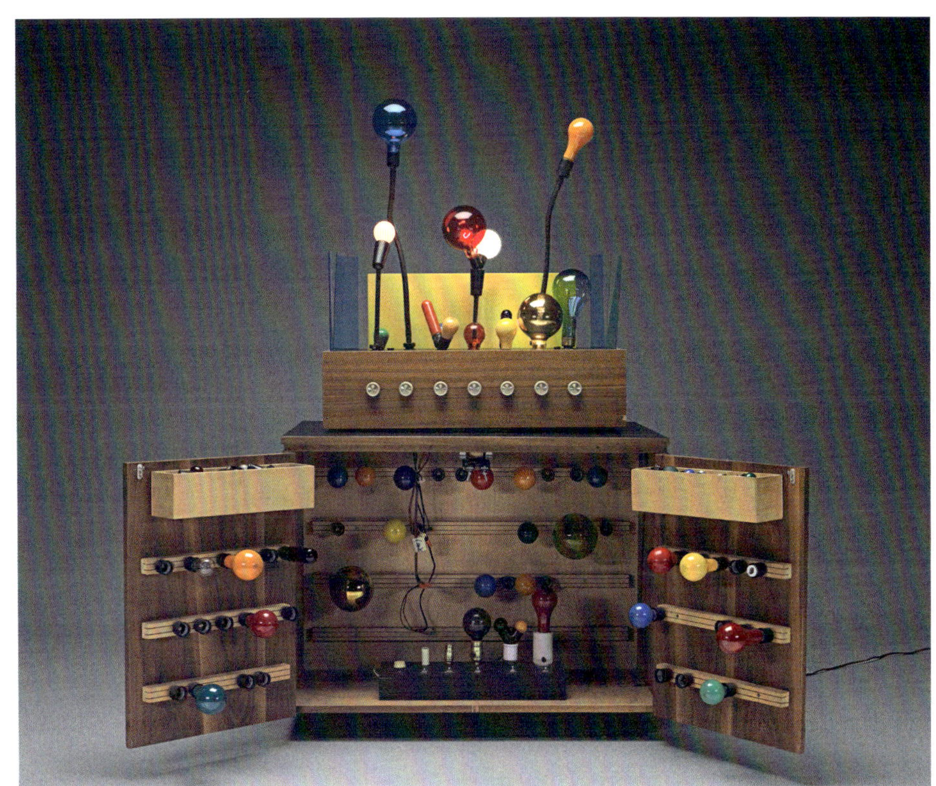

Fig. 2. Allan Chasanoff, Light Table, 1969. Motorized cabinet with light bulbs, 38 1⁄2 × 39 3⁄8 × 26 3⁄8 in. (97.8 × 100 × 67 cm) (closed). Allan Chasanoff Archive, Yale University Art Gallery

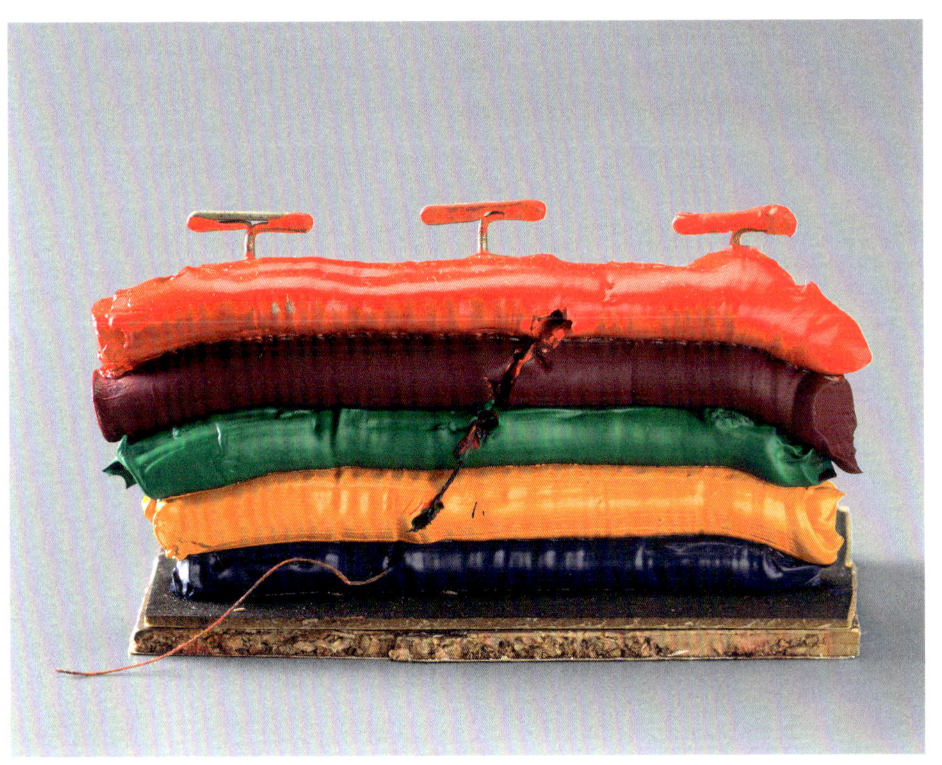

Fig. 3. Allan Chasanoff, Paint Squeezing Sculpture, ca. 1971–75. Oil paint with support pins, 2 1⁄16 × 3 1⁄2 × 1 7⁄8 in. (5.2 × 8.9 × 4.8 cm). Allan Chasanoff Archive, Yale University Art Gallery

Chasanoff could manipulate, they were also reminiscent of Abstract Expressionism. Compositions using horizontal paint squeezings (pl. 56), like the color fields in some Light Bulb pictures (pls. 4, 54), may refer to the paintings of Mark Rothko, while marks and streaks (pls. 52, 55, 57) may be seen as gestural or calligraphic allusions to Jackson Pollock or Cy Twombly. Visual references to these Abstract Expressionists persist in Chasanoff's later pictures (pls. 13, 22–23, 28–29, 63, 68, 93) and relate to his view of their paintings as an attempt to "return to culture" after the horrors of World War II. As he suggested, a sort of memory awoke that "yes, there used to be reading and writing—there was civilization before all the destruction." Chasanoff thought of the color blocks in Rothko's later-period works as resembling blurred paragraphs in a book. Pollock's work he associated with ink scribbling, and Twombly's with the first attempt to utter words again, in writing, through a return to ancient Greek and Roman sources. For Chasanoff, the work of these artists brought to mind the reed and stylus, papyrus and paper—the basic instruments of early Western writing—as well as a child's first venture into culture through color, line, and then the word.[32] And, in a sense, his own work in photography evokes these as well: the experience of optical confusion relates to preverbal infancy, and the creation of still lifes and digital montages from shards and fragments relates to uttering and connecting words to speak and write.

Constructed Images and the Optical

Starting in 1976, Chasanoff reduced the time he spent on photography in order to turn his attention to his family's real estate business.[33] An intense

seven-year period devoted to new construction brought both financial security and burnout, which together led him to retire in 1983. He then returned to his creative endeavors.[34] As Postmodern photography broke into the New York art world in the 1980s,[35] Chasanoff was working out his own statement on the nature of the medium along two parallel paths: he continued to build what became a historically significant photography collection, initiated during his creative hiatus, and, in about 1982, he started to construct increasingly complex studio still lifes (see pls. 16, 18, 62–63). Both the collected and made pictures were taken through the camera lens and unmanipulated,[36] and both explored, among other concerns, what Khasanoff called “the optical”—short for optical problem or optical confusion in straight, or unaltered, photographs.[37] He described the issues at stake in the following way:

> What is “the optical”? When an individual looks at the photographic image and—at the instant of perception—the image is visually confused or the subject matter’s identity is compromised, that is what I call “the optical.” Typically, within a short period of time, this confusion is resolved. For a few images, the visual reconciliation takes more time. . . . In some cases the image, once deciphered, does not necessarily remain resolved, meaning that upon subsequent viewings, the observer will likely confront the visual disturbance again. It was “the optical problem” as an endless quandary of vision that governed my major preoccupation with photography.[38]

Khasanoff traced his preoccupation with optical confusion back to the primal experience of obstructed vision in his baby carriage. However, the optical problem in photography, a consequence of the disjunction between humans’ binocular vision and the camera’s monocular view, is present throughout the history of the medium. Many celebrated photographers had taken optical—or purposely ambiguous—pictures, among them Brassaï, Larry Fink, Jan Groover, and, one of Khasanoff’s favorites, Ray Metzker. Khasanoff’s collection of them is unique, as is his own sustained exploration of the issue.

The photographs Khasanoff made encompass various forms of the optical. In those perhaps most closely referencing his baby carriage memory, a blunt obstruction may partially block sight of an object (pls. 2, 22, 61; p. 10), or a disorienting blur, reminiscent of Metzker’s *Pictus Interruptus* series (fig. 4), may disrupt the satisfactory perception of it (pls. 66–67, 80; p. 9). In others, the balancing of positive and negative space (pls. 64–65, 70, 89), alignment of objects (pl. 34), reflections on glass (pls. 77, 81), play of light and shadow (pls. 38, 76), and camouflage effects (pls. 26, 87)

may challenge the viewer in distinguishing foreground from background and understanding the position of objects in space. So does dense visual cacophony (pls. 30, 72–73), while also possibly evoking, through sensual chaos, how our minds process multiple layers of information simultaneously.[39]

Across Khasanoff’s oeuvre, the optical remained important as much in his studio still lifes (see pls. 20, 61–75) as out in the world (see pls. 32, 76–89, 94–97), and later in his digitally created images (pls. 33, 43, 90, 99–100, 108–9, 113, 141). In the 1990s, distrust of photography resulting from digital manipulation became a pervasive cultural issue. But Khasanoff’s collection and practice make the case that

Fig. 4. Ray Metzker, *Pictus Interruptus*, 1978. Gelatin silver print, 7 13/16 × 11 in. (19.8 × 27.9 cm). Museum of Fine Arts, Houston, The Allan Chasanoff Photographic Collection

photographs had been unreliable all along, not only after the digital revolution. Even if unmanipulated pictures are technically a trace of the real, he suggested we had still better doubt our perception and understanding of what the real may be.

This need for doubt is especially pressing in a Postmodern consumer age when photographic images are ubiquitous: their presumed truth status seeps into our psychology and, by extension, our social, legal, and political lives. The stakes in how we respond to content received through mass media—Chasanoff called this unidirectional flow "uni-munication"—were existential for him both personally and culturally. Because mass media images often appear seamless (manipulation is hidden), we trust them instinctually, making our vulnerability to propaganda inevitable.[40] Yet the individual may respond in kind, as Chasanoff and many Postmodern artists proposed. Video equipment and personal computers connected to the Internet provide at least some production power and a platform from which to speak. Further, appropriation, subversion, or other modes of making images from images may allow one "to speak with the words in which one has been spoken to," as Chasanoff described it.[41] He elucidated his own practice as follows:

> Amongst the efforts to respond to the rejection of the seam, such as surrealism and photocollage, I fell upon the strategy of photo-visual disruption. It is a surreptitious device that questions the image from the inside, within the platform of the so called real. Pictures aren't what they se a/e m, or are they? I doubt it.[42]

In a related vein, Chasanoff saw potential for "photo-visual disruption" and the disorienting quality of the optical to cast doubt on the institutional power of the museum. "The other idea," he said, "is [that] hopefully these things infiltrate the museum, and if so, then it will question within the museum itself, or of the pictures being shown."[43] His relationship to museums was likely influenced by his thoughts on psychological castration, which he connected to inhibited speech.[44] He was preoccupied with preserving the voice of the artist, or maker, in the context of powerful museums, and resisting the idea of artworks as completed rather than as phases of infinite inquiry. He repeated frequently, and half-jokingly, "The artwork is

executed by the artist, and hung by museums. It's all about death. I don't like that!" He associated the selective and restrictive power of the museum with the necktie—"The tie is a restriction. The tie is the museum. . . . It hangs me, it chokes me"[45]—seeing in this cultural symbol a choking, splitting (head from body), hanging male garment pointing to the penis. On, and resisting, this premise, he built a tie collection focusing on pieces decorated with images or language proving the potential of individual expression, as opposed to the usual restrained abstract patterns.[46] Ties also appear in some of his images (pl. 72; p. 9).

While Khasanoff continued to photograph out in the world throughout his life and left his props and studio setup ready for play in the basement of his townhouse, in the late 1980s he dove into the digital universe and enthusiastically embraced the personal computer as soon as it became available. By the time the first version of Adobe Photoshop was released in 1990, he had already experimented with making digital compositions, or montages (for an early example, see pl. 25).[47] In the 1990s he also collaborated to develop software and hardware applications for use in scanning, reading, and annotating texts and images—projects he would engage in intermittently over the next three decades.[48]

It is possible, especially across the arc of Khasanoff's trajectory, to think of digital montage as a natural extension of photographic still life, for they share some similarities in the creative process. In both cases, outcomes are controlled by moving around things, physical or virtual. And in both cases, the process of layering may raise psychological questions, as he was particularly aware: "If something lies behind another thing what do we see? To cover and to try to expose what is covered is a continual provocation and purpose in life. The photographic issue of voyeurism is hereby engaged. After all, the eye is a sexual organ."[49] Indeed, the visual complexity of his analog still lifes was created mostly by the layering of fragmented objects and painted glass plates (see fig. 1); through the camera's tendency to flatten space, the setups collapsed into confusing photographs (see pls. 16, 18, 20, 22, 24, 69). The shooting process often involved several revisions, achieved by literally breaking or rearranging props, or moving the camera in order to disturb preconceived ideas of what the image "should" look like. The result was a series of "findings" that reflected an incrementally morphing

reality (see pls. 24, 71).[50] Such studio experimentation, combining selective and additive and iterative ways of working, anticipated not only his own digital process but arguably some aspects of digital image making in general. (See some of the paired images in "From Analog to Digital: A [World in] Transition," pls. 16–31; for digital iterations and versioning, see pls. 122–23, 149)

Though many of Photoshop's features replicated analog darkroom techniques, such as cropping and color and density adjustment, Photoshop also included tools for simulating painting, drawing, outlining, and font work, and others that streamlined montage through virtual selecting, cutting, pasting, and layering. As it became a dominant software, its specificities played a role in forming the practices of its users, especially those of a younger generation of digital image makers, who, as Charlotte Cotton states, "may have little or no psychic baggage of allegiance to photography's analog past."[51] Khasanoff's analog studio experiments, however, did not seem to burden him with such baggage but serendipitously to have prepared him for a wholehearted transition to digital work at an age when many would have proceeded with cold feet or hardly at all.

Digital photomontage may be thought of as combining selective and additive processes, like Khasanoff's studio practice, through fragmenting and reassembling digital "traces of the world." Such montage differs crucially from collage made by other means, using materials such as paper, in that photomontage tends to be seamless.[52] While this is problematically deceptive in mass media, for Khasanoff it had positive implications when done on a personal computer, at home: "The local environment, formerly a receiver and only occasionally a media producer, now realizes the greatness of mixed media. Via digital underpinnings and transformations, the computer with its new peripherals and configurations can receive and bespeak in text, picture, sound, and moving image. The individual can create the seamless in his own machine."[53] Khasanoff's digitally produced images would take up this challenge, interweaving pictorial and textual elements to speak back in the language in which he had been spoken to.

Contour and Content: A Graphic Turn

Contour and outline were always major features of Khasanoff's images, whether analog or digital, straight or manipulated. His attention to these visual elements may be related to the moment of joy in the optical viewing experience when visual confusion is resolved and the image is seen—and understood—clearly.[54] This primal sensual—and cognitive—pleasure is traceable, Khasanoff believed, to the infant's experience of gradually clearing vision by defining the edges and

boundaries of objects during the first year of life.[55] In many of his 1980s studio still lifes, objects are outlined either by paint applied on glass in front of them (pls. 16, 18, 63, 69, 93) or by painting directly on them (pls. 16, 66, 91). At the same time, in certain photographs made out in the world, though still sensed as optical, there is clear delineation and separation of the compositional elements (pls. 38, 40, 94–97). It thus seems that both the "confusion phase" and the "resolution phase" of the optical experience are reflected in Khasanoff's straight photography, the former more often in images where visual cacophony dominates and the latter where the composition is more compartmentalized.[56]

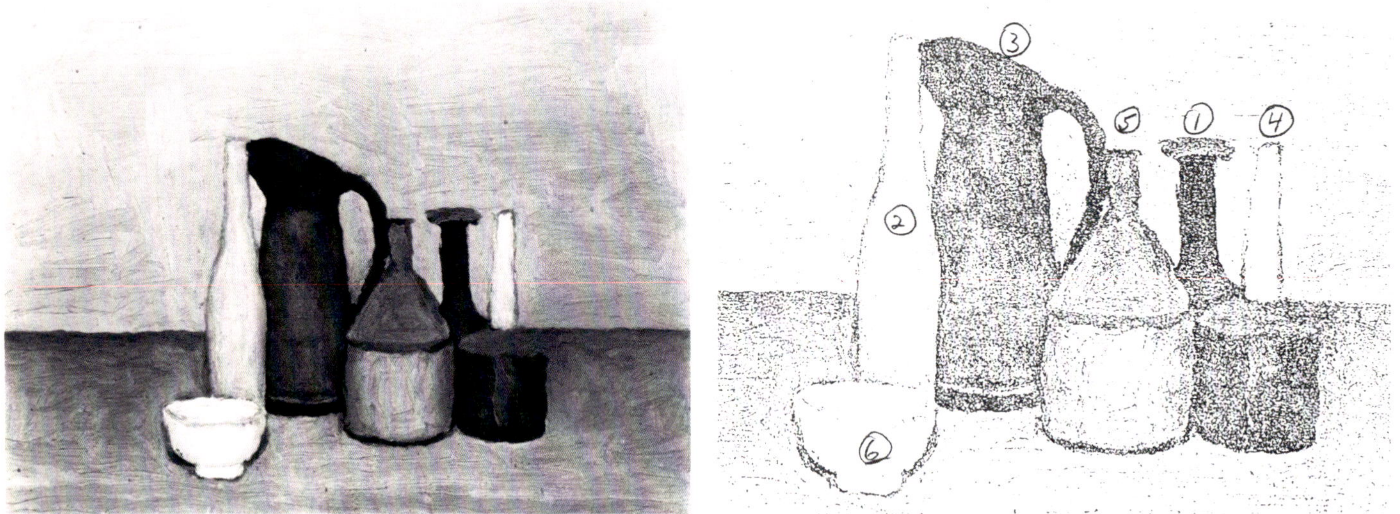

Fig. 5. (left) Giorgio Morandi, *Still Life*, 1952 (Vitali no. 819). Oil on canvas, 11 3/4 × 15 1/2 in. (30 × 39.5 cm). From: *Giorgio Morandi* (Des Moines: Des Moines Art Center, 1982), 112. (right) One of Chasanoff's photocopies of Morandi's painting, or a related drawing, with added numbers, ca. 1985–90. Allan Chasanoff Archive, Yale University Art Gallery

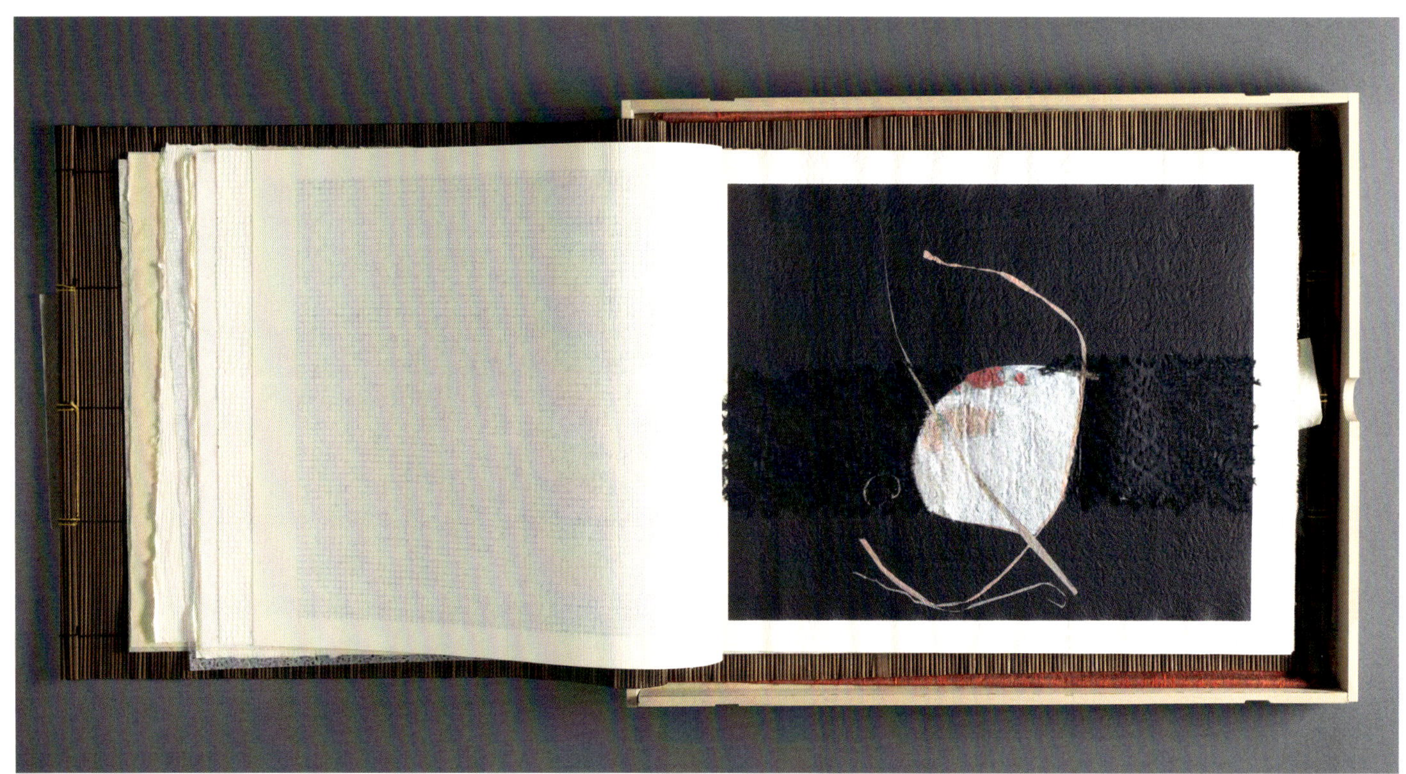

Fig. 6. Allan Chasanoff, *Touch-See*, 2000–2001. Hand-bound volume of Japanese paper with bamboo cover, protective cloth, and wood case, book (closed): 14 × 17 × 1/2 in. (35.6 × 43.2 × 1.3 cm); case: 15 1/4 × 18 3/4 × 1 1/2 in. (38.7 × 47.6 × 3.8 cm). Allan Chasanoff Archive, Yale University Art Gallery

With the leap to digital montage, Chasanoff's playing with outlines veered toward graphically neat silhouettes filled with diverse imagery. In his various outline series, both contour and content reflect persistent motifs that were part of his personal vocabulary: the outline series include Baseball (pls. 37, 105), Box (pls. 11, 106–7, 110, 139), Chair (pls. 99–100), Fan (pls. 107–8), Kimono (pl. 110), and Staircase (pls. 90, 104). Content includes black residue on photographs torn from photo albums (pls. 104, 113),[57] cotton (pls. 11, 105), erasure/erasing (pls. 104, 112), rubber bands (pls. 104, 113), and Chasanoff's own fonts (pls. 106–10) and drawings (pl. 37) (see "Visual Vocabulary," p. 90). Sometimes he borrowed contour and content from reproduced artworks—often elements of still lifes and interiors—by artists such as Giorgio Morandi, Henri Matisse (pls. 101–3), and Paul Klee (pl. 161).[58] It is tempting to think that he saw outlined shapes as empty vessels—digital crockery, to play with the still life analogy—asking to be filled and refilled, making these works a part of his effort to counter our propensity to become locked into finite meaning(s) assigned to lines, shapes, and by extension texts, images, symbols, and logos.[59]

Chasanoff's interest in edges and contours likely explains his enduring attraction to the work of Morandi.[60] References and borrowings from the Italian still life artist emerge in his pictures in the mid-1980s (pls. 28, 65, 91) and continue to the end of his life (pls. 157, 161, 167). What might have particularly drawn him to Morandi is the way individual objects in his paintings touch each other, visually merge, and relate to the background. These factors, and Morandi's use of color, reduce distinction between figure and ground to the extent that many of his paintings could qualify as optical.[61] In about 1985, Chasanoff focused his attention on one Morandi work in particular (fig. 5),[62] possibly because of what he perceived as a compositional flaw in the arrangement of the depicted objects—a flaw evoking not only the optical but also "the shock and rupture" of the seam.[63] He would then riff on this still life setup for three decades (see pls. 28, 34, 39, 166–67). In 2015, as a culmination of this involvement, he spent six months on a digital Morandi outline series working with the setup's contour (pls. 27, 35, 43, 90, 112–13). In two of these compositions he highlighted the four areas where the touching of the objects struck him as optical by overlaying them with colored rectangles (see pl. 35). Given his statement, "I learned to stare when they told me I couldn't touch,"[64] it is intriguing that he found the optical where touch is—and at the same time alluded to

the prohibition with the *X*s of the harlequin pattern, which may be interpreted as forbidding or canceling touch. He had combined vision and touch deliberately in his artist's book *Touch-See* (fig. 6), in which he printed his images on different types of Japanese paper with varying texture. To apprehend this book fully, touching it is essential; furthermore, the physical quality of the pages relates to their degree of transparency, which generates a form of layering that recalls Chasanoff's use of glass sheets in analog still lifes and Photoshop layers in digital montages.

Another outline Chasanoff explored, primarily in 2006, was that of the cardboard shipping box, when unfolded. Its silhouette is featured in many digital montages where it serves as a container of myriad cultural and personal significations, its rectangular and flap shapes inviting repeated filling (pls. 11, 106–7, 110, 139). Khasanoff considered the convertible cardboard box "a defining characteristic of the urban, modern information society," as the preferred packaging for many products circulating within consumer capitalism.[65] As such, a box outline filled with imagery may relate to actual boxes filled with consumables. It may also evoke the rules or boundaries of psychological inhibition, which keep all that is unspoken inside and contained. Further, the transformation of the flat box into three-dimensional container, and back, may relate to photography's transformation of the three-dimensional world into a two-dimensional picture, often rectangular. But in purely compositional terms, the outline can simply be an empty, negative space used to hold new content—and the idea of content as interchangeable, or exchangeable, makes meaning slippery and infinite or, conversely, hermetic and in need of translation.

Visual Vocabulary

Khasanoff typically filled outlines such as the box, and other containers of negative space, with his "object-subjects" of interest—a vast vocabulary of things in the world and graphic shapes that drew his attention. Many were established as visual "words" in his analog still lifes, where they are among the props used in his setups. These include cups, teapots, bottles, ceramic shards, toy or model chairs, picture frames, neckties, photographers' "barn door" light modifiers, cotton wool or balls (made into "constructs"), rubber bands, and the letter *X*, to name but a sample.[66] They were loaded with meaning for Khasanoff, no matter how small or commonplace. In the teapot, receiver and pourer of liquids, he saw a hermaphrodite (pls. 3, 18,

21, 26, 67).[67] In the chair, he saw a structural support for the "weakness of sitting," the position most comfortable for humans (pls. 30, 73, 99–100, 165).[68] Frame is what surrounds the artwork and separates art from non-art (pls. 32, 48). The barn door—a four-flapped studio device that attaches to a light source and thus stands between the viewed and the viewer—he saw as "prepositional" in a linguistic sense, or "pre-positional" in a spatial sense, being "pre/before/in front of" the camera's subject (see pls. 15, 17, 109, 113, 140, 157). Its four flaps, shaping the direction and intensity of the light, have the ability to "sculpt" the image of the subject.[69] Khasanoff associated this transformational quality between two and three dimensions, as well as the modular and versatile design of the flaps, with the convertible shipping box[70] and also the kimono (pl. 110). Cotton is material suitable to support highly saturated color (pls. 11, 37, 105; p. 17), and as such may be related to Khasanoff's Light Bulb and Paint Squeezing series. As is the case with many of his props, they are interesting sculptural objects in their own right. Cotton balls additionally carried personal meaning for Khasanoff as reminders of visiting his friend Carole Kismaric in the hospital toward the end of her life.

Some "words" in the vocabulary carry complex trains of thoughts. Rubber bands (pls. 103–4, 106, 113, 124, 127) may recall a special sensual memory attached to what Khasanoff called "indented skin."[71] After sleeping, if the sheet or pillow made a mark on his skin, the indentation, when touched, had a peculiar feel to him. He related this sensation to his infant years and to the memory (real or imagined) of feeling his mother's skin, indented from wearing a bra, while she was breastfeeding him. He observed that, even into adulthood, his tongue moved a bit when he touched his indented skin, or if he saw indented skin on others.[72] Such a mark may also relate to Khasanoff's interest in showing the seam—in a collage, or after something breaks or cracks—and his thoughts on mass media and the importance of uncovering clues to production, manipulation, failure, and correction.[73] Rubber bands may also take on calligraphic shapes when twisted (see pl. 127), or the shape of a circle when relaxed, and so relate to writing or to the connecting function of holding things together—as do boxes—and thus may allude to the seemingly faraway realm of relational databases.[74]

Another complex "word" in his vocabulary, "erasings," refers to the tiny objects produced during erasure and composed of paper, graphite or ink, and the eraser material (see pls. 90, 104, 112, 160, bottom; p. 18). Khasanoff differentiated between "the act" and "the remnant" of erasure/erasing. Part of the act is sweeping away the remnants, a gesture he found grand and offensive, even if necessary in the everyday. As to the remnants, he imagined attempts, in this age of micro-analysis, to reconstitute the meaningful content they hold—but knowing that would be impossible, he saw in erasings a rebuke to technological hubris. He kept a collection of tiny erasings, used them as props, and also generated fonts with characters similar to Japanese kanji from scans and photographs of them. A way to give their hidden content new life, he

thought to turn them into writing, which he in turn used in image making.[75] For example, in a montage made in 2018 (pl. 156), he typed *X* in his Erasure font (the solid black shape at center, partially covered by the red seal impression), complicating and merging the meanings carried by this letter with those carried by erasings. This use of erasings relates to Khasanoff's interest in the concept of *sous rature*, or "under erasure," first developed by Martin Heidegger and expanded by Derrida. In crossing out a word but leaving it visible, the philosopher indicates that the term is inadequate or inaccurate, but no satisfactory substitute is available; for Derrida, language as a whole is inadequate and *sous rature*. Khasanoff may have felt similarly about verbal language, as well

Fig. 7. Cy Twombly, *Roman Notes V*, 1970. Offset color lithograph, 34 1⁄4 × 27 1⁄2 in. (87 × 69.9 cm). Yale University Art Gallery, Richard Brown Baker, B.A. 1935, Collection

as visual language or symbols. Though he continued to employ his vocabulary, he intended to elude fixed meaning.

The objects Khasanoff used as words in his visual language, modest in scale but vast in number, reflected perhaps his early feeling of “an amorphous infinity of things. Sort of a direct mental correspondence to the endless universe.”[76] Rather than trusting in big symbols, he found meaning in the multiplicity and variation of the small. He interpreted everyday objects through analysis of their shape, utility, and associated personal memories, applying the same mental care with which he approached scarce and culturally revered art objects, which he also studied and collected extensively. While nurturing his interest in art through weekly visits to galleries and museums around Manhattan and extensive travels in Europe and Asia—especially Japan[77]—he also accumulated over seven thousand art books, four thousand of which were on photography. Because his art purchases of the 1970s to 1990s—photographs, ceramics, book art, and more[78]—were relatively affordable, the objects could be collected in large numbers around specific ideas to generate cultural statements—one important outcome of Khasanoff’s Postmodern practice. As a corollary to his belief in multiplicity, he distrusted idols (other than Jackie Robinson, he would joke) and felt offended by dismissal and elitism.[79] Instead of the noun or verb, he said, “my favorite linguistic form is the preposition, the exemplar of position.”[80] In the world of words, prepositions are small, unpretentious, and do a lot of work, as connectors, away from the limelight. In this way, they may symbolize the nature of Khasanoff’s personal vocabulary.

Line, Shape, Meaning: Asemic Writing and Multivalent Letters

In keeping with Khasanoff’s thinking about art and language, within his photographic work we may consider straight optical images as explorations of seeing, and digital montages as writing-like processes in which picture fragments may function as words, and their combination as phrases or sentences. A related field that was present on Khasanoff’s radar consists of writing without language: the phenomenon of “asemic writing.” Somewhere between visual art and written text, it has been explored by artists like Paul Klee, Cy Twombly, and Xu Bing; poets like

Henry Michaux; and theorists like Roland Barthes.[81] Their work draws our attention to writing as a series of lines and shapes that slide on the spectrum between realistic and abstract, and between “meaning-full” and “meaning-less” in terms of their relationship to a referent, and by extension to any possible meaning as we try to “read” them (fig. 7).

Khasanoff’s excursions into the blurred territory between image and writing, and each medium’s relationship to meaning, are already evident in some of his mid-1980s still lifes (see pl. 128). Digital tools later eased the ways in which he could play with type and picture, as if each were both text and image. Some of these works explore the Roman alphabet for the abstract qualities of the letters’ lines and the shapes they engender (pls. 126, 138). In others, winking at logographic characters, particularly the Japanese kanji, Khasanoff plays with fonts he created by combining stylized renderings of his own pictures with letter fragments.[82] In a few such fonts—AMF (see pls. 31, 108–9, 139–40), BAPHT (see pls. 113, 131–34, 136, 157), and FBT (see pls. 7, 114, 136–37, 140)—each letter combines shapes generated from Khasanoff's photographs of bamboo branches and telephone poles with alphabetic forms, bringing together nature, technology (pole wires carry electricity and speech), and writing.[83] Other fonts were made using only pictures, either from his image collections, such as baseball players in newspaper photos, or from his own photographs of bamboo plants (pls. 122–23, 132), telephone pole wires (pls. 121, 135–36), erasings (pl. 156), and tree roots.[84] He used individual characters from these fonts in digital montages as he would any other image or outline (pls. 31, 106, 108–9, 119, 122–23, 135–37), or he would use them as an alphabet, to type in and over his images (pls. 7, 107, 113, 121, 132, 140).

Unless the viewer can decipher which character corresponds to which key on the standard keyboard, the texts in Khasanoff's montages are illegible. But this would not be the only obfuscation of meaning. It is very possible that he typed randomly. It is also possible that he typed nonsense poetry—he had a life-long practice of writing strings of words without intended meaning, but with the expectation that some meaning would nonetheless be generated by the viewer, because the words would adhere somewhat to grammar, a hard structure for our minds to shed (see p. 103).[85] Considering reading text and seeing or reading images as related experiences, he perceived an essential parallel between his font work and the optical:

> ELIZABETH HANSEN (interviewer): You want people not to trust the photo. Is there a relationship to that in the Font world?

> KHASANOFF: Yes, it's all related to that. How else can I stop the reading of the word? If you just read the word "tomorrow," it is immediately gonna go into your head. . . . But if I fuck around with the font . . . there's a chance I have disturbed the system enough, in order to maybe think about "tomorrow" in a little bit different way. It's a stoppage.
>
> HANSEN: It's then optical, interestingly, in the font world.

KHASANOFF: Yeah, because the font world is reading, and what else is reading but optical? It is optical.[86]

In connection with his interest in fonts, as well as his continued exploration of psychological symbols, Khasanoff pursued a collection and project on the letter *X* and integrated this letter/symbol into the vocabulary of his photography (pls. 55, 86, 116, 152). He saw *X* as a uniquely image- or kanji-like character in the otherwise abstract Western alphabet, given its shape. As a visual representation of its meaning(s), *X* may be related to the notion of castration, and so to cutting, cancelation, and elimination, but paradoxically also to support, literally as in construction scaffolding, for example, and figuratively as in physical or emotional support to recover, remake, or reinvent the body or the self.[87] Khasanoff's visual interest in *X* also made him notice that the pattern on the traditional costume of the harlequin, formed by adjacent equilateral triangles that form diamonds, can also be seen as a pattern of *X*s (pls. 33, 35, 112, 157). He was interested in the diamond as a shape marking the onset of Cubism, in particular, in depictions of harlequins: Paul Cézanne's *Harlequin* dates from 1888–90, followed by several increasingly Cubist versions by Pablo Picasso and others.[88] As a symbol, then, *X* bore personal meaning for Khasanoff beyond the commonplace function of the letter. If his interest in asemic writing could relate to the elusiveness, or inaccessibility, of meaning, *X*—just two lines crossing each other, which could signal *in*access—proved to be the source of a well of meanings, some contradictory, as in "parad*ox*," a word carrying, as Khasanoff saw it, a castrated bull.[89] He playfully embraced both the randomness and the prolific associations in his thinking.

Late Years: Multi-Line and 3-D Projects

Throughout his creative life, it was typical for Khasanoff to transition from one project to the next in an associative, "one thing leads to another" fashion, while also working in a cyclical way, revisiting ideas from his previous investigations. In about mid-2015, he felt he was done

with using a single Morandi still life as an outline (see fig. 5). He also took a break from his *X* project and slowed down on exploring erasure.[90] In his last major project, informally called Multi-Line (pls. 141–61), which spanned 2015 to 2019, he returned to several themes by working with fragmented lines: some were found on street pavements, some were appropriated from other artists, and many of the images used were deconstructed and reconstructed using Photoshop. They allowed him to (re)examine decay and erasure; the physical and emotional connections signaled by skin lines (as with rubber bands); and the significance of seams or cracks.

Khasanoff had addressed his interest in the line—a most basic mark—in various ways over decades, exploring its relationship to positive and

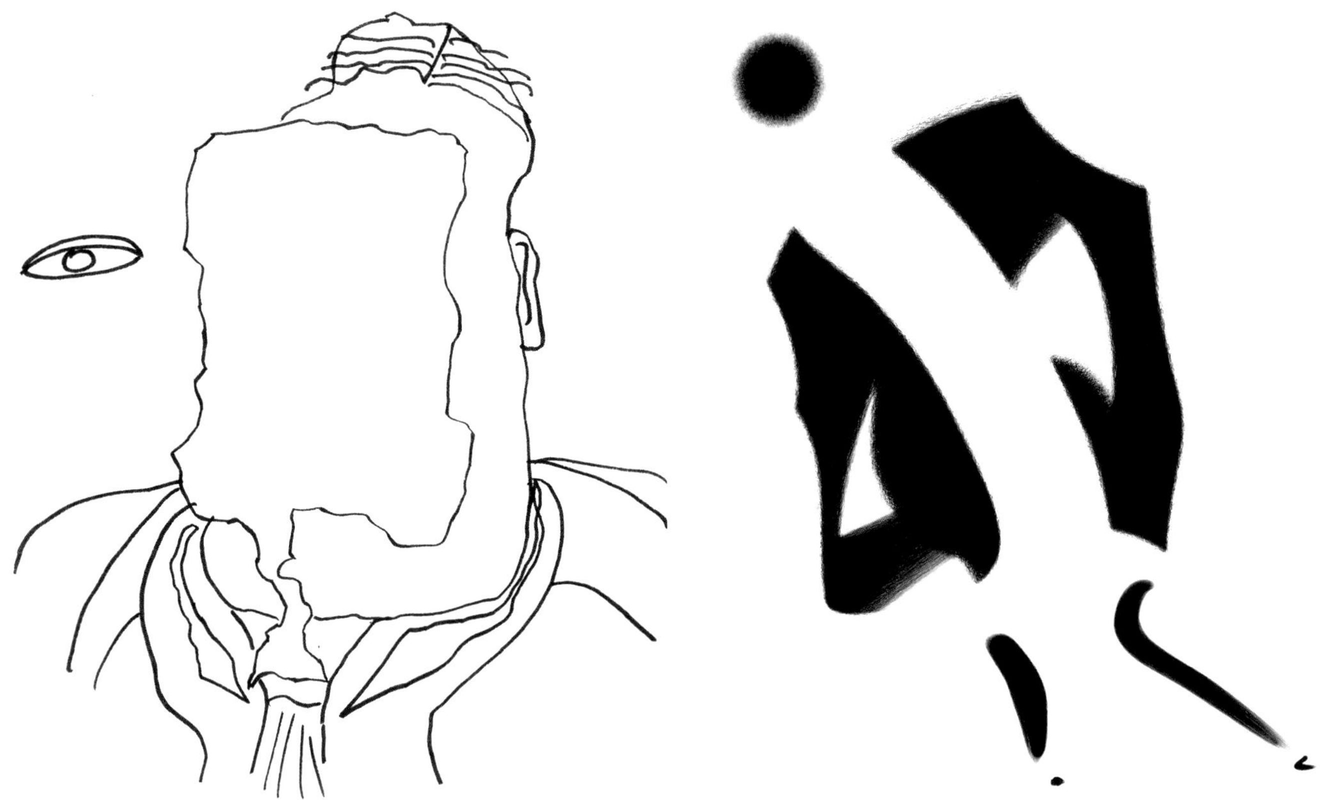

Fig. 8. (left) Allan Chasanoff, Sketchbook Drawing, ca. 1985–95; (right) Allan Chasanoff, Zen Brush Drawing, 2016. Allan Chasanoff Archive, Yale University Art Gallery

negative space and, arguably, to the optical. His line-related projects included a roughly ten-year sketchbook drawing practice starting in the mid-1980s, experimentations with sumi-e (East Asian ink brush painting) in the 1990s, and digital drawings using the Zen Brush application on the iPad and iPhone during the 2010s (fig. 8).[91] In his photography, the fractured props and painted lines in his analog still lifes (see pls. 24, 70, 91) and the cracks and lines in his digital montages (see pls. 9, 92, 111) had been important features and help explain his enthusiasm when he realized real-world ground and pavement could be a rich source for "collecting" lines—by photographing them.

During the last decade of his life, aging and difficulty with balance forced Khasanoff to look down more while walking, and he started taking pictures of what he saw below his feet: tree roots during his numerous visits to Japan, which reminded him of kanji characters; shadows of artworks during museum visits in Manhattan;[92] and cracks in the pavement around his Murray Hill neighborhood. Some of the roots turned into fonts (see p. 206), and the cracks came to be the raw material for Multi-Line. Editing the digital contact sheets on his computer screen, with slow and thorough looking, allowed him to play with the phenomenon of pareidolia—the human ability to see meaningful images in a random or ambiguous visual pattern (for the multiple images associated with one photograph, see pl. 144). Often he extracted the shapes and lines he found (pls. 145–46, 148, 153) and composed them into delicate, sometimes whimsical montages, evoking hand-drawn lines and shapes (pls. 147, 154, 156) and asemic writing (pl. 155). In other words, through pareidolia he identified some meaning in the abstract patterns of straight photographs, and then used those "meaning-filled" elements, or "image-fragment-words," to make "less meaning-full" statements (montages), reminiscent perhaps of his nonsense poetry.

Following his pattern in some previous series, deeper into the Multi-Line project he added imagery and lines from his own work to his newly developed "crack" vocabulary, including favorite motifs such as his fonts (pls. 156–57), drawings (pls. 150–51), museum floor shadows (pl. 141), Japanese seal impressions (pl. 156),[93] Andrew Jackson stamps (pl. 152),[94] erasings (pl. 160, bottom), and, in one image, a barn door, harlequin diamonds, and Morandi bottles (pl. 157). He also took lines from other artists, including Georg Baselitz (pl. 150), Camille Pissarro (pl. 149), Jenny Saville (p. 21), and Lee Friedlander.[95]

Eventually he chose a particular shape in his pavement photographs—reminiscent to him of the Pietá and perhaps evoking his love for his mother and awareness of his own impending death—created an outline from it, and filled it with various content (pls. 160–61). At the time of his passing, two of these Pietá outline images were pinned on his office wall, and it is possible he would have continued to play with them had he had more time. Whether through poetic coincidence or premonition, they were filled with fragments of paintings by Morandi and Klee (see pl. 161)—connecting Khasanoff to artists working in still life, the optical, and asemic writing in one final embrace.

In 2013–14, just before starting Multi-Line, and again toward its end in 2019, Khasanoff acted on his interest in 3-D modeling and printing,

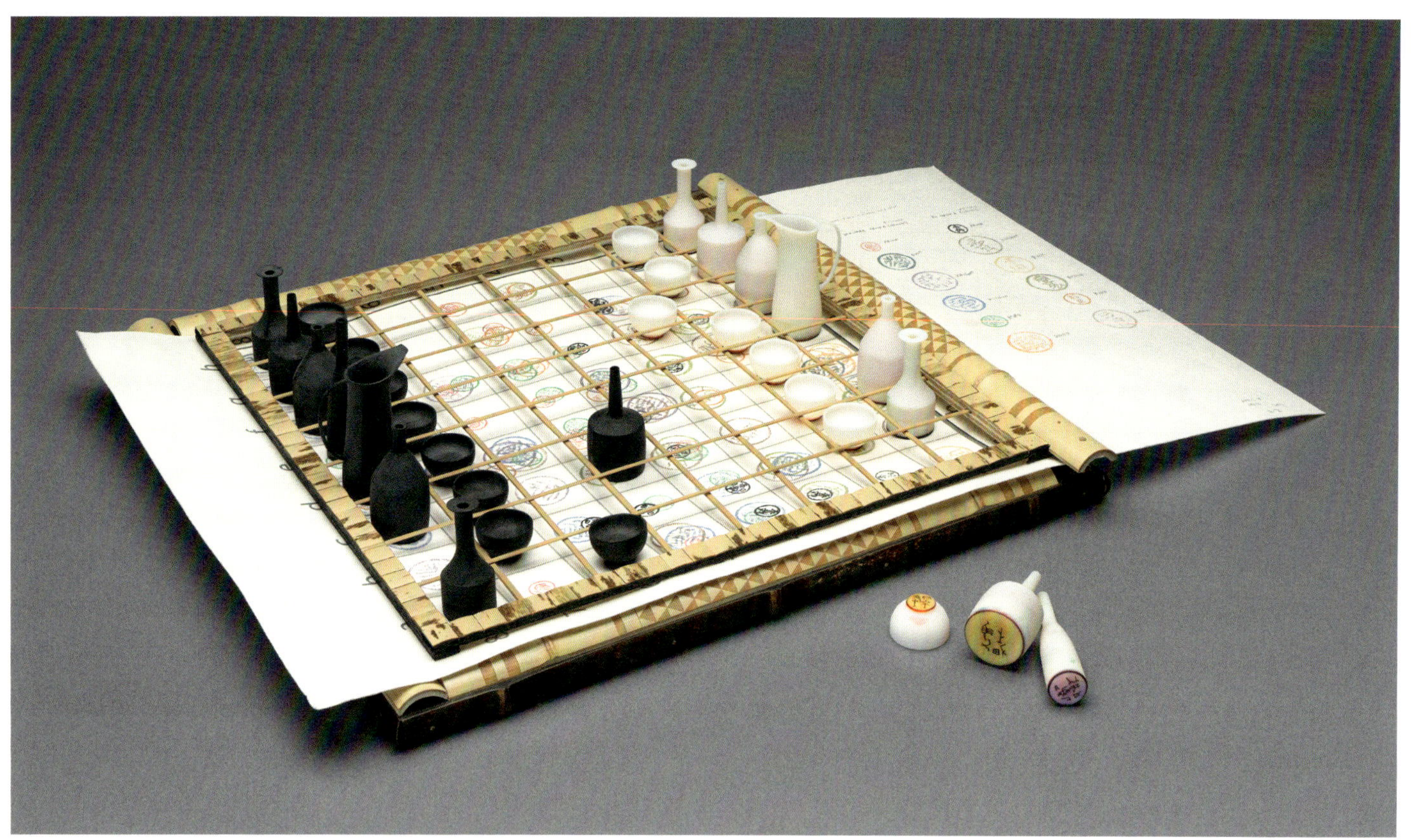

Fig. 9. Allan Chasanoff, Morandi Chess Set, ca. 2011. Playing pieces: 3-D-printed polylactic acid, with seals designed by Atsuko Segawa and carved by Gao Feng, dimensions variable; board: bamboo and wood, 17 7⁄8 × 17 11⁄16 × 2 1⁄16 in. (45.4 × 45 × 5.3 cm); sheet tracing the moves of a Bobby Fischer–Boris Spassky game played in Reykjavik in 1972, replayed by Chasanoff and Zoë Sheehan Saldaña, April 4–11, 2013: 16 15⁄16 × 21 15⁄16 in. (43.1 × 55.8 cm). Allan Chasanoff Archive, Yale University Art Gallery

which went back to his early engagement with digital tools in the 1990s. Initially using a MakerBot printer, he produced prints from scanned three-dimensional objects, sometimes manipulating the results (pls. 162–64). New equipment acquired in 2019 allowed him to make a leap in scale, color, and texture, with which he played all the way through the last months of his life in 2020 (see pls. 165, 167–69).[96] He thought of the 3-D process as a form of digital ceramic but also as the latest frontier of digital photography: objects are scanned using visible white light, manipulated and "merged"—his preferred word for 3-D compositing—in an image-editing software, and printed.[97] He saw a parallel between the unpredictable line produced by Photoshop's "magic wand" selection tool, which he used in the Multi-Line project, and the deterioration of objects through scanning and printing errors in the 3-D process. Both types of imprecision may be thought of as misinterpretation, as when meaning slips due to the problematic nature of language, or during translation from one language to another.

Working with old props in his townhouse basement, such as a small Pietá-like figurine made from book binding leather (pl. 163, left), plastic Freud figurine, or paint tube "sitting" on a chair—reminiscent to him of Francis Bacon's studies of Pope Innocent X after Diego Velázquez—he produced 3-D prints marked by signs of error or incompletion (pls. 162–65). These works may prompt us to see a parallel between the deterioration of objects in the scanning, manipulating, and printing process and the fading or failure of memories. Another feature of the works is the presence of visible support elements. While these may be read as production clues, they also summon up similarities between the role of supports in the 3-D printing process and in physical and emotional life, which in turn may be related back to the symbolism of the letter *X* in Khasanoff's work and the role of pins in his paint squeezing sculptures (see fig. 3).

Unlike these imprecise pieces, the 3-D prints of Khasanoff's preferred Morandi setup, comprising four bottles, a pitcher, and a cup or bowl, have clean lines (pl. 166). Printed in multiple iterations, they served as the point of departure for his Morandi chess sets (fig. 9).[98] Also used in some of Khasanoff's late still lifes and montages (pls. 39, 75, 166), they allowed him to create variations on the original configuration, play with contour and overlap, and—by placing a black pitcher in front of a white one, for example (pl. 166)—invert the usual relationship

between object and shadow, circling back to such explorations in his earlier still lifes (see pl. 62). In a few of his last 3-D prints, he merged the Morandi pieces with 3-D scans of a take-out cup carrier (pl. 167). A deceptively random choice, the cardboard carrier—not unlike the convertible shipping box—is an ingenious, practical tool of convenience in the consumer capitalist packaging arsenal. Combining this disposable element with the pure Morandi forms elevates it; or perhaps it is a gesture of campy humor. Khasanoff's inclination for preserving the accidental and (otherwise) derogatorily discarded, also expressed in his interest in erasure, extended to his enthusiasm for whimsical, frothy pieces made accidentally by the 3-D printer (pl. 168), as well as for stand-alone compact pieces spit out by the printer's algorithm as printer's waste or produced as "purge blocks" when purging the printer of one color before using another (pl. 169). None of these he had much control in making, yet he often ended up preferring them to "perfect" pieces.

Life Anew

Giving new life to artworks (his own and those of other artists), to ordinary objects in which he saw great significance, and to the ideas that underpinned his understanding of the individual and society was Allan Thasanoff's observable insistence across his numerous activities. What's more, he would have included people and pets if he could. Interestingly, the seed of this devotion may have been his emphasis on doubt, especially questioning what we are prone to believe instinctually, and above all the photographic image. Belief put aside, or at least under scrutiny, opens paths to free play. Through the optical, he placed everything we see under the sign of confusion. Through appropriation, he found a way to have conversations with other artists. In collecting and connecting, breaking and reassembling, or deconstructing and reconstructing, he saw ways to foster the emergence of unintended new meanings. In contours and outlines of recognizable shapes, such as that of a convertible flat box or a Morandi setup, he saw empty negative spaces to be filled with unexpected new content. Through the preservation of tiny, overlooked objects, such as "erasings," he resisted the idea and gesture of discarding, and by transforming them into fonts, he proposed that they be reused, and elevated (back) into new writing.

Related perhaps to this inclination toward recycling, he would have loved to see museums reveal the "seams" of production on images and objects in

their care, show traces of their transformations, and let the individual (viewer) take them apart and play with them rather than worship them based on values defined by the institution. In line with this notion, he was toying with the idea of creating a mobile phone or tablet app as an aid to a future exhibition of his work, through which the Photoshop layers of his Multi-Line works would be available for viewers to look at alongside the "executed" prints "hung" on the wall. In a similar spirit, he thought to make all of his digital line and crack vocabulary available online for anyone to use in their own montages, or visual sentences. Given the chance, maybe he would have played with elements of virtual reality, too—he was aware of VR as the next photographic frontier. Moreover, he would most likely encourage the reader of this book to do what he would have done: cut these pages off their spine, unbind, shuffle, annotate, scan, rip, tear, wrinkle them, and file them for future reference and/or transform them into something new—of their own making.

All are creative inasmuch as we can all create a new sentence.
—Allan Chasanoff

A dote on the ’note

The footnote
Has been the goat
In the recent lacuna declension

But I vote
To tote the ’note
(From inside the moat)
And resurrect its immense intention.

—Allan Chasanoff

Notes

1. Allan Chasanoff, “2-18-09 items formal listing,” 2009, p. 4, Allan Chasanoff Archive, Yale University Art Gallery. Hereafter this archive is abbreviated as Chasanoff Archive, YUAG.
2. Chasanoff’s photography collection is divided between the Museum of Fine Arts, Houston, and the Yale University Art Gallery. See *Tradition and the Unpredictable: The Allan Chasanoff Photographic Collection*, exh. cat. (Houston: Museum of Fine Arts, Houston, 1994); and Joshua Chuang, *First Doubt: Optical Confusion in Modern Photography; Selections from the Allan Chasanoff Collection*, exh. cat. (New Haven, Conn.: Yale University Art Gallery, 2008). Chasanoff’s ceramics collection was donated to the Mint Museum, Charlotte, North Carolina; see *Allan Chasanoff Ceramic Collection*, exh. cat. (Charlotte, N.C.: Mint Museum of Craft + Design, 2000). For his book art collection, now at the Gallery, see *Odd Volumes: Book Art from the Allan Chasanoff Collection*, exh. cat. (New Haven, Conn.: Yale University Art Gallery, 2014).
3. Solo exhibitions took place at the Marcuse Pfeifer Gallery in New York in 1983 and 1988, each accompanied by a catalogue: *Allan Chasanoff: Situate, Lying and Being: Still Life Photographs*, and *The Party of the First Pot: Allan Chasanoff, Photographs*. Soon after the second New York event, some of Chasanoff’s photographs were shown at Studio 666 in Paris. Chris Insinger, communication with the author, September 22, 2022; see also http://www.lavrillier.com/carol-marc-lavrillier-studio-666.
4. He would also say, cheekily, that he didn’t file his taxes as an artist, meaning it wasn’t his profession.
5. Friends and collaborators included the multidisciplinary artists Raymon Elozua and Doug Beube; playwright, actor, and theater historian Errol Hill; engineer, computer programmer, and photographer Francis Olschafskie; cardiologist Dr. Michael Poon; entrepreneur and programmer Rick Ross; photography dealers and gallerists Howard Greenberg and Peter McGill; architects Hani Rashid and Lise Anne Couture; photographer and educator Charles H. Traub; and librarian and author Richard Ovenden (see the preface to this volume).
6. The Richard Benson and Allan Chasanoff Classrooms at the Gallery’s Wurtele Study Center, where the pair’s respective archives can be accessed, are the result of Reynolds’s vision.
7. Allan Chasanoff, “AC—Structure Development,” ca. 2000, p. 6, Chasanoff Archive, YUAG.
8. Chasanoff often called these works simply “digital” and sometimes “collages.”
9. See Allan Chasanoff, “PM,” 1998, pp. 1, 4, Chasanoff Archive, YUAG: “Post-Modernism is an inexact term. . . . It has something to do with using and mixing up something from the past. What past? All the past”; “Post-Modernism is a recognition and usage of the new enabling technology of computer and Internet that combines with the older content of the mass media. . . . I am a Post-Modernist.”
10. In this volume, series names are drawn from the terms applied in the photography databases to repeated subjects and themes (“categories”). These are mostly descriptive and were generated

by Chasanoff, Hansen, and myself. They sometimes vary slightly from the terms used in Chasanoff’s writings, interviews, other databases, and print box labels. Some categories have been edited for clarity: for instance, “Light Bulb” here is “Light Table/Bulbs” in Hansen’s database; “Paint Squeezing” here is “Paint Tube and/or Squeezing” in Hansen’s database; “Multi-Line” here is “Multi-Line/Crack Project” in my database. Some images belong to more than one series. Some series identified in the databases are not mentioned in this volume.
11. Allan Chasanoff’s father, Harris Chasanoff, was born in New York City in 1906; Harris’s parents were born in present-day Belarus, then Russia. Chasanoff’s mother, Hanna Korner, was born in Manhattan in 1907; her parents were born in Poland and present-day Ukraine. Biographical details per Robert Chasanoff, Allan’s nephew; communication with the author, March 29, September 27, and October 6, 2022.

12. Chasanoff's collection of newspaper images of baseball players is preserved in the Chasanoff Archive, YUAG. His Baseball (outline) series (found by searching "Baseball/sports" in Hansen's database) is a response to noticing that the same types of photograph showing the same body movements of players were constantly repeated. See Hansen's notes in the "Baseball/sports" entries, likely paraphrasing Chasanoff's thoughts.
13. Quotations from "ACV9586, Allan and Doug Beube interview 12-18-08," videotape 1, mins. 2–4, Chasanoff Archive, YUAG.
14. *The Standard Edition of the Complete Psychological Works of Sigmund Freud*, translated from the German under the general editorship of James Strachey (London: Hogarth Press and the Institute of Psycho-Analysis, 1953–74).
15. Chasanoff, "AC—Structure Development," 8. Chasanoff referred to this seminal memory as his "infant rattle memory."
16. In 1973–74 he took a class on semiotics at the New School, taught by Marshall Blonsky, and snuck a tape recorder into the lectures for his own reference. According to an entry in the Allan Chasanoff Collection Database (ACDB)—a repository of information on his collections and archive, maintained at his studio by Nicole DeGeorge—he collected materials about Blonsky and Roland Barthes from 1974 to 1985. At some point Chasanoff wanted to put on a play about Barthes. He approached Blonsky about writing it and spoke to Richard Howard (translator of Barthes), but the project was eventually abandoned. See "Semiotics & semiotics related material," ACDB, Chasanoff Archive, YUAG.
17. "He teaches us not how to live but how to read. In short, the postmodern Freud is Freud the interpreter—not the interpreter of dreams, or of the psyche, or of culture, but the interpreter *tout court*." Allan Megill, *Prophets of Extremity* (Berkeley: University of California Press, 1985), 325.
18. "ACV9587 Allan and Doug Beube Interview 12-18-08," videotape 2, mins. 2–3, Chasanoff Archive, YUAG: "This is deeply engrained in my psyche. This is not an intellectual, thought out thing. This was just attacking me."
19. "Sentenced to the sentence" was a phrase Chasanoff used frequently in conversation, as in "ACV9586 Allan and Doug Beube Interview 12-18-08," videotape 1, mins. 29–30. In "AC—Structure Development," 10, he wrote: "When [in school years] practicing vocabulary words often I would struggle and first think whether it was a 'good' or a 'bad' word. The super-ego infected the simple sign event. And when I had to write a composition in freshman year in high school I agonized over it. The main problem being how to go from sentence to sentence. What is the space in between, what is in the transition? This is a remark-able [*sic*] situation."
20. Robert Chasanoff, communication with the author, March 29, 2022.
21. "The appeal of deconstruction for those in the visual arts is not hard to grasp: if existing images, like words, are not fixed representations but capable of being refashioned and reinterpreted to yield new, critical meanings, then the entire universe of pictures is a

subject for artists—from Marlboro ads to Edward Weston photographs." Andy Grundberg, *How Photography Became Contemporary Art* (New Haven, Conn.: Yale University Press, 2021), 149–50. It is important to note that while Chasanoff embraced appropriation, he thought Richard Prince (working with Marlboro ads) and Sherrie Levine (working with Edward Weston photographs) stopped short, as they did not create new phrases or statements with what they appropriated.
22. Other artists Chasanoff appropriated from by using cutouts and painted ceramics in still life setups include Georges Braque, Giorgio Morandi, and Cy Twombly. His digital works include appropriations from still more artists.
23. "If you see something iconic, and like it, study it and then break it up and mash it up. That's speech (with words and memory): we don't own words, we learn them (collect them in

childhood) and use them." Chasanoff, quoted in Mónika Sziládi, "AC Photography—Looking Down—Crack Project," 2016–18, p. 45, Chasanoff Archive, YUAG.

24. Chasanoff worked on a variety of puzzle projects intermittently from the early 1970s until as late as 2016. These include constructions, sculptures, and commissioned custom-made jigsaw puzzles, all preserved in the Chasanoff Archive, YUAG. Two jigsaw puzzles were made from scans of pages from Derrida's *Of Grammatology* (p. 9 and p. 46 from the first American edition, published by John Hopkins University Press in 1976). One (p. 9) was produced two-sided, with a digital montage by Chasanoff on the reverse. As a pair, the two puzzles can be intermixed, producing fragmented text and image when completed. See the "Puzzle Projects" and "Object 235: Custom Puzzles – 2016" entries in the ACDB. Puzzle pieces are used as props in select images.
25. "ACV9586 Allan and Doug Beube Interview 12-18-08," videotape 1, mins. 15–16.
26. Vince Aletti and Anne Wilkes Tucker, "An Interview with Allan Chasanoff," in *Tradition and the Unpredictable*, 6.
27. This image could be a double exposure, but it is much more likely that the newspaper is reflected in the window. The newspaper image may be better discerned if the photograph is rotated 90 degrees clockwise.
28. Plato's allegory of the cave *(Republic* 514b–518d) was definitely on Chasanoff's mind in the 2010s in relation to his "Museum shadows" series. See Sziládi, "AC Photography—Looking Down," 5, 34. It is very possible that shadows reminded him of the cave earlier, as well.
29. Allan Chasanoff, "Lux, et tu, Veritas?" in Chuang, *First Doubt*, 214.
30. The light table is referred to as "Lamp Table" and "Lamp Project" in some databases. See the entry "Object 31: Lamp Project," ACDB, 1969: "This self-contained prop system is a unification of storage, and use, order and change."
31. "Object 40: Paint Tube Squeezings," ACDB, 1971–75. See also Victoria Miguel's entry "Paint Squeezings Sculptures," in Nicole DeGeorge and Victoria Miguel, "Allan Chasanoff Archive Asset and Inventory Report," 2012, p. 28, Chasanoff Archive, YUAG.
32. Sziládi, "AC Photography—Looking Down," 37.
33. "In 1976 professional business obligations required my complete attention, so I had to limit drastically the time spent on photography for the following seven years." Allan Chasanoff, "Lux, et tu, Veritas?" in Chuang, *First Doubt*, 214.
34. Robert Chasanoff, communication with the author, July 12, 2022.
35. For more on this, see Grundberg, *How Photography Became Contemporary Art*.
36. "Chasanoff focused on collecting so-called straight images understood to be 'seen through the taking lens,' or otherwise unmanipulated by the human hand." Chuang, *First Doubt*, 13.
37. See Chasanoff, "AC—Structure Development," 7: "When I started to photograph seriously again in the early 1980s it was directed at still life and the optical. So there was now a certain relatedness between what I was collecting and what I was photographing.

Certainly not in any direct correspondence but most assuredly both activities were concerned with the optical."

38. Chasanoff, "Lux, et tu, Veritas?" in Chuang, *First Doubt*, 215.
39. Chasanoff explored cacophony and sensual chaos in some of his audio and video projects as well, all preserved in the Chasanoff Archive, YUAG. In those, he layered sounds, recorded texts, and moving images, "allowing meaning to come forward via the connections, overlaps and serendipitous moments of syncopation." JoAnn Wasserman, "Double-doing-Videos," project description, ACDB; also in the "projects" and "projects continued—monika" databases (as "Double-doing videos"), Chasanoff Archive, YUAG. For more, see the entries "Double-doing-Videos"/"Double-doing videos" and "Sound Projects," ACDB and "projects continued—monika."

40. In a recorded interview, Chasanoff explains the significance of the seam: "Seam has meant for me personally the ability to see the production technique, and not hiding the one into the other. The world of consumer capitalism does not want us to see the production. So therefore the seam to me is an absolutely critical thing." He goes on to describe how photographs conceal seams: "The flatness of the photograph is gonna pretty much get rid of the seam. The medium is pretty much gonna absolutely overtake the seam. . . . It's hard for a photograph really to expose the seam. So, if I make it 'sensitive,' rather than 'exposed,' maybe I can get at the issue. But it's very very hard. The only way really to do it with a photograph is to rip the photograph . . . one of the powers of a photograph is that it gets rid of the seam." "ACV9529 AC Optical 8-06-2007," videotape 1, mins. 32–34, 35–38.
41. Allan Chasanoff, "Media Article," section 8, "To Answer in Kind," p. 14, Chasanoff Archive, YUAG.
42. Ibid., section 9, "Seam," 22.
43. "ACV9529 AC Optical 8-06-2007" videotape 1, mins. 5–7, Chasanoff Archive, YUAG.
44. See Allan Chasanoff, "no speak, language," 2010, p. 1, Chasanoff Archive, YUAG: "One of my main media ideas is that there is a pressure to speak—whether from the inside or from the outside there is a pressure—and the controlling of this utterance is a basic condition for culture—the psych castration—inhibit the inkling and then displace." See also Chasanoff, "Media Article," section 6, "The So Called Listening Process."
45. "ACV9587 Allan and Doug Beube Interview 12-18-08," videotape 2, mins. 46–47.
46. For more on the tie collection, now in the Chasanoff Archive, YUAG, see the "Tie Collection" description in the ACDB. See also "Tie Collection," description by Victoria Miguel, in DeGeorge and Miguel, "Allan Chasanoff Archive Asset and Inventory Report," 23.
47. "Chasanoff's first foray into the digital realm was his purchase of a Mindset microcomputer in 1985 and DOS-based Lumena software in 1988, both of which at the time were state-of-the-art tools for editing and processing computer graphics." Chuang, *First Doubt*, 17n16.
48. In 1991–94, with artist and software engineer Francis Olschafskie, Chasanoff patented and prototyped a scanning pen called Read In Bed. In 1995–2000, working with Java programmer Rick Ross, he developed two softwares for forming and annotating cross-media linkages, called Objects in the Universe and IRelate. (The lines in the image on the half-title page of the present catalogue evoked, for Chasanoff, the connectivity explored in Objects in the Universe. See "ID 7289," Hansen's database.) The culmination of these efforts for Chasanoff was Read and Note, a software he developed in the 2010s with Olschafskie. A web-based multimedia platform, it integrates reading, annotating, quoting, collecting, and linking texts, images, audio, and video. Dates from the ACDB.
49. Allan Chasanoff, introduction to *Allan Chasanoff: Situate, Lying and Being: Still Life Photographs*, exh. cat. (New York: Marcuse Pfeifer Gallery, 1983), 3.

50. "A still [life] photographer is active. He is one of the few photographers who makes his scene. He makes then takes. Some still [life] photographers make the scene and then embrace it from end to end. I make the scene with such a preconception, pre-visualization. Often, after it is constructed and conforms to what I had in mind, it fails. Either it is too rigid, or it bores me. However, rarely do I leave the scene. There remains a tension, so I go inside and therein take my pictures. I insert the break between make and take." Allan Chasanoff, introduction to *The Party of the First Pot: Allan Chasanoff, Photographs*, exh. cat. (New York: Marcuse Pfeifer Gallery, 1988), 3.
51. Charlotte Cotton, *Photography Is Magic* (New York: Aperture, 2015), 5.
52. On the relationship to collage, Chasanoff writes: "Photocollage [montage] is a hybrid, a monster. In a manner, it acknowledges the collage [as by Picasso and Braque], but it hides behind the

achieved photographic process to present itself. Bows to the mass media production sensibility. It is a precursor but not a progenitor of hypermedia." "Media Article," section 9, "Seam," 21.

53. Ibid., 22.
54. Chasanoff, "AC—Structure Development," 8: "The culmination of this in my aesthetic sensibility is that after not seeing the object well and then I do [it] makes me feel better. But the infantile repetition activity is then exercised so that I make the optical problem again and then resolve it."
55. Chasanoff, "Lux, et tu, Veritas," in Chuang, *First Doubt*, 215: "Consider the moment when a baby clarifies what was previously just a blur. I believe that this original, sensual completion process is reactivated when one looks at the pictures that I identify as possessing 'optical' characteristics."
56. For more on how these two phases of the optical engender Chasanoff's aesthetics, see Mónika Sziládi, "An introduction to how I approached Allan Chasanoff (AC) Photography," 2015–17, pp. 9–14, Chasanoff Archive, YUAG.
57. Chasanoff collected photographs he tore from photo albums for the abstract shapes created by the black backing paper. A selection of these is preserved in the Chasanoff Archive, YUAG. He scanned many of them—referring to the resulting images as the "Back of Photo" series (see p. 13)—and used some of the scans as digital props in his montages. For more, see the "Object 16: Back of Photo (BOF)" description in the ACDB. See also "Back of Photo," description by Victoria Miguel, in DeGeorge and Miguel, "Allan Chasanoff Archive Asset and Inventory Report," 24–25.
58. The appropriations in plate 161 come from two sources: Morandi's *Still Life* (1963; see Lamberto Vitali, *Morandi dipinti: Catalogo generale* [Milan: Electa, 1983], no. 1313) and Klee's *Girl in Mourning* (1939; Metropolitan Museum of Art, New York, 1984.315.61), a portrait.
59. Allan Chasanoff, "Arch with Hani- aka Harch," 1996–97, p. 6, Chasanoff Archive, YUAG: "Probably it is the silhouette that is the basic design and symbolic attribute of Postmodernism. A defined shape, exterior dominated, which asks to be filled. But the filling does not have to be in 2 dimensions. It can be violated or snubbed and depth and multiplicity can be used as the filling."
60. Chasanoff's interest in Morandi included the creation of ceramic, papier-mâché, and glass objects, 3-D prints, and chess sets (see fig. 9). The objects are works in their own right, and they were used in setups for photographic still lifes and videos (see pls. 28, 34, 91, 166). The still lifes were often reused in digital montages (see pl. 39). See Allan Chasanoff and Mónika Sziládi, "Allan Chasanoff (AC): Morandi Projects," 2015, Chasanoff Archive, YUAG.
61. "In Morandi they [figure and ground] were never really separate. In fact, even with the figurative elements, there were cases where his ground actually got in front of the figures or in many cases couched them so intimately that there was no separating the two." Lawrence Weschler, *Seeing Is Forgetting the Name of the Thing One Sees: A Life of Contemporary Artist*

Robert Irwin (Berkeley: University of California Press, 1982), 56–57. Cited in Elizabeth Hansen, "The Optical Problem in Photography: The Allan Chasanoff Collection," 2008, Chasanoff Archive, YUAG. See also Mónika Sziládi, "Painted Edges—Optical," 2019, p. 2, Chasanoff Archive, YUAG.

62. Chasanoff worked with photocopies of what he believed was a drawing related to Morandi's painting *Still Life* (1952; Vitali, *Morandi dipinti*, no. 819), but the location of the drawing and its actual medium are unknown. The author has not been able to identify this indeterminate work in Morandi catalogues raisonnés. Chasanoff photocopied the work, or possibly the painting, from a source he later could not find.
63. "Allan's fascination with that particular Morandi drawing [or work] stems from a compositional flaw he perceives in the arrangement of the bottles. His fascination with this composition that 'does not work,' its dissonance, or lack of harmony, has a parallel in his interest in the

optical in photography as well as the shock and rupture that he describes as the seam in his *Media Article*; the seamlessness of media in Modernism substantiates its authority[;] by drawing attention to the seam, to flaws, he questions authority. In the still life images and Morandi based works he does so by using the quintessentially authoritarian form of Western art." Victoria Miguel, "BEING THINKING MAKING," in DeGeorge and Miguel, "Allan Chasanoff Archive Asset and Inventory Report," 10.

64. Allan Chasanoff, quoted in Anne Wilkes Tucker, "The Challenge of Confusion," in *Tradition and the Unpredictable*, 15.
65. "ACV9478 Box Talk with AC and Elizabeth 1-15-2007," videotape, 2007, mins. 5–6, Chasanoff Archive, YUAG. See also Chasanoff's two-page statement "The BOX," 2006, Chasanoff Archive, YUAG.
66. A large selection of the props is preserved in the Chasanoff Archive, YUAG.
67. Allan Chasanoff, conversation with the author, ca. 2015–20.
68. Ibid., ca. 2015–20.
69. During his travels in Japan, Chasanoff commissioned three barn door–inspired bamboo objects in Sakai, preserved in the Chasanoff Archive, YUAG. Two were made by Tanabe Chikuunsai III in 2007, and one by his son Tanabe Chikuunsai IV (Shouchiku Tanabe) in 2011.
70. Riffing on the convertible box, between 2009 and 2012 Chasanoff collaborated with the artist and book binder Barbara Mauriello to create a series of modular folding boxes adorned with Japanese paper. See Mónika Sziládi, "Barbara Mauriello Boxes," 2019, Chasanoff Archive, YUAG; and Barbara Mauriello's two-page project statement, "Boxness, Houseness," ca. 2012, Chasanoff Archive, YUAG.
71. "Recently I had a visual discovery whereby I related my interest in rubberbands to Indented skin—that is, the way a batch of rubberbands laying indiscriminately around and on top of each other looked like what the indented skin configuration looked like after sleep, etc." Chasanoff, quoted in the entry "Indented Skin," ACDB.
72. See Sziládi, "AC Photography—Looking Down," 3n9.
73. Ibid., 36.
74. Chasanoff, conversation with the author, 2020.
75. See Sziládi and Chasanoff, "JAPAN—An Introduction," 3. See also Mónika Sziládi, "Erasure, Byte—Soutine—Rothko Erasure project with MSZ," 2019, Chasanoff Archive, YUAG.
76. Chasanoff, "AC—Structure Development," 2.
77. Chasanoff visited Japan about a dozen times between 1990 and 2012, including eight trips between 2007 and 2012 for the purpose of learning about Japanese culture while working with seal makers and calligraphers. For more, see Sziládi and Chasanoff, "JAPAN—An Introduction." See also the handwritten travel diaries by Akiko Ito, Chasanoff's guide in Japan, with drawings. Digital resources include a "digest" of Ito's diaries (Japan-Akiko-AC-DIGEST-final.doc) and an Excel spreadsheet detailing projects, as well as towns, seal makers, and calligraphers visited (Japan_table.xls). All preserved in the Chasanoff Archive, YUAG.

78. His photography collection likely started in the late 1970s, though the first acquisitions are dated 1980 in his photography collection database, called the "photo" database; the ceramic collection, in 1978; the book art collection, ca. 1994. Chasanoff also collected Russian posters from ca. 1993; neckties from ca. 1994; recordings of the song "Amazing Grace" from the early 1990s, and more. Dates here are drawn from the ACDB, Chasanoff's "projects" and "projects continued—monika" databases, and correspondence with Raymon Elozua, September 13, 2022.
79. "If you said to me, Allan, what are you? I'm not gonna say I'm an American, I'm not gonna say I'm a Jew. I'm gonna say to you—tongue and cheek—I'm a Brooklyn Dodger fan. . . . Jackie Robinson was my favorite ball player"; "ACV9586 Allan and Doug Beube Interview 12-18-08," videotape 1, mins. 8–10. Regarding elitism, Chasanoff said, "Post modernism is not a production system for the elite constructor"; "Media Article," section 10, "Post Mod and the receiver," p. 24.

80. Chasanoff, "AC—Structure Development," 3.
81. The first "full-length exploration of the history and meaning of asemic writing," Peter Schwenger's *Asemic: The Art of Writing* (Minneapolis: University of Minnesota Press) was published in 2019 and cherished by Chasanoff during the last year of his life.
82. "Keep feeling that our speech limited to words alone in alphabet is not rich enough. . . . Need to re-instate the image into our writing. Do not need the usual correlation between words of speech and words of writing. . . . So this morning—[I] realize [I] can also add to the font base the assembly parts of the font into a pictorial realist sense and add it to the font that made it. It will have some uniquey attributes. Merge the pictorial and the abstract. Is this what the Japanese do?" Allan Chasanoff, "Fonting—and other stuff," 2006, p. 2, Chasanoff Archive, YUAG.
83. See Chasanoff and Sziládi, "JAPAN—An Introduction," 9. See also "ACV9476 Font Talk with AC and Elizabeth 1-3-2007," videotape 1, mins. 7–9, Chasanoff Archive, YUAG. According to Zoë Sheehan Saldaña, Chasanoff's collaborator in creating fonts, the alphabetic forms (font fragments) were created by modifying or erasing parts of "half characters" that were made by cutting roughly in half letters from existing font sets: in AMF the font fragments were created mainly from Chasanoff's Half Linotext; in BAPHT from his Half Bauhaus, Half Didot, and possibly others; in FBT from Half Didot, Half Linotext, Half Notre Dame, and two other Chasanoff fonts, Font 6 and Play; communication with the author, October 7, 2022. We may speculate that the font name BAPHT stands for BAmboo-PHone-fonT and FBT for Font-Bamboo-Telephone. For AMF, other than the remote possibility of it standing for Alphabet-Manipulated-Font, Saldaña cheekily proposed it could stand for Allan-Making-Fun.
84. Zoë Sheehan Saldaña, communication with the author, August 4, 2022.
85. "If I write nonsense poetry, once in a while I try to get away from the sentence, but it's very hard to break apart noun, verb, etc." "ACV9586 Allan and Doug Beube Interview 12-18-08," videotape 1, mins. 29–30. Chasanoff was not enthusiastic about comparisons of his nonsense poetry to surrealist or spiritual automatic writing. He also wrote nonsense prose; see section 16 of his "Media Article."
86. "ACV9476 Font Talk with AC and Elizabeth 1-3-2007," videotape 1, mins. 10–12.
87. For more on Chasanoff's *X* project, see Mónika Sziládi, "X—Symbol *and* Letter (*also* Shape)," 2016/19, Chasanoff Archive, YUAG.
88. Paul Cézanne, *Harlequin*, 1888–90, National Gallery of Art, Washington, D.C.; Pablo Picasso, *Seated Harlequin*, 1901, Metropolitan Museum of Art, New York; Pablo Picasso, *Acrobat and Young Harlequin*, 1905, Barnes Foundation, Philadelphia; Pablo Picasso, *Harlequin Leaning*, 1909, private collection. Georges Braque and Juan Gris also painted Cubist harlequins. See Sziládi, "X—Symbol *and* Letter (*also* Shape)," 8.
89. For more on Chasanoff's interest in the ox, or castrated bull, see Sziládi, "X—Symbol *and* Letter (*also* Shape)," 5–7, 11–12.

90. See Sziládi, "AC Photography—Looking Down," 3.
91. Dates here are drawn from the ACDB, except in the case of sumi-e, which he mentions in "AC—Structure" (started in 2000) as "10 years ago."
92. Mostly shot in 2012, predominantly in the Metropolitan Museum of Art, New York.
93. During his 2007–12 Japan travels, Chasanoff commissioned roughly two hundred seals "translating" or representing concepts such as erasure, ember, upside/downside, and wedge. They are preserved in the Chasanoff Archive, YUAG, along with information on their meanings compiled by Miho Suzuki. "He was interested in the realistic graphic elements in the language, as well as in the older art/artisan practice of carving seals. . . . Each year, for four years, he chose a different idea/theme to see how different seal makers would interpret and craft it." He explained his concepts to the seal makers with the help of his

guide and translator, Akiko Ito. See Sziládi and Chasanoff, "JAPAN—An Introduction," 2–4; for the quotation, see p. 2. Chasanoff's exploration of seals began when he had his signature Bamboo Boy seal created in Japan in ca. 2006 (see pls. 7, 31, 90, 107–8, 133).

94. Chasanoff collected stamps in childhood; discussions with his friend Richard Benson in about 2011 drew him back into collecting. Benson was particularly interested in the "Black Jack," a stamp depicting President Andrew Jackson (issued in 1863), and the "Black Bull," showing a bull running ahead of its herd (issued in 1898). As a result of their shared interest, Benson and Chasanoff collaborated on a project called *Jackson Cancellation* in 2013–14. Benson photographed, enlarged, and printed noncanceled Jackson stamps in several sizes. Chasanoff then took these on his last trip to Japan, in 2012, and commissioned calligraphers and seal makers to cancel them by painting calligraphy and stamping seals created specially for this project over them. For more, see Mónika Sziládi, "Jackson paragraphs from two texts," 2018, Chasanoff Archive, YUAG.
95. "He [also] extracted lines from works by Pollock, van Gogh, Marden, Léger, Johns, Held, and many more." Sziládi, "AC Photography—Looking Down," 12. In the case of Saville, he extracted the lines from a picture he took of one of her works at the Gagosian gallery, West 21st St., New York, in 2018. Other images came mostly from published sources.
96. See Mónika Sziládi, "Notes on 3D Prints and Sculpture," 2018, Chasanoff Archive, YUAG. In the 1990s, Chasanoff worked with the software Crystal to create 3-D images. During this period, he had 3-D files made of his preferred Morandi setup (four bottles, a pitcher, and a cup or small bowl). In ca. 2009–11, he learned about new 3-D processes and had his Morandi files 3-D printed. He then utilized the pieces in his Morandi chess sets (see fig. 9) and still life photographs (see pl. 166). In about 2013, he bought his own MakerBot 3-D printer and spent about a year scanning and printing paint tubes and chairs. He stepped away from the work because of time issues—it took up to twenty-two hours to output a small object. In 2019 he returned to it, now using a Prusa i3 3-D printer, and experimented with scanning and printing objects in his vocabulary. He used some of his 3-D prints in his late still life setups. The late 3-D prints are dated ca. 2019–20, because of difficulties ascertaining what was accomplished in the studio during the winter months from late 2019 to spring 2020. According to David Pattillo, who operated the 3-D printers during this time, four-color pieces were likely made in 2020 (see pls. 165, 167), the others in 2019; communication with the author, April 27, 2022.
97. See Sziládi, "Notes on 3D Prints and Sculpture," 1.
98. The chess pieces in these sets are carved on the bottom with Japanese kanji. Functioning like seals, they can trace the steps of a game, recording chess moves in kanji statements with fluid meanings. The Morandi chess sets are preserved in the Chasanoff Archive, YUAG. For more about them, see Miho Suzuki, "Morandi Chess Kanji," 2013, Chasanoff Archive, YUAG; and Sziládi and Chasanoff, "JAPAN—An Introduction," 6–7.

Plates II

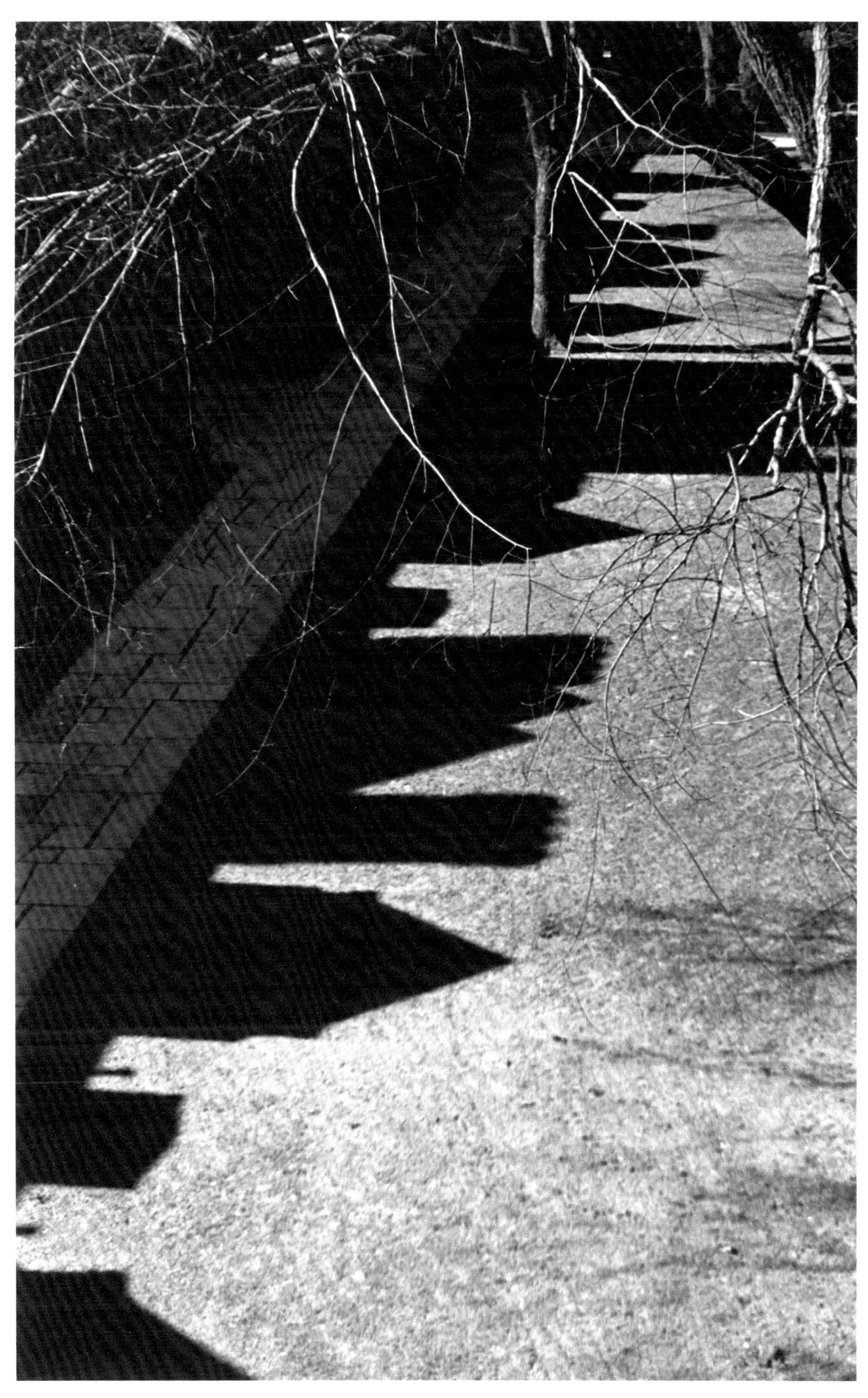

Plate 44
No. 4285, ca. 1963, gelatin silver print.
Allan Chasanoff Archive, Yale University Art Gallery

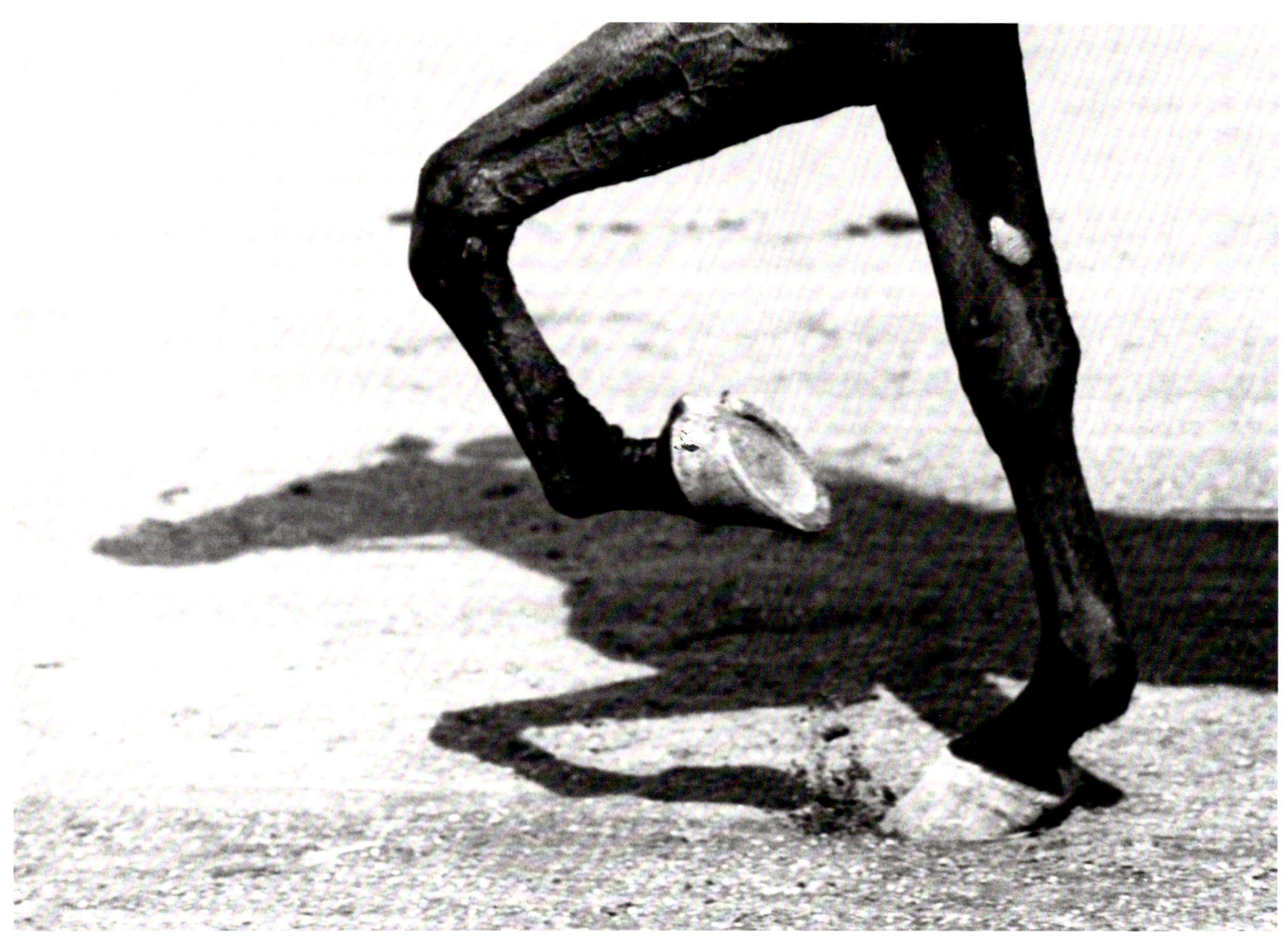

Plate 45
No. 4289, ca. 1965–70, gelatin silver print.
Allan Chasanoff Archive, Yale University Art Gallery

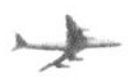

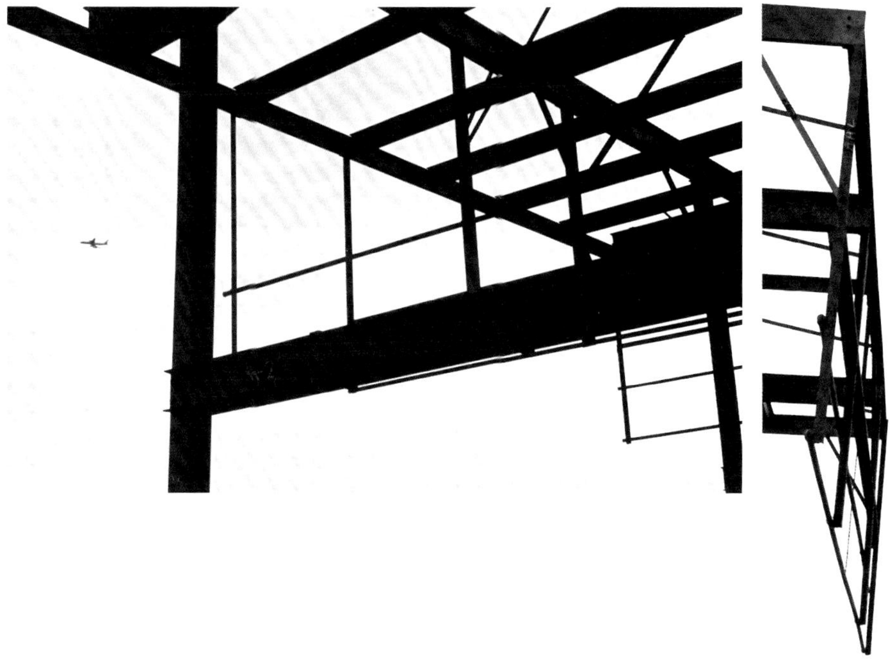

Plate 46
No. 4392, ca. 1965–70, gelatin silver print.
Allan Chasanoff Archive, Yale University Art Gallery

Plate 47
No. 4395, ca. 1965–70, gelatin silver print.
Allan Chasanoff Archive, Yale University Art Gallery

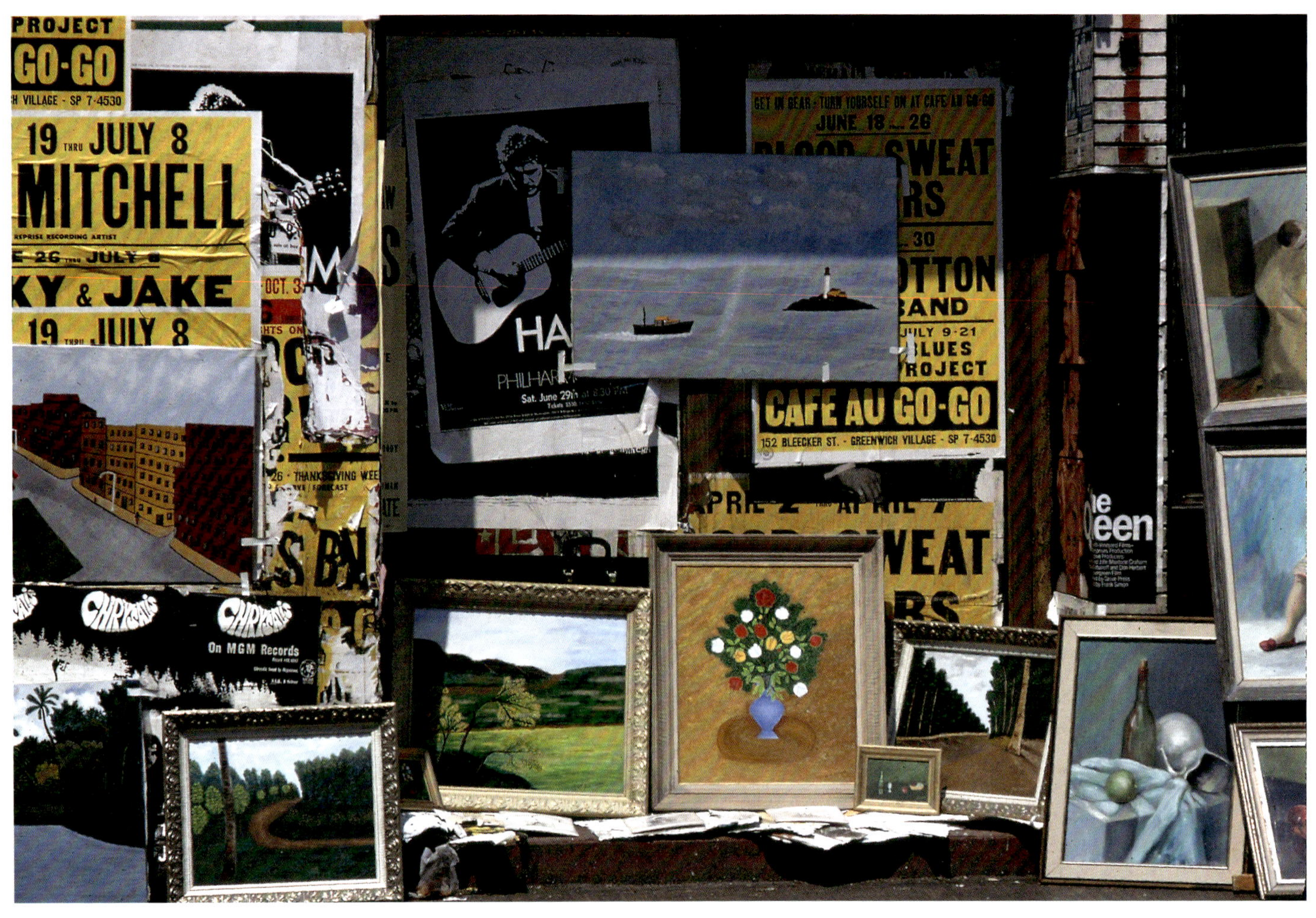

Plate 48
No. 2630, 1968, color transparency. Poster series.
Allan Chasanoff Archive, Yale University Art Gallery

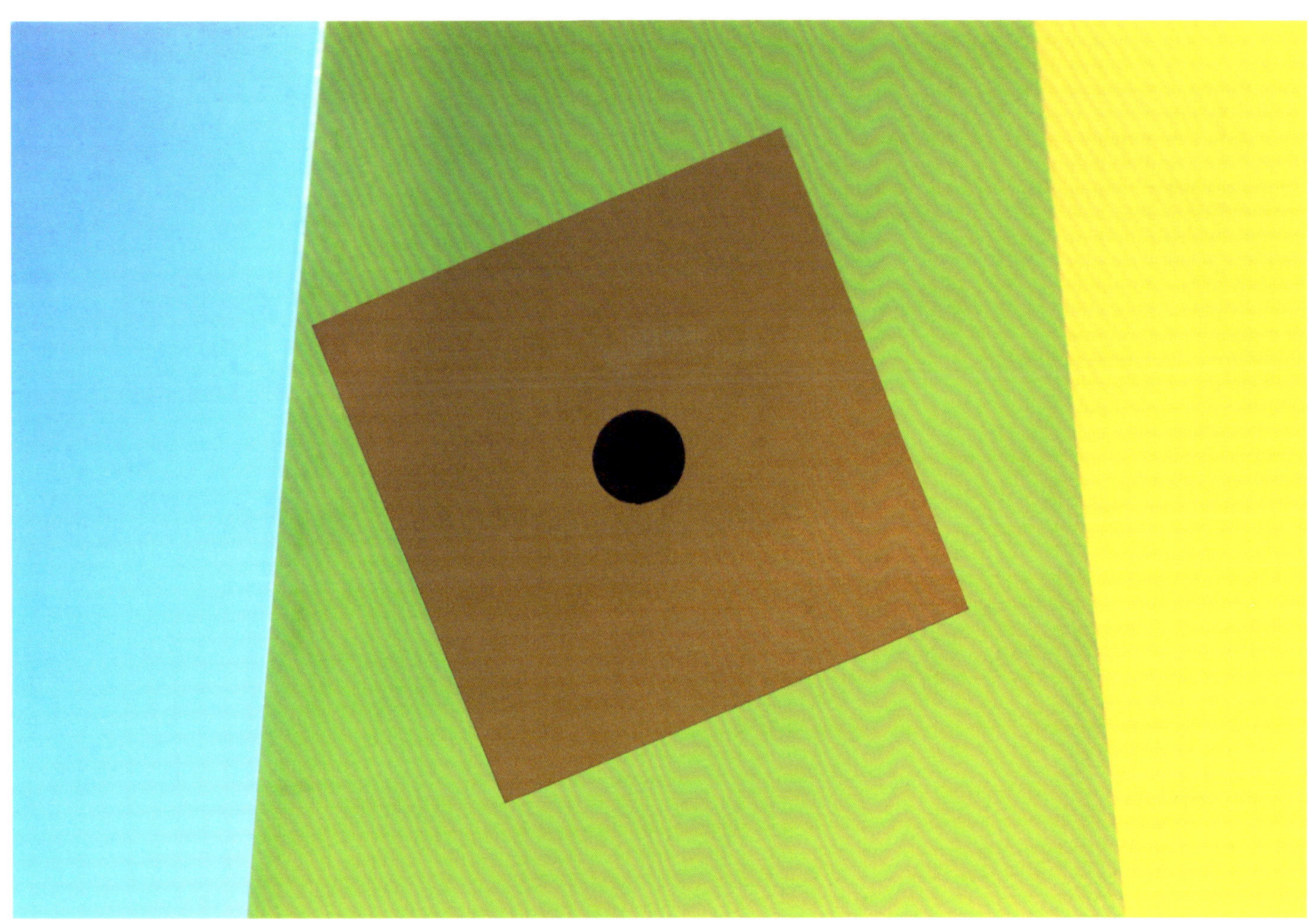

Plate 49
No. 2324, 1968, color transparency.
Allan Chasanoff Archive, Yale University Art Gallery

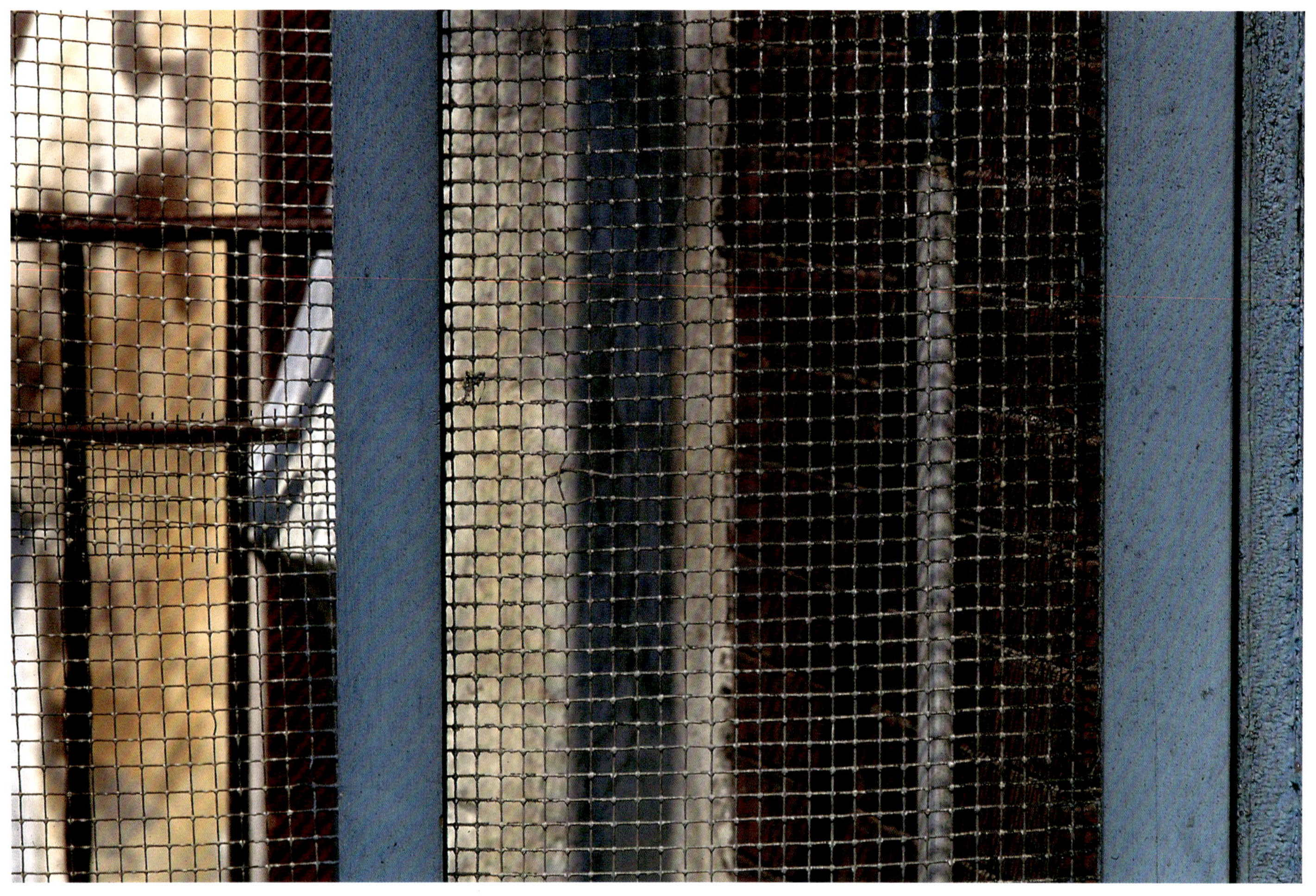

Plate 50
No. 2628, 1968, color transparency.
Allan Chasanoff Archive, Yale University Art Gallery

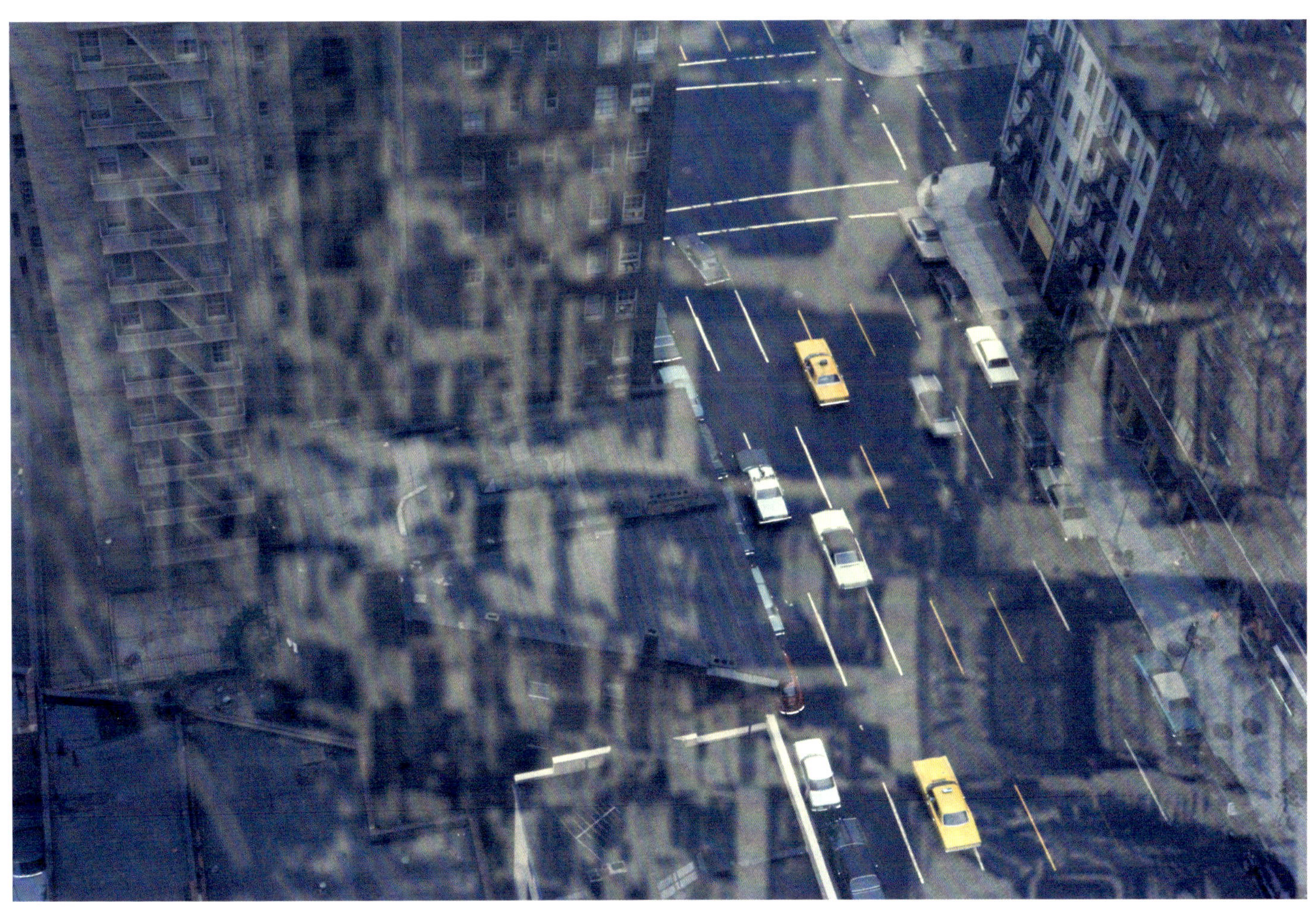

Plate 51
No. 2312, 1969, color transparency.
Allan Chasanoff Archive, Yale University Art Gallery

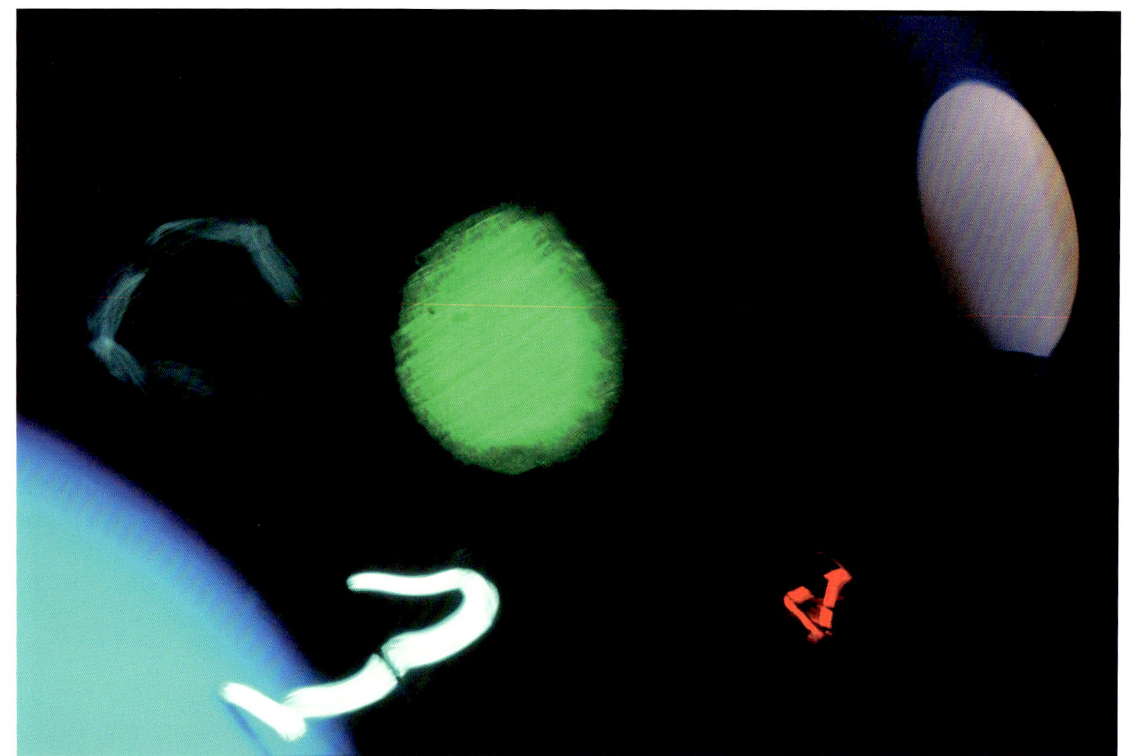

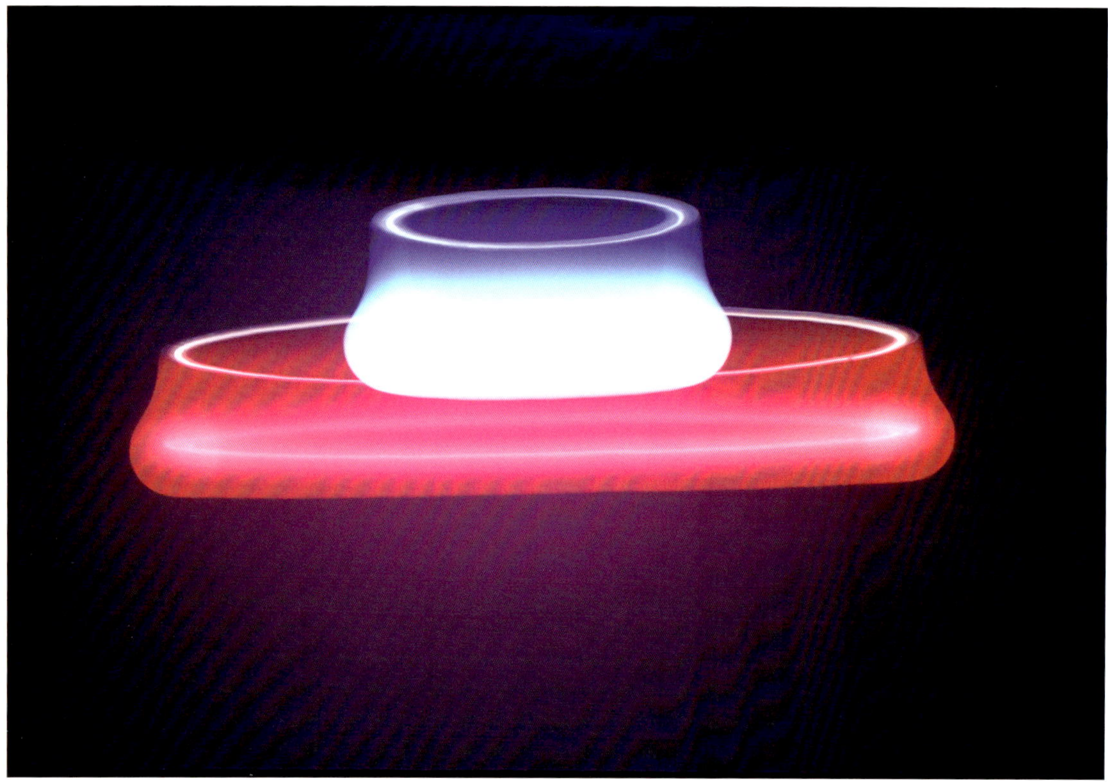

Plate 52
No. 1252, 1973, color transparency. Light Bulb series.
Allan Chasanoff Archive, Yale University Art Gallery

Plate 53
No. 2429, 1972, color transparency. Light Bulb series.
Allan Chasanoff Archive, Yale University Art Gallery

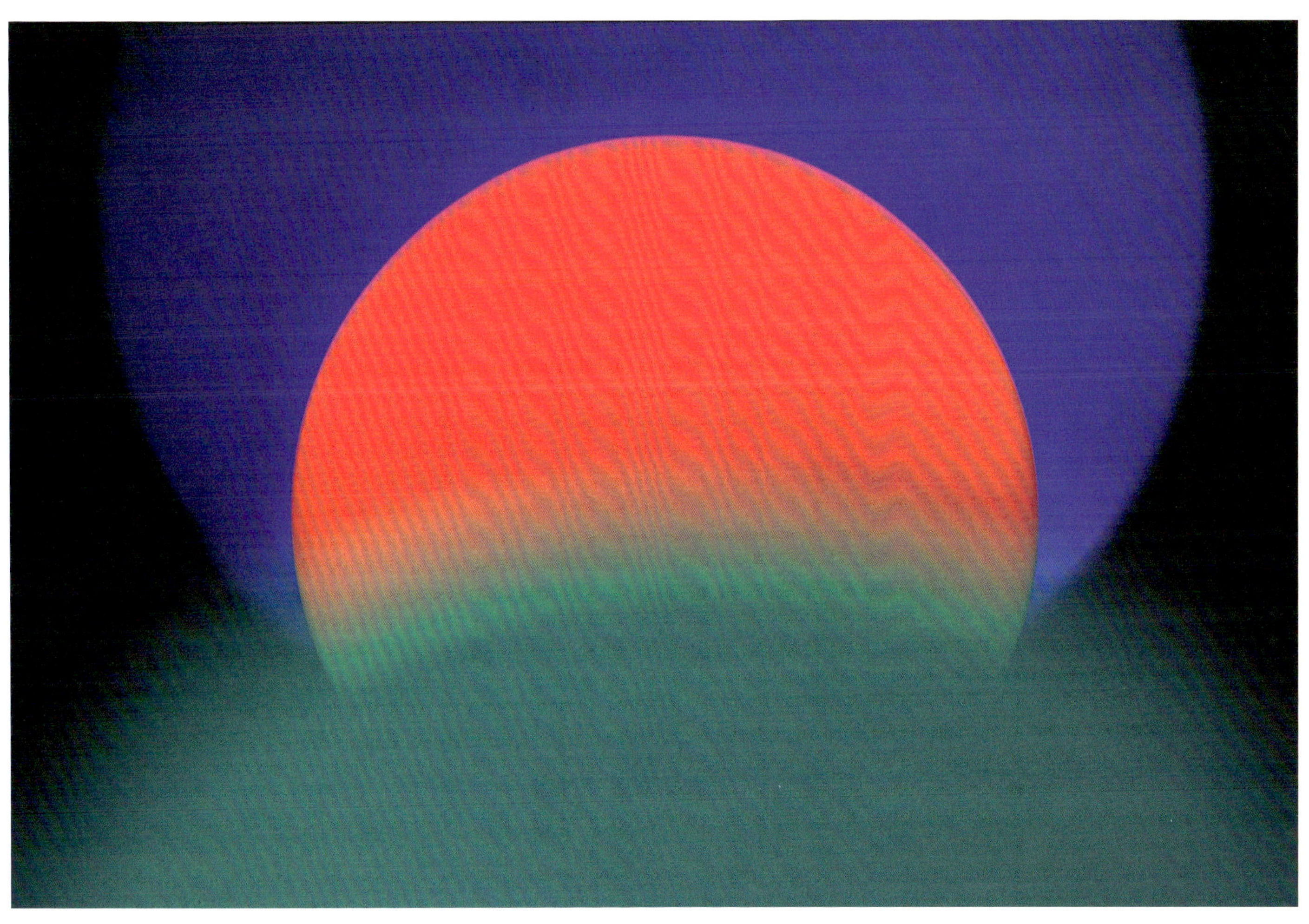

Plate 54
No. 1253, 1975, color transparency. Light Bulb series.
Allan Chasanoff Archive, Yale University Art Gallery

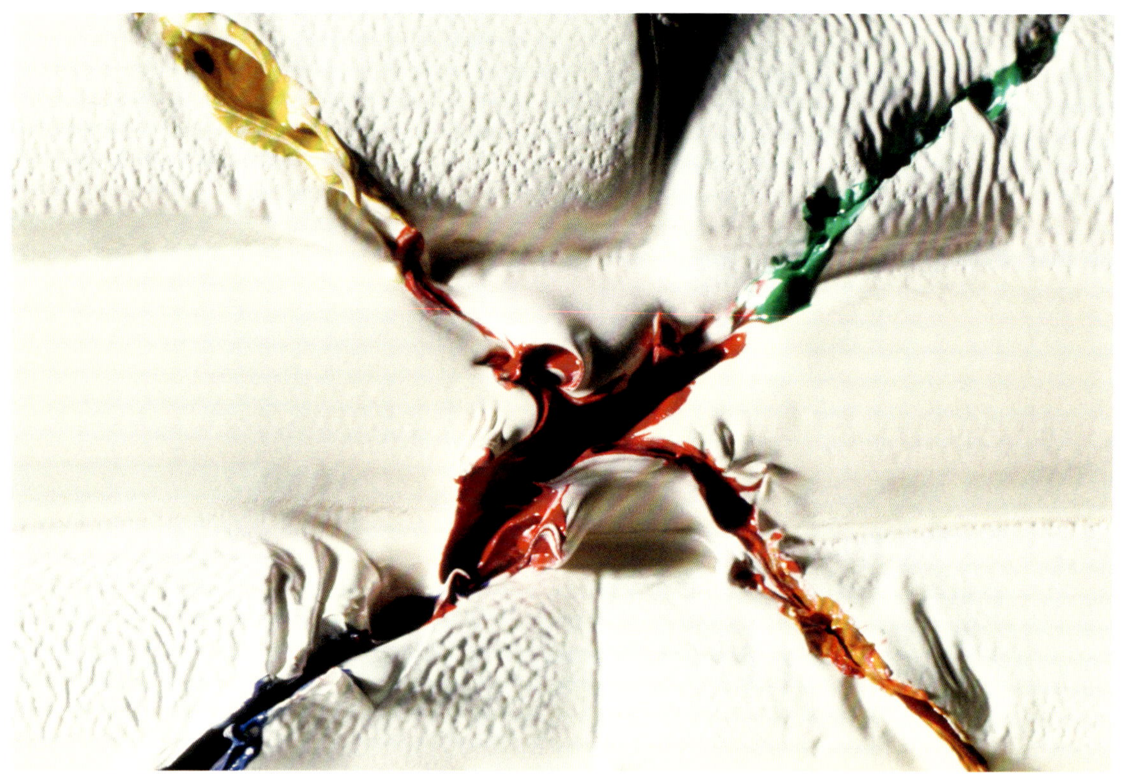

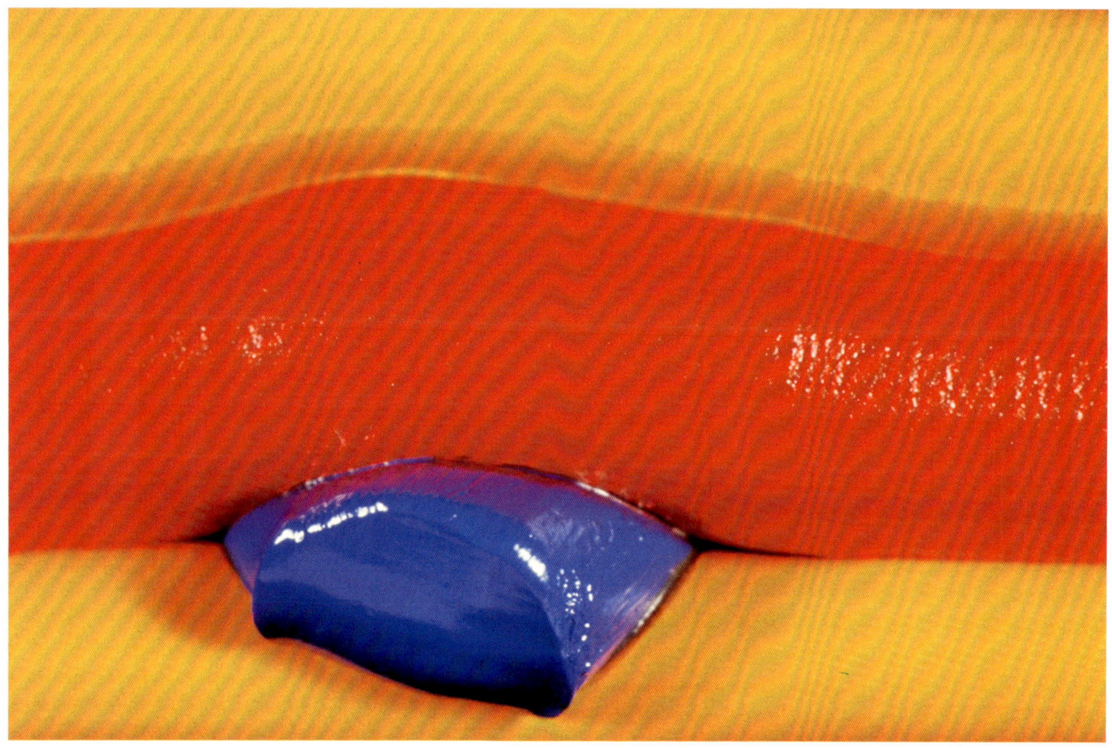

Plate 55
No. 1299, 1974, color transparency. Paint Squeezing series.
Allan Chasanoff Archive, Yale University Art Gallery

Plate 56
No. 1243, 1975, color transparency. Paint Squeezing series.
Allan Chasanoff Archive, Yale University Art Gallery

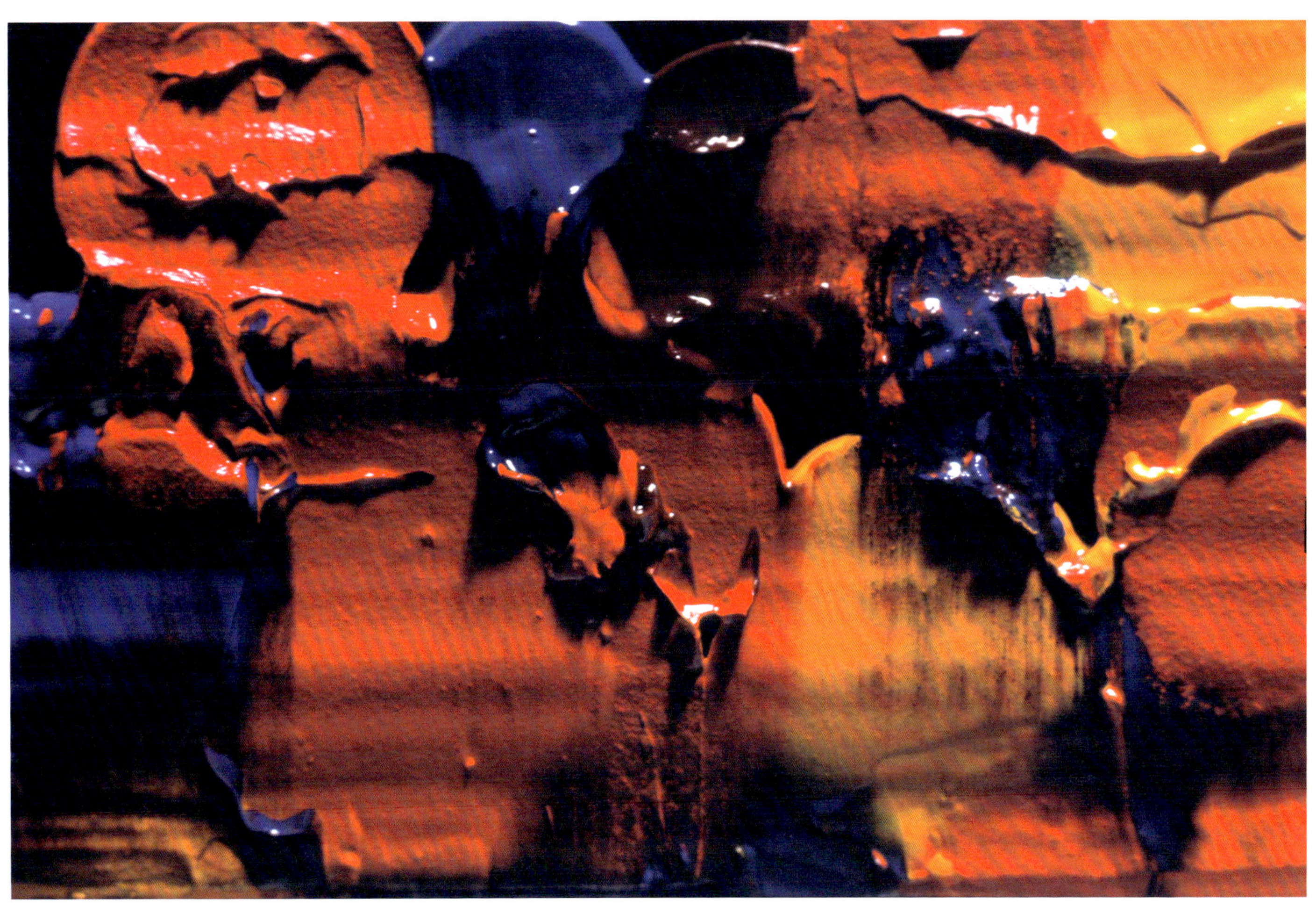

Plate 57
No. 2347, 1975, color transparency. Paint Squeezing series.
Allan Chasanoff Archive, Yale University Art Gallery

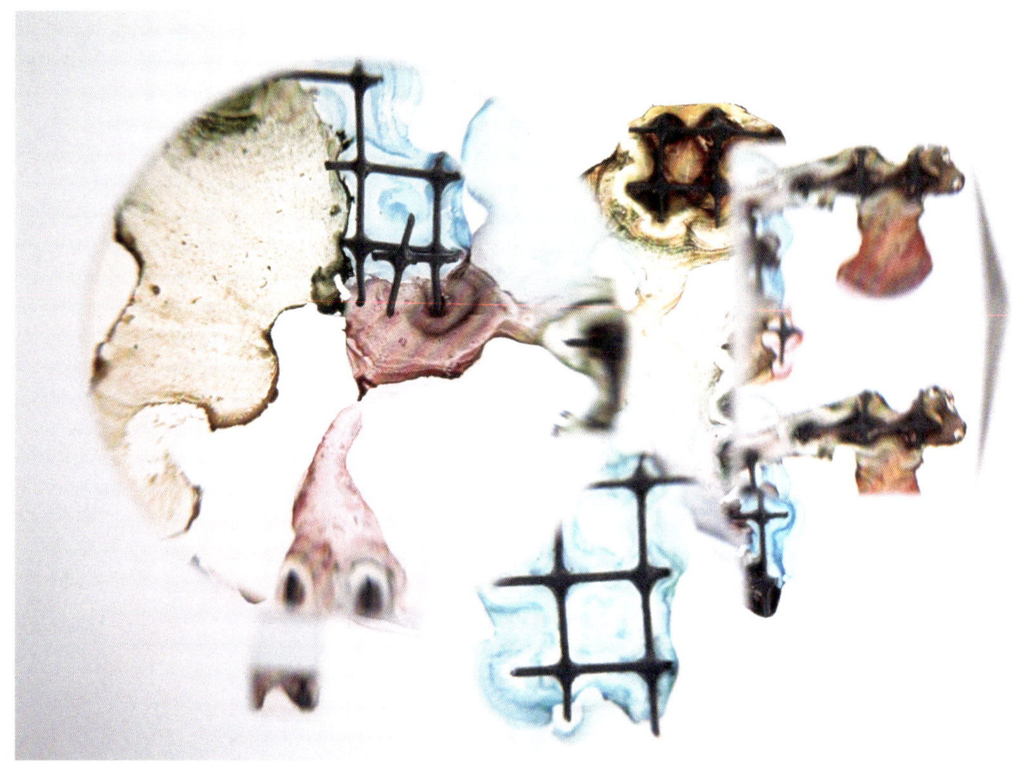

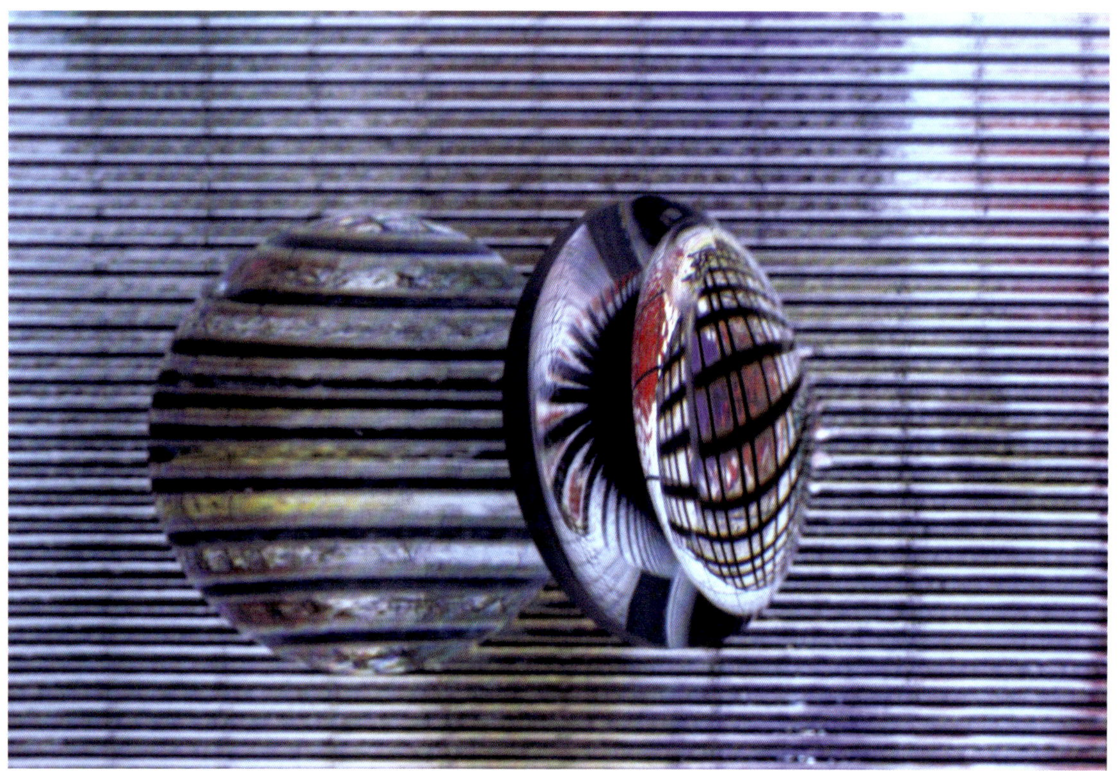

Plate 58
No. 2857, 1976, color transparency. Lens series.
Allan Chasanoff Archive, Yale University Art Gallery

Plate 59
No. 2413, 1976, color transparency. Lens series.
Allan Chasanoff Archive, Yale University Art Gallery

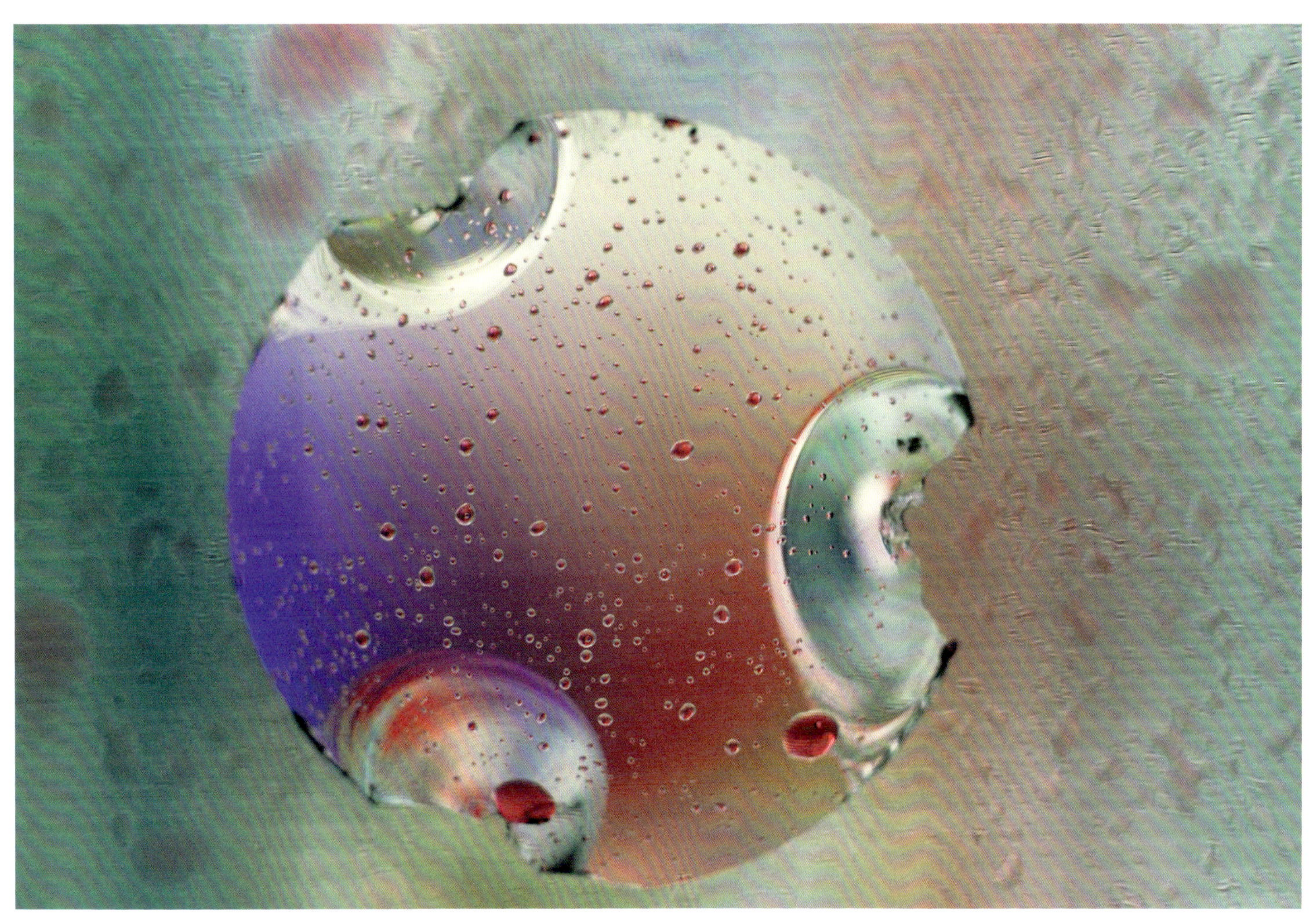

Plate 60
No. 1277, 1976, color transparency. Lens series.
Allan Chasanoff Archive, Yale University Art Gallery

Confusion, Not Illusion:
The Optical

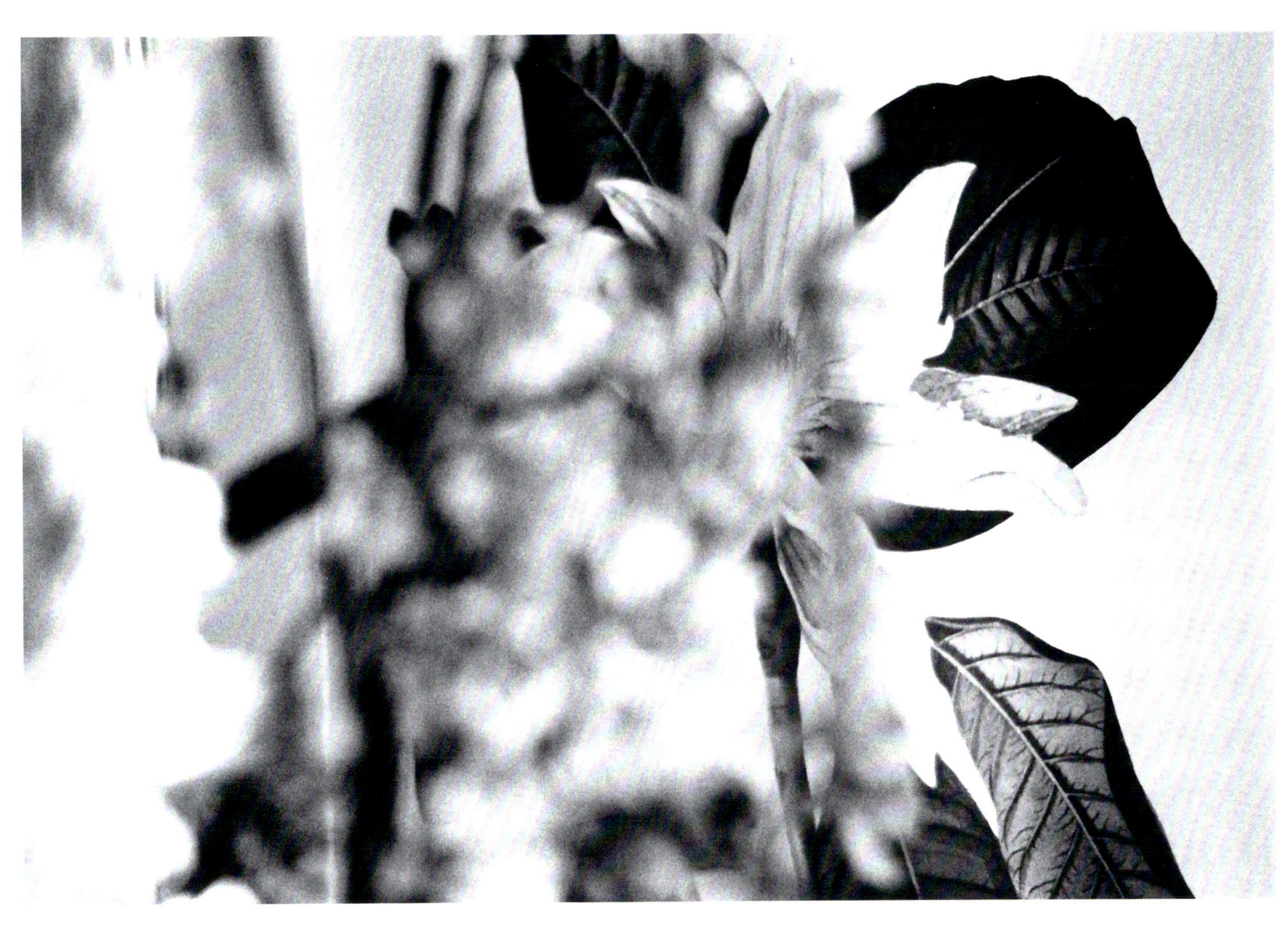

Plate 61
No. 4380, 1994, gelatin silver print.
Allan Chasanoff Archive, Yale University Art Gallery

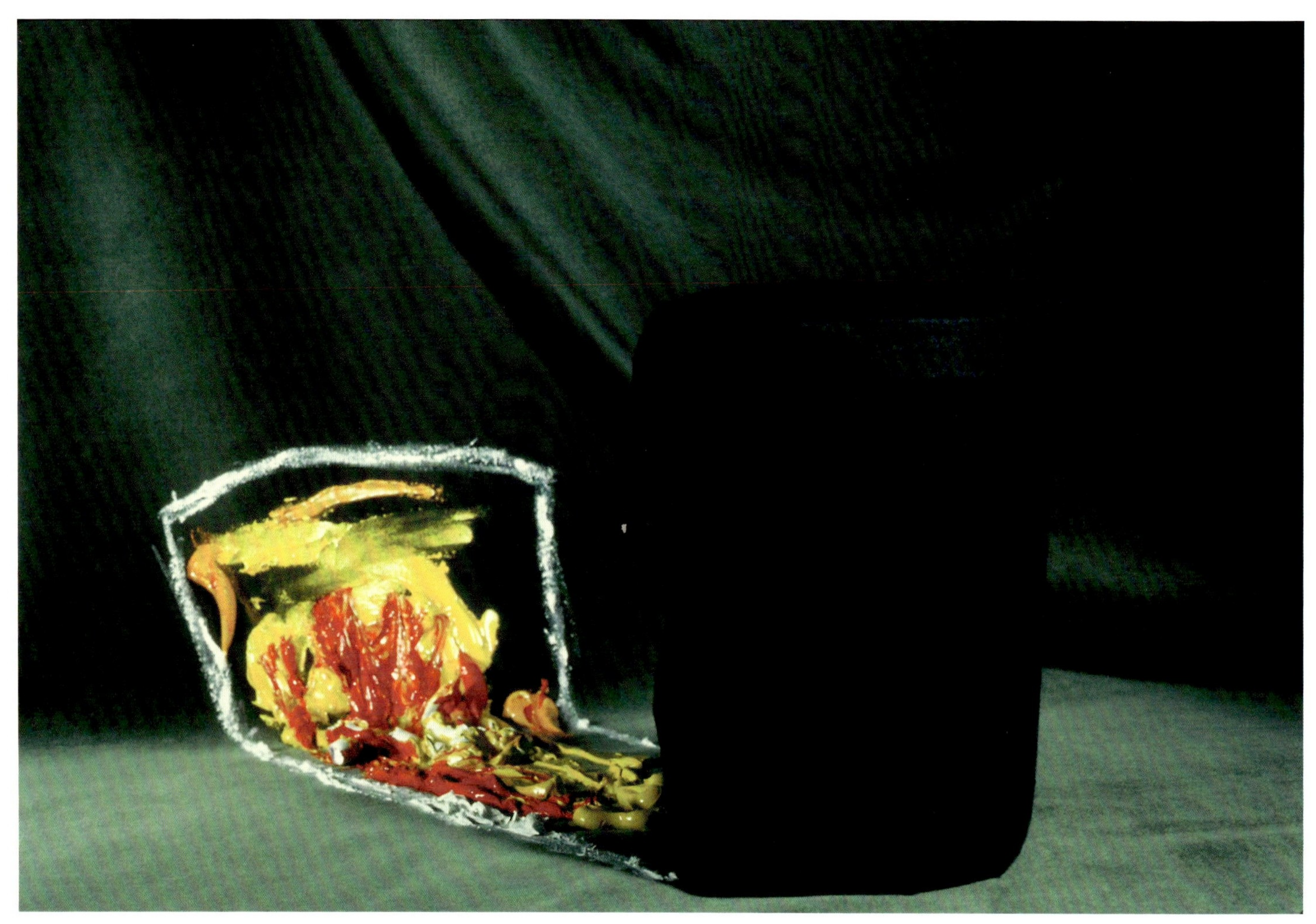

Plate 62
No. 1369, 1982, color transparency.
Allan Chasanoff Archive, Yale University Art Gallery

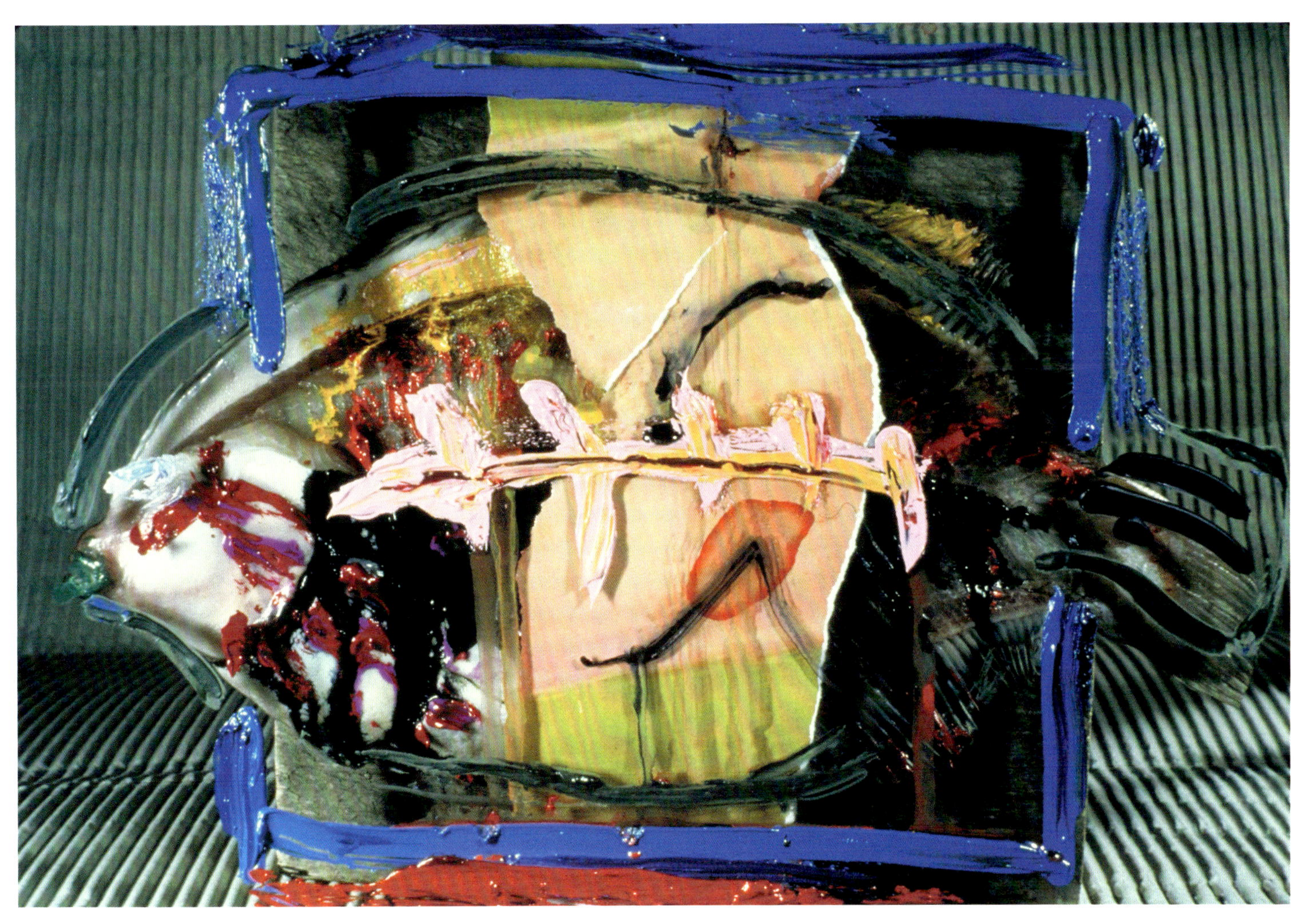

Plate 63
No. 1337, 1983, color transparency.
Allan Chasanoff Archive, Yale University Art Gallery

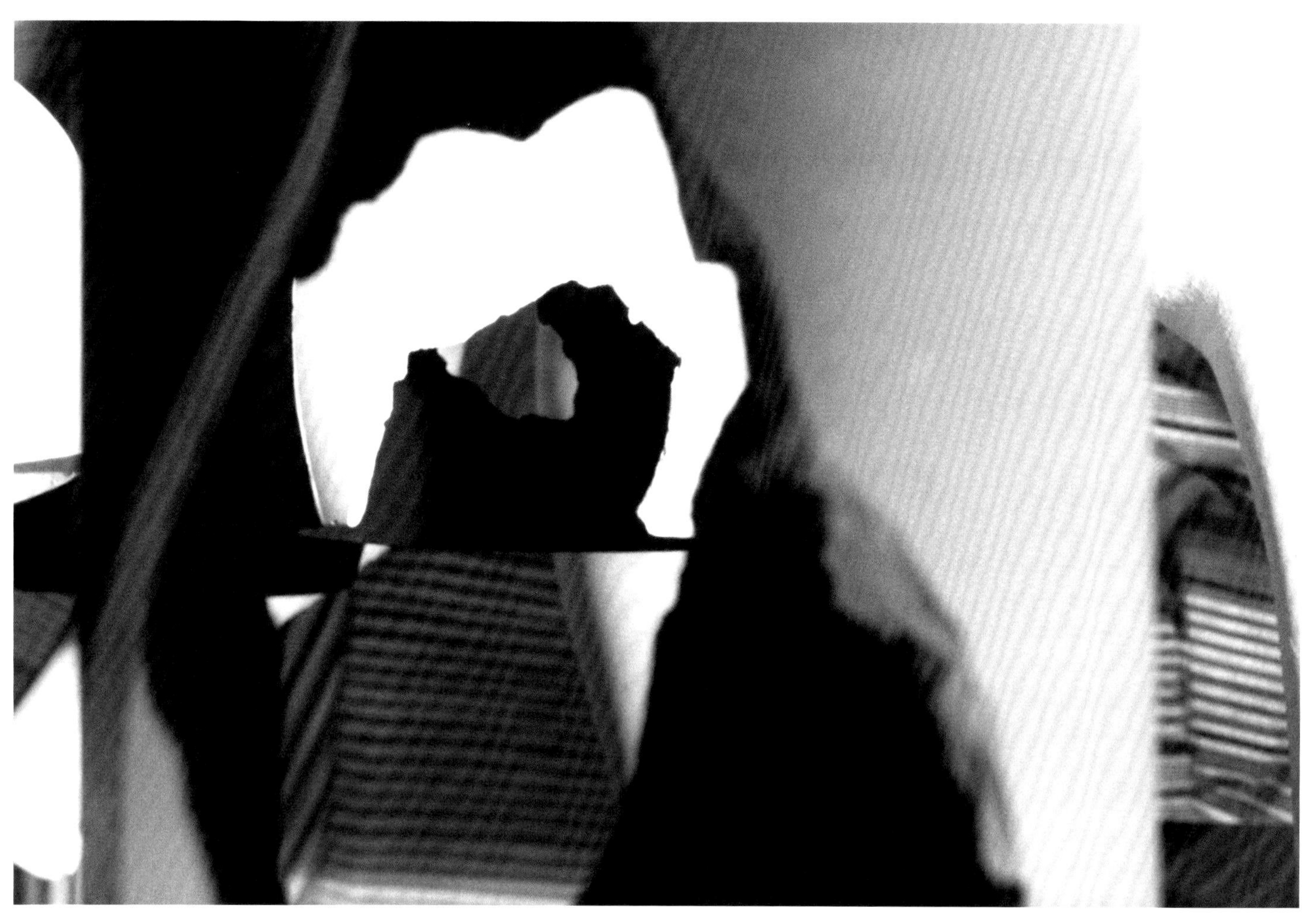

Plate 64
No. 1579, 1985, black-and-white negative.
Allan Chasanoff Archive, Yale University Art Gallery

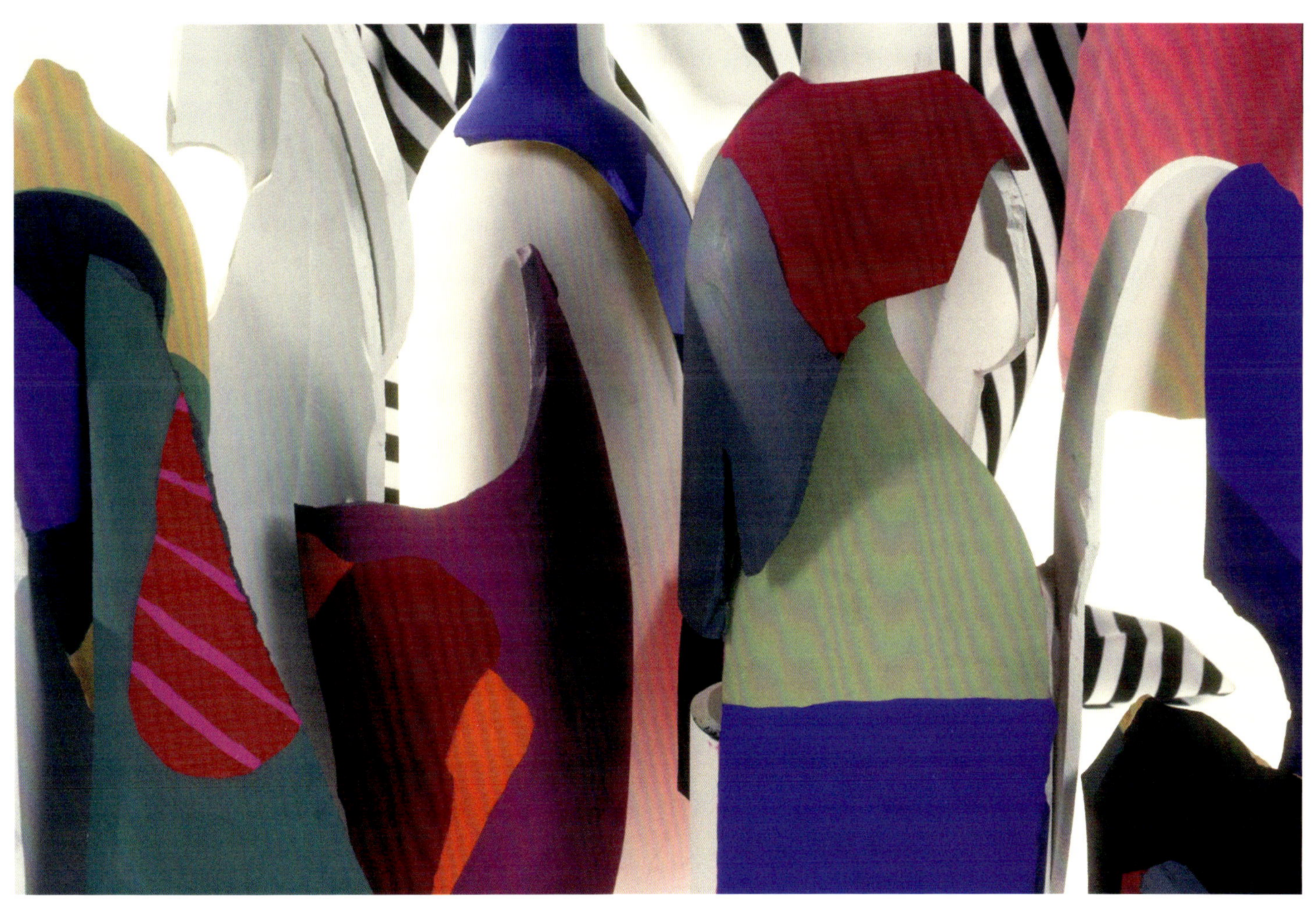

Plate 65
No. 1386, 1985, color transparency.
Allan Chasanoff Archive, Yale University Art Gallery

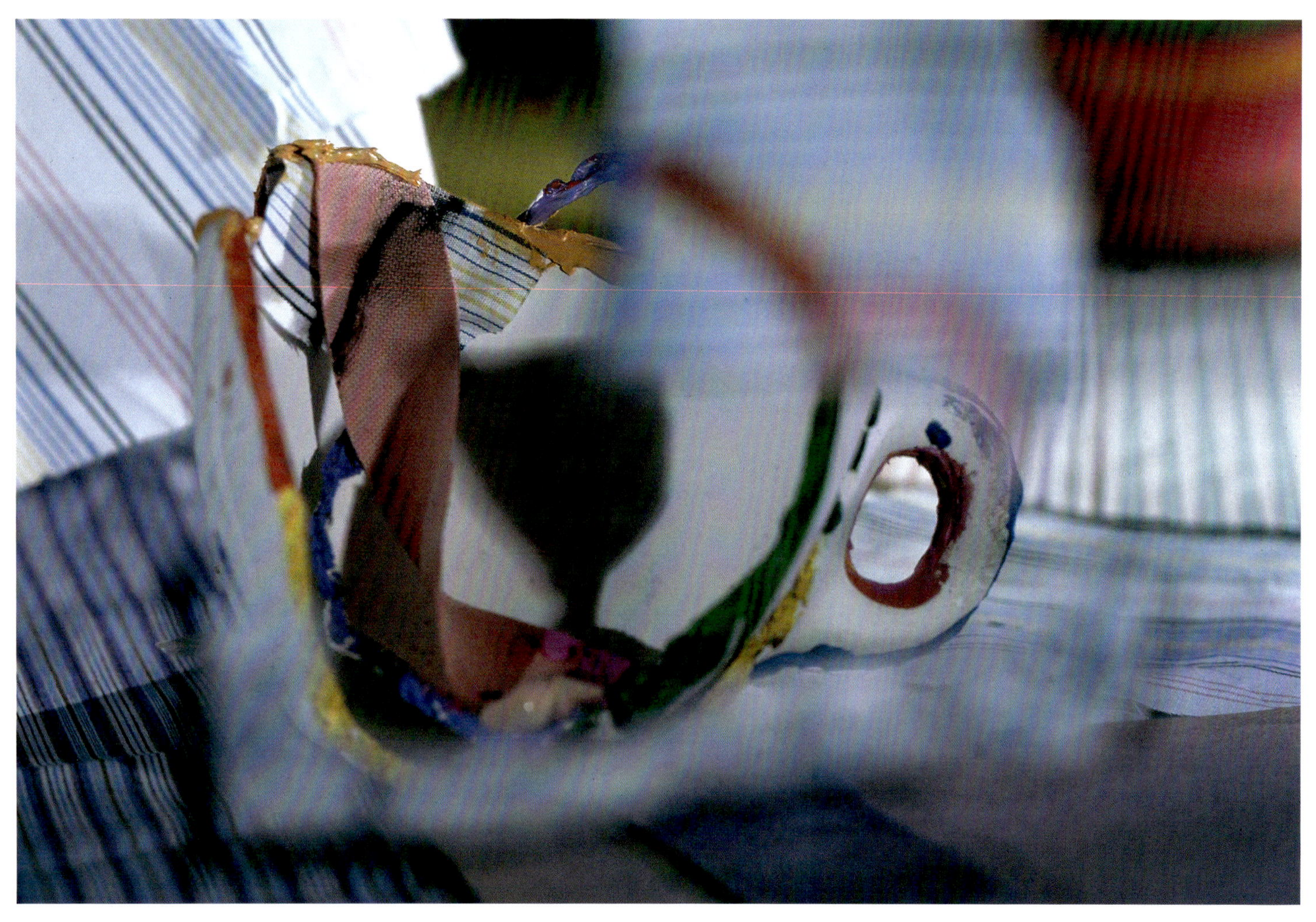

Plate 66
No. 3232, 1985, color transparency. Cup series.
Allan Chasanoff Archive, Yale University Art Gallery

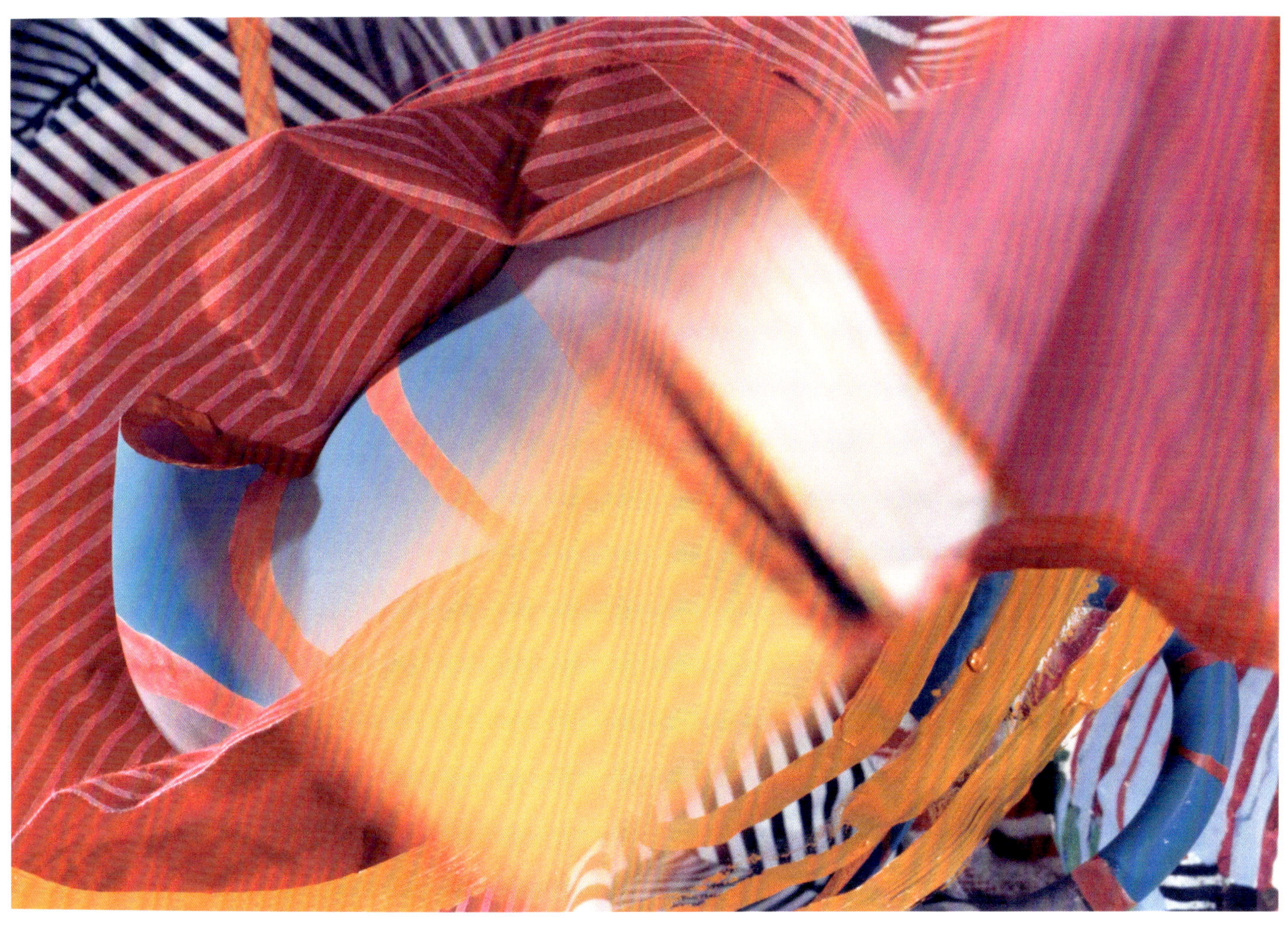

Plate 67
No. 3734, 1986, color negative. Teapot series.
Allan Chasanoff Archive, Yale University Art Gallery

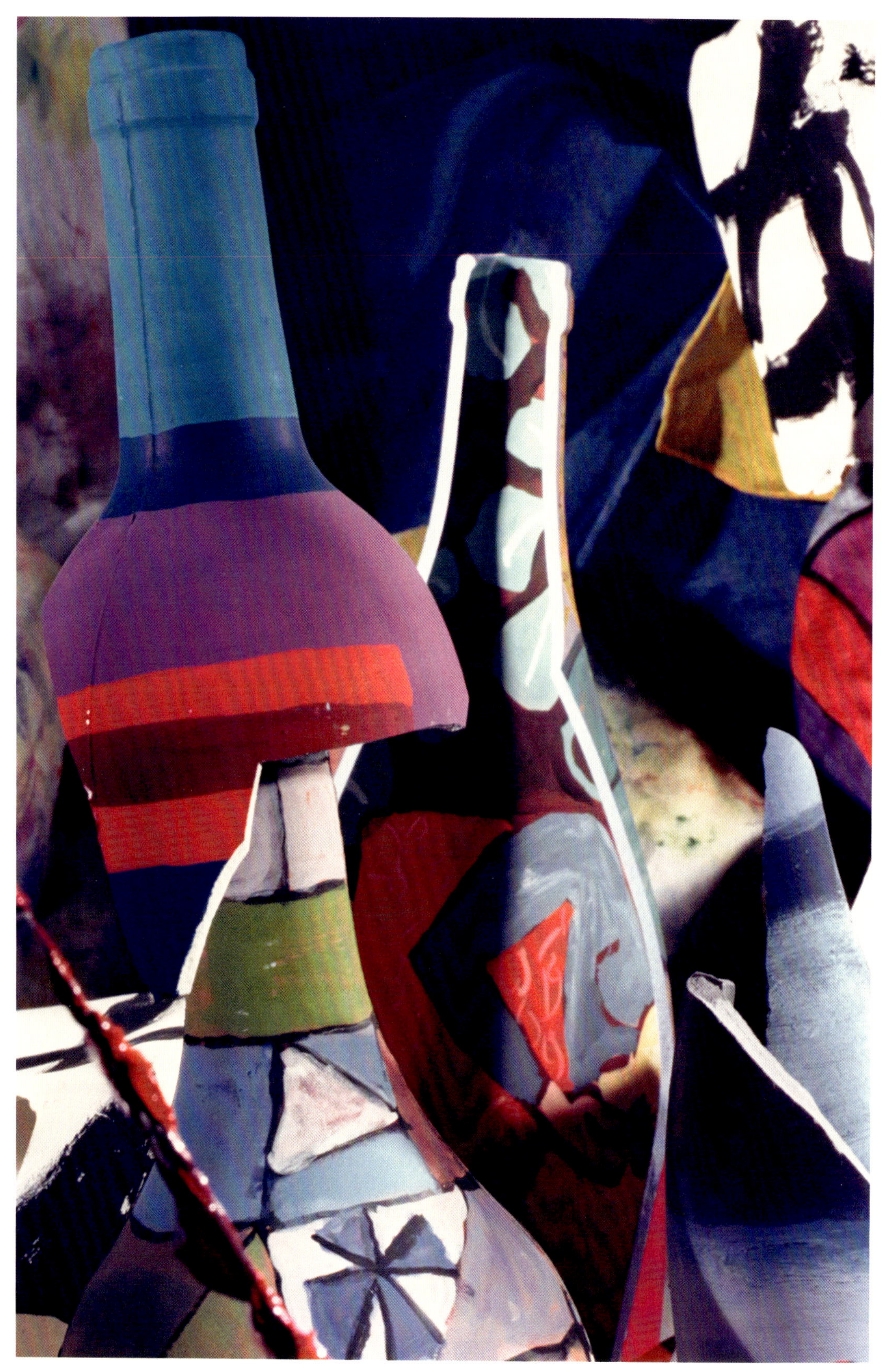

Plate 68
No. 3756, 1986, color negative.
Allan Chasanoff Archive, Yale University Art Gallery

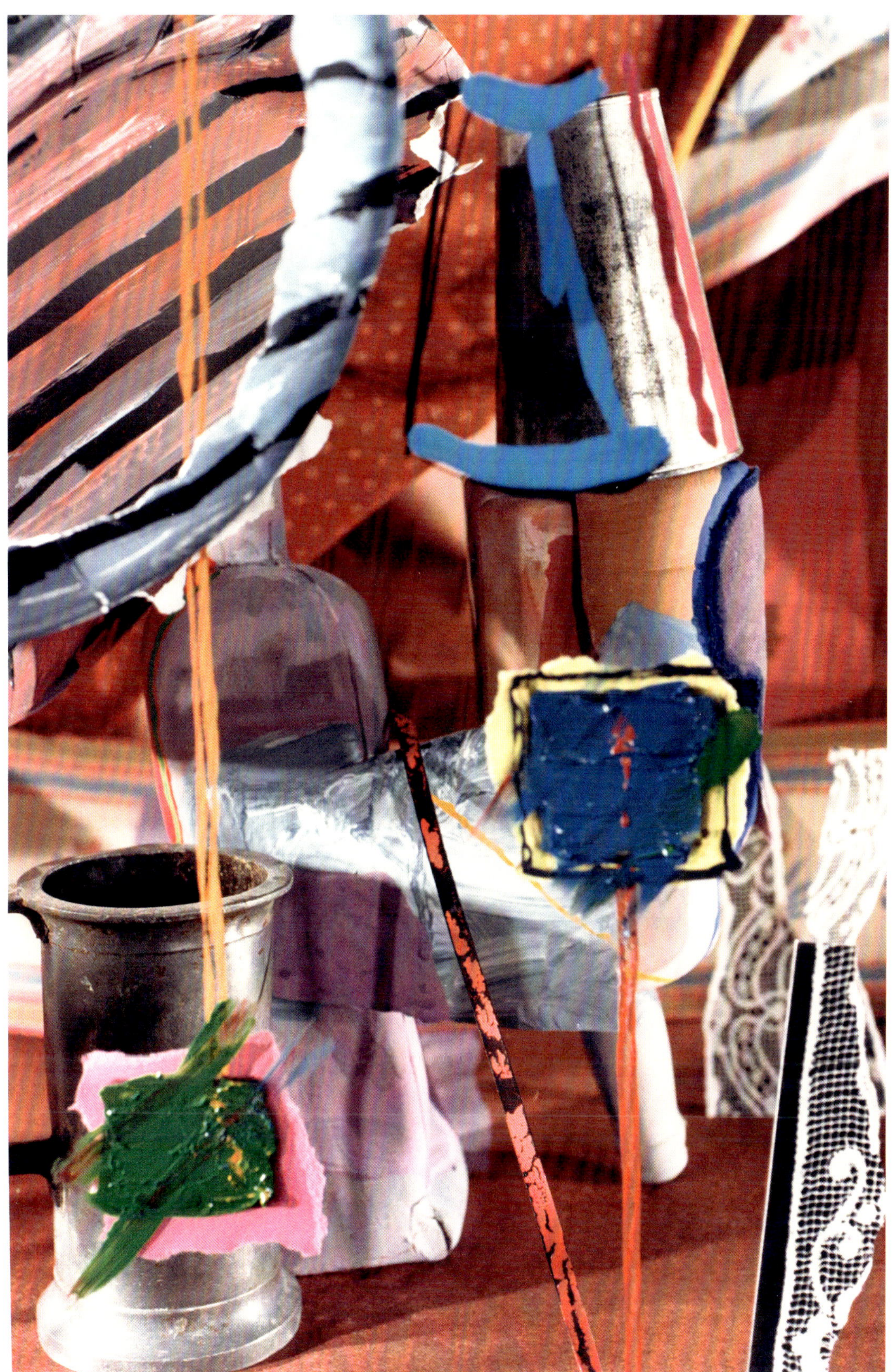

Plate 69
No. 3737, 1986, color negative.
Allan Chasanoff Archive, Yale University Art Gallery

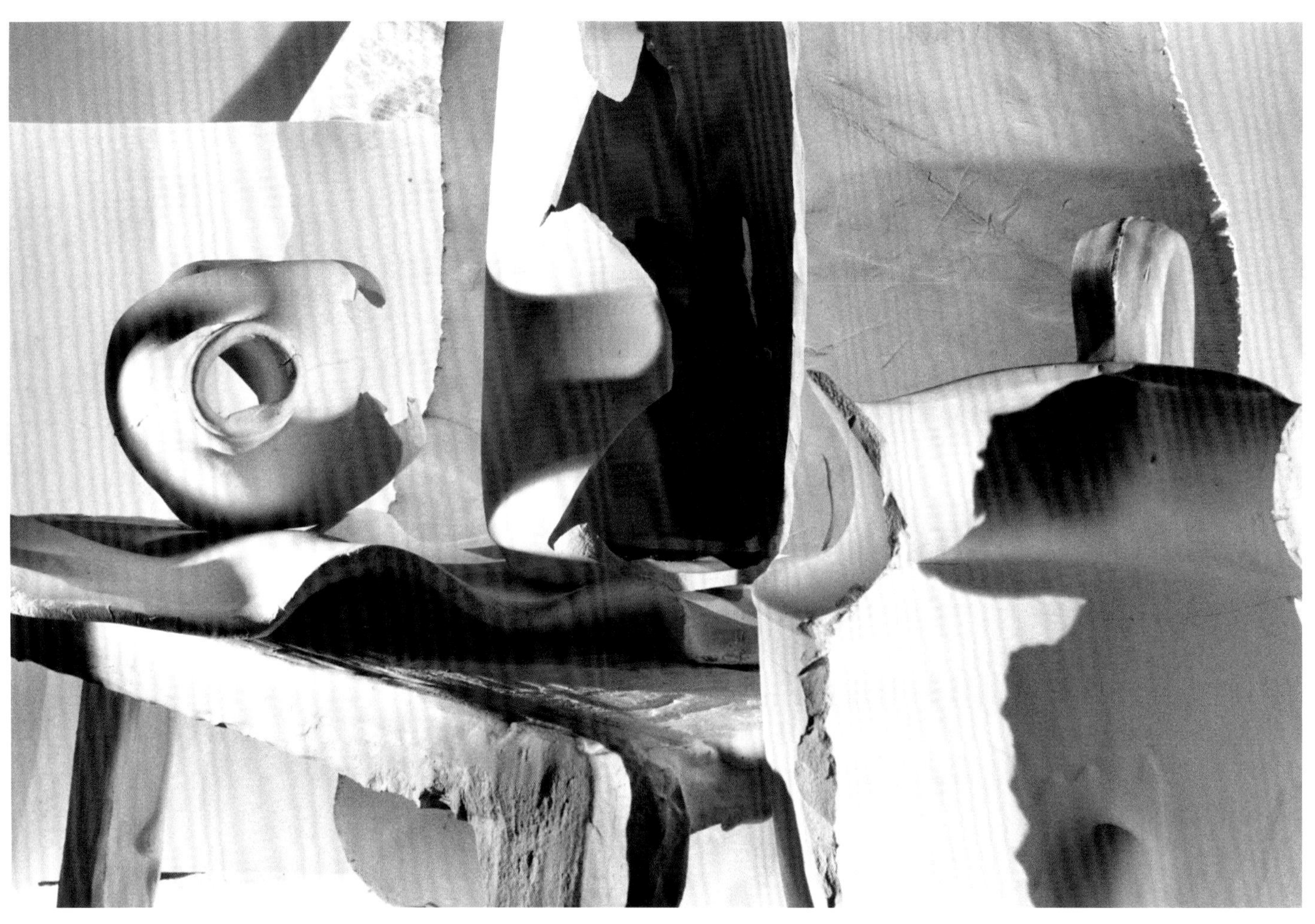

Plate 70
No. 1442, 1986, gelatin silver print.
Allan Chasanoff Archive, Yale University Art Gallery

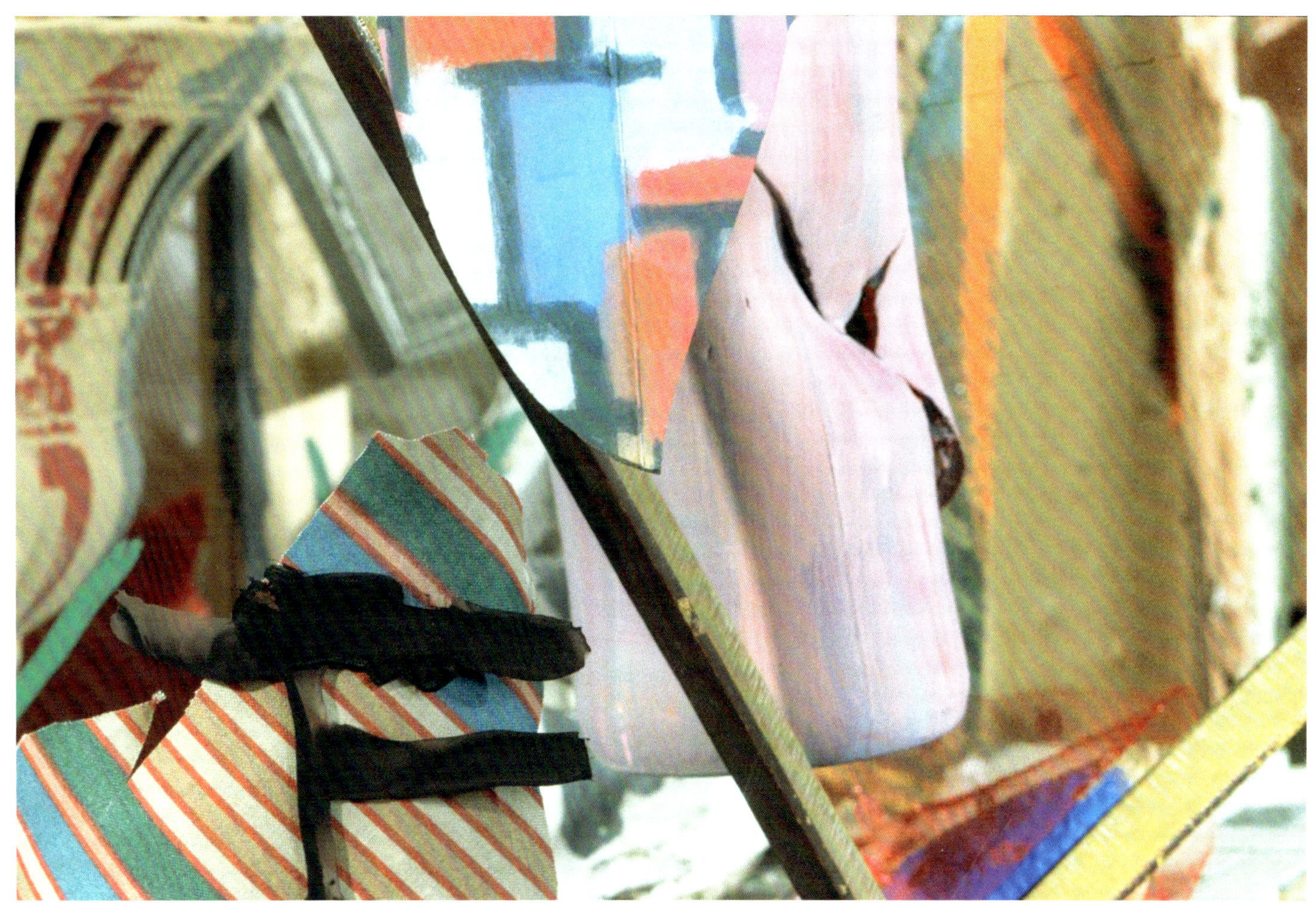

Plate 71
No. 1485, 1986, color negative.
Allan Chasanoff Archive, Yale University Art Gallery

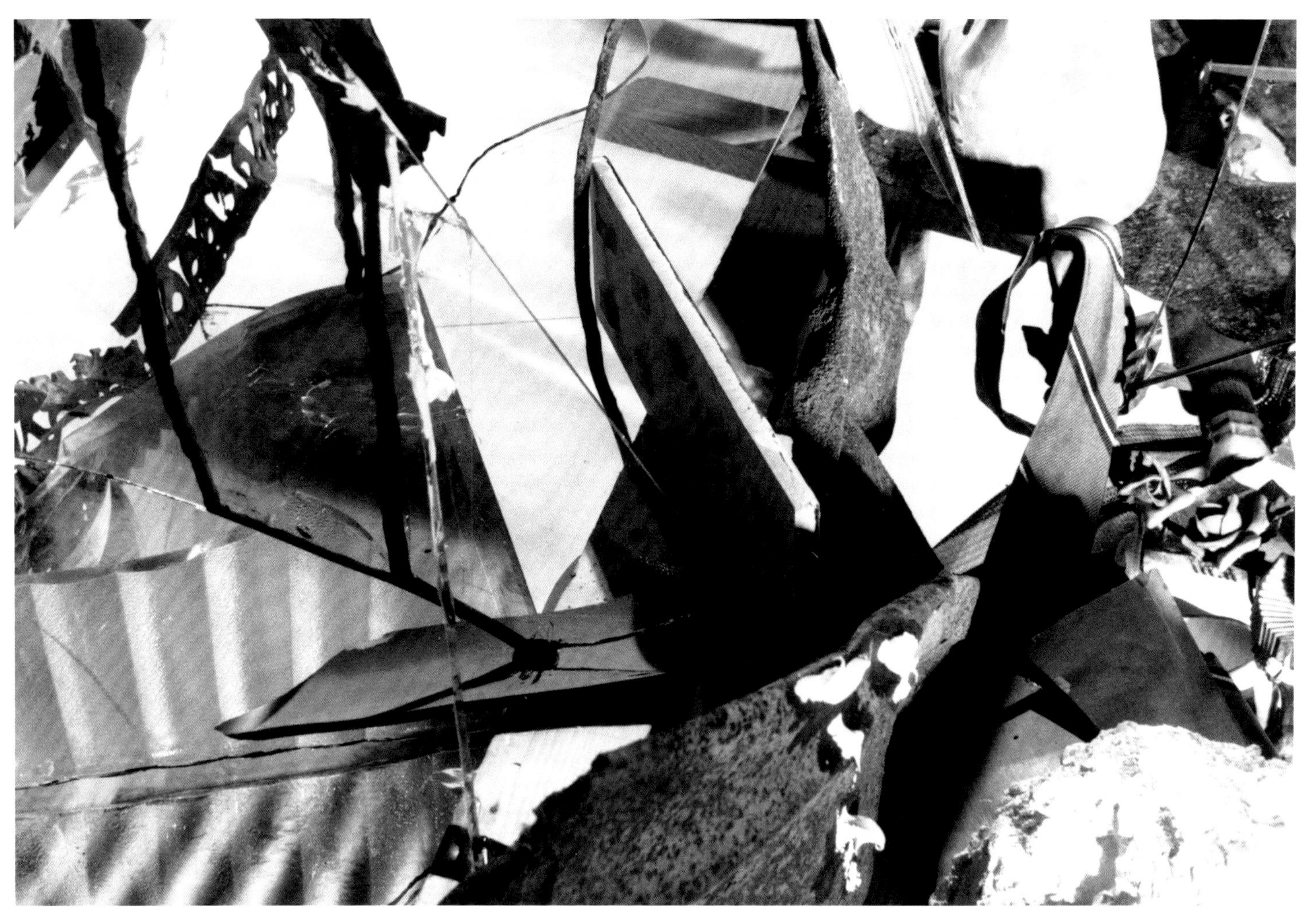

Plate 72
No. 3860, 1986, gelatin silver print.
Allan Chasanoff Archive, Yale University Art Gallery

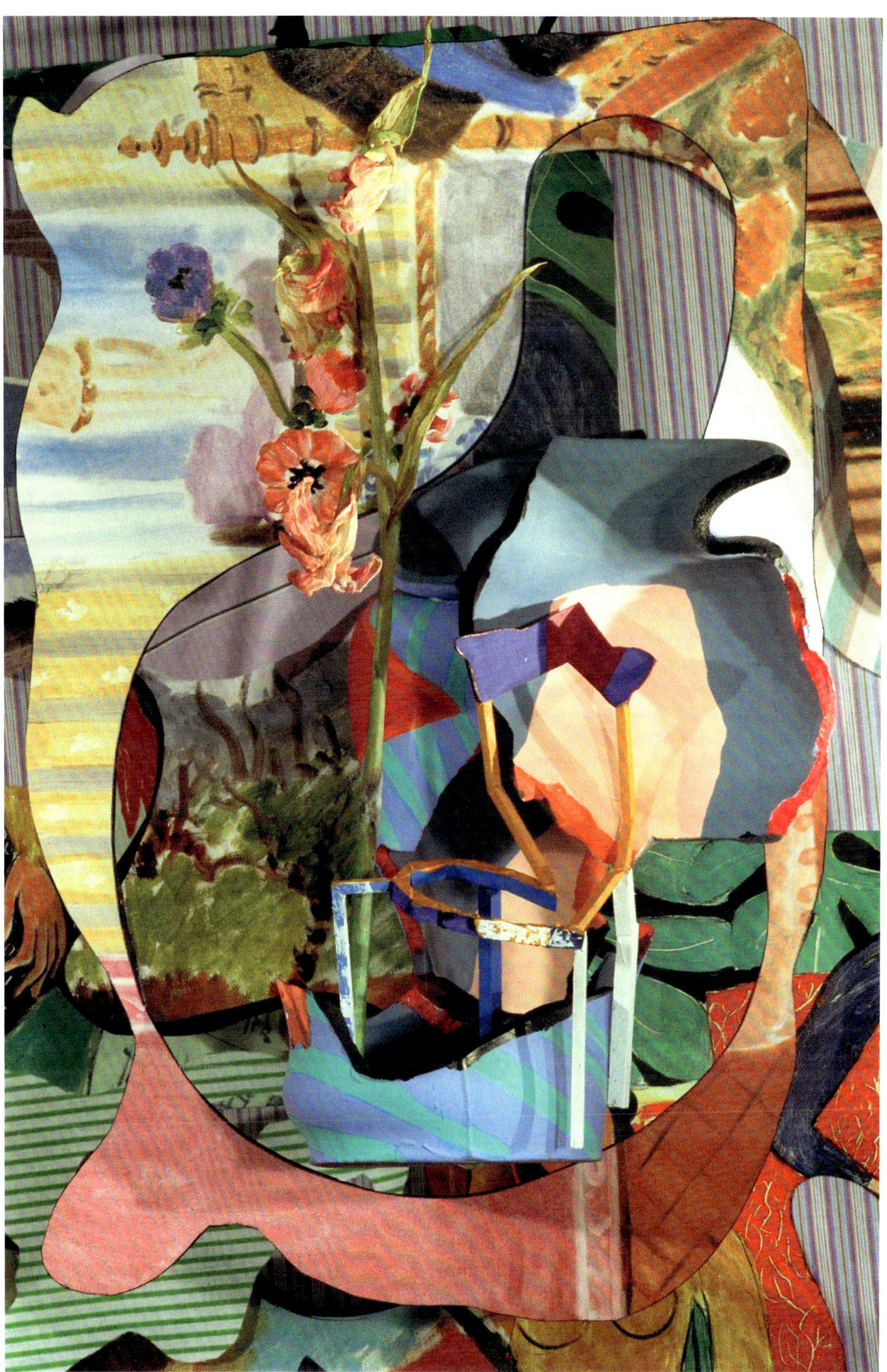

Note
The still life setup here, like the one for plate 30, included pieces of fabric, cutouts from reproductions of paintings by Henri Matisse, ceramic shards, and a small chair assembled from painted modeling wood.

Plate 73
No. 1413, 1987, color negative.
Allan Chasanoff Archive, Yale University Art Gallery

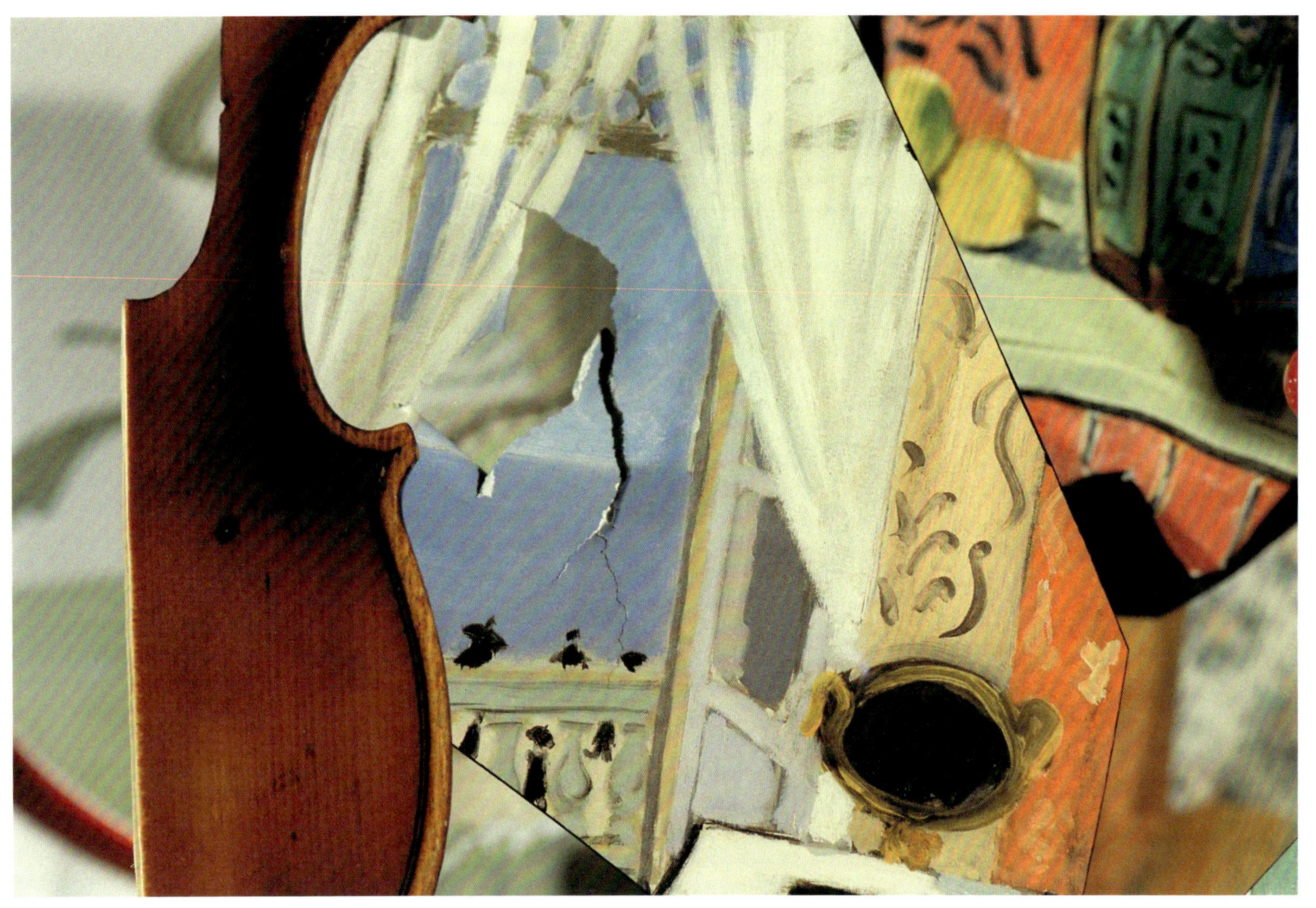

Note
The still life setup for this photograph included cutouts from reproductions of paintings by Henri Matisse.

Plate 74
No. 1407, 1988, color negative.
Allan Chasanoff Archive, Yale University Art Gallery

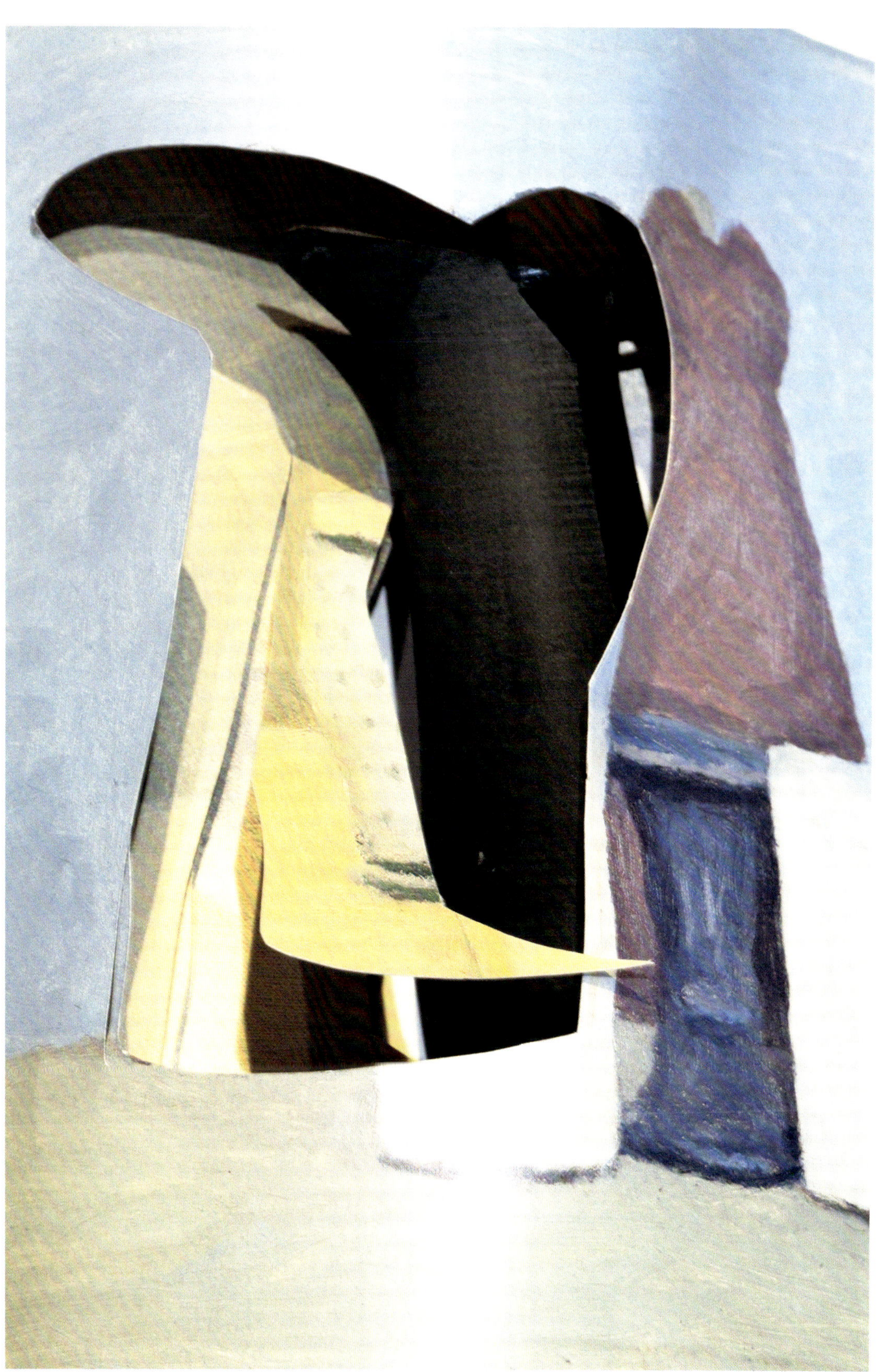

Note
In the Morandi book project, Chasanoff cut out pieces from his books on Giorgio Morandi and created setups with them. The black pitcher is a 3-D print inspired by one of the vessels in his preferred Morandi work (see fig. 5).

Plate 75
No. 10296, 2010, digital image file. Morandi book project.
Allan Chasanoff Archive, Yale University Art Gallery

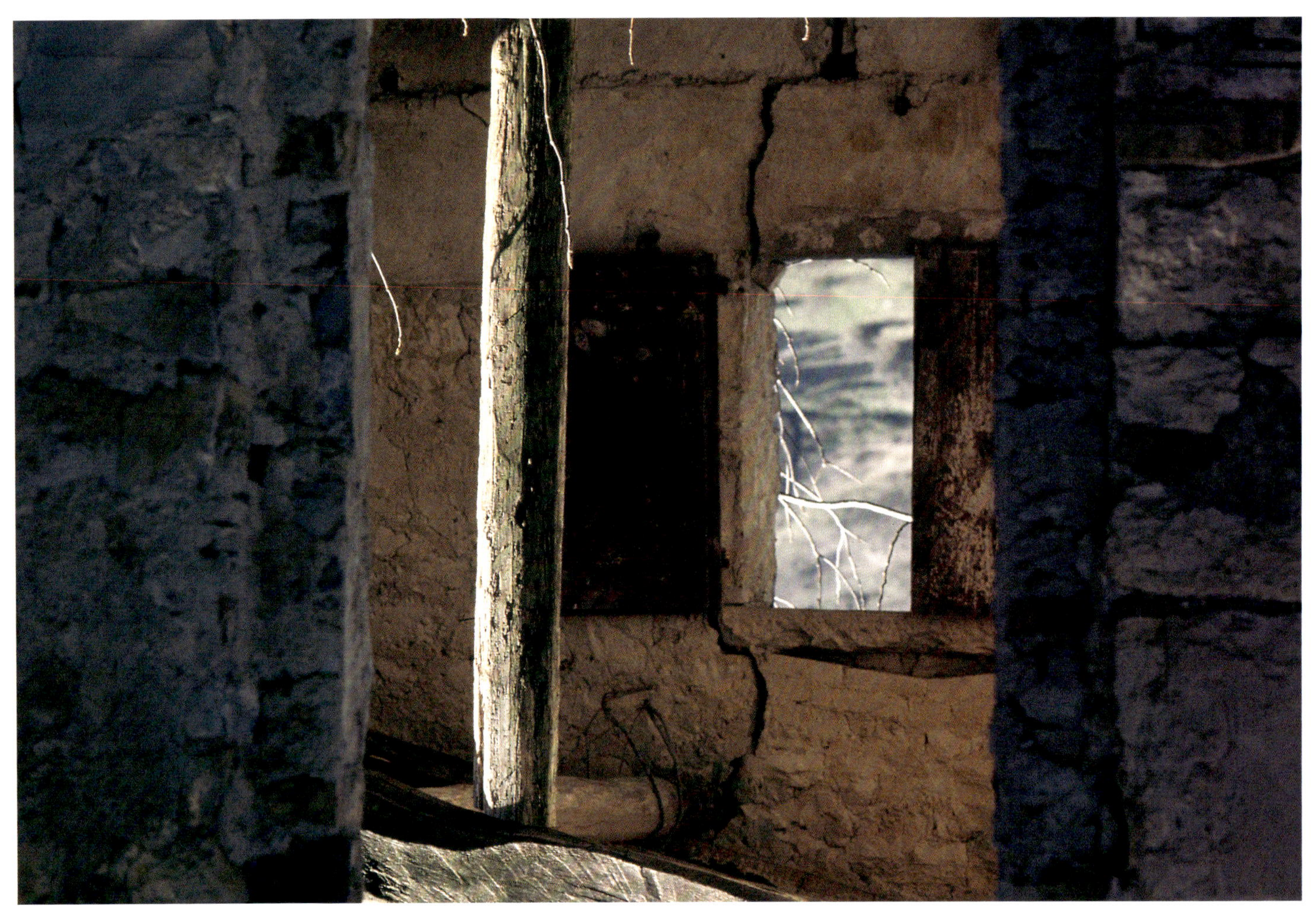

Plate 76
No. 2521, 1975, color transparency.
Allan Chasanoff Archive, Yale University Art Gallery

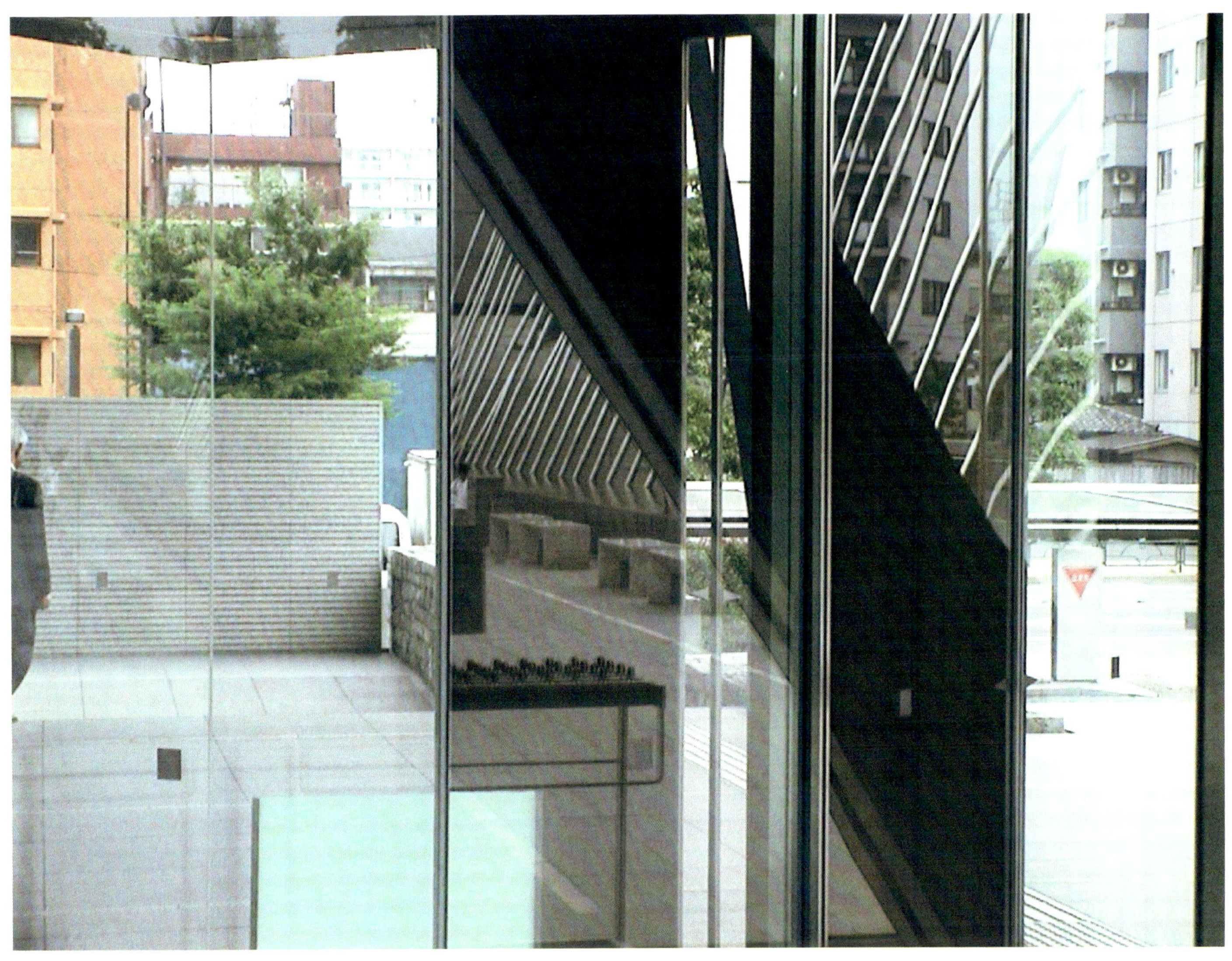

Plate 77
No. 4685, 2000, pigmented inkjet print (still from digital video).
Allan Chasanoff Archive, Yale University Art Gallery

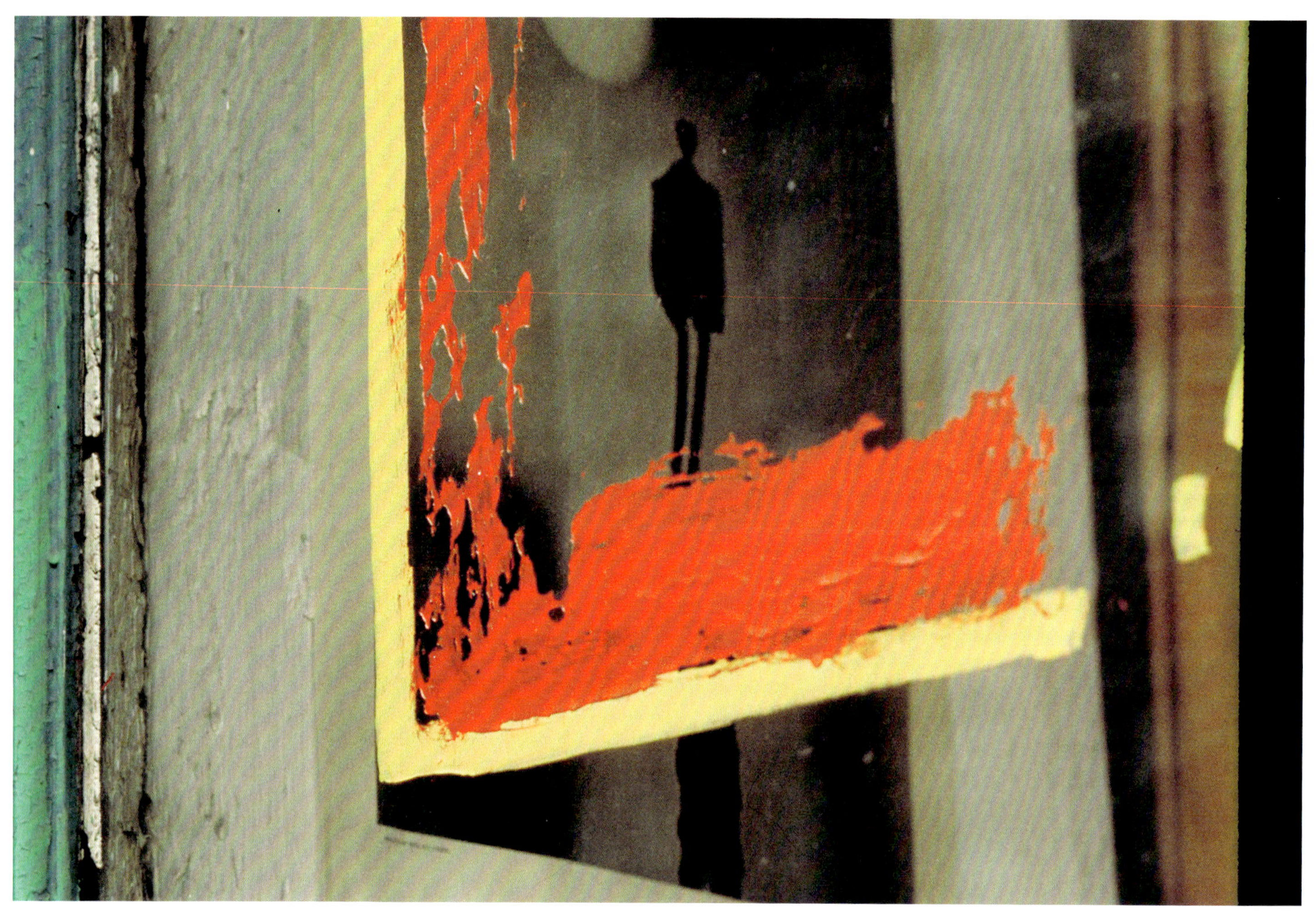

Plate 78
No. 1272, 1977, color transparency.
Allan Chasanoff Archive, Yale University Art Gallery

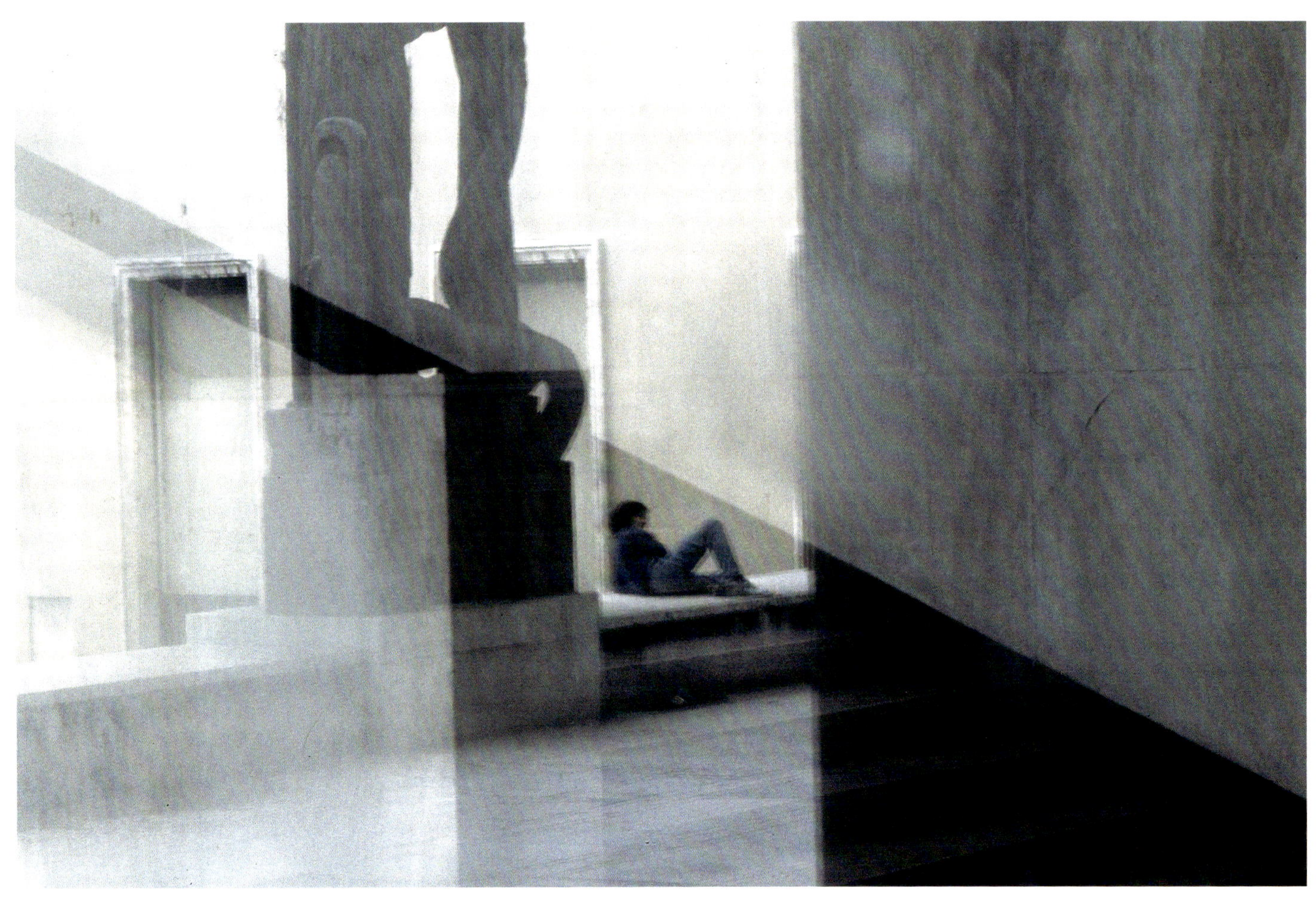

Plate 79
No. 2803, 1978, color transparency.
Allan Chasanoff Archive, Yale University Art Gallery

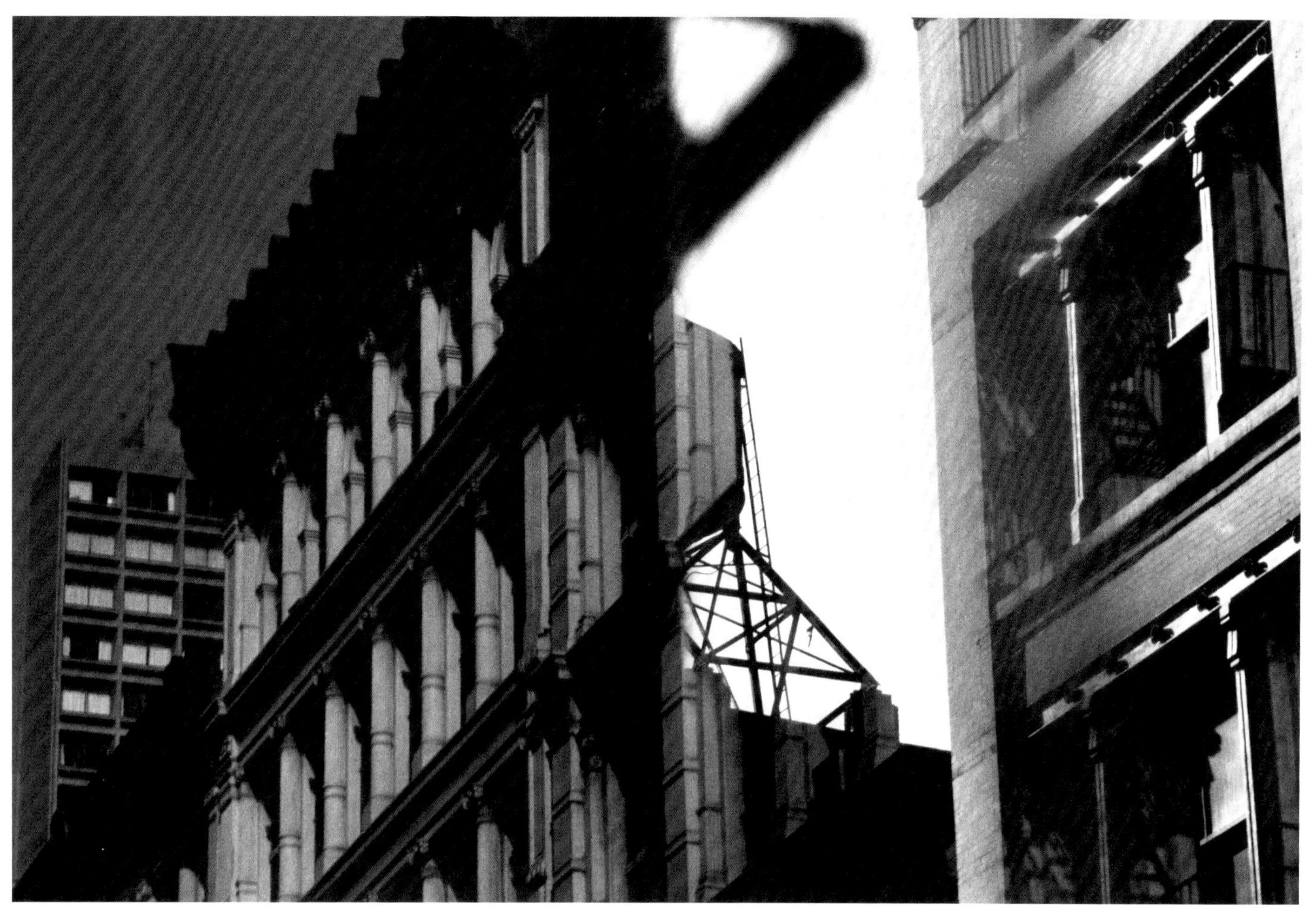

Plate 80
No. 3423, 1982, gelatin silver print.
Allan Chasanoff Archive, Yale University Art Gallery

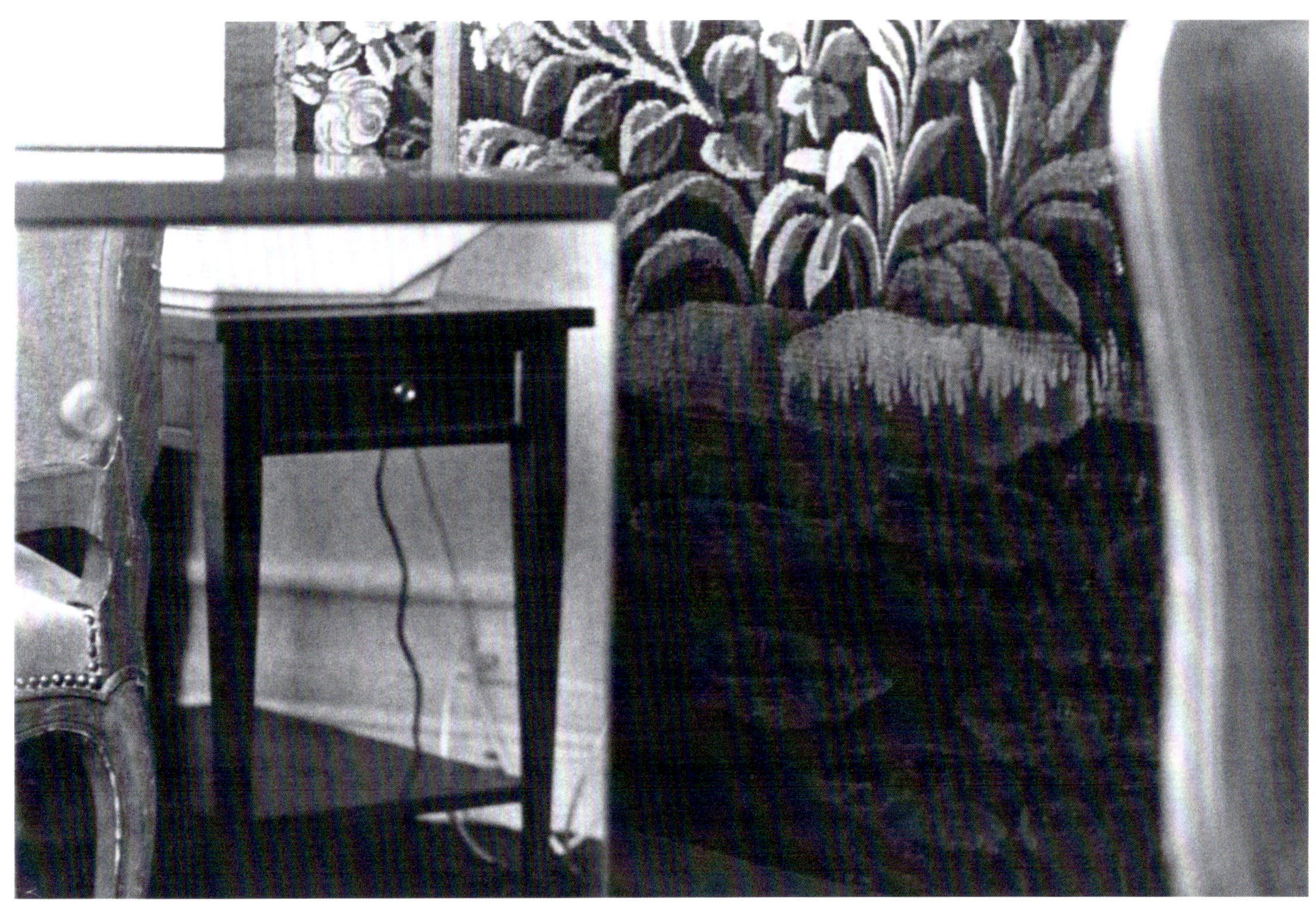

Plate 81
No. 3502, 1983, gelatin silver print.
Allan Chasanoff Archive, Yale University Art Gallery

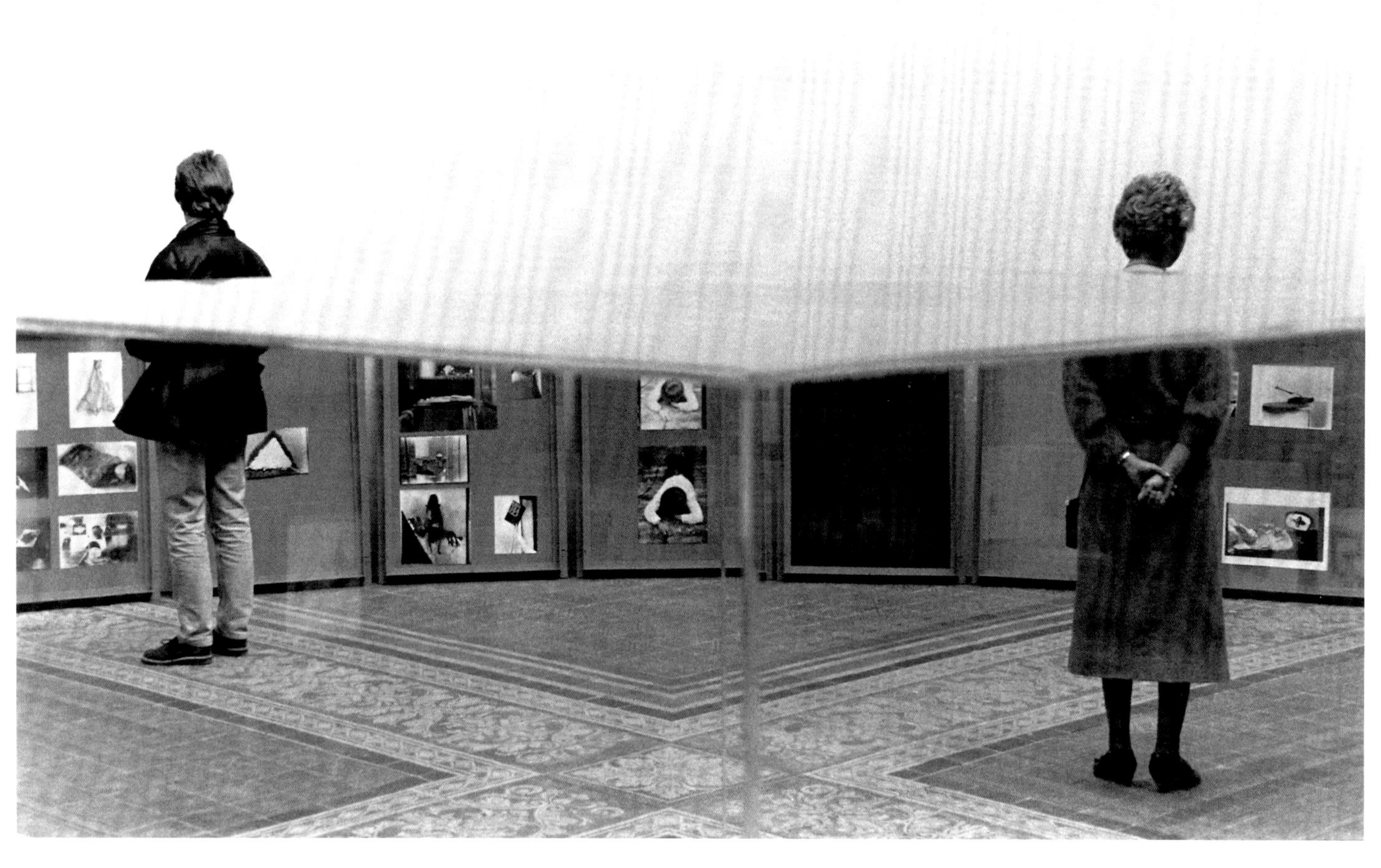

Plate 82
No. 4049, 1988, gelatin silver print.
Allan Chasanoff Archive, Yale University Art Gallery

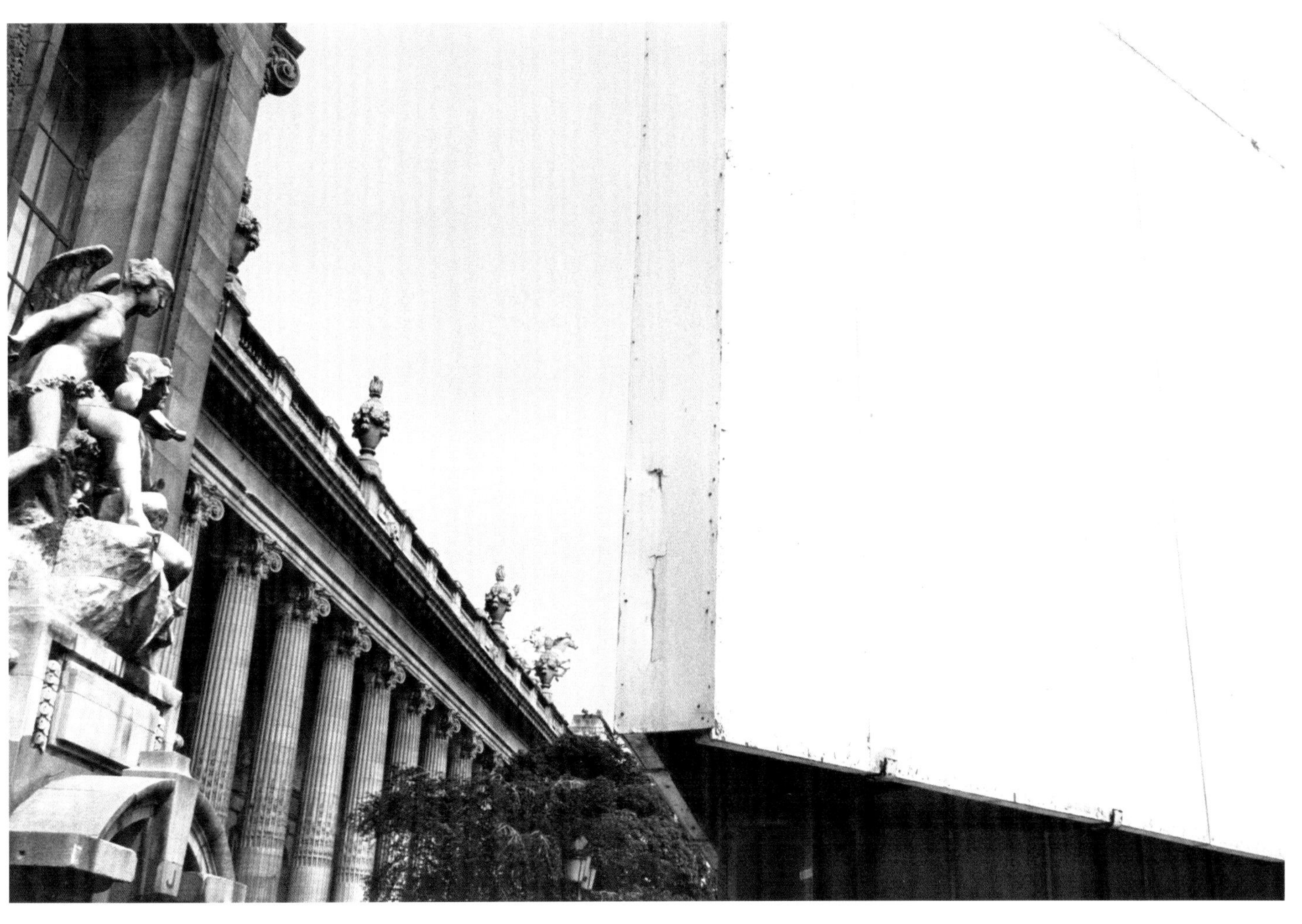

Plate 83
No. 4123, 1991, gelatin silver print.
Allan Chasanoff Archive, Yale University Art Gallery

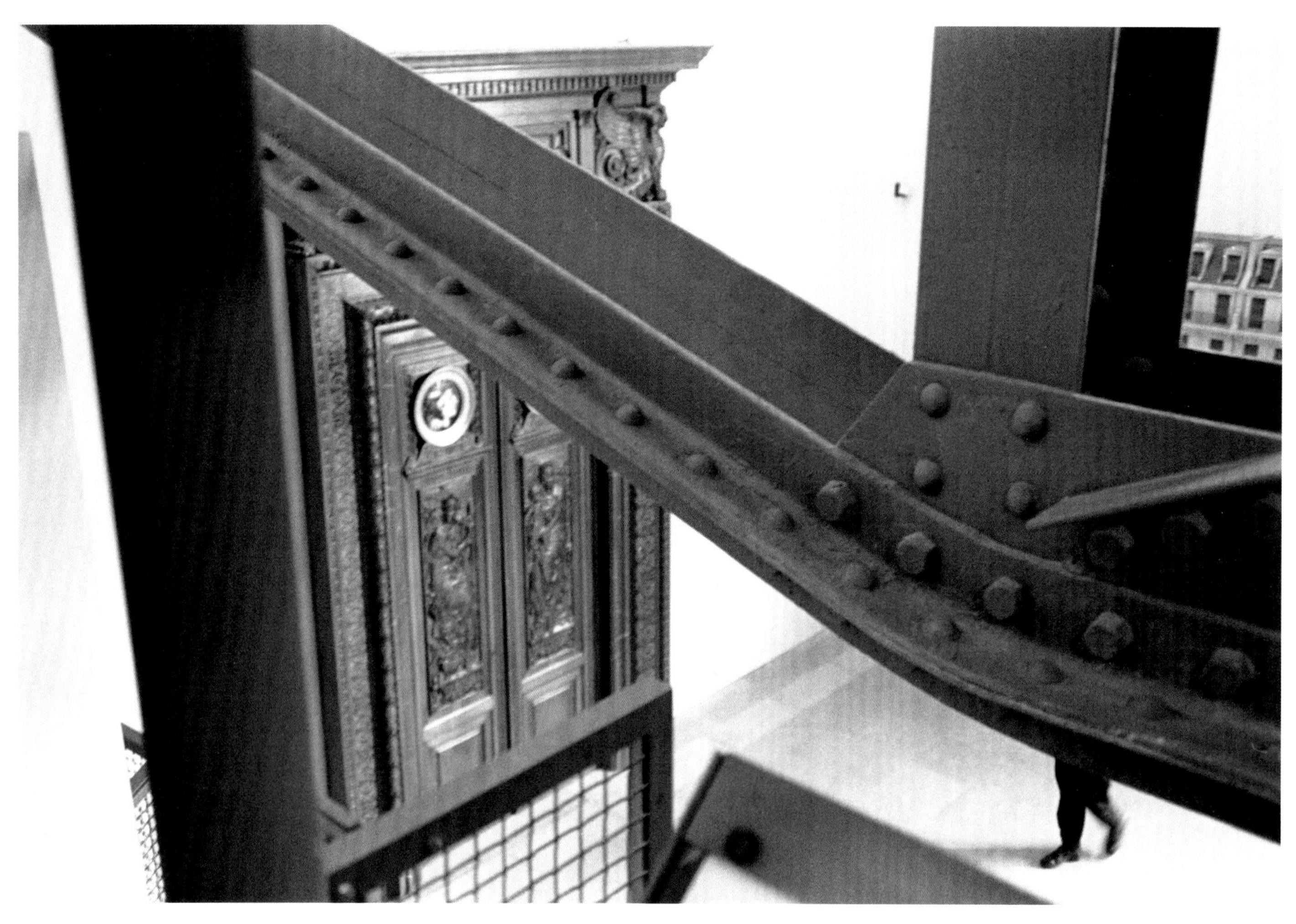

Plate 84
No. 4029, 1988, gelatin silver print.
Allan Chasanoff Archive, Yale University Art Gallery

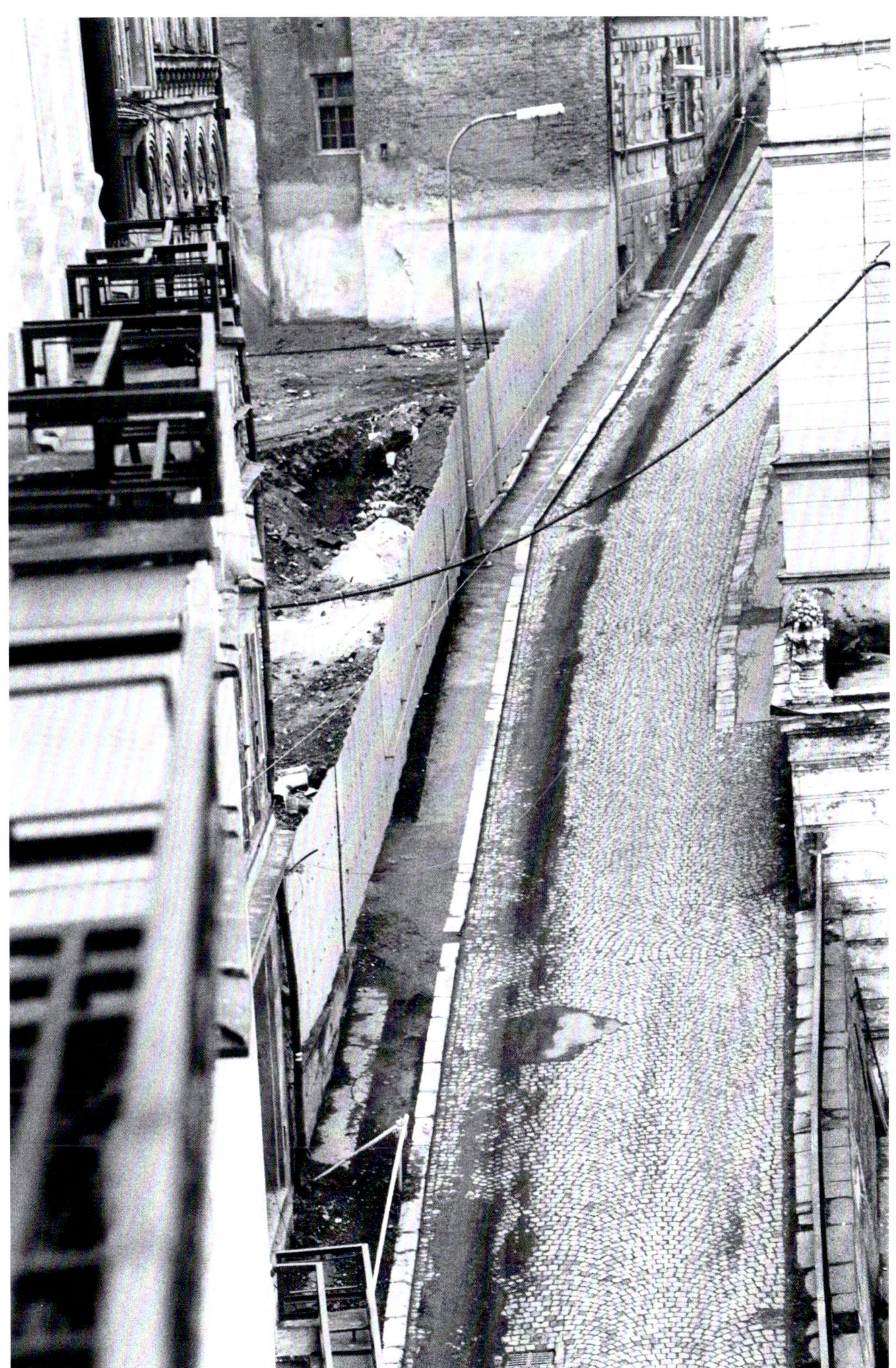

Plate 85
No. 4133, 1991, gelatin silver print.
Allan Chasanoff Archive, Yale University Art Gallery

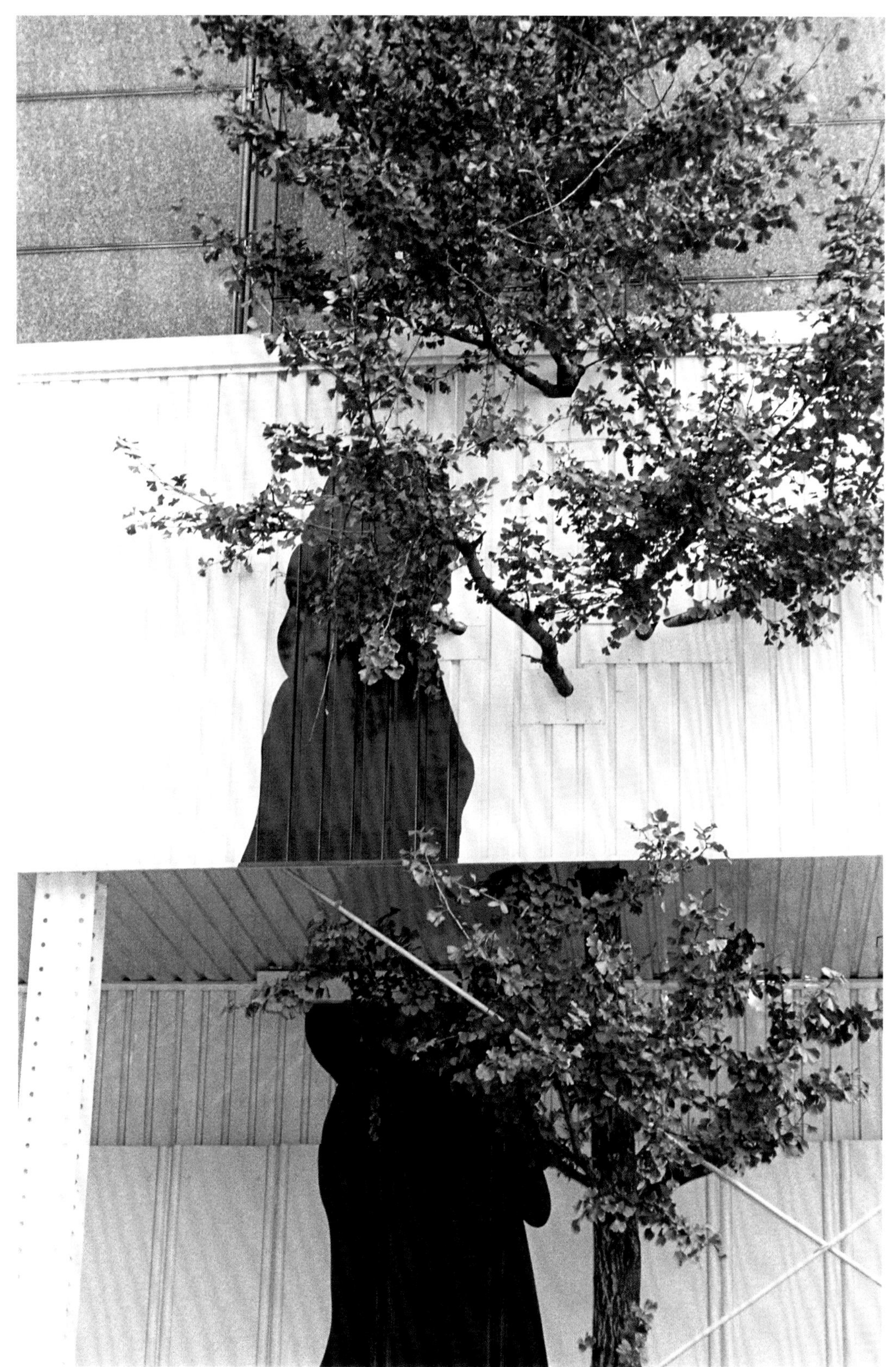

Plate 86
No. 1602, 1990, gelatin silver print.
Allan Chasanoff Archive, Yale University Art Gallery

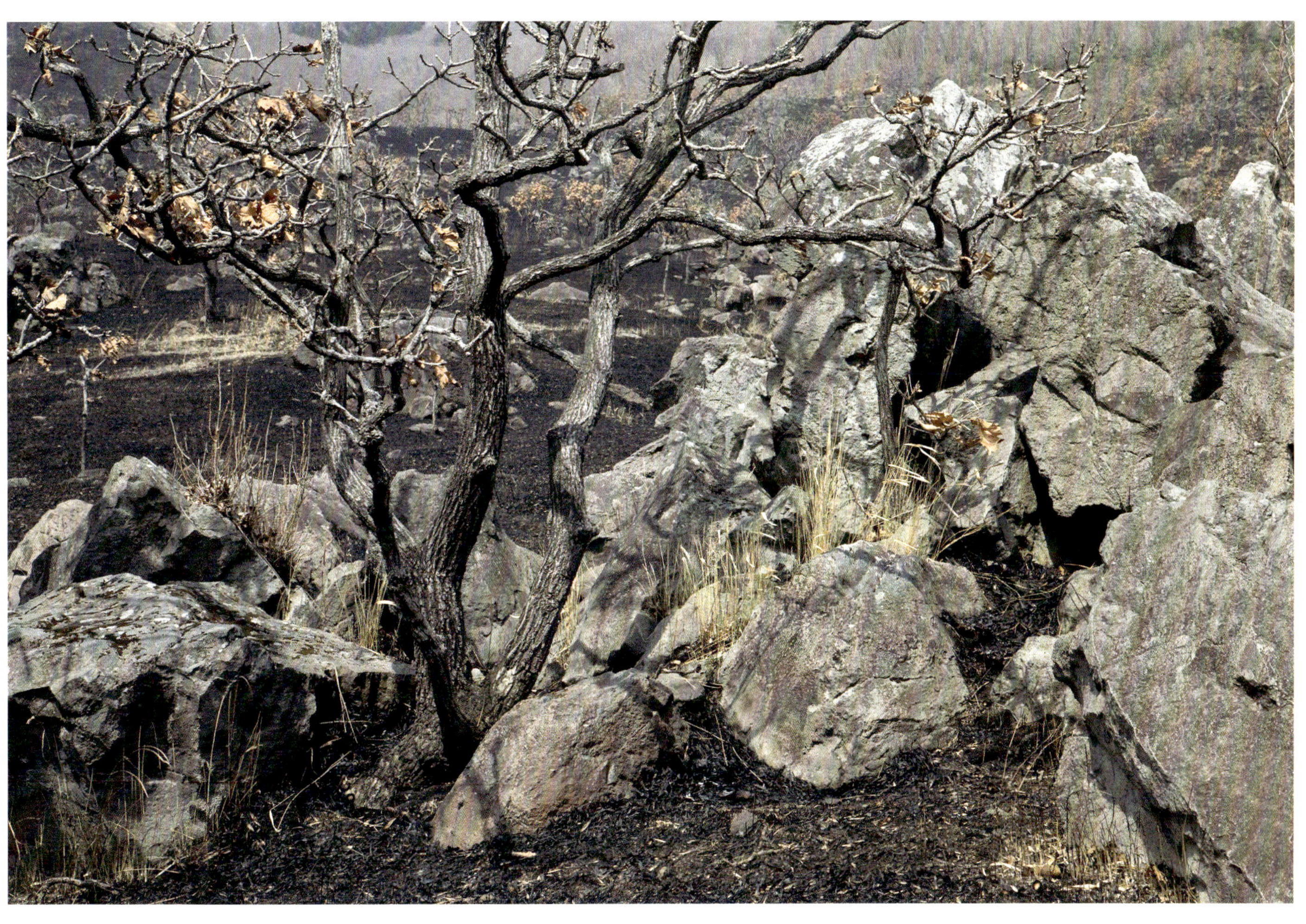

Plate 87
No. 8324, 2008, digital image file.
Allan Chasanoff Archive, Yale University Art Gallery

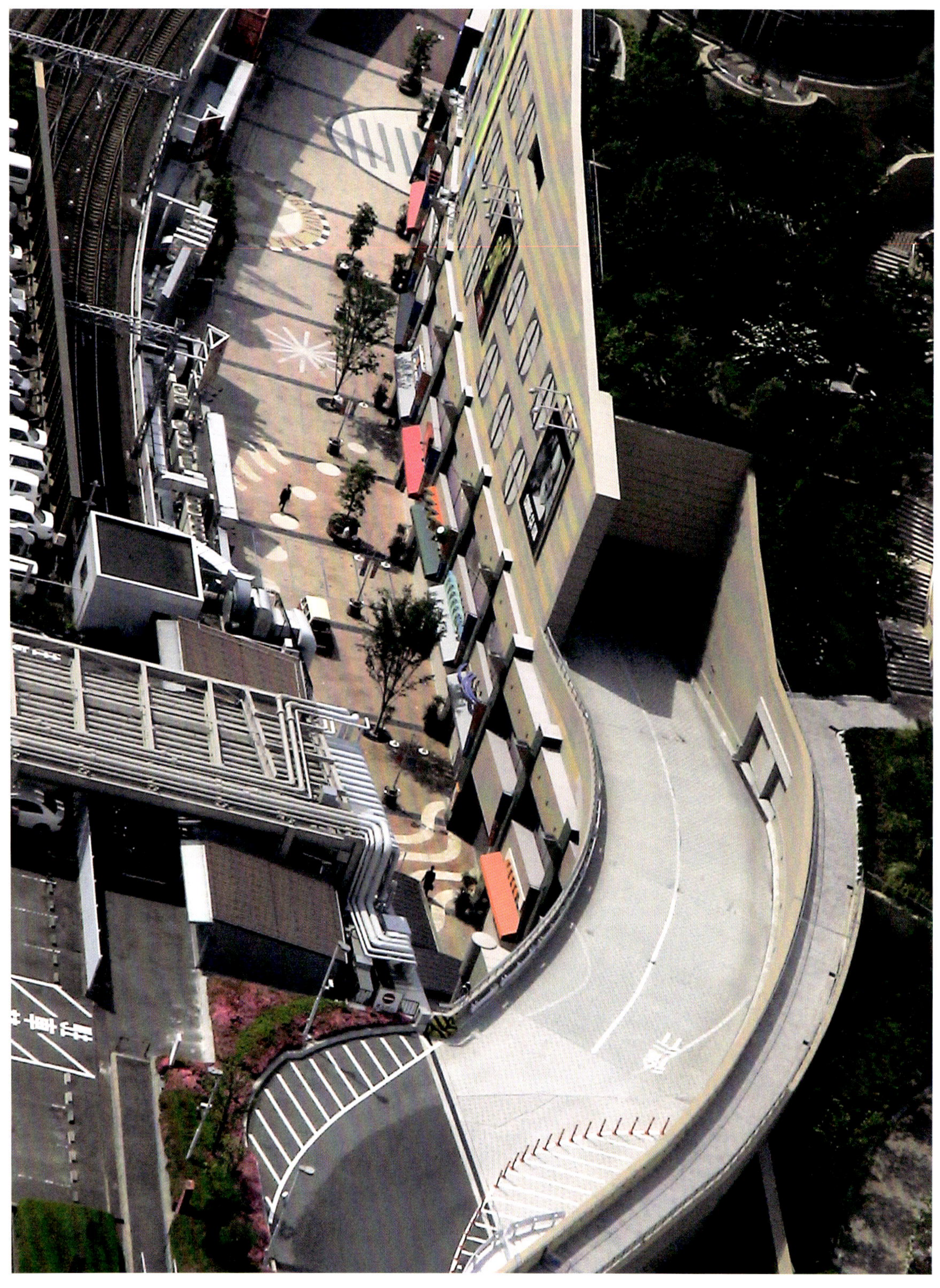

Plate 88
No. 6125, 2004, digital image file.
Allan Chasanoff Archive, Yale University Art Gallery

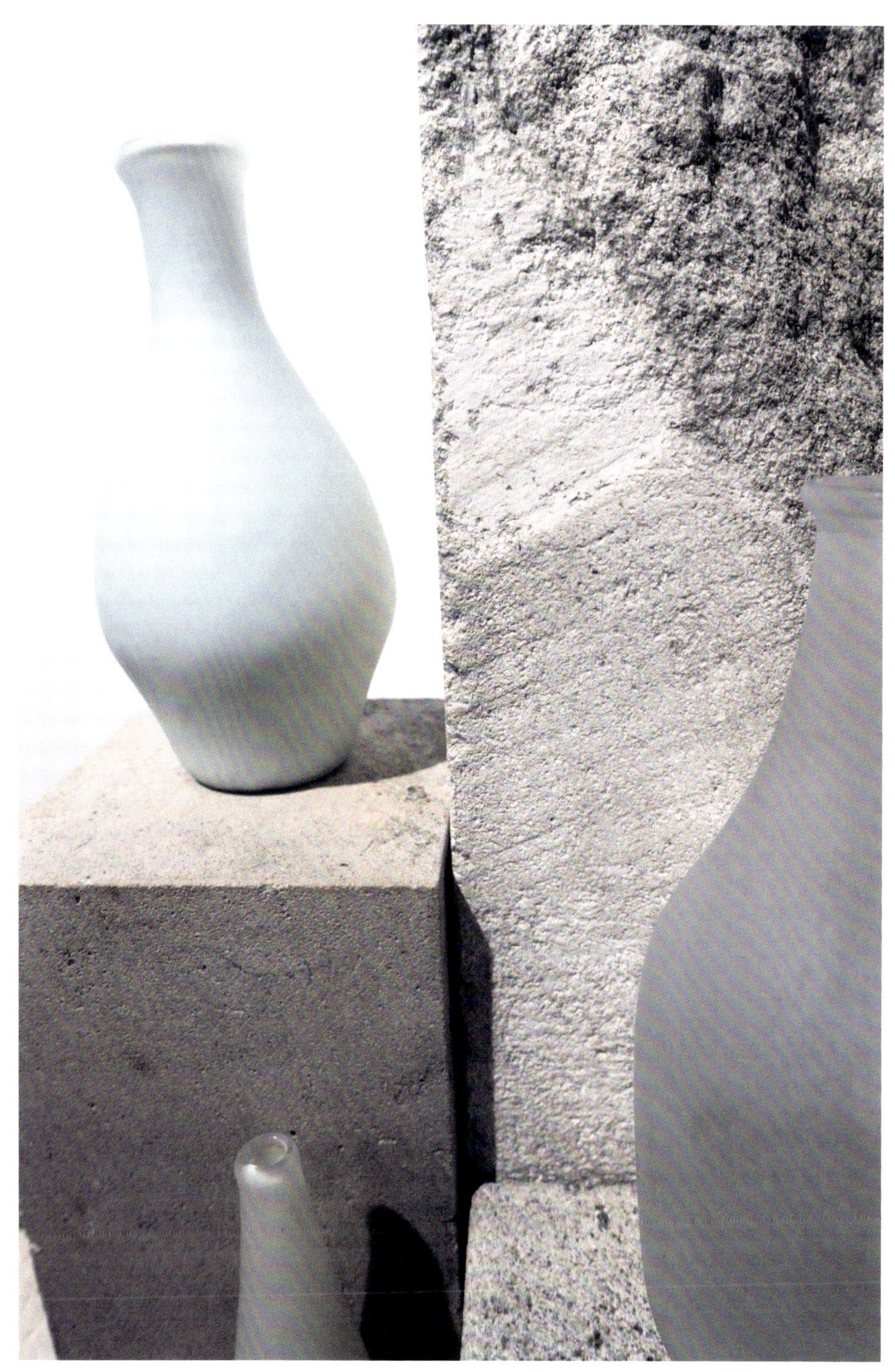

Note

Plates 88 and 89 exemplify Chasanoff's concept of "upside/downside." He thought certain shapes, when repeated in reverse orientation, force the viewer's eye upward, then downward, on a circular course. He kept a collection of such images found in signs (e.g., two opposing arrows), advertisements, and elsewhere. As a visual rhetorical device, he saw this as "dominating speech," which doesn't allow for response or dialogue.

Plate 89

No 11998, 2015, digital image file.
Allan Chasanoff Archive, Yale University Art Gallery

Contour
and Content

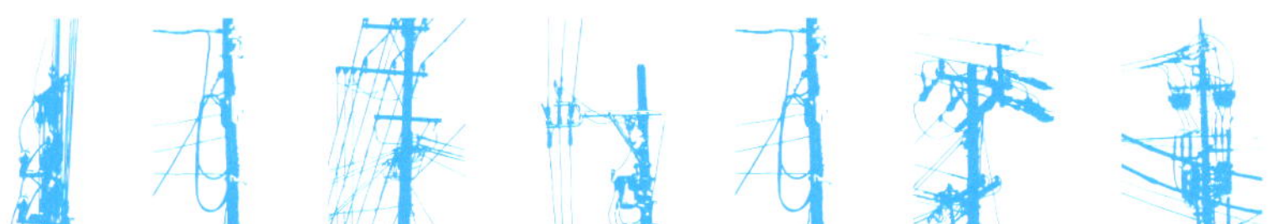

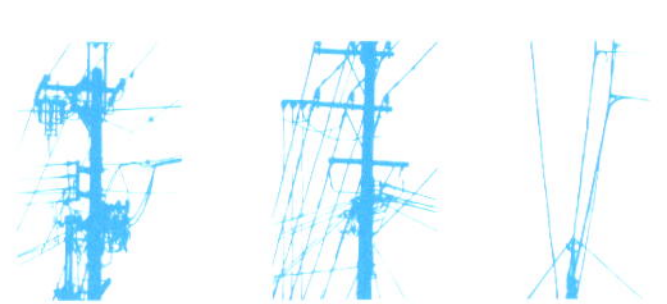

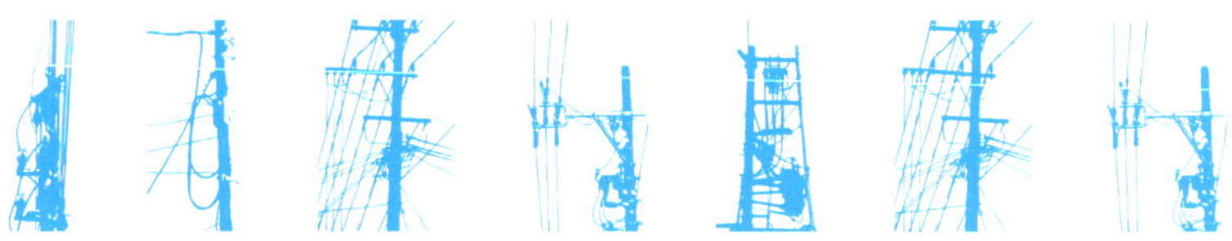

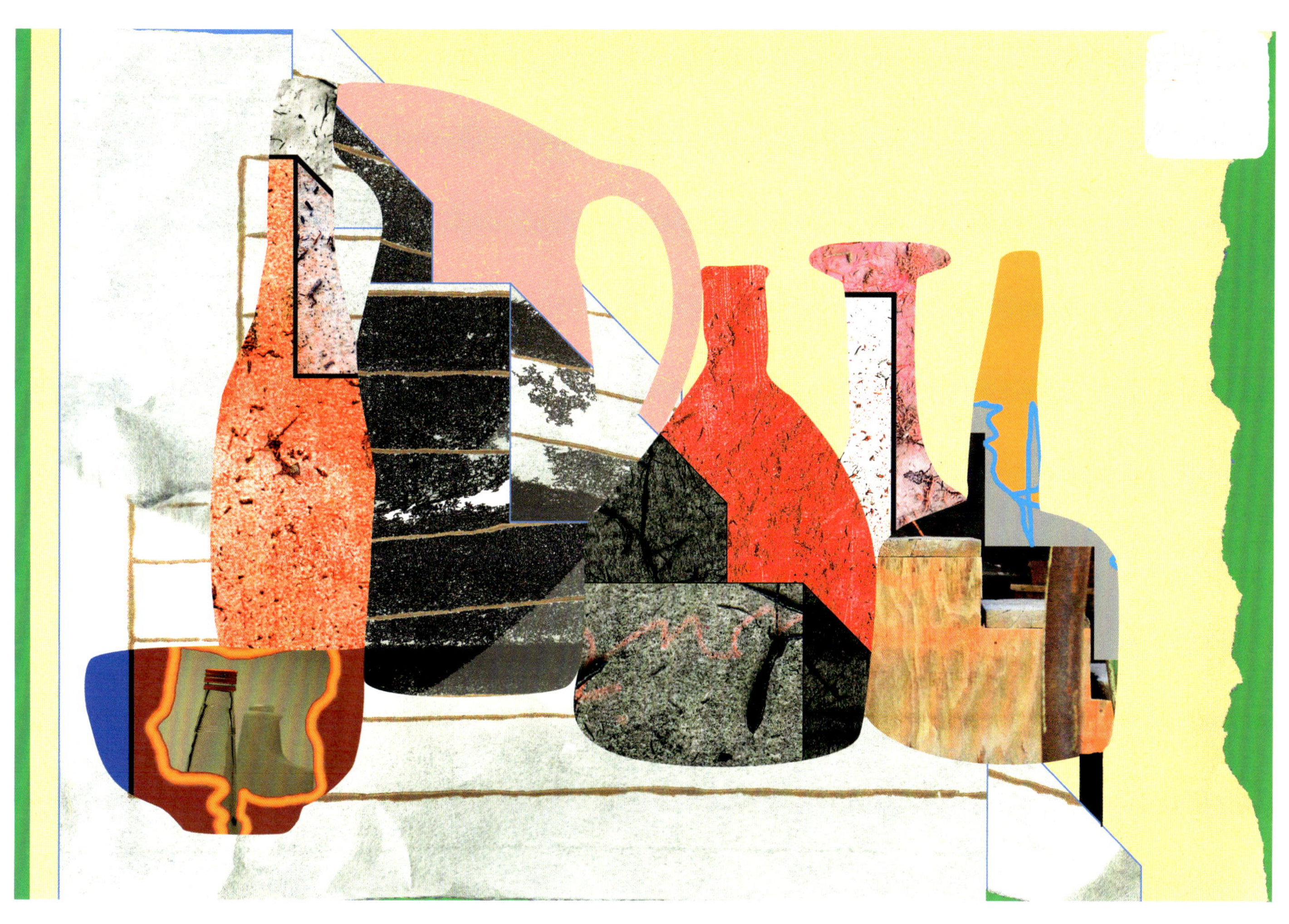

Note
Chasanoff's Bamboo Boy seal appears faintly at top right. Other elements included here are "erasings" and Japanese paper.

Plate 90
No. 11863, 2015, digital montage. Morandi (outline), Staircase (outline) series.
Allan Chasanoff Archive, Yale University Art Gallery

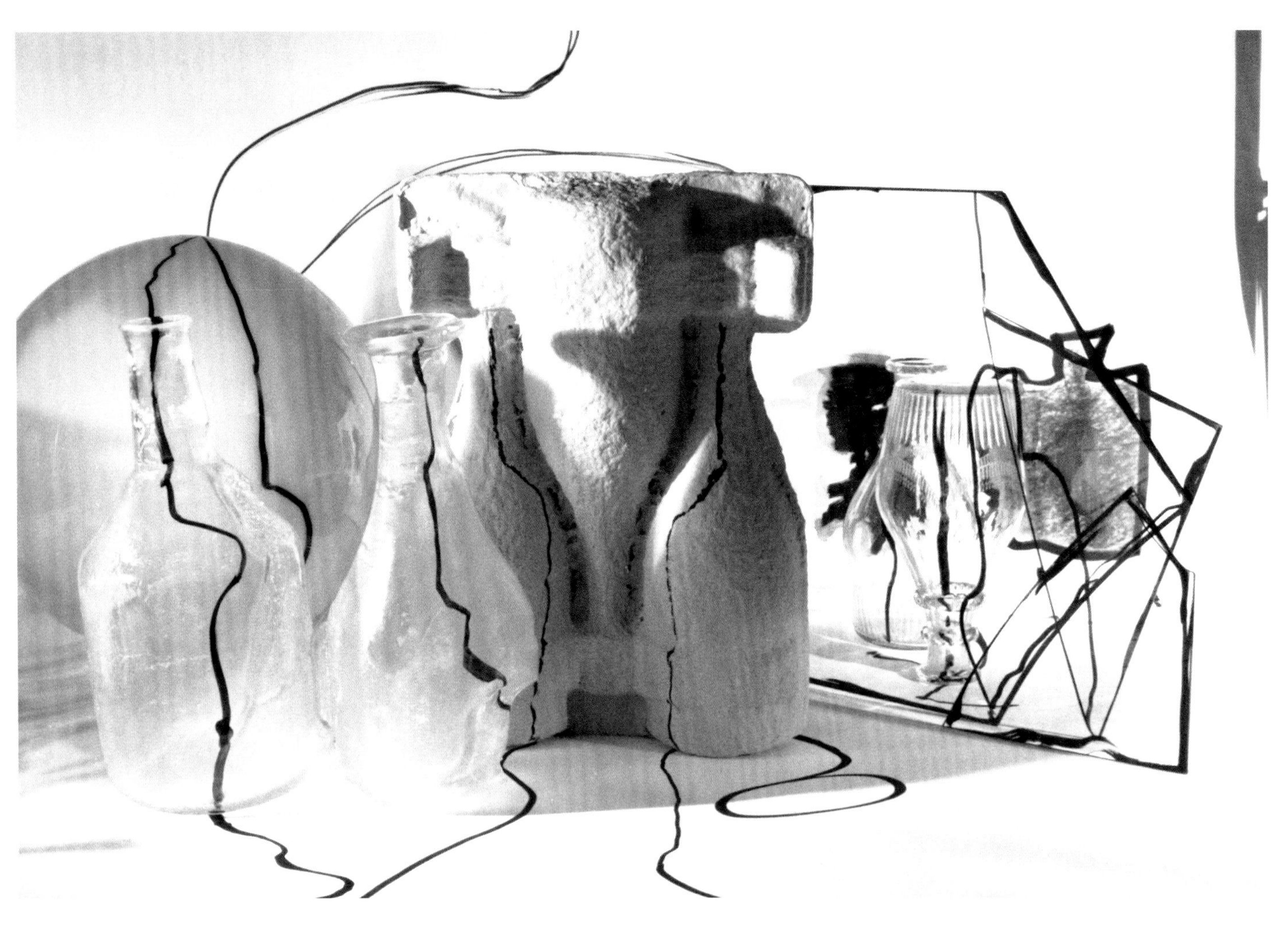

Plate 91
No. 3952, 1988, gelatin silver print.
Allan Chasanoff Archive, Yale University Art Gallery

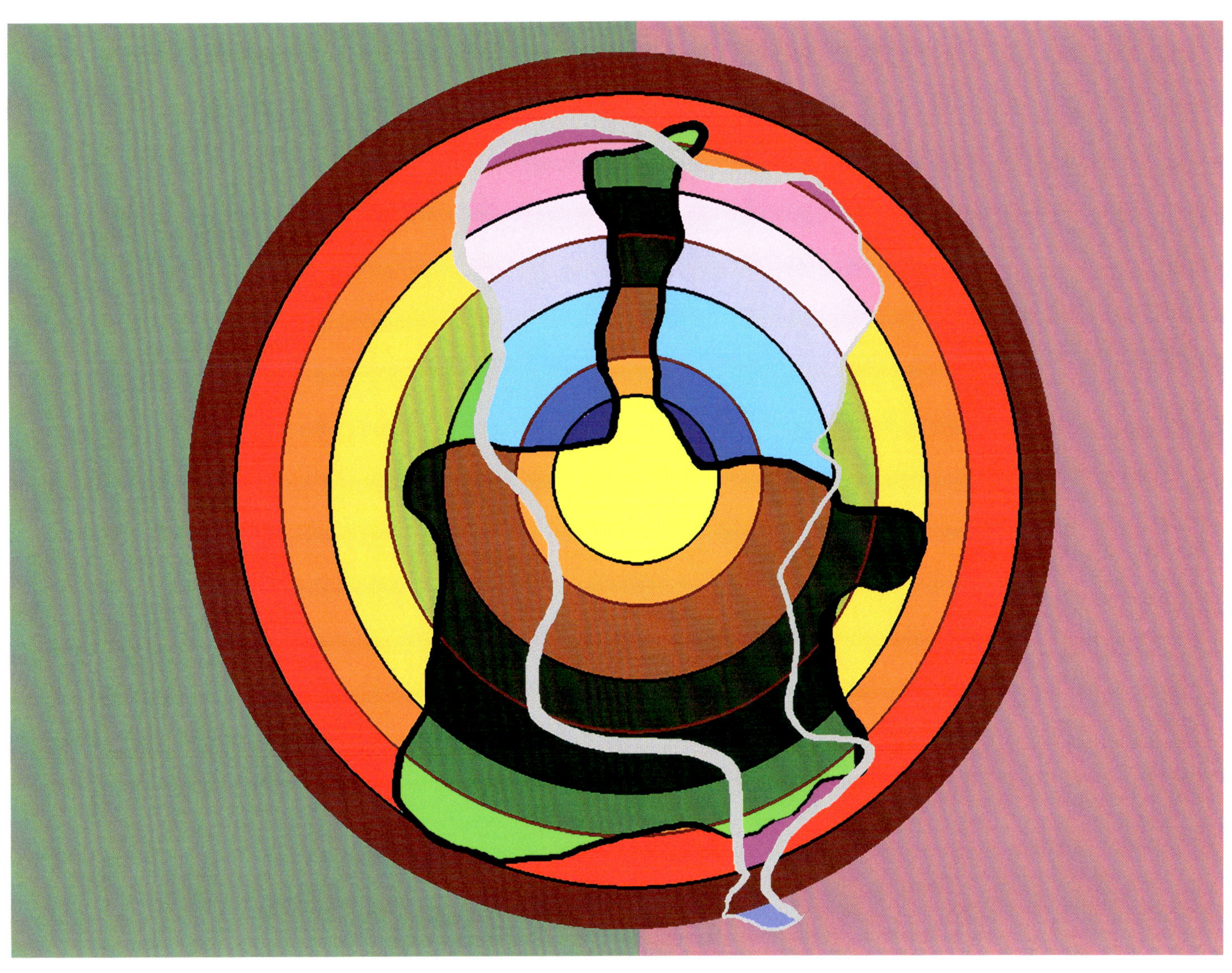

Note
This image was used as cover art for the CD of Chasanoff's audio project Sen-te-nse (1992).

Plate 92
No. 4586, 1992, digital montage or drawing.
Allan Chasanoff Archive, Yale University Art Gallery

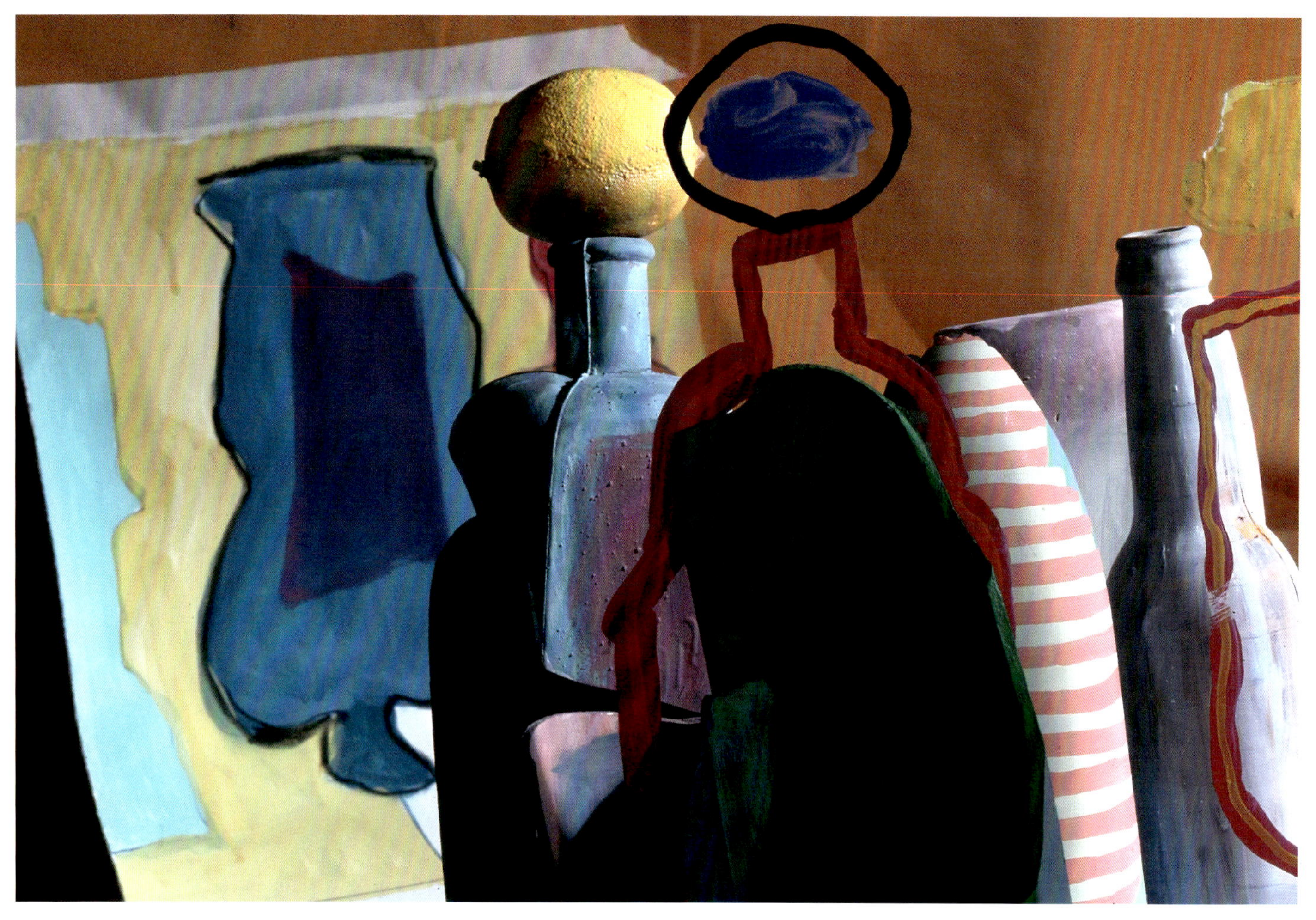

Plate 93
No. 3238, 1986, color transparency.
Allan Chasanoff Archive, Yale University Art Gallery

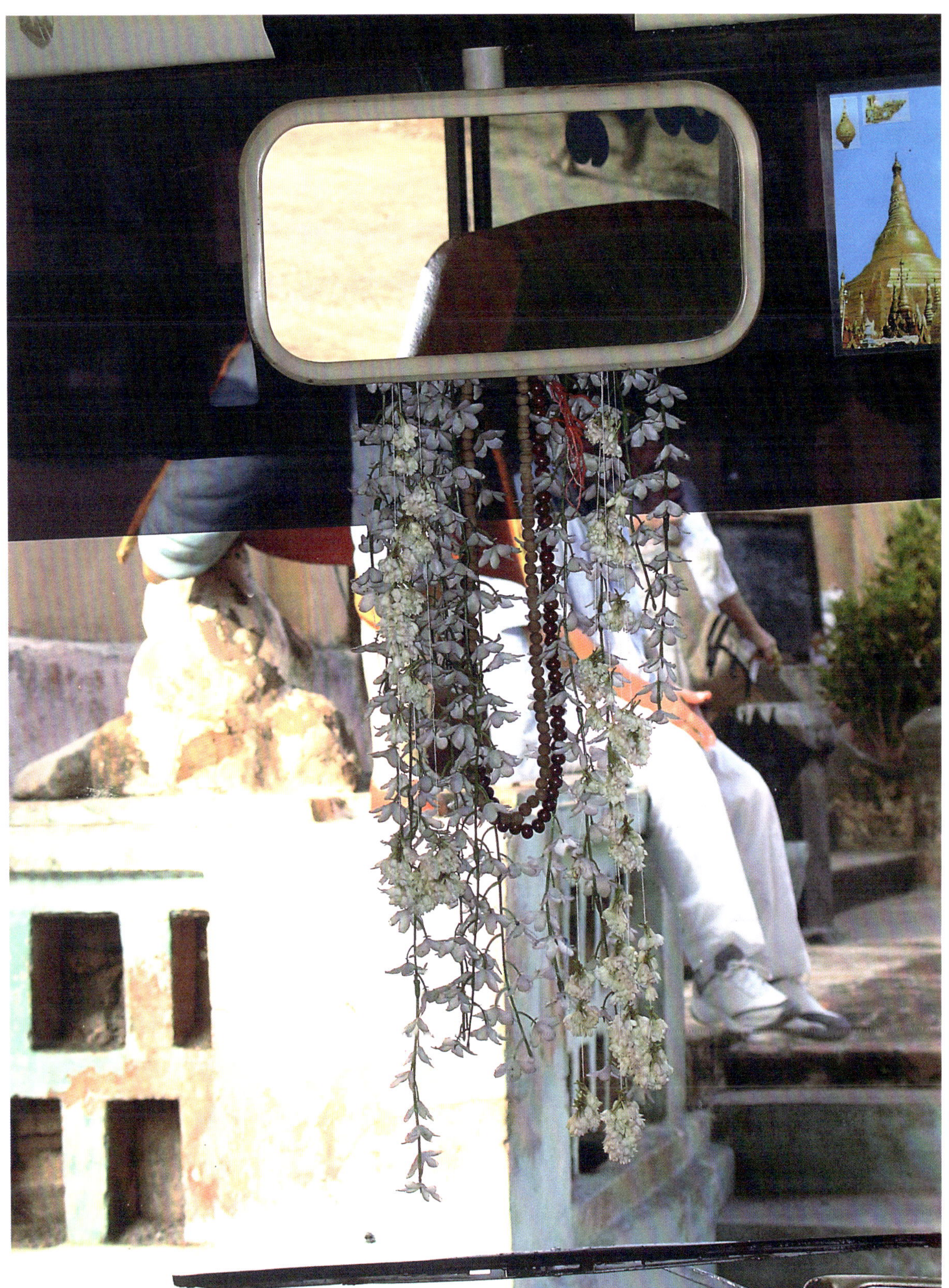

Plate 94
No. 6821, 2005, pigmented inkjet print.
Allan Chasanoff Archive, Yale University Art Gallery

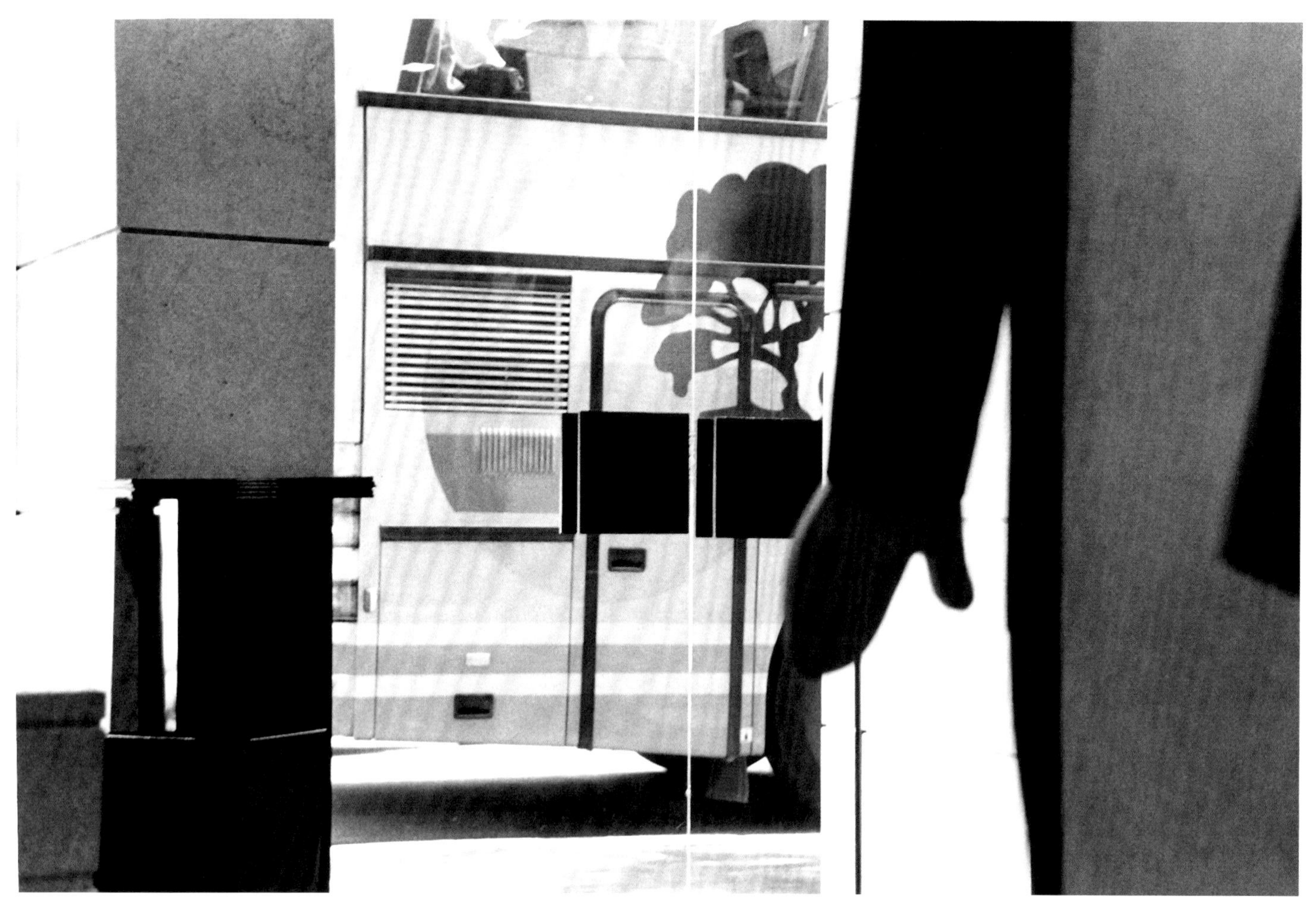

Plate 95
No. 4094, 1991, gelatin silver print.
Allan Chasanoff Archive, Yale University Art Gallery

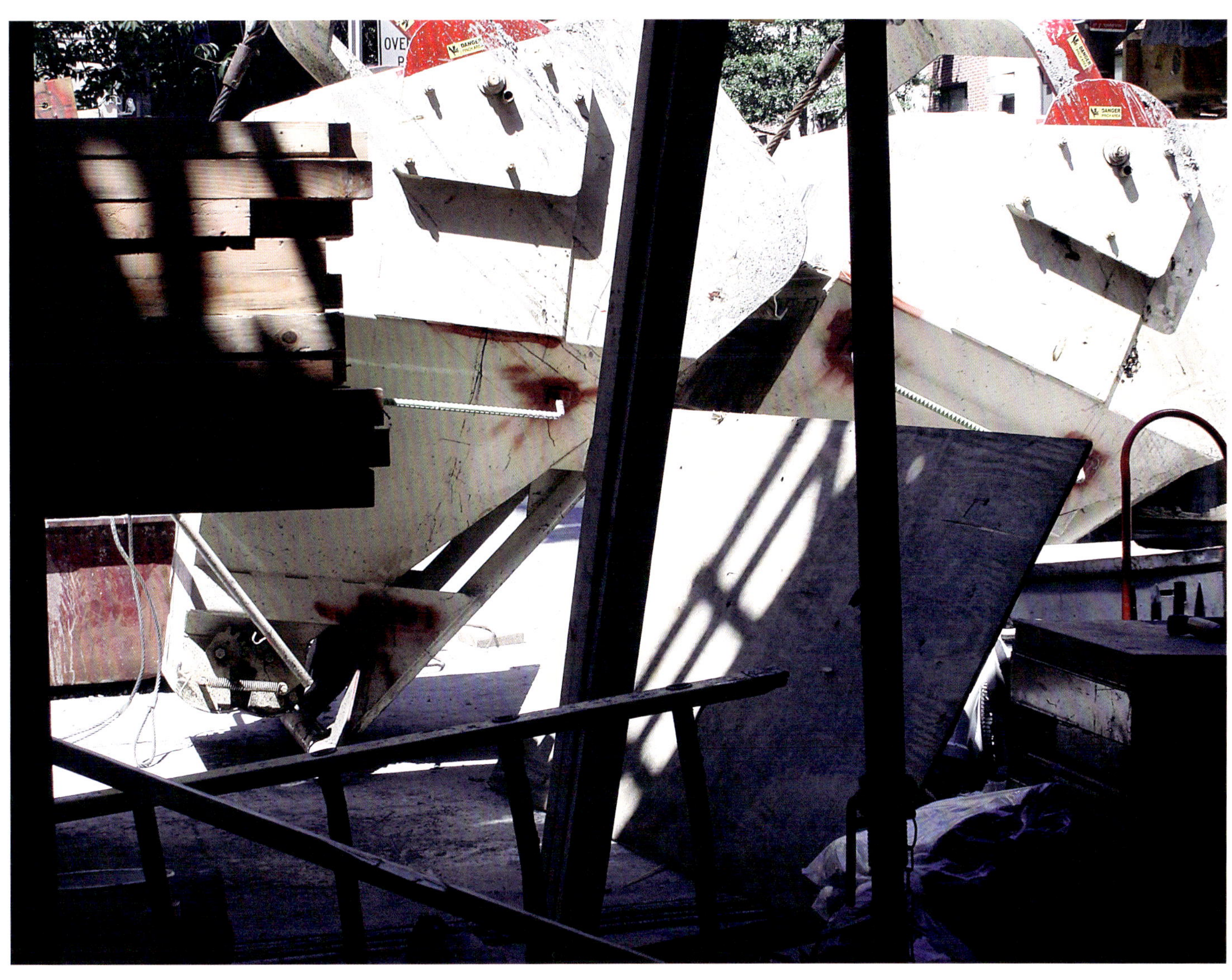

Plate 96
No. 7302, 2006, digital image file.
Allan Chasanoff Archive, Yale University Art Gallery

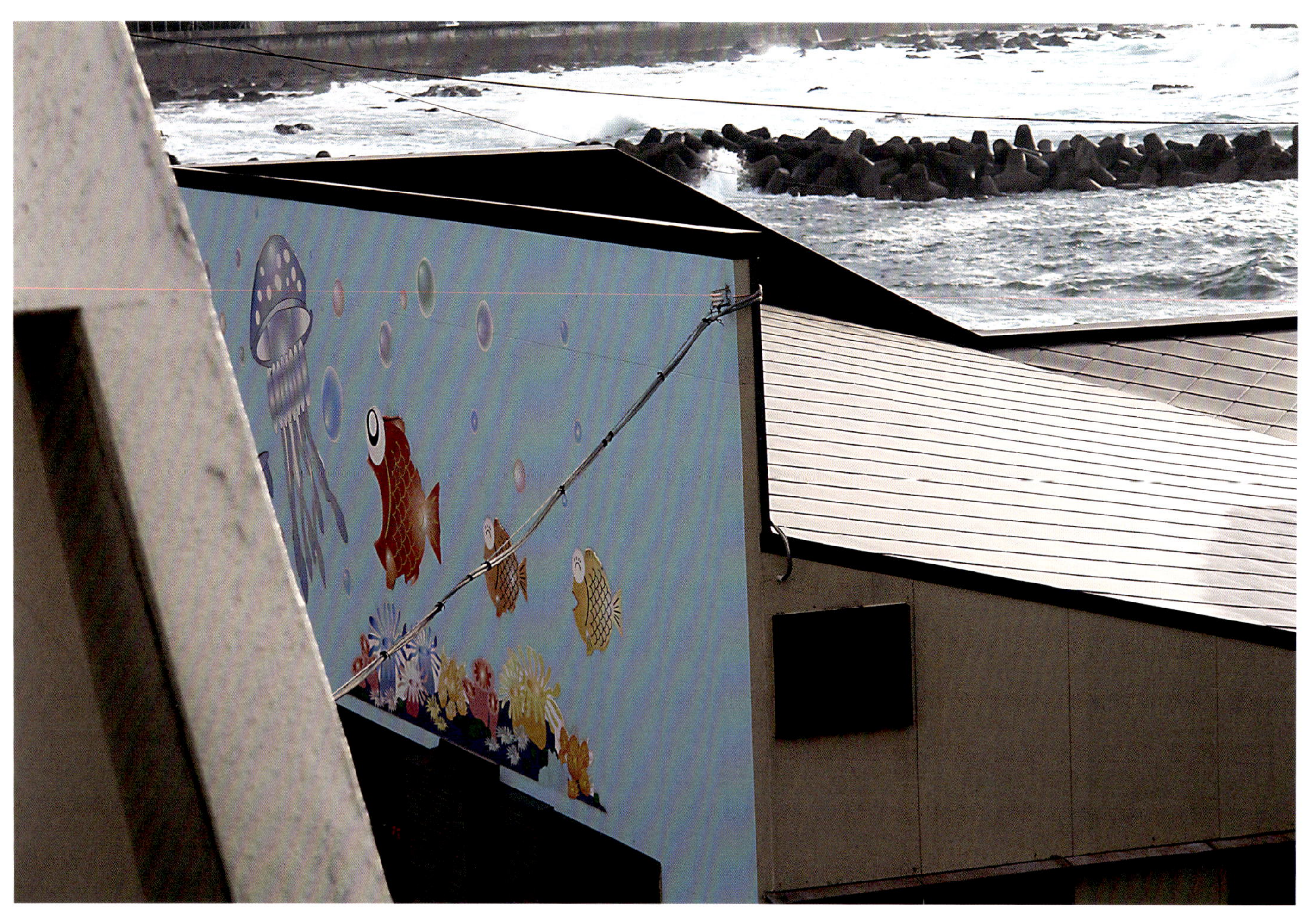

Plate 97
No. 8428, 2007, digital image file.
Allan Chasanoff Archive, Yale University Art Gallery

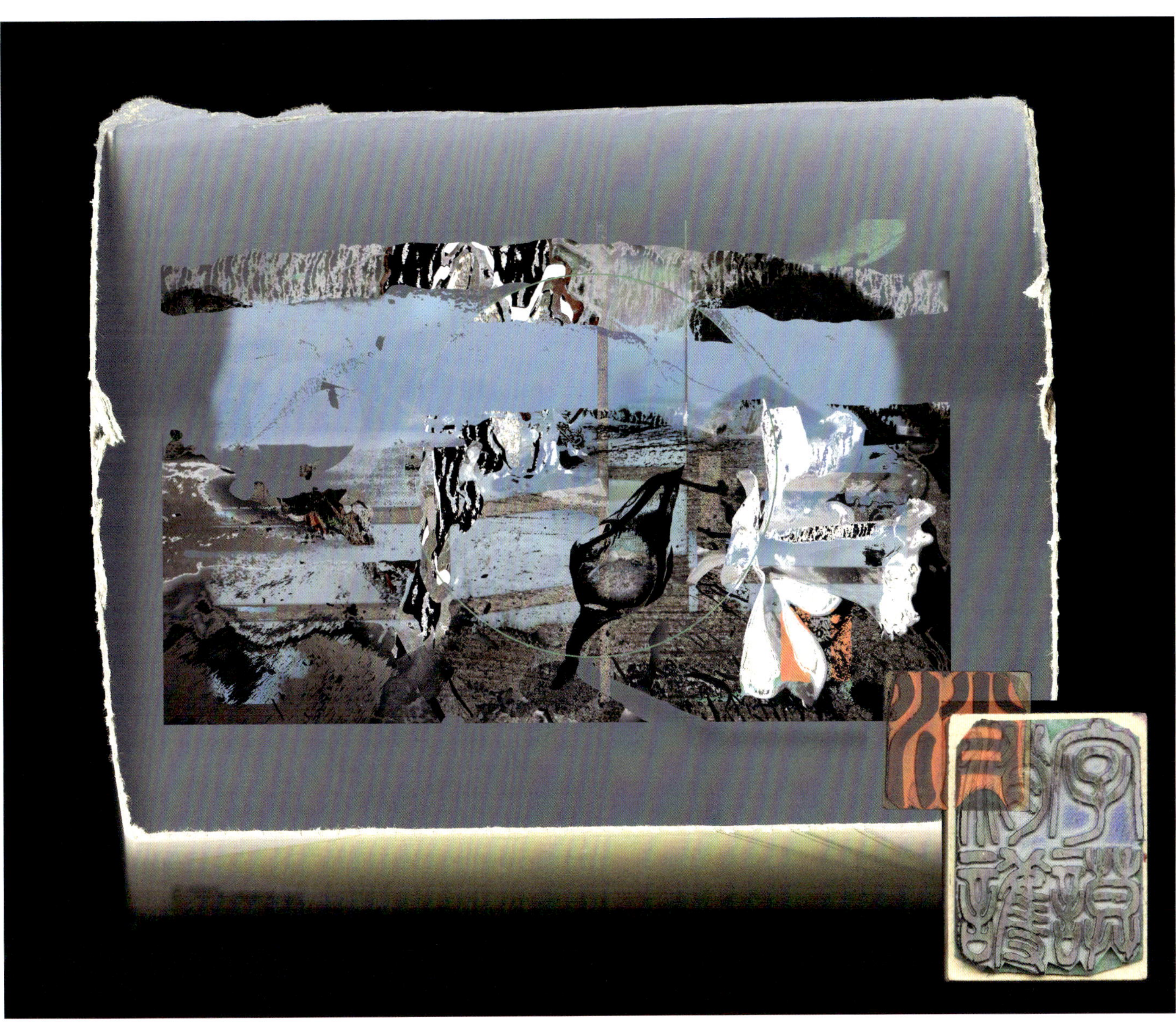

Note

The scanned seals at bottom right were commissioned by Chasanoff in 2007 during one of his trips to Japan as interpretations of his concept of "erasure." The smaller one was made by Yukichi Hoshina, the larger by Touru Hideshima. The image layer with flowers at center, one of Chasanoff's montages, is erased back digitally to show another of his montages.

Plate 98

No. 8466, 2008, digital montage.
Allan Chasanoff Archive, Yale University Art Gallery

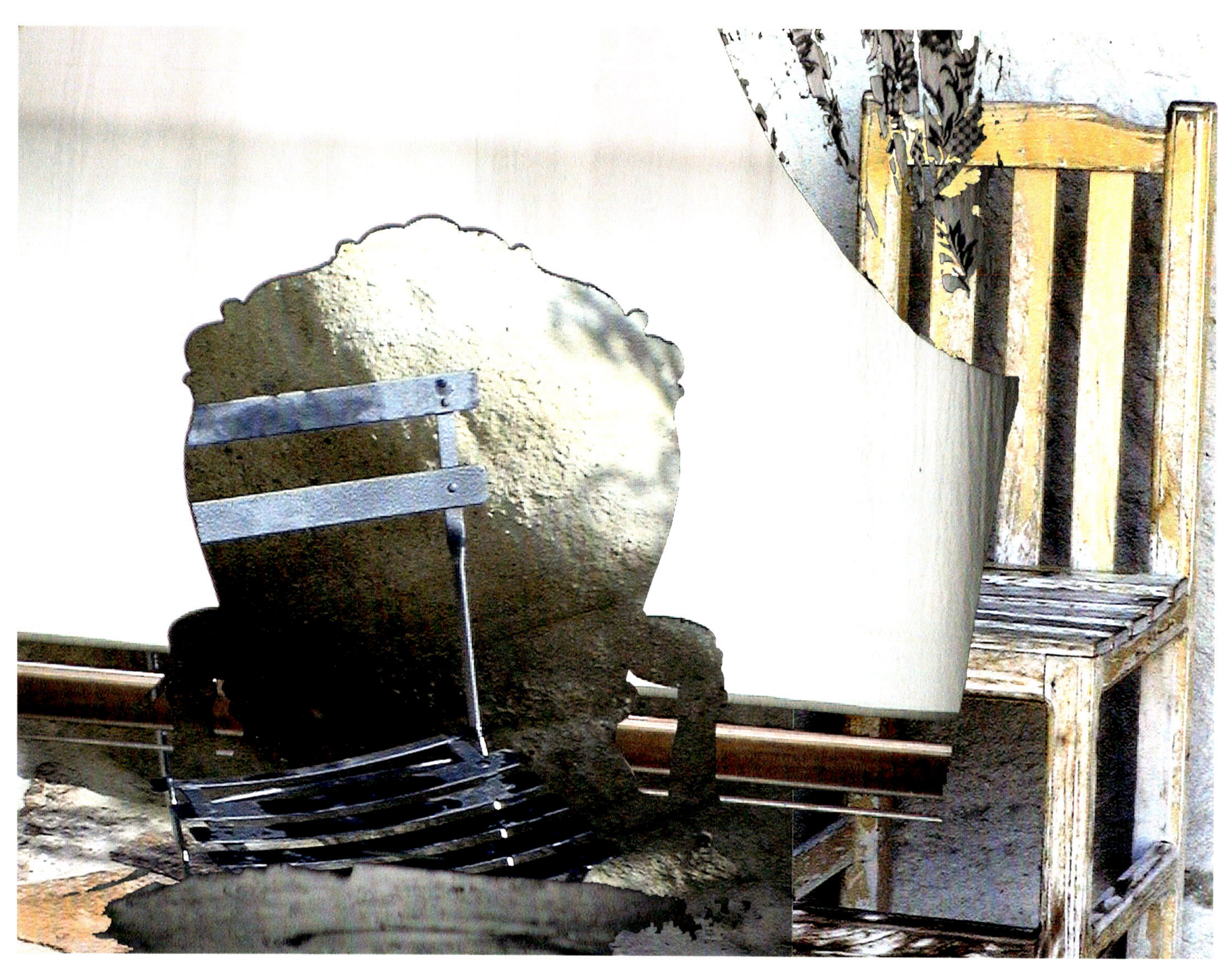

Plate 99
No. 4832, ca. 2001, digital montage. Chair (outline) series.
Allan Chasanoff Archive, Yale University Art Gallery

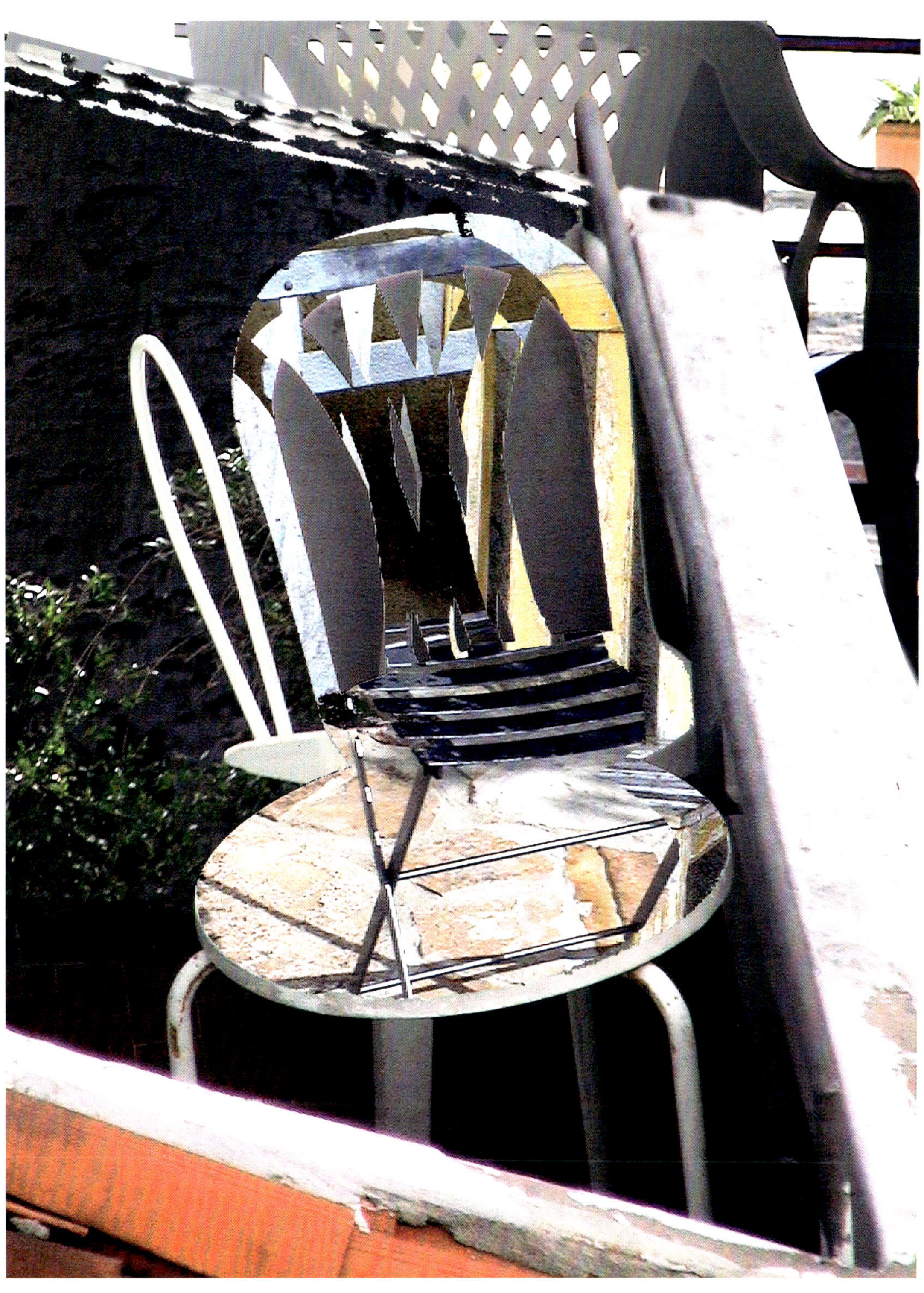

Plate 100
No. 4834, ca. 2001, digital montage. Chair (outline) series.
Allan Chasanoff Archive, Yale University Art Gallery

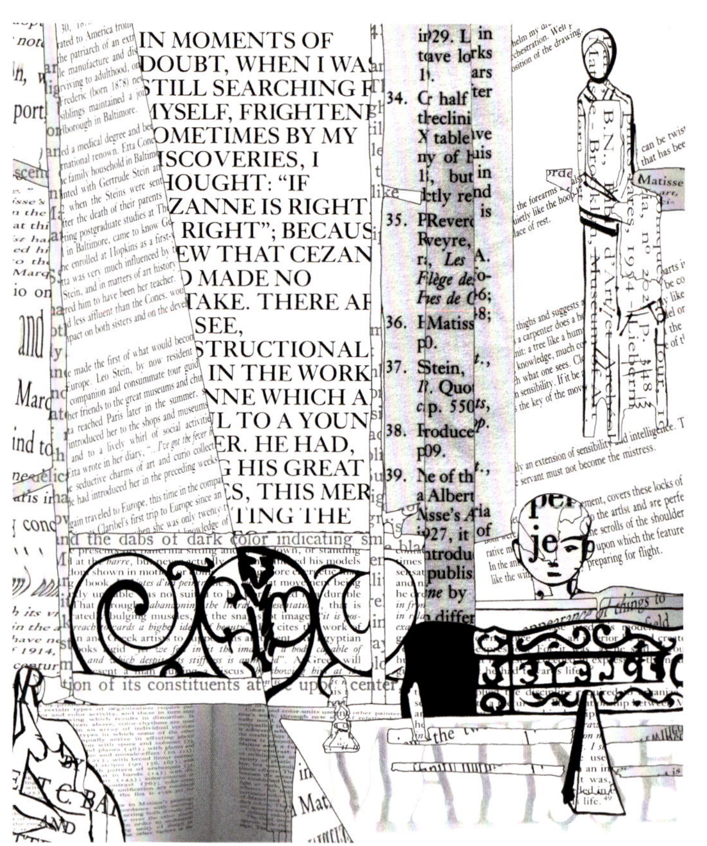

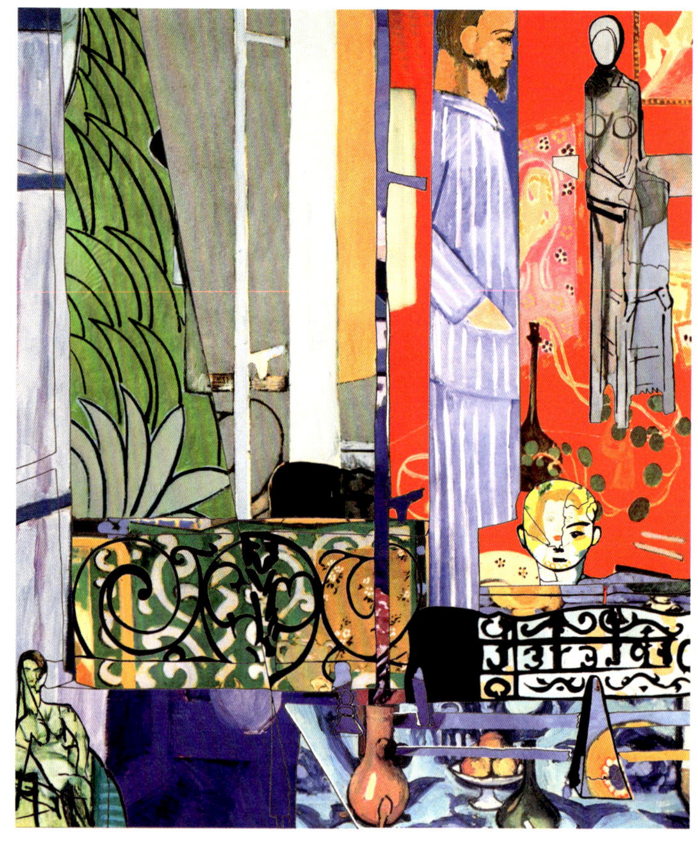

Note
In plate 102, several paintings by Henri Matisse are appropriated to fill in the outline created from the artist's *Piano Lesson*.

Plate 101
No. 1137, 2000, digital montage. Matisse, *Piano Lesson* (1916) series. Allan Chasanoff Archive, Yale University Art Gallery

Plate 102
No. 1140, 2000, digital montage. Matisse, *Piano Lesson* (1916) series. Allan Chasanoff Archive, Yale University Art Gallery

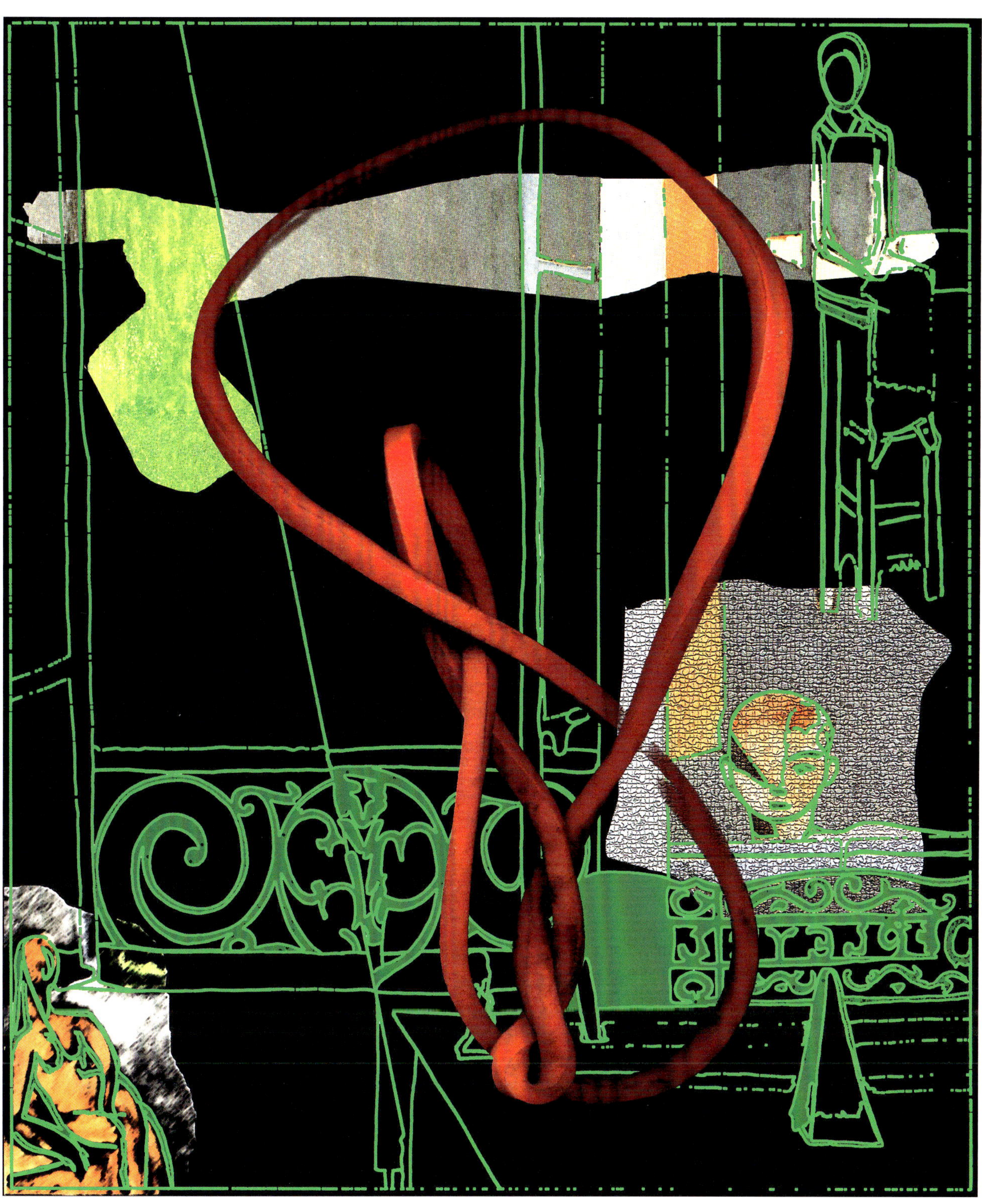

Plate 103
No. 1150, 2000, digital montage. Matisse, *Piano Lesson* (1916) series.
Allan Chasanoff Archive, Yale University Art Gallery

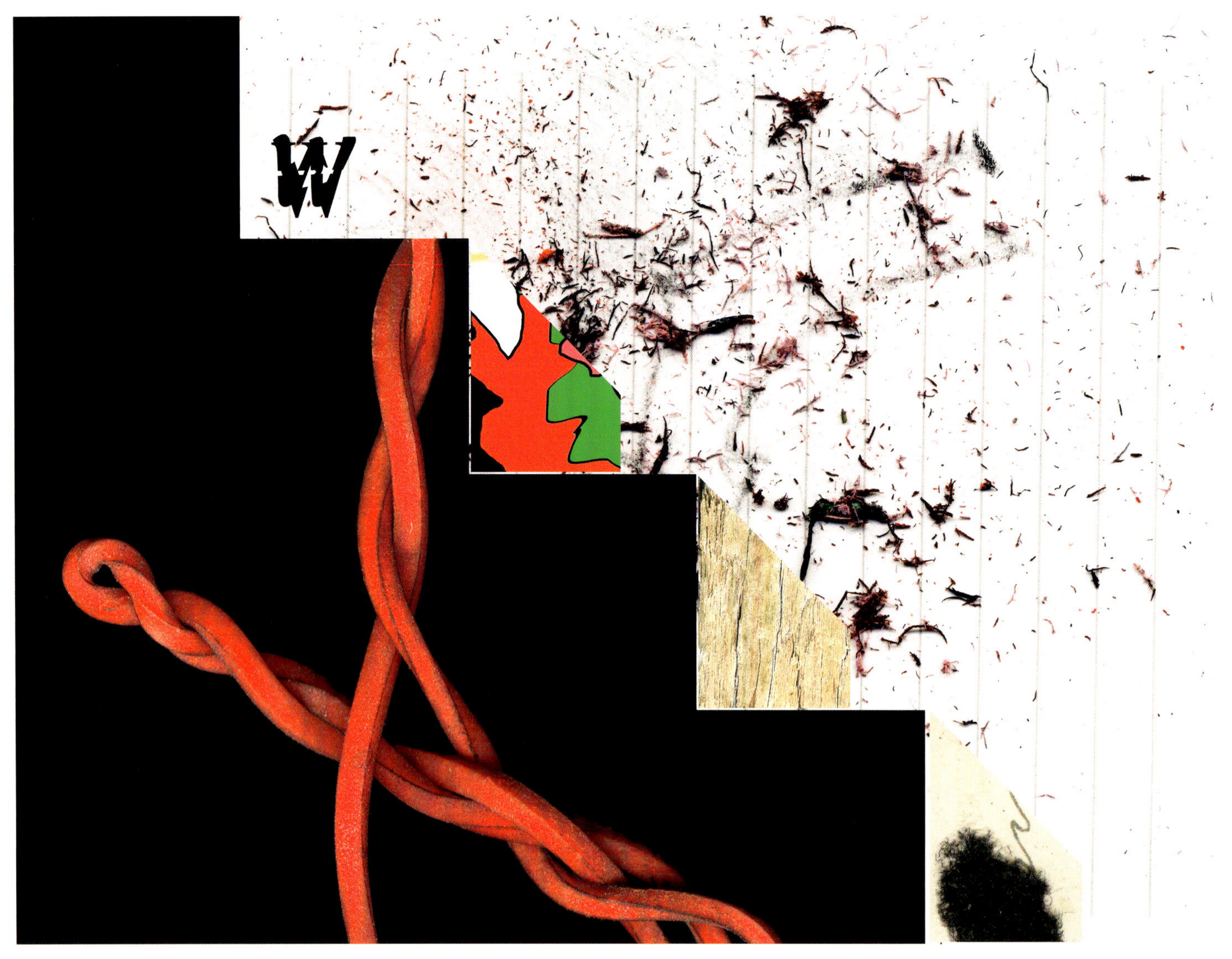

Note
The *W* is from Chasanoff's Play font. Other elements include a rubber band, erasings, and a back-of-photo detail at bottom right.

Plate 104
No. 6395, 2005, digital montage. Staircase (outline) series.
Allan Chasanoff Archive, Yale University Art Gallery

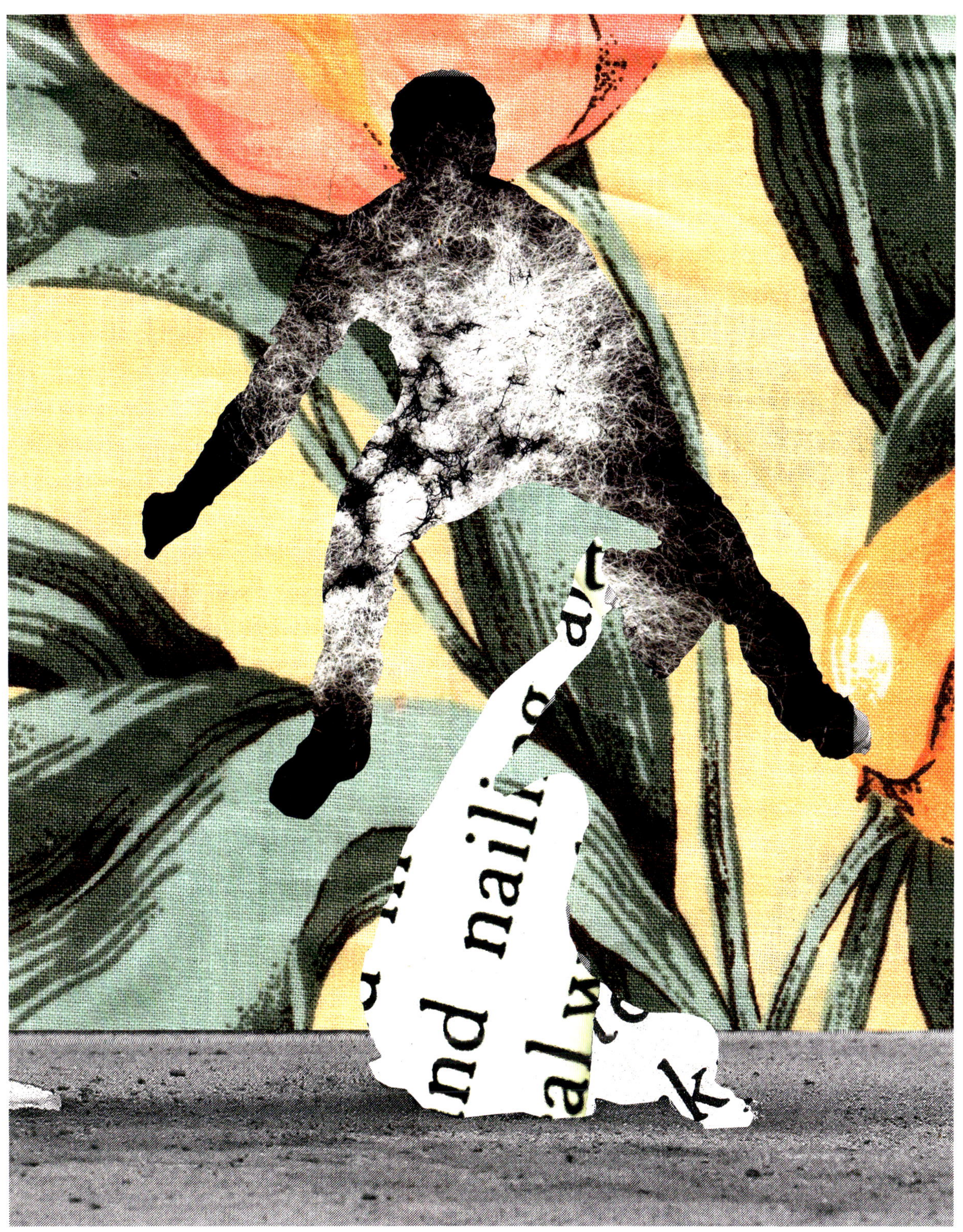

Note

Inside the outlined figure, top center, is scanned painted cotton.

Plate 105

No. 6404, 2005, digital montage. Baseball (outline) series.

Allan Chasanoff Archive, Yale University Art Gallery

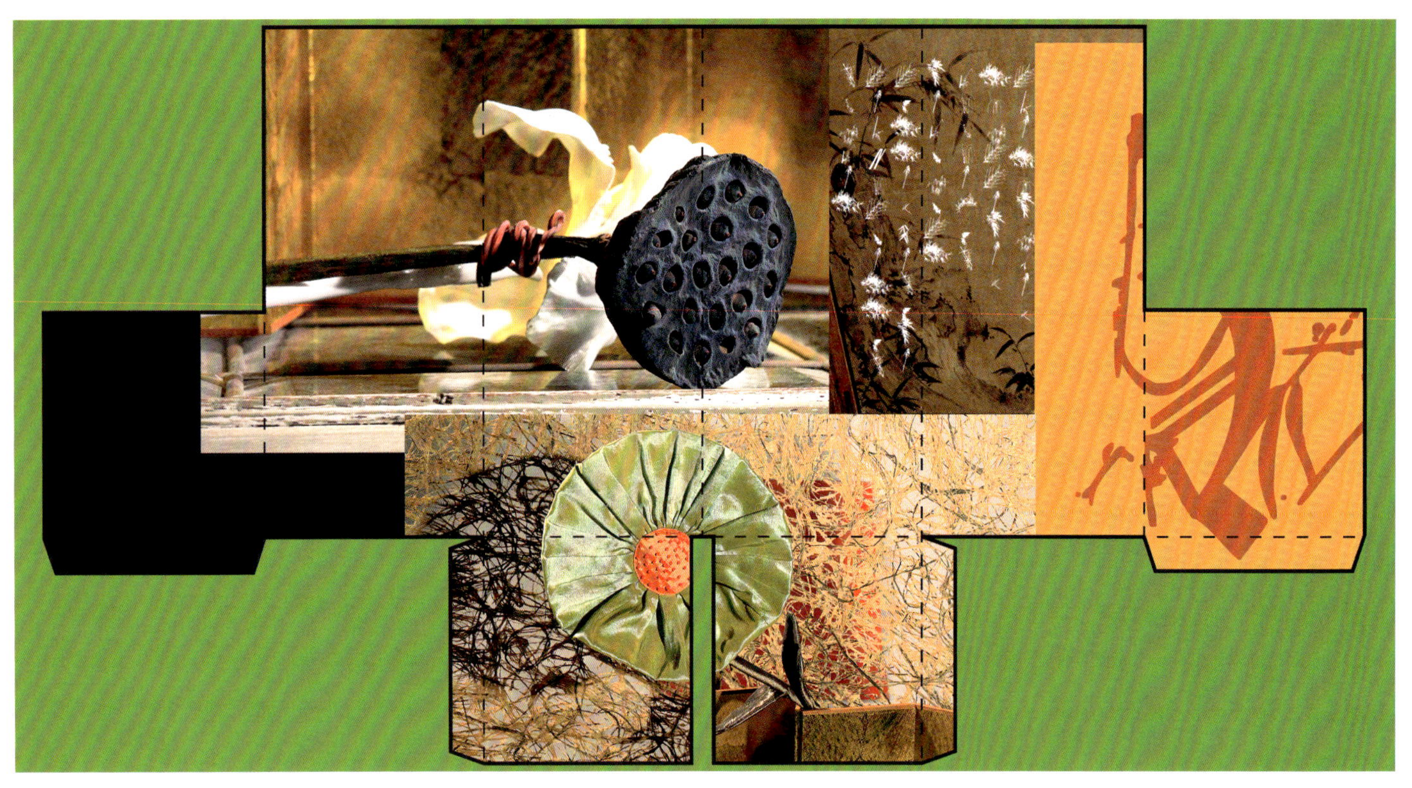

Note
Chasanoff's Bamboo A font appears in white at center right, and a character from his BAPHT font is at far right.

Plate 106
No. 7401, 2006, digital montage. Box (outline) series.
Allan Chasanoff Archive, Yale University Art Gallery

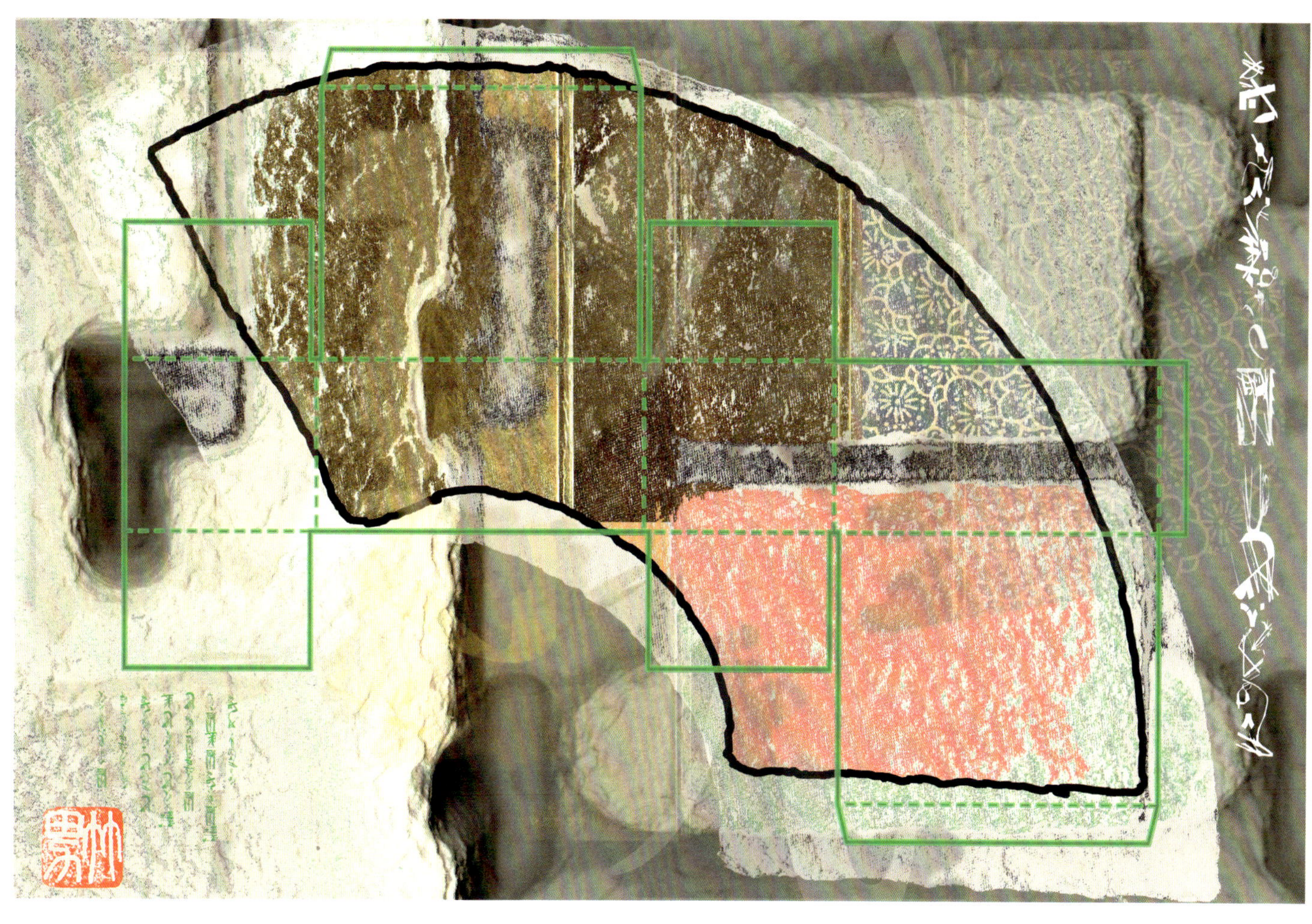

Note

A packing insert from a shipping box, blended with other elements, makes up the background. Chasanoff's BAPHT font appears at bottom left and far right, and his Bamboo Boy seal is at bottom left.

Plate 107

No. 7388, 2006, digital montage. Box (outline), Fan (outline) series.
Allan Chasanoff Archive, Yale University Art Gallery

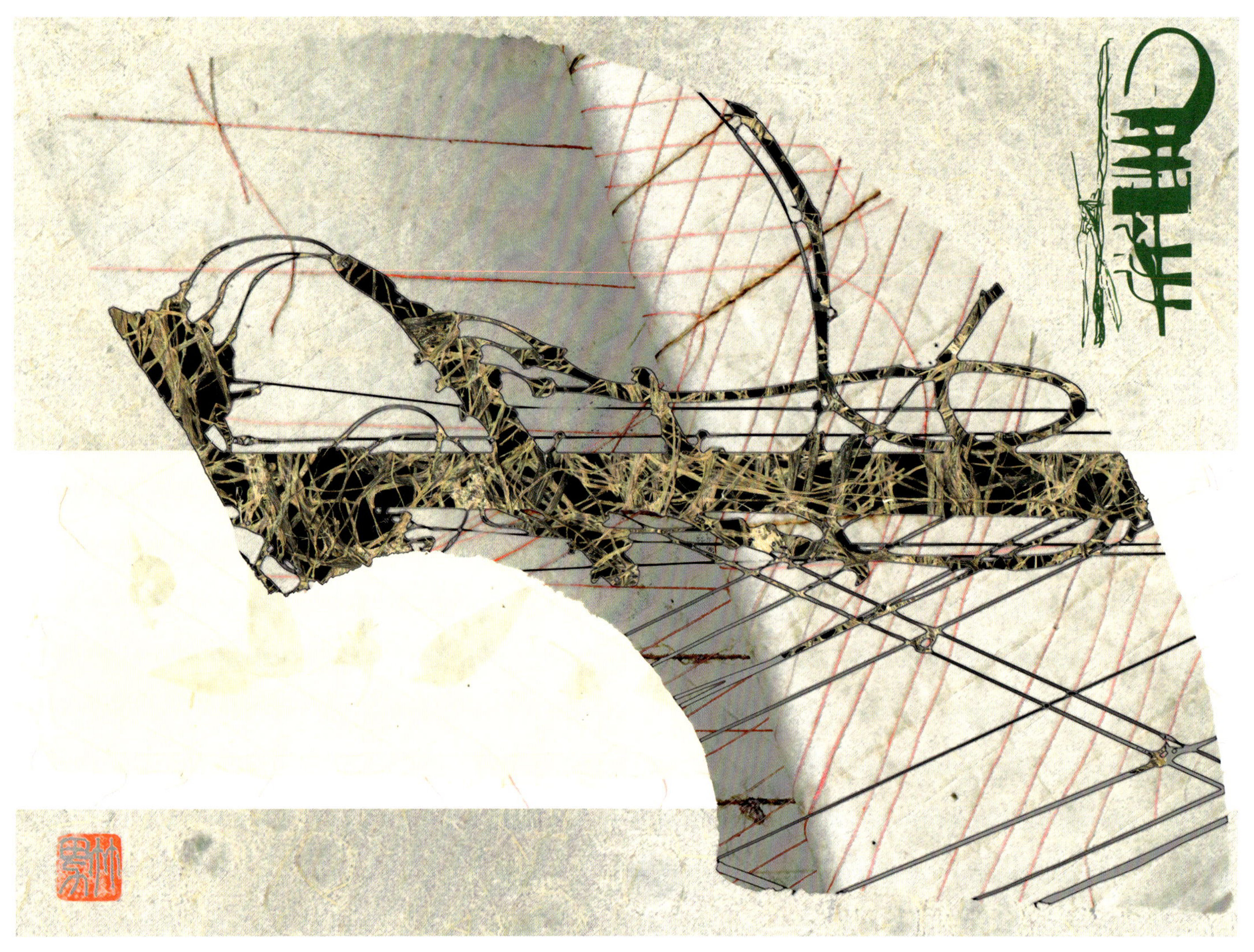

Note
A character from Chasanoff's AMF font appears at top right, and his Bamboo Boy seal is at bottom left. Various textures come from scanned Japanese paper.

Plate 108
No. 7386, 2006, digital montage. Fan (outline) series.
Allan Chasanoff Archive, Yale University Art Gallery

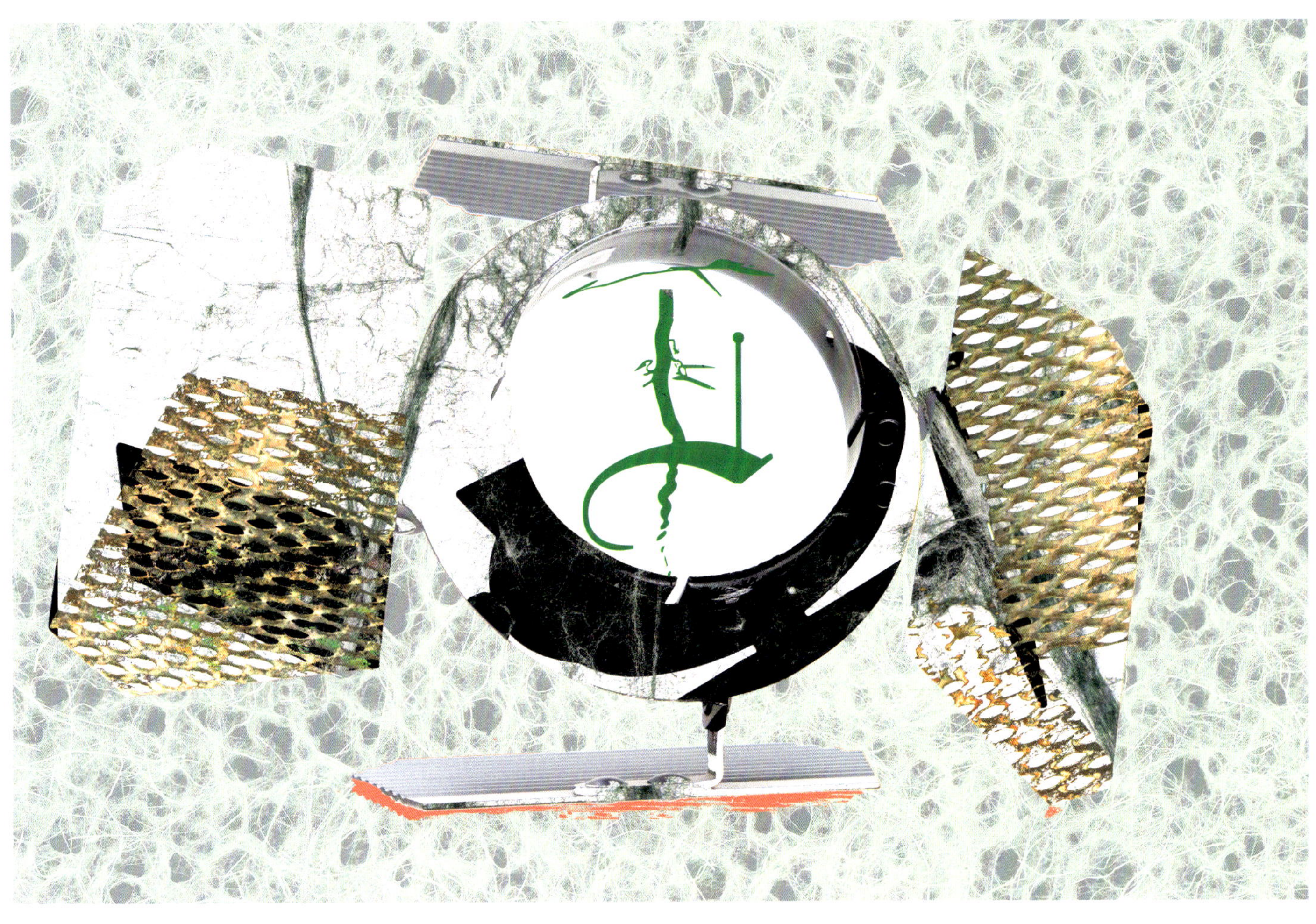

Note
A character from Chasanoff's AMF font appears at center.

Plate 109
No. 11224, 2008, digital montage. Barn Door (outline) series.
Allan Chasanoff Archive, Yale University Art Gallery

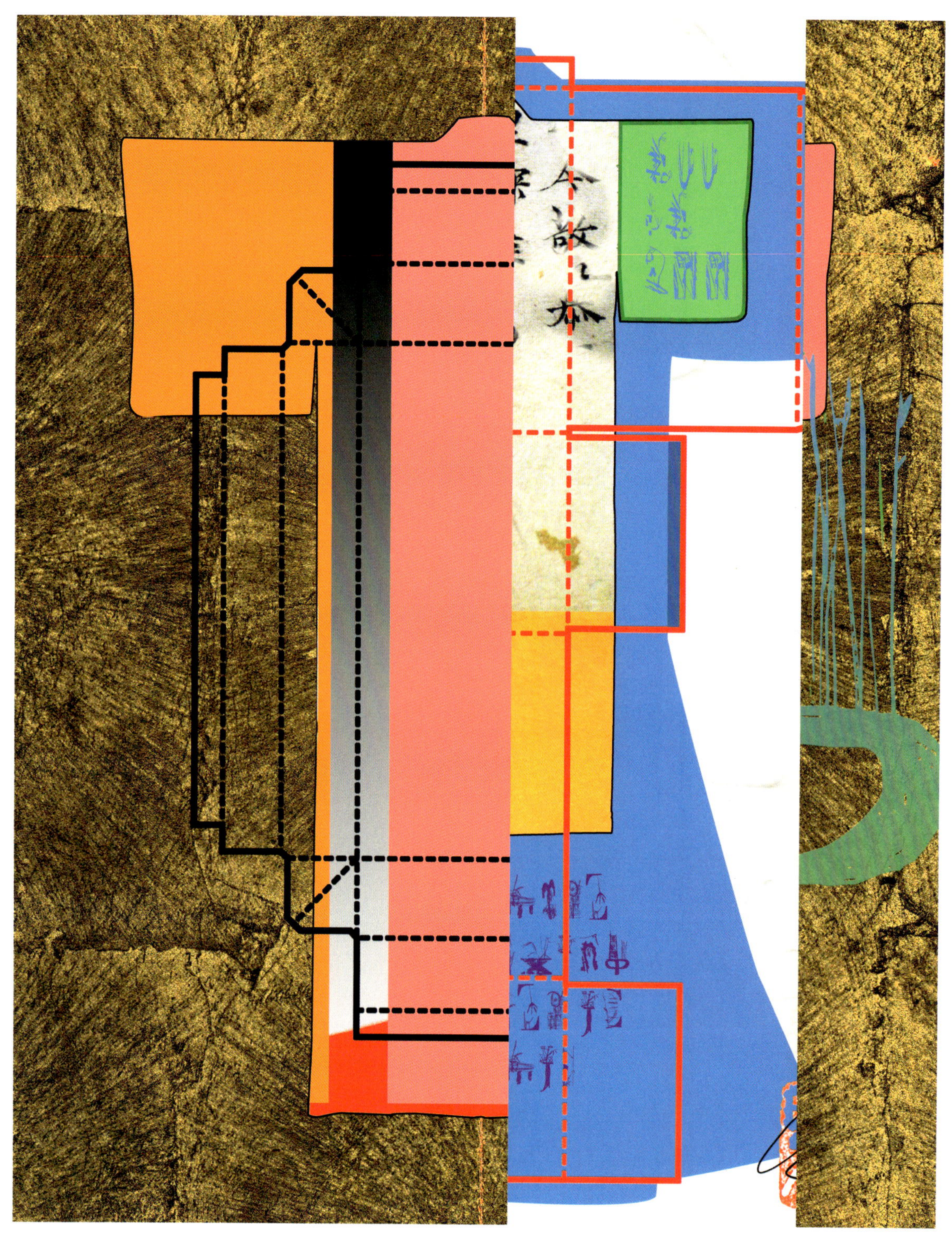

Note
Chasanoff's BAPHT font appears at top right, and his FBT font is at bottom center.

Plate 110
No. 7424, 2006, digital montage. Box (outline), Kimono (outline) series.
Allan Chasanoff Archive, Yale University Art Gallery

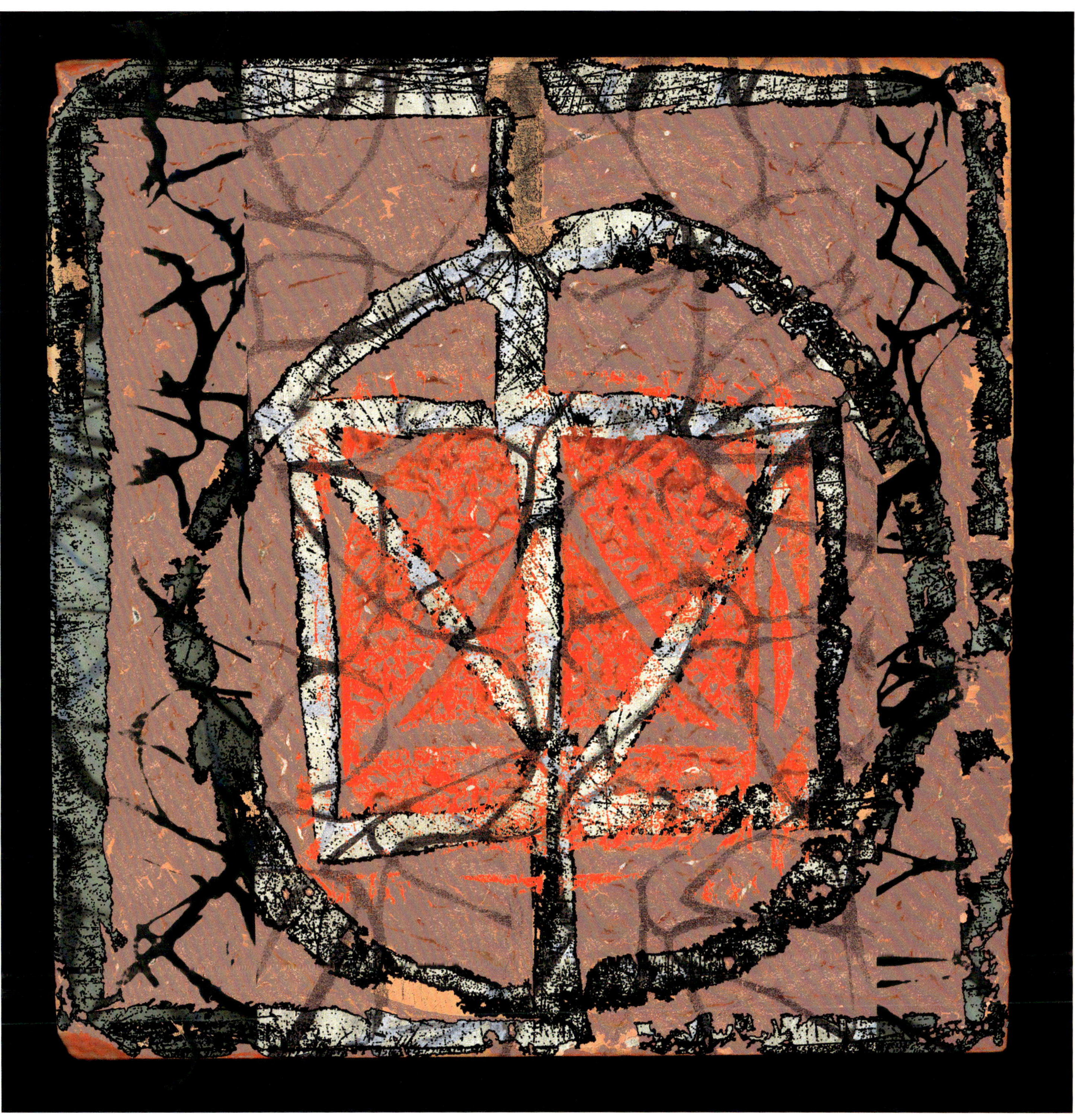

Note

In 2009 Chasanoff commissioned several seals in Japan to complement his screenplay "Mother's Tongue." They include symbolic imagery: the square, triangle, and circle of the Buddhist monk Sengai Gibon's depiction of the universe (Edo period); and the line, representing the cut or castration, and female genitalia. The two seals here, in black and red, were made by Seia Manabe and Shashin Iwaasa, respectively.

Plate 111

No. 11227, 2010, digital montage. Mother's Tongue Seal (outline) series.
Allan Chasanoff Archive, Yale University Art Gallery

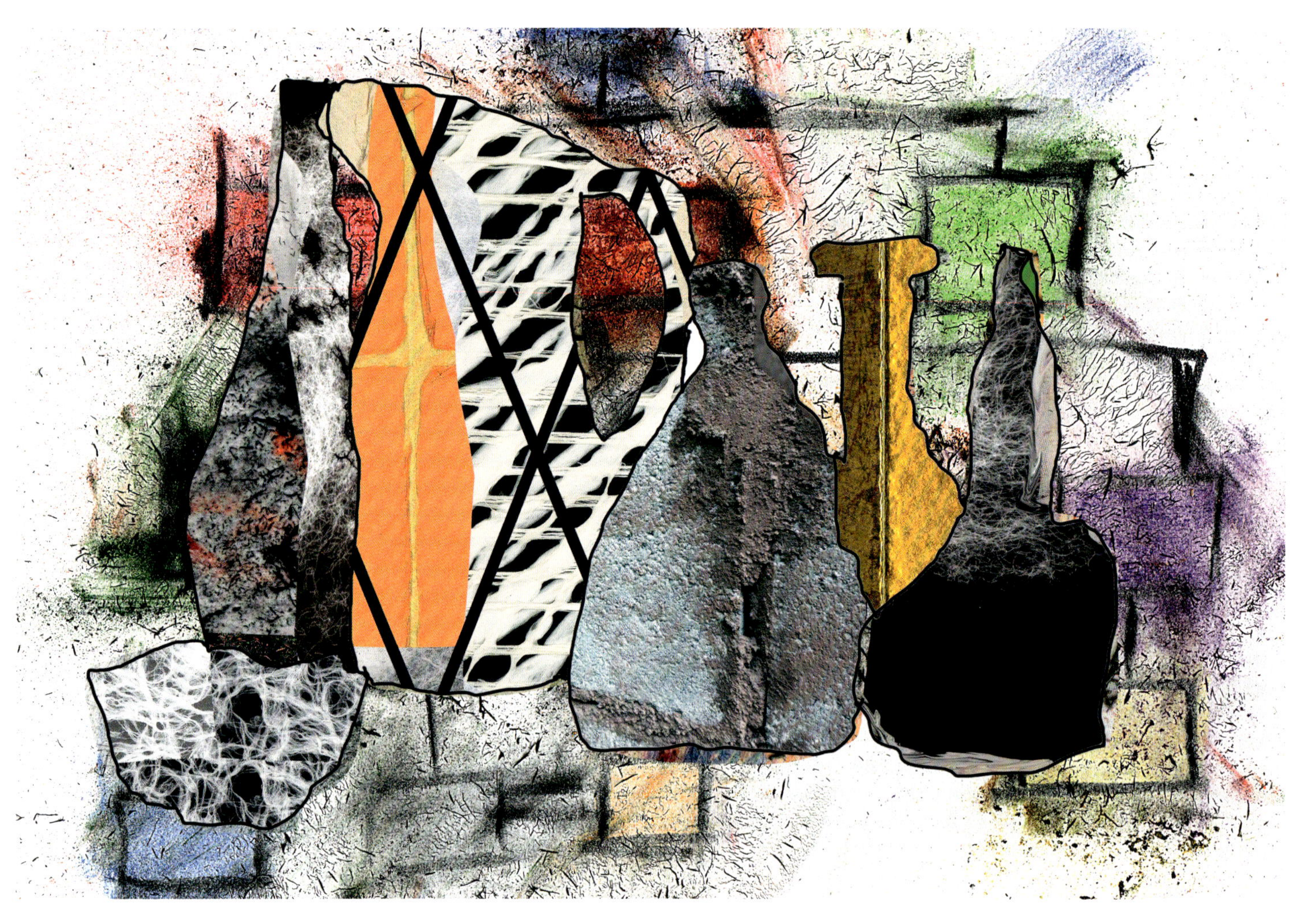

Note

Elements of Chasanoff's vocabulary present here include the diamond (or *X* or harlequin) pattern, cinder block and grout alluding to his experience in construction, erasings, painted cotton, and (likely) Japanese paper.

Plate 112

No. 11827, 2015, digital montage. Morandi (outline) series.
Allan Chasanoff Archive, Yale University Art Gallery

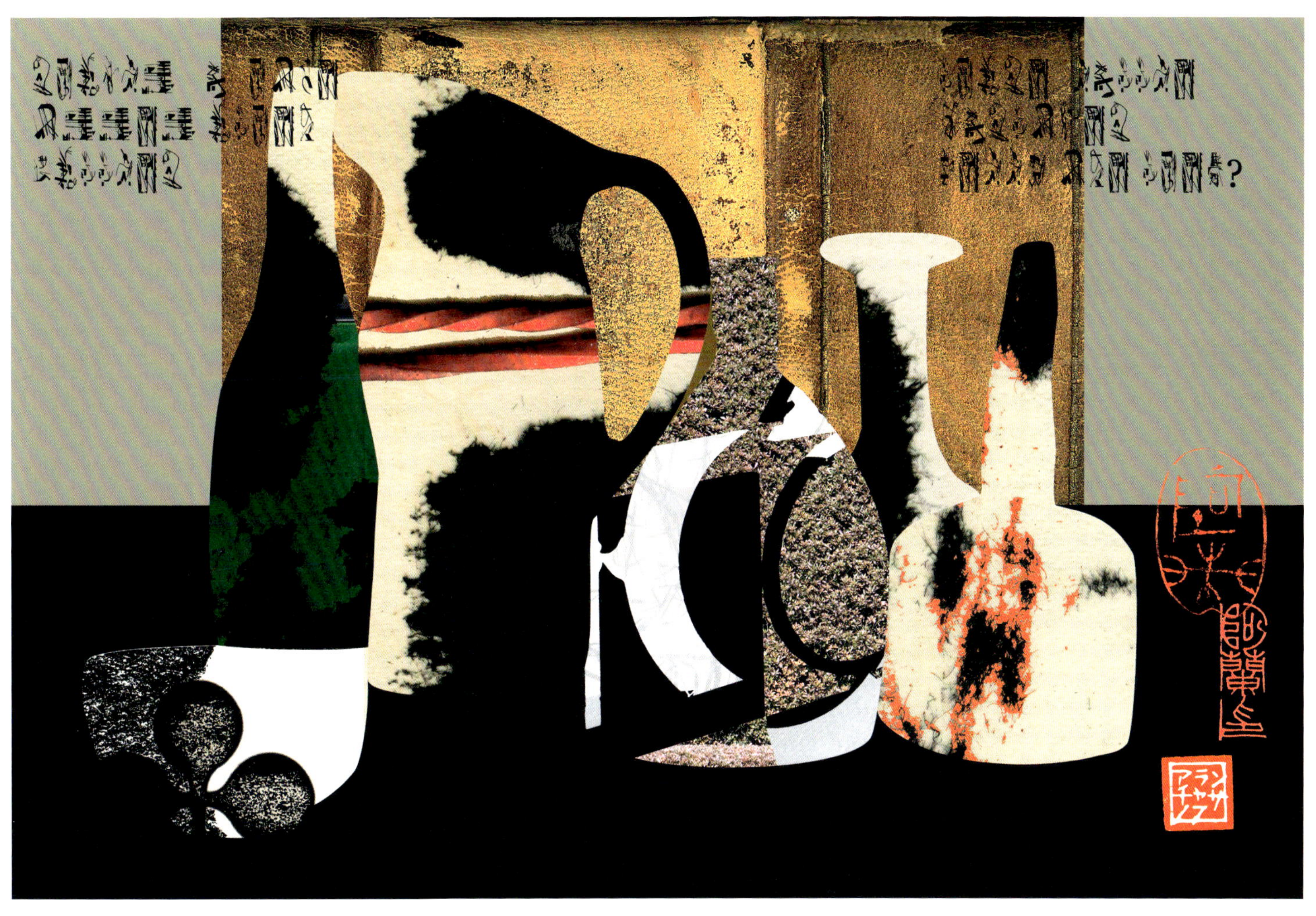

Note

Elements of Chasanoff's vocabulary inside the Morandi outline include rubber band, back of photo, and (partial) barn door. Outside the outline are Japanese seal impressions, most likely a scanned book cover (in golden brown), and his BAPHT font.

Plate 113

No. 11846, 2015, digital montage. Morandi (outline) series.
Allan Chasanoff Archive, Yale University Art Gallery

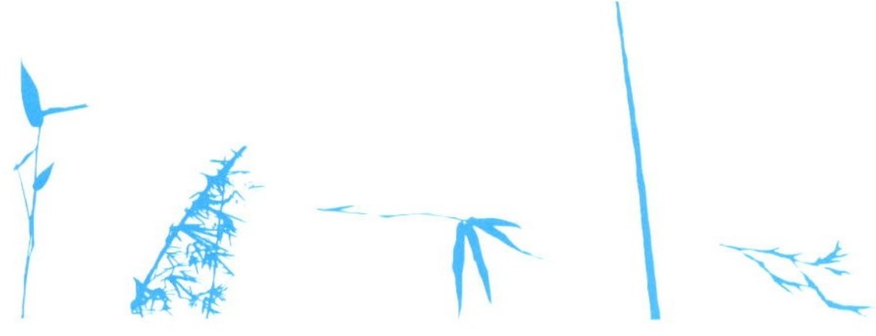

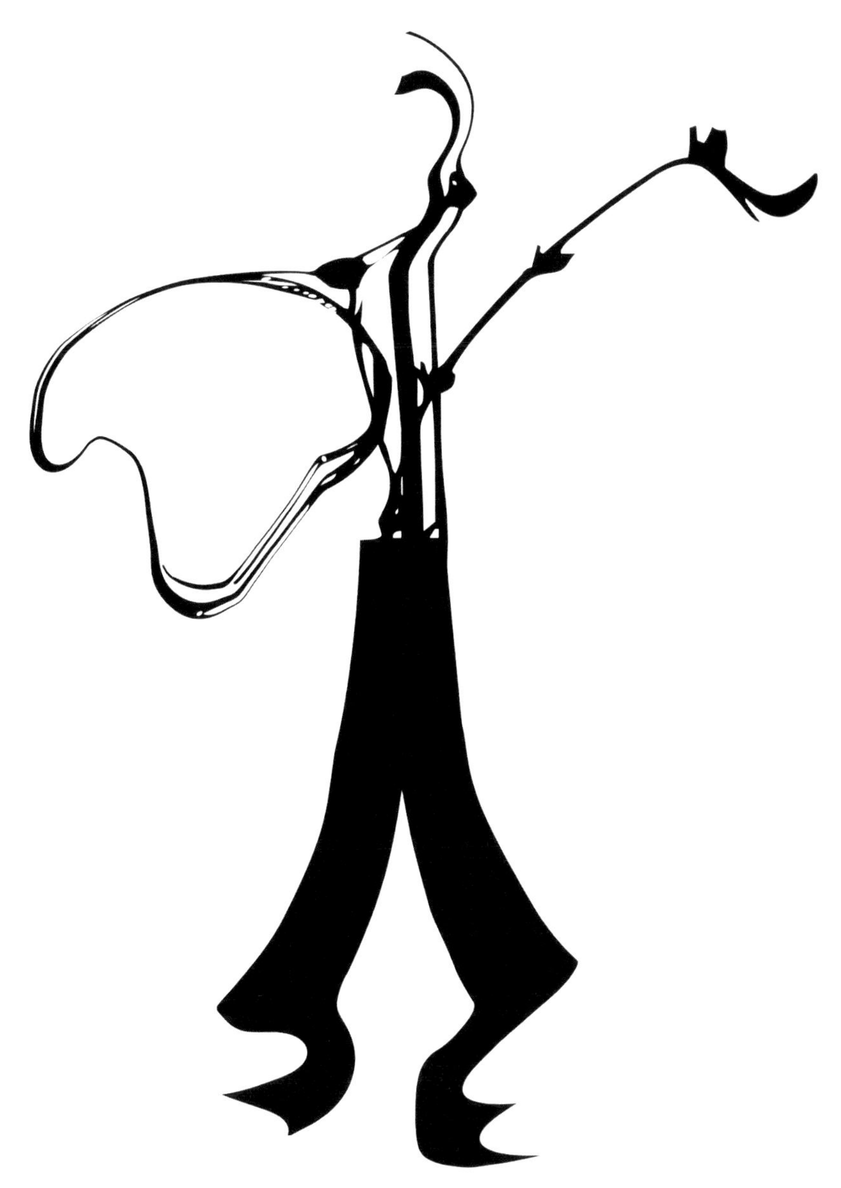

Note
Chasanoff distorted a character from his FBT font using Photoshop tools to create this image.

Plate 114
No. 7511, 2006, digital montage. AC Fonts series.
Allan Chasanoff Archive, Yale University Art Gallery

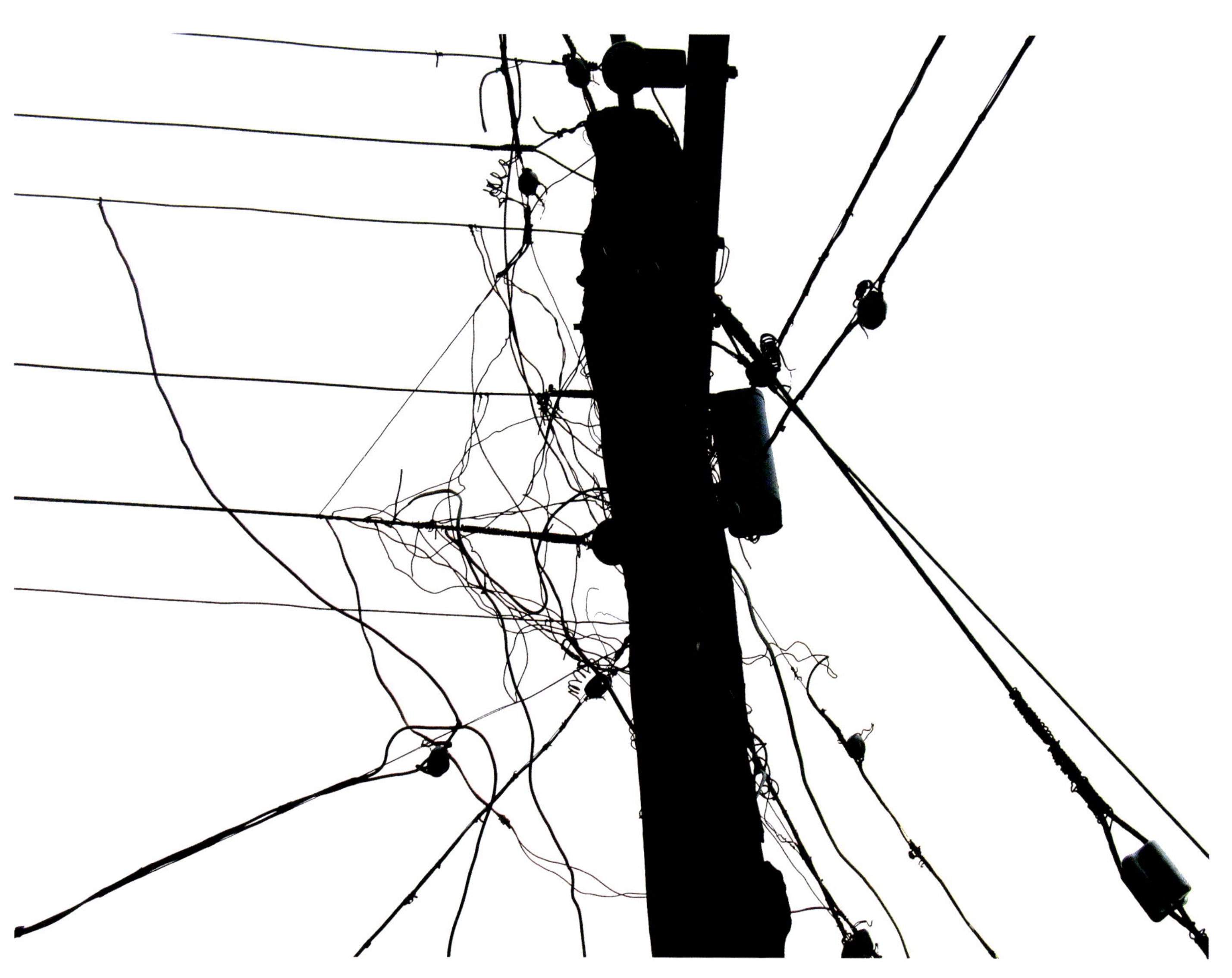

Plate 115
No. 6825, 2005, digital image file.
Allan Chasanoff Archive, Yale University Art Gallery

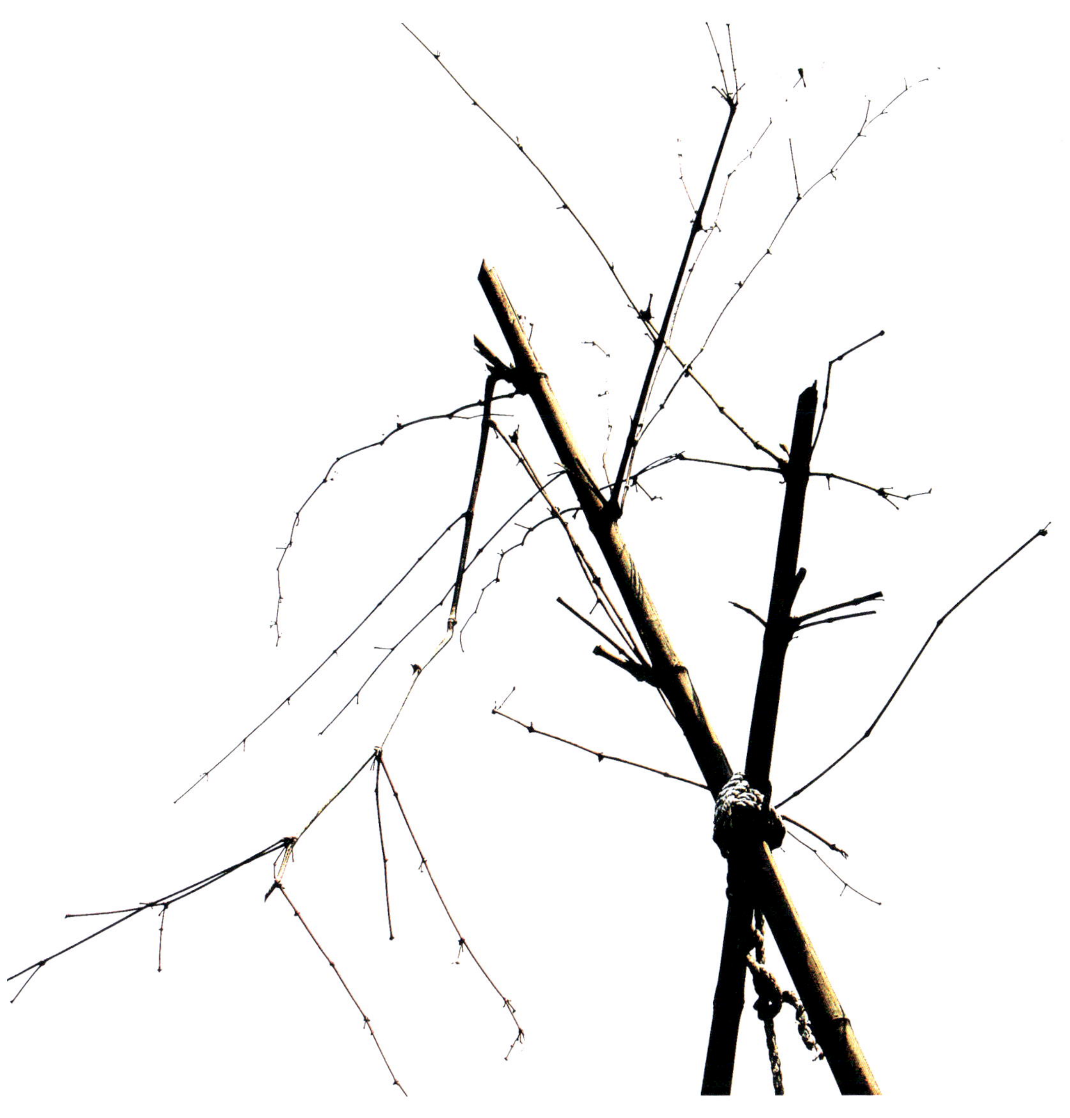

Plate 116
No. 6986, 2005, digital image file.
Allan Chasanoff Archive, Yale University Art Gallery

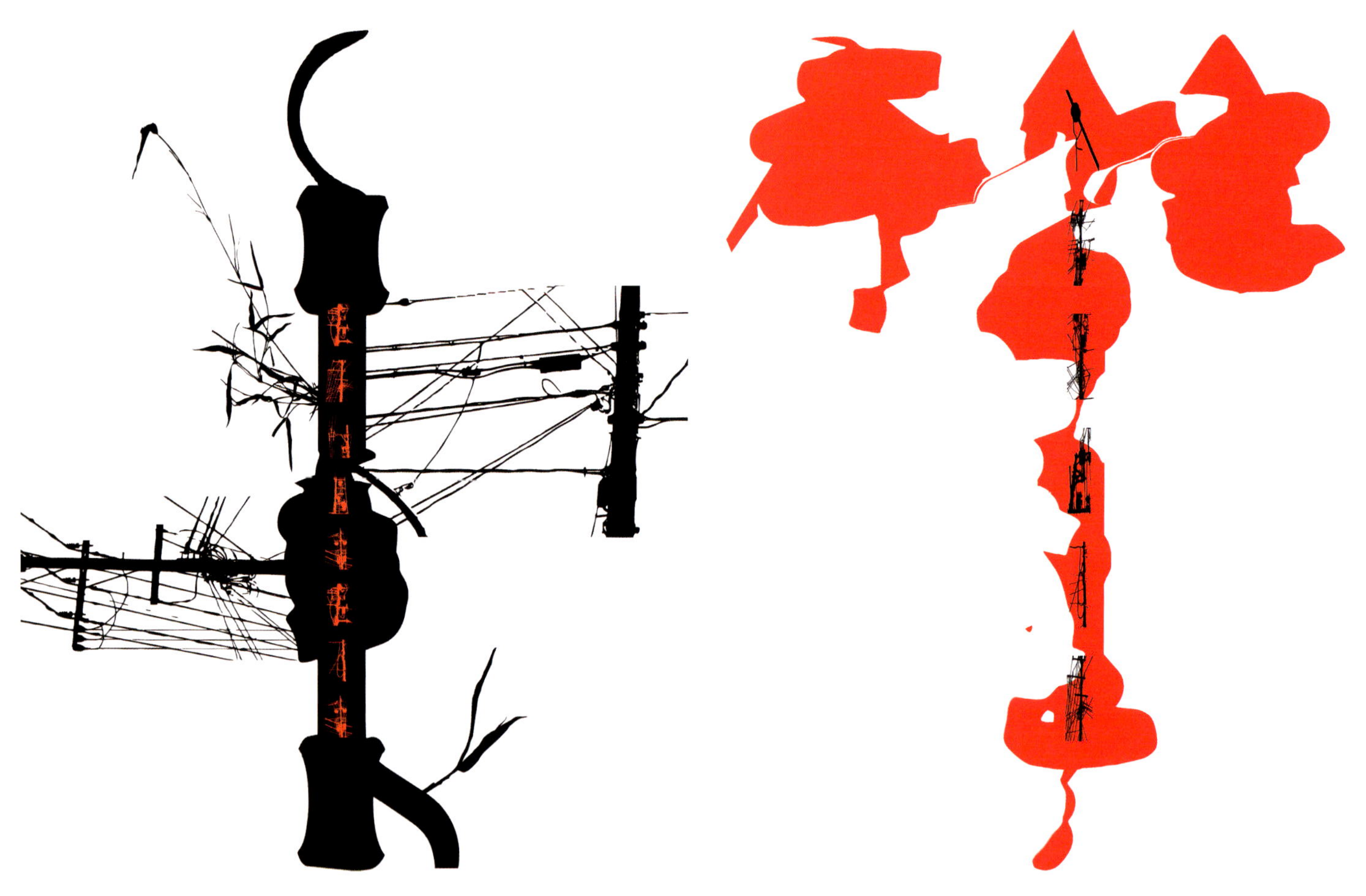

Note

Chasanoff created several fonts from photographs of telephone poles and bamboo. The black shape at left includes characters from his Pole A, Pole B, Bamboo A, and Bamboo B fonts and is superimposed with characters in red from Pole B. The red shape at right is superimposed with characters from Pole A and Pole B.

Plate 117

No. 7492, 2006, digital montage. AC Fonts series.
Allan Chasanoff Archive, Yale University Art Gallery

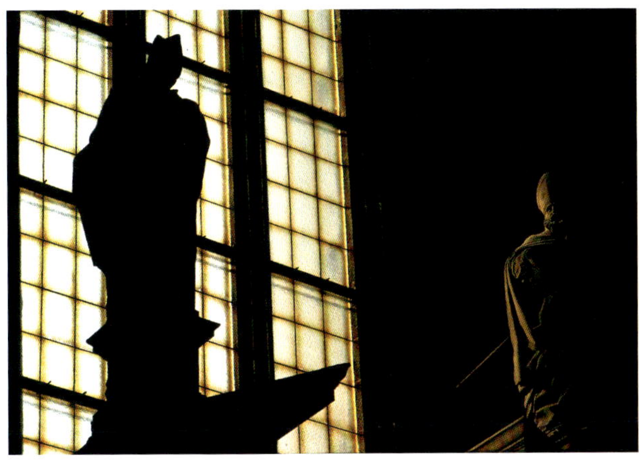

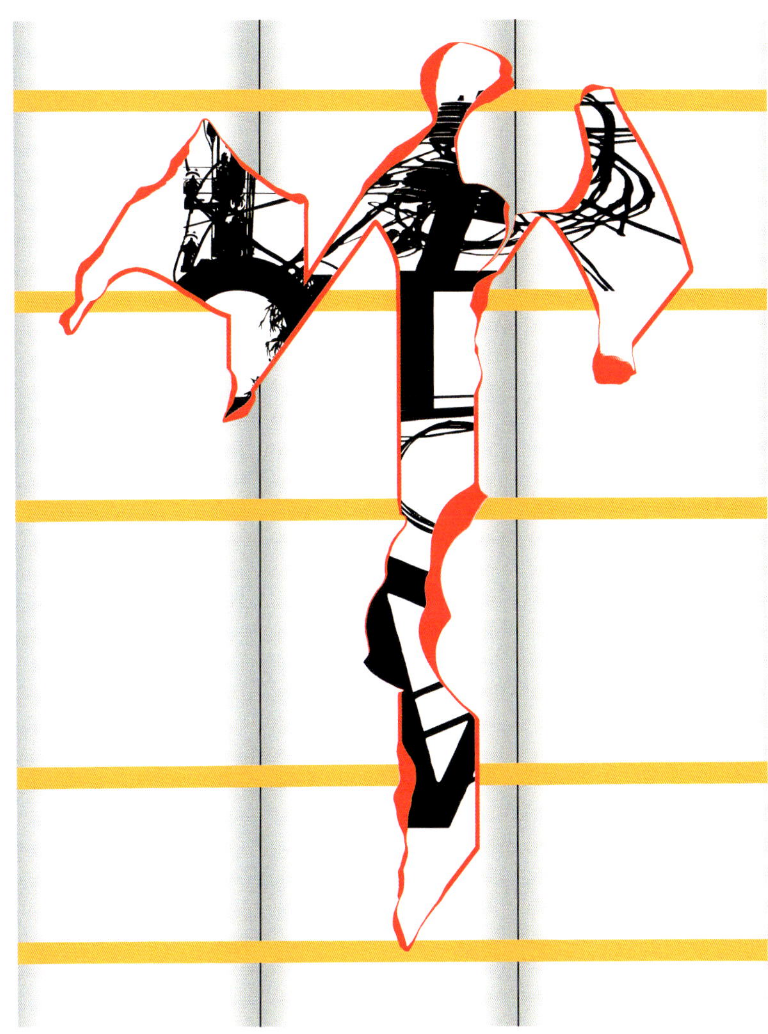

Note

187 The central figure in plate 119, which Chasanoff associated with the Devil, a bat, or Dracula, is likely a font character, distorted and outlined in Photoshop. Inside, a character from the font Pole A and fragments of other fonts can be identified. Plate 118 shows two statues, one silhouetted against a grid, in a photograph made more than thirty years earlier. It is tempting to imagine these elements merged or rearranged to make an image similar to plate 119.

Plate 118
No. 2621, 1974, silver dye-bleach print.
Allan Chasanoff Archive, Yale University Art Gallery

Plate 119
No. 7494, 2006, digital montage. AC Fonts series.
Allan Chasanoff Archive, Yale University Art Gallery

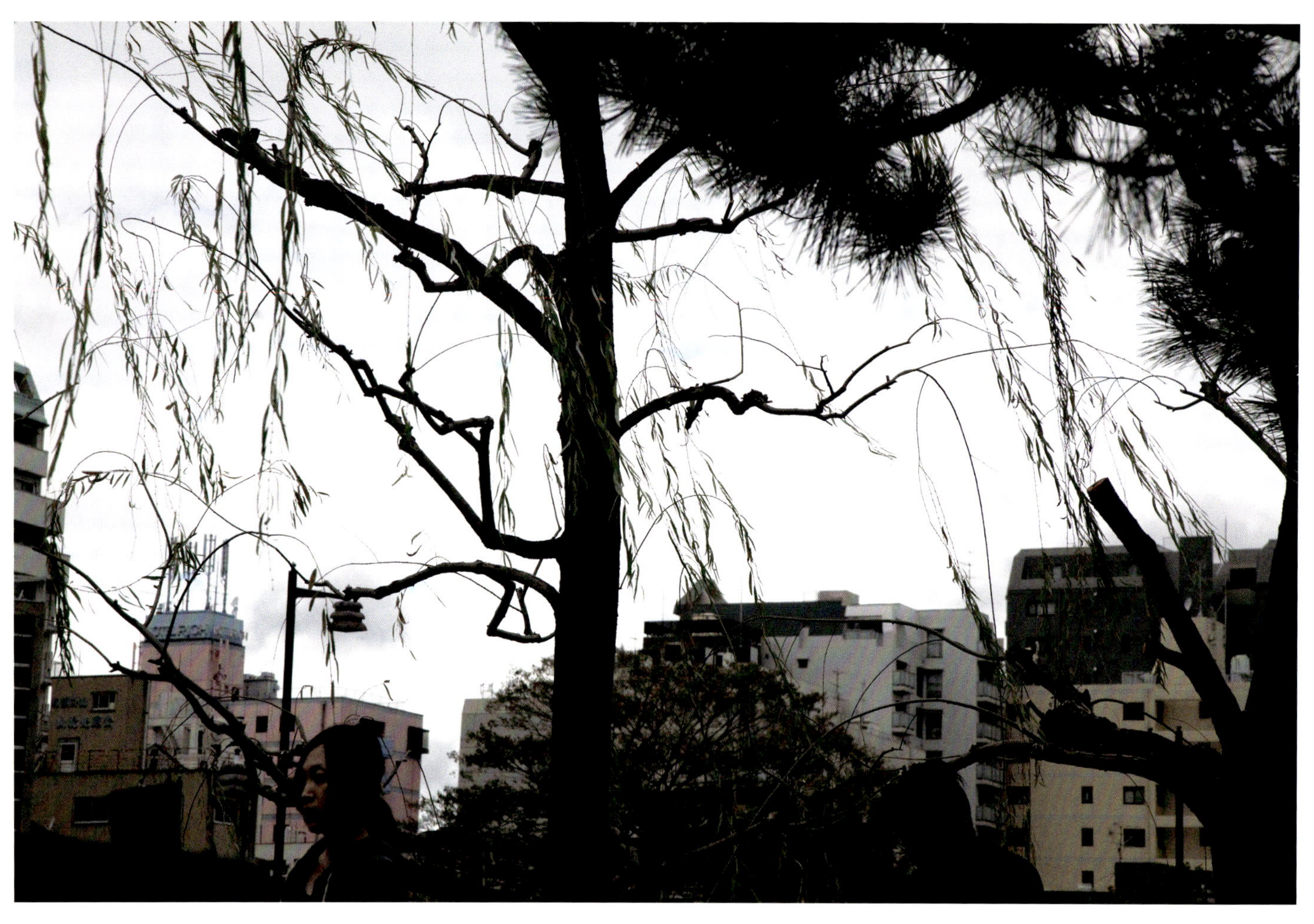

Plate 120
No. 10572, 2009, digital image file.
Allan Chasanoff Archive, Yale University Art Gallery

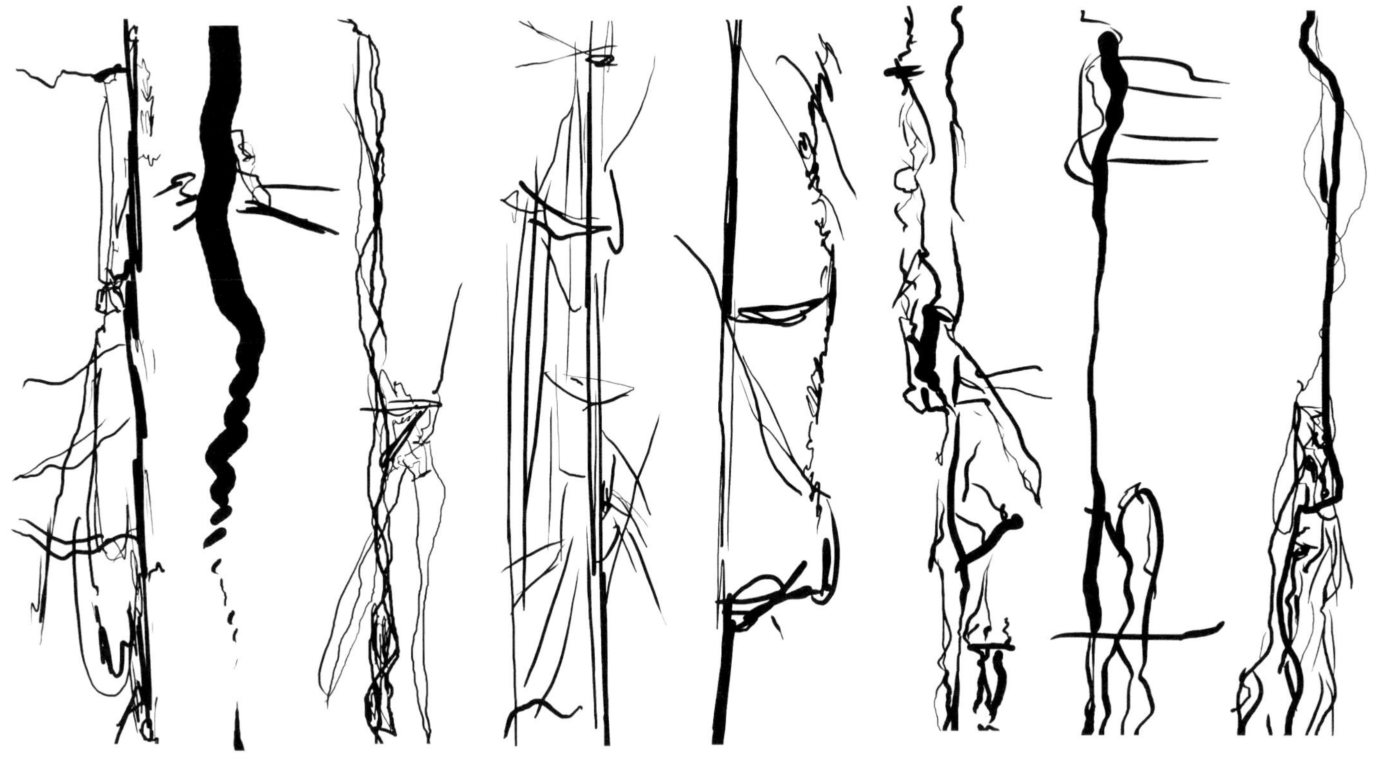

Note

These characters from Chasanoff's Tpolesum font—created from his images of telephone poles—spell "DFBECIGH," a nonsense word. Their similarity to the branches in plate 120 may be seen as ironic, given our tendency to visualize nature and technology in contrasting ways.

Plate 121

No. 7514, 2006, digital montage. AC Fonts series.
Allan Chasanoff Archive, Yale University Art Gallery

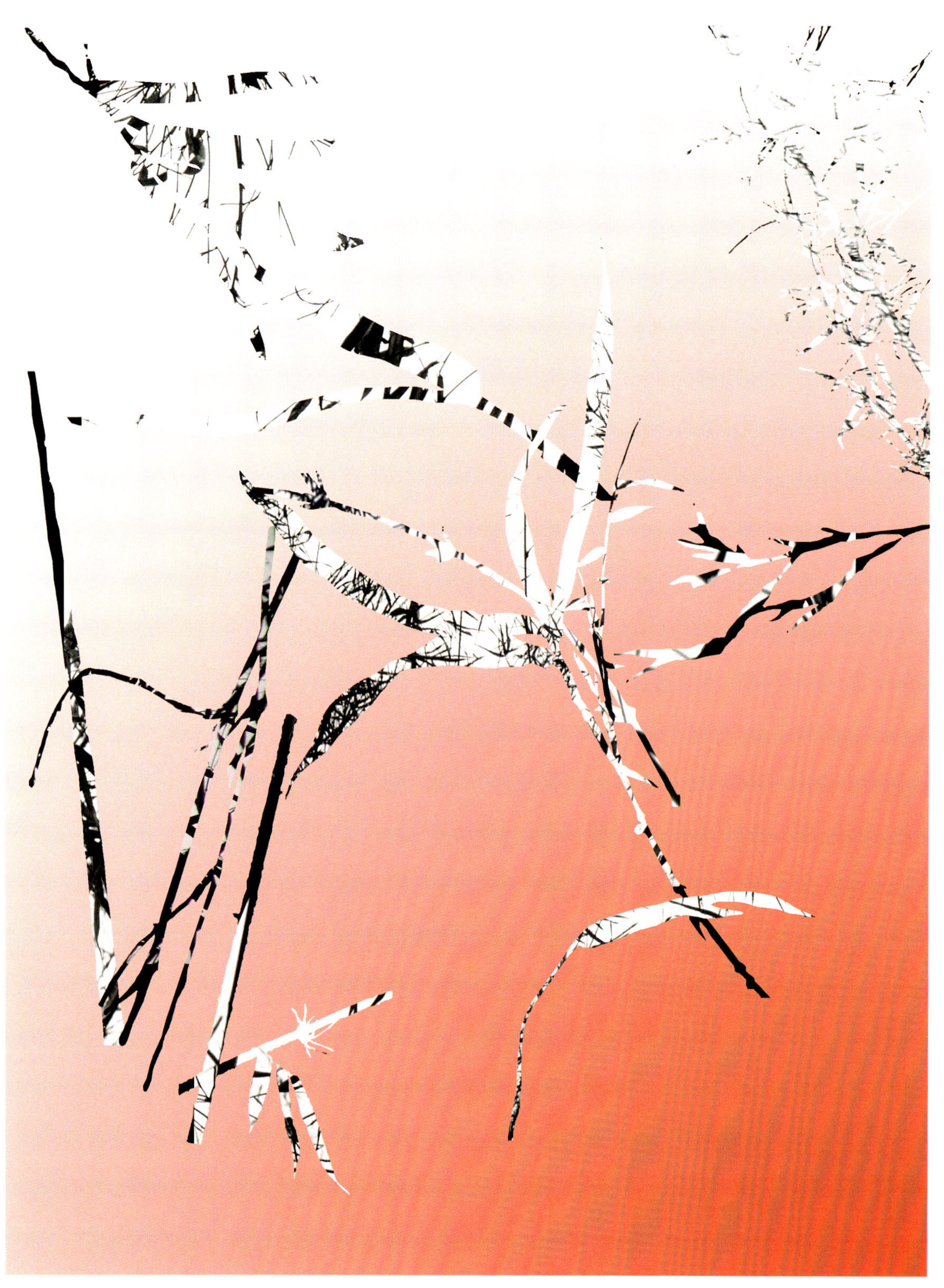

Note
Characters from Chasanoff's Bamboo A and Bamboo B fonts are silhouetted and filled with his photographs of bamboo—placing inside the font its referent, he explained.

Plate 122
No. 7497, 2006, digital montage. AC Fonts series.
Allan Chasanoff Archive, Yale University Art Gallery

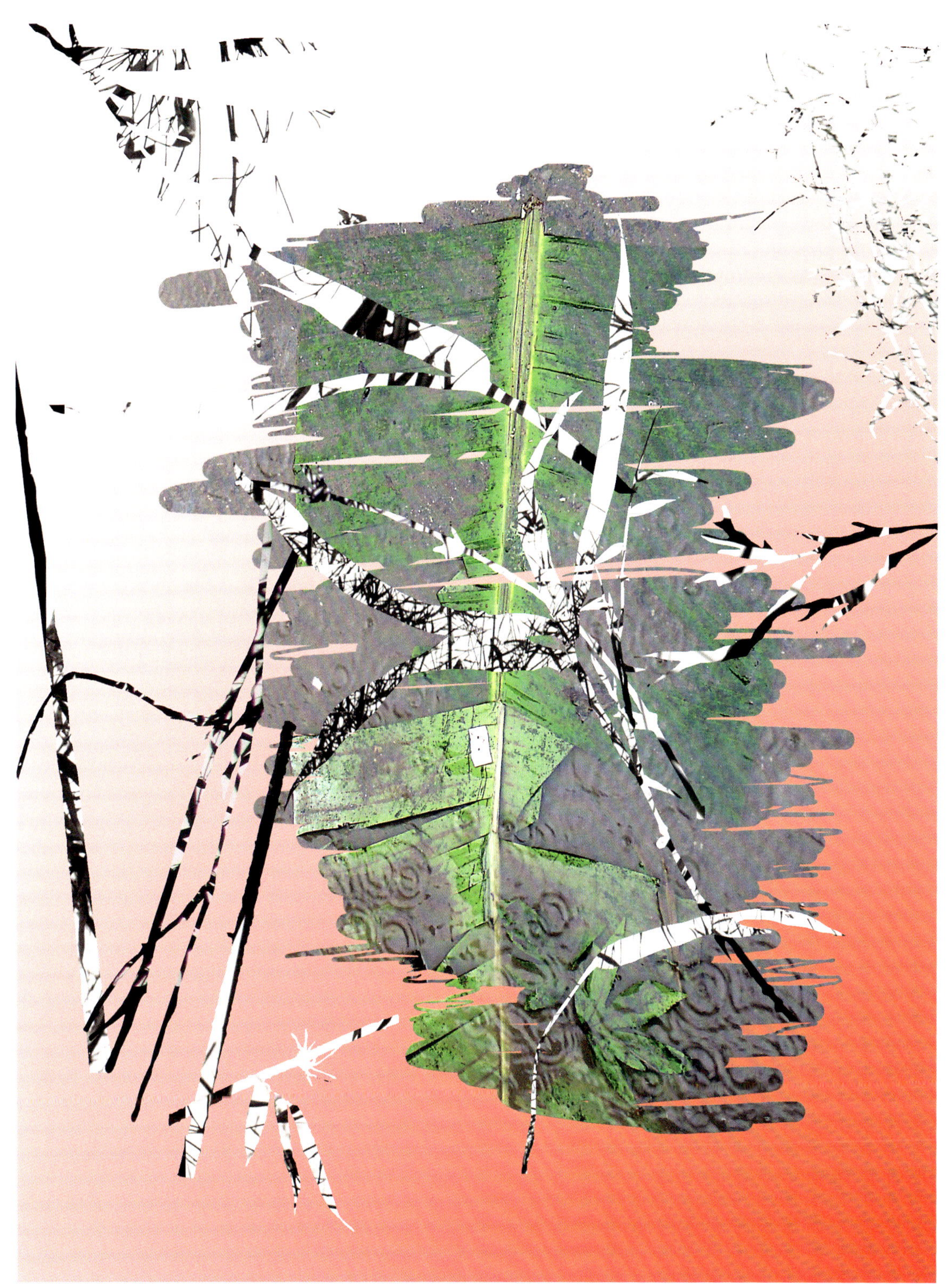

Note

The configuration in plate 122 is here placed against blended elements, including green leaves, that are digitally scraped back.

Plate 123

No 7505, 2006, digital montage. AC Fonts series.
Allan Chasanoff Archive, Yale University Art Gallery

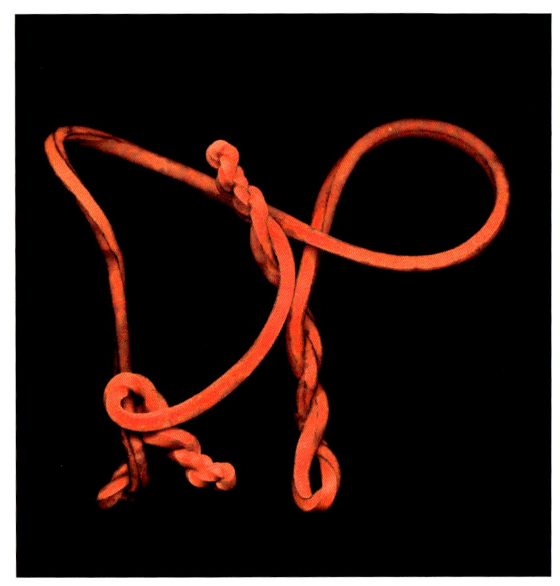

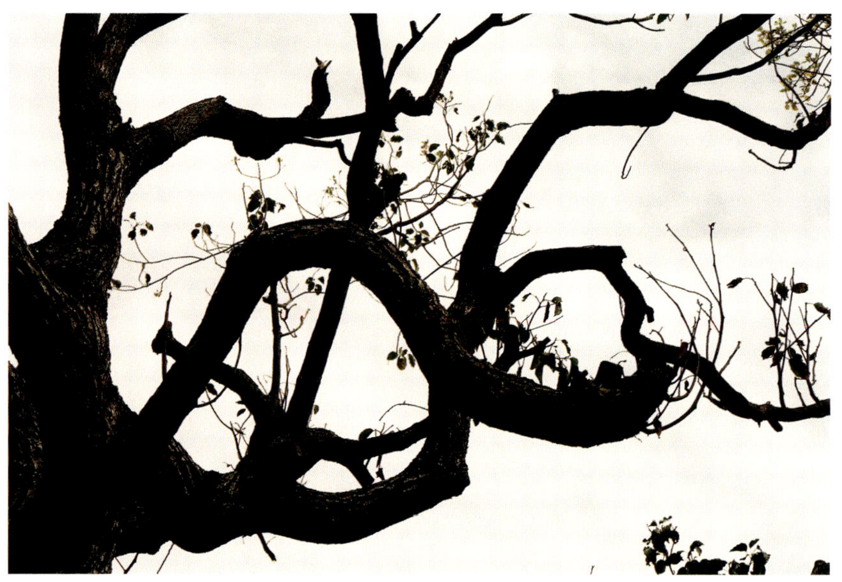

Plate 124
No. 4897, 2000, digital scan. Rubber Band series.
Allan Chasanoff Archive, Yale University Art Gallery

Plate 125
No. 7729, 2007, digital image file.
Allan Chasanoff Archive, Yale University Art Gallery

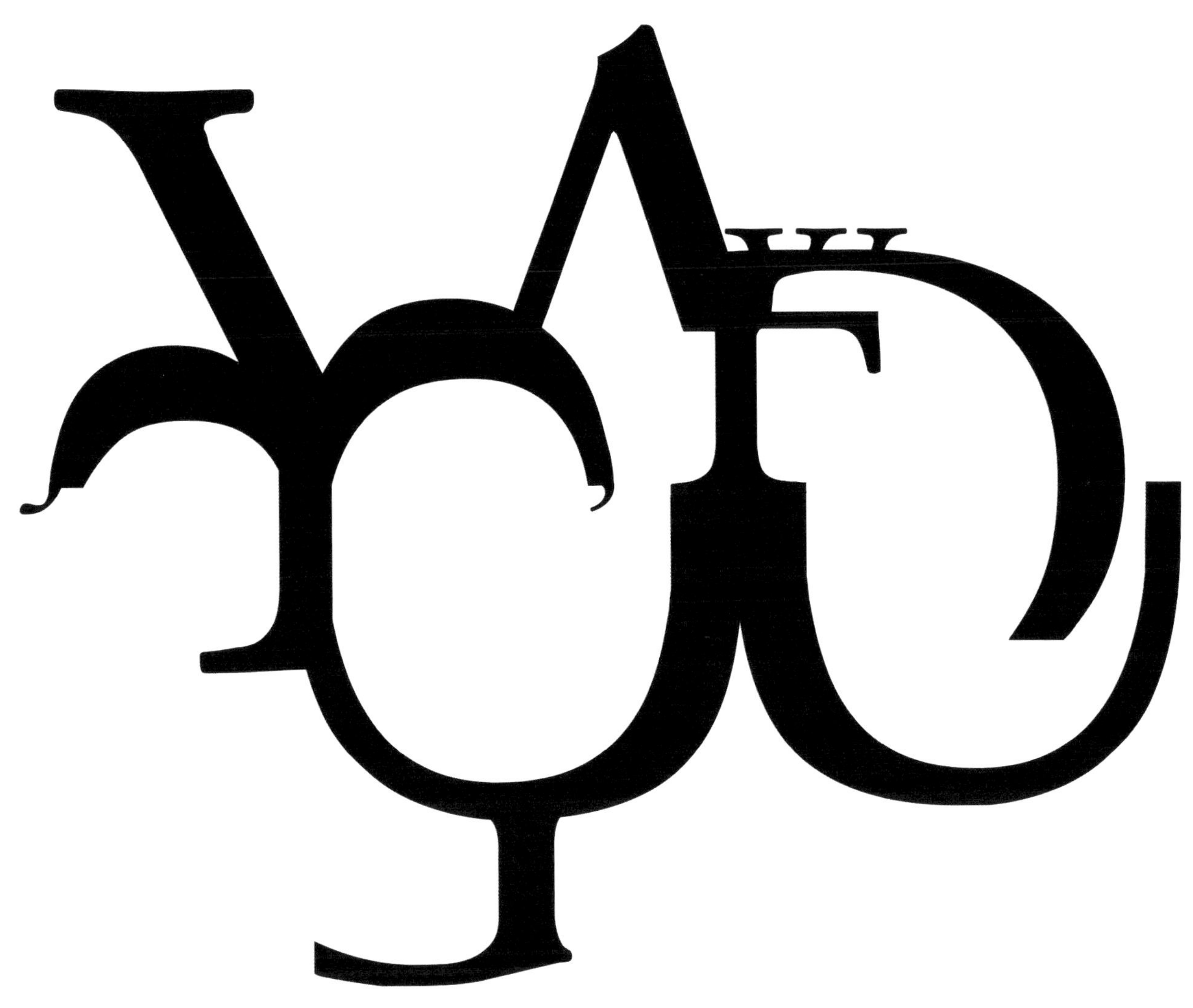

Plate 126
No. 6409, 2005, pigmented inkjet print (from digital montage). Fonts series.
Allan Chasanoff Archive, Yale University Art Gallery

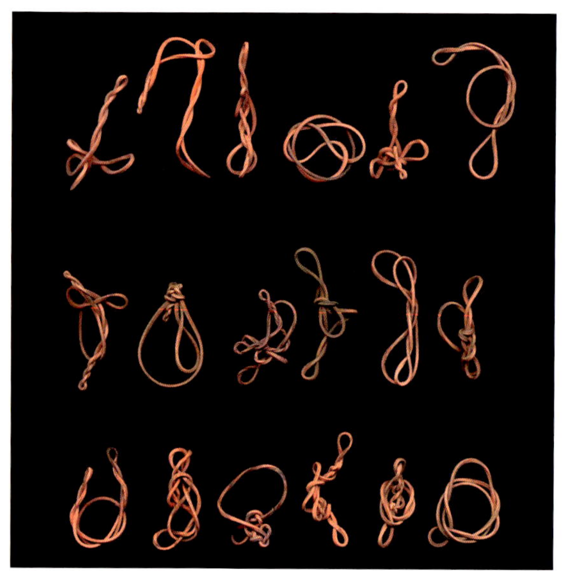

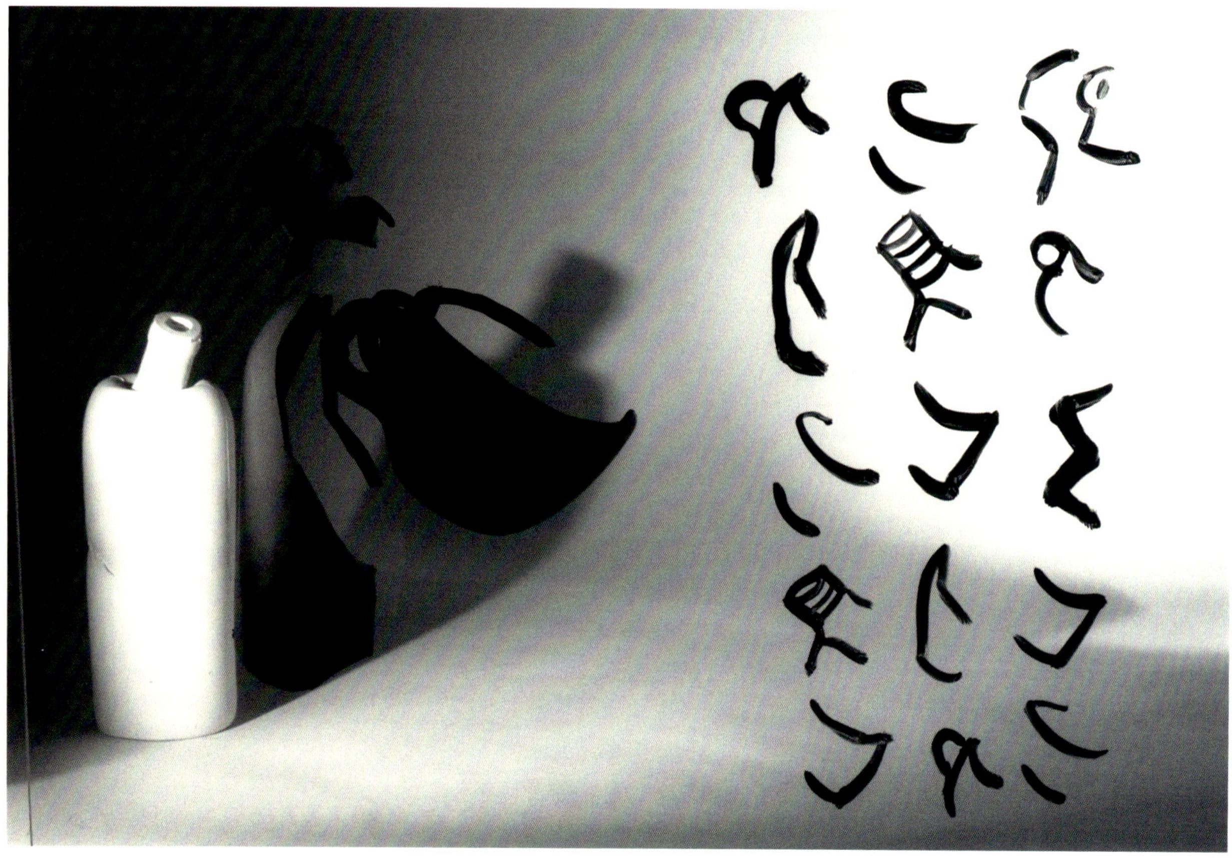

Note
A single scan of eighteen rubber bands produced the image in plate 127; compare plate 134.

Plate 127
No. 4935, 2000, digital scan. Rubber Band series.
Allan Chasanoff Archive, Yale University Art Gallery

Plate 128
No. 1521, 1986, black-and-white negative.
Allan Chasanoff Archive, Yale University Art Gallery

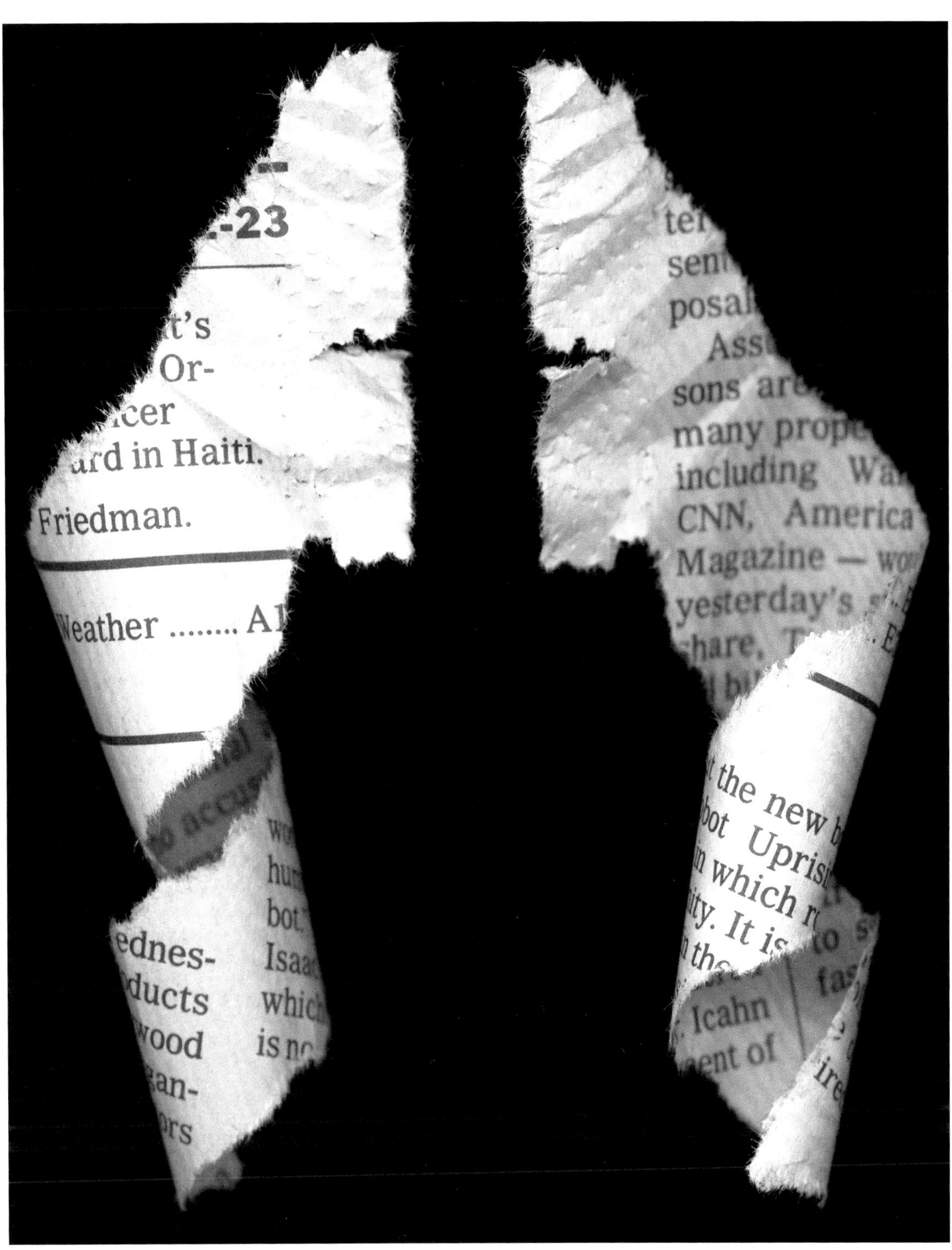

Note
Scans of two sides of the same piece of newspaper are combined here. The tears can be seen as mouths, giving us text and speech in one image, while the negative space forms a bottle.

Plate 129
No. 7291, 2006, digital montage.
Allan Chasanoff Archive, Yale University Art Gallery

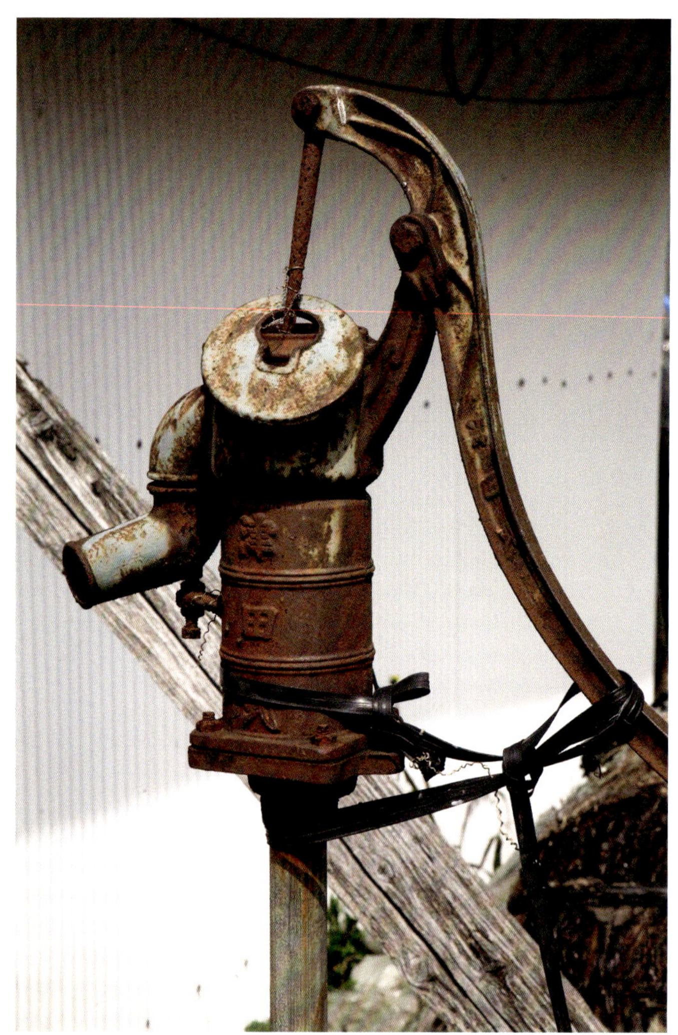

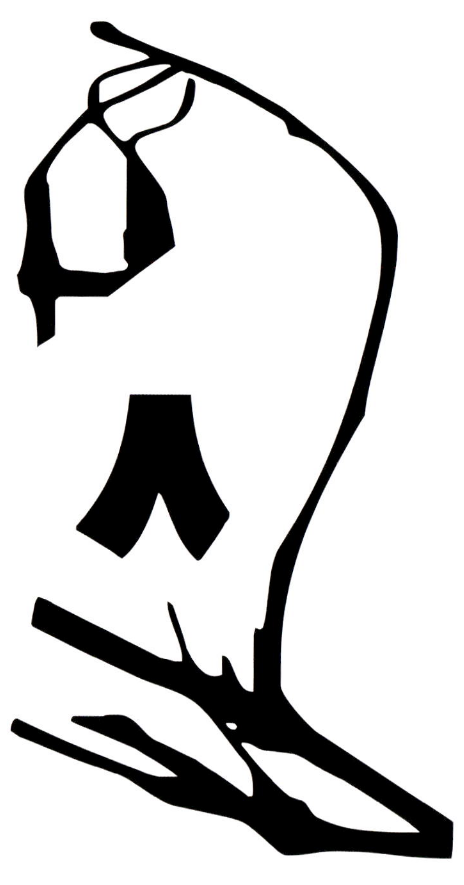

Note

The character in plate 131, from Chasanoff's BAPHT font, stands for the letter *S*. It happens to echo the lines of the pump in plate 130. The formal coincidence suggests a potential slip or expansion of the character's meaning beyond its phonic referent and pictorial components (bamboo, telephone poles). See also plate 132, top right.

Plate 130

No. 8239, 2008, digital image file.

Allan Chasanoff Archive, Yale University Art Gallery

Plate 131

No. 11271, 2009, font.

Allan Chasanoff Archive, Yale University Art Gallery

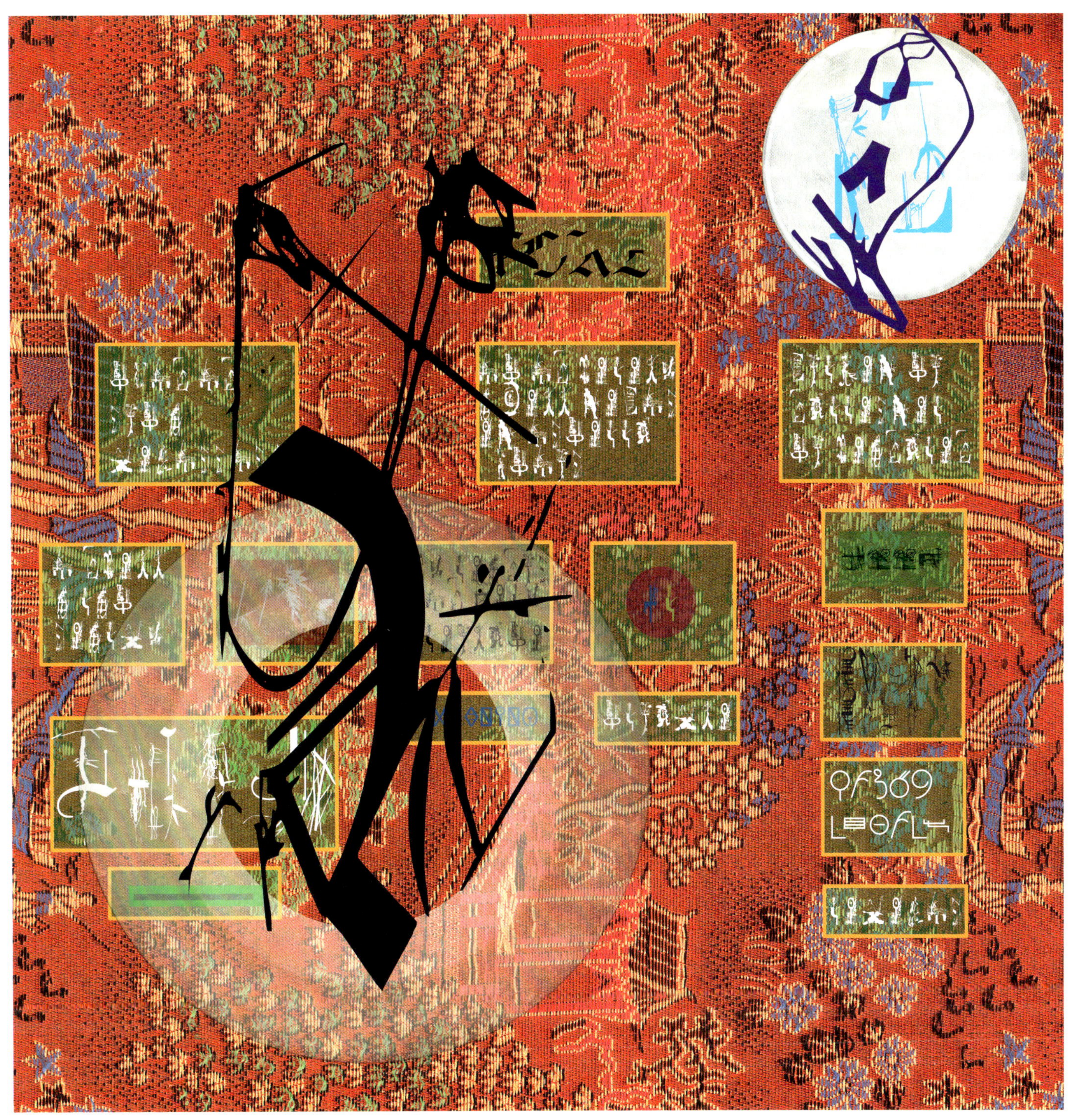

Note
Chasanoff used several of his fonts here: AMF, Bamboo A, BAPHT, FBT, Font 6, Half Notre Dame, Origin, and Tpole-etc.

Plate 132
No. 7464, 2006, digital montage. Competition-Hierarchy series.
Allan Chasanoff Archive, Yale University Art Gallery

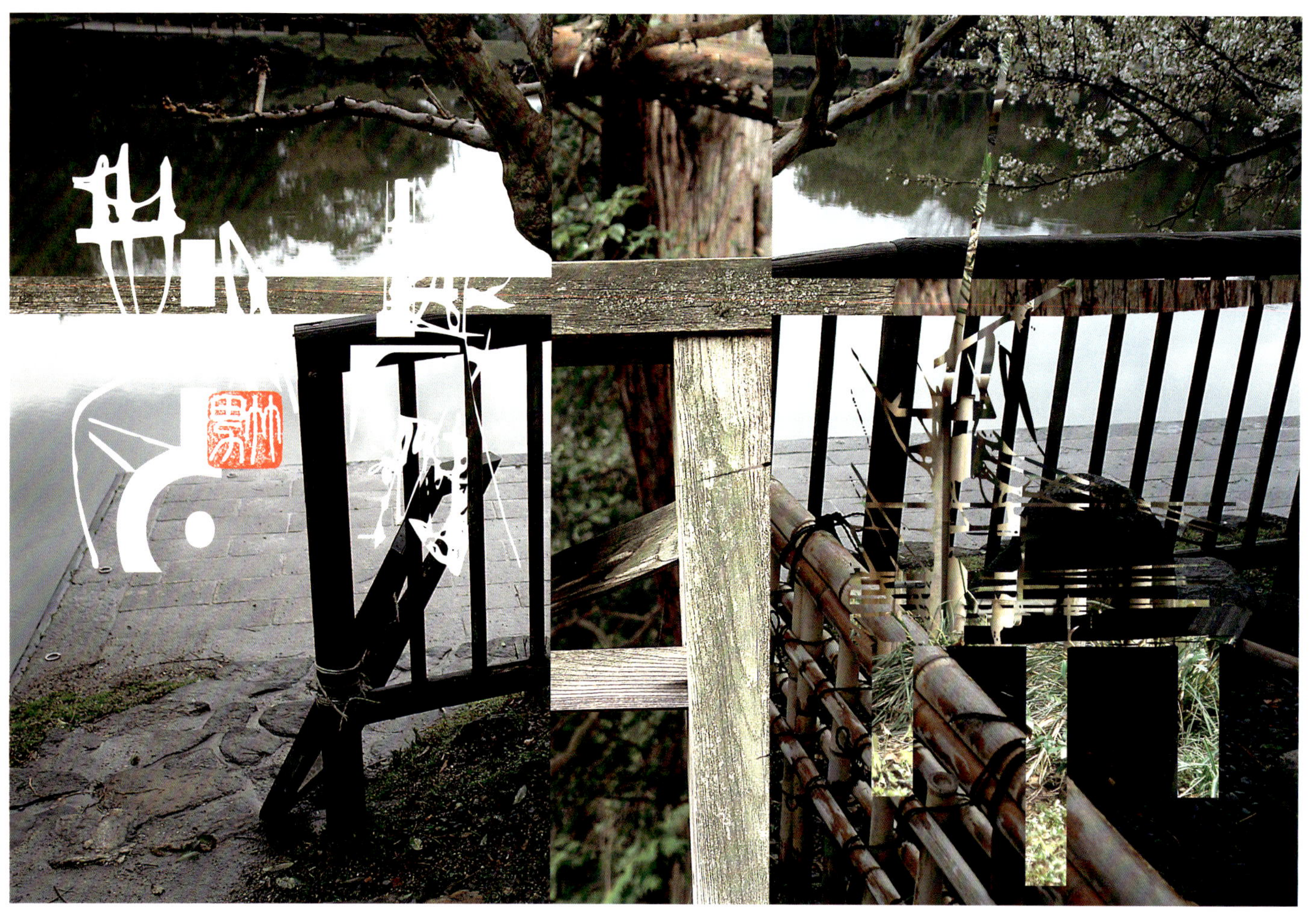

Note

Two characters from Chasanoff's BAPHT font appear at left in white, along with his Bamboo Boy seal in red. At right a character from his FBT font is filled with a photograph.

Plate 133

No. 7476, 2006, digital montage. AC Fonts, 2006 Asia Trip series.
Allan Chasanoff Archive, Yale University Art Gallery

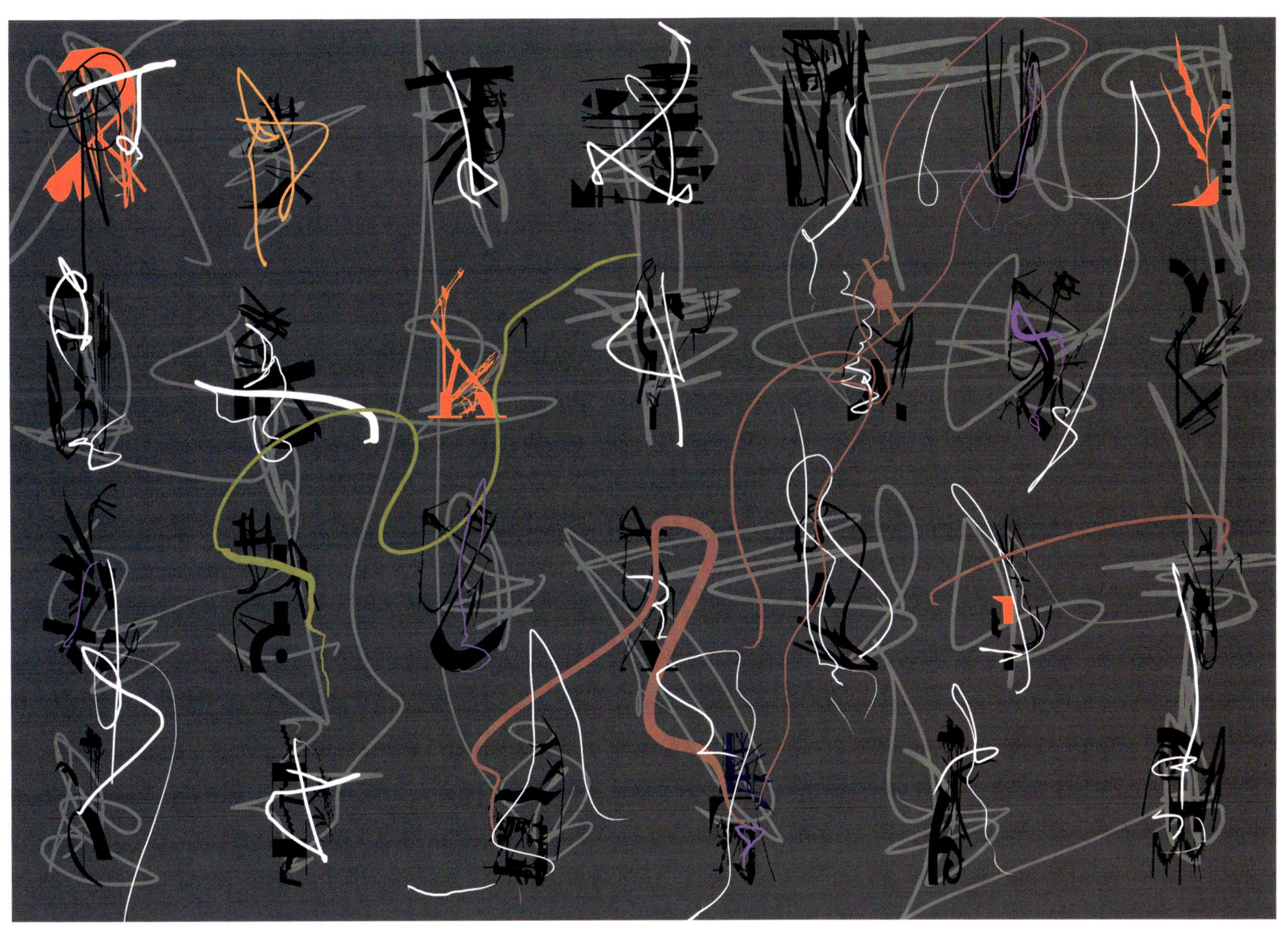

Note
Characters from Chasanoff's BAPHT font are here layered between drawn, or scribbled, lines.

Plate 134
No. 7532, 2006, digital montage. AC Fonts series.
Allan Chasanoff Archive, Yale University Art Gallery

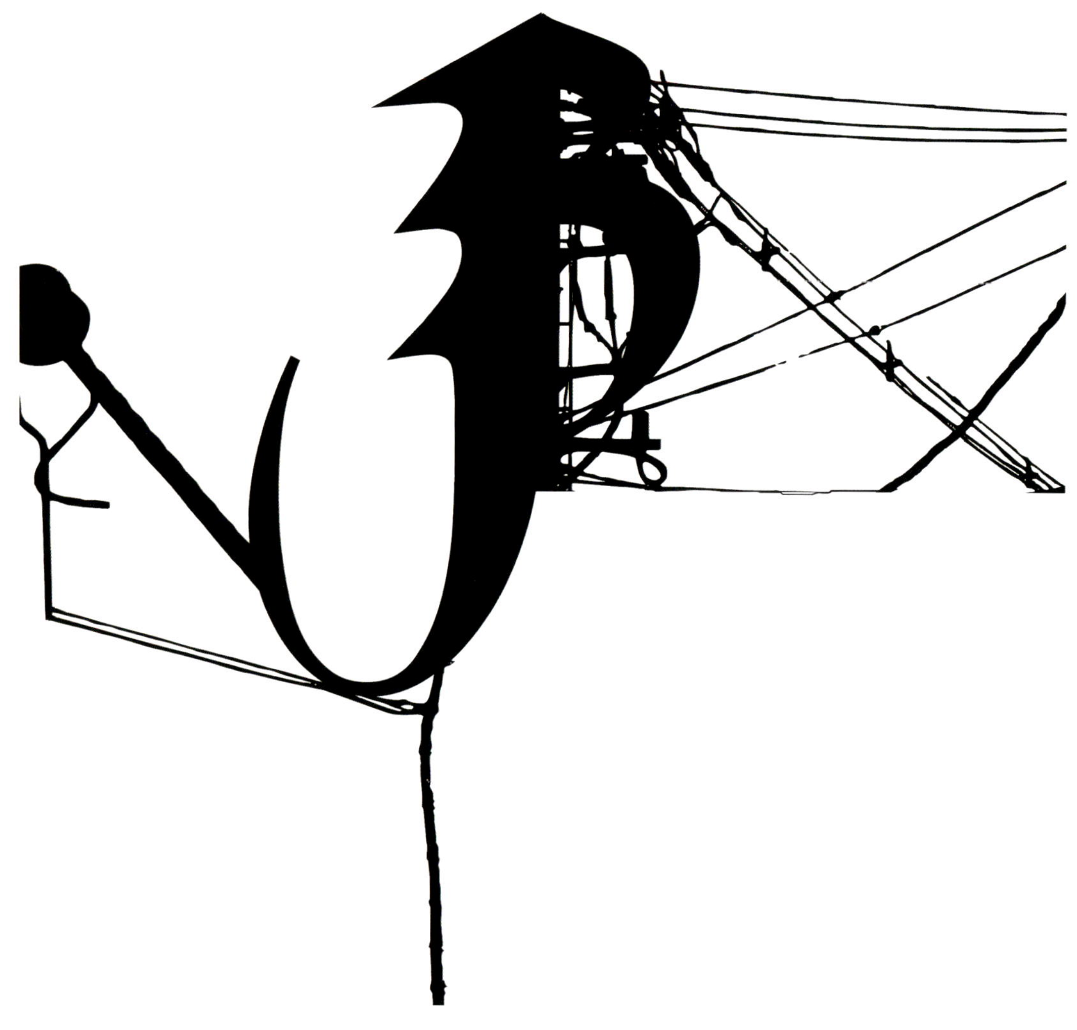

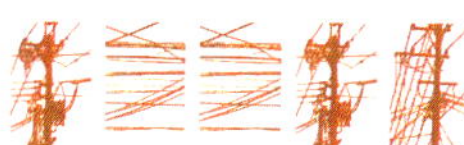

Note
Chasanoff layered font characters in plates 135 and 136 to achieve a form of pictorial writing, similar to hieroglyphics (pl. 135 fonts: Half Notre Dame, Pole A, and Pole B; pl. 136 fonts: AMF, BAPHT, FBT, and Pole A).

Plate 135
No. 7517, 2006, digital montage. AC Fonts series.
Allan Chasanoff Archive, Yale University Art Gallery

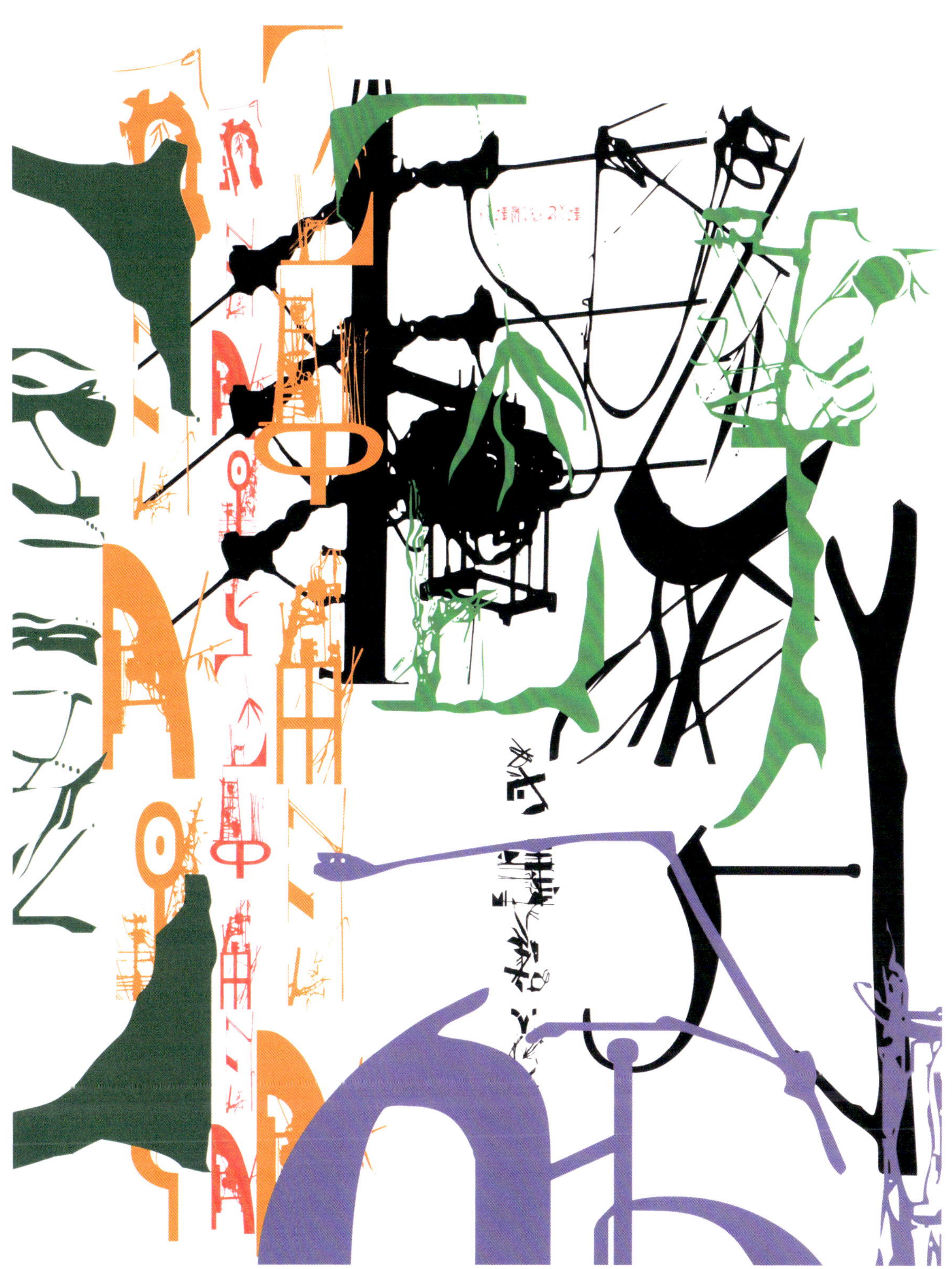

Plate 136
No. 7523, 2006, pigmented inkjet print (from digital montage). AC Fonts series.
Allan Chasanoff Archive, Yale University Art Gallery

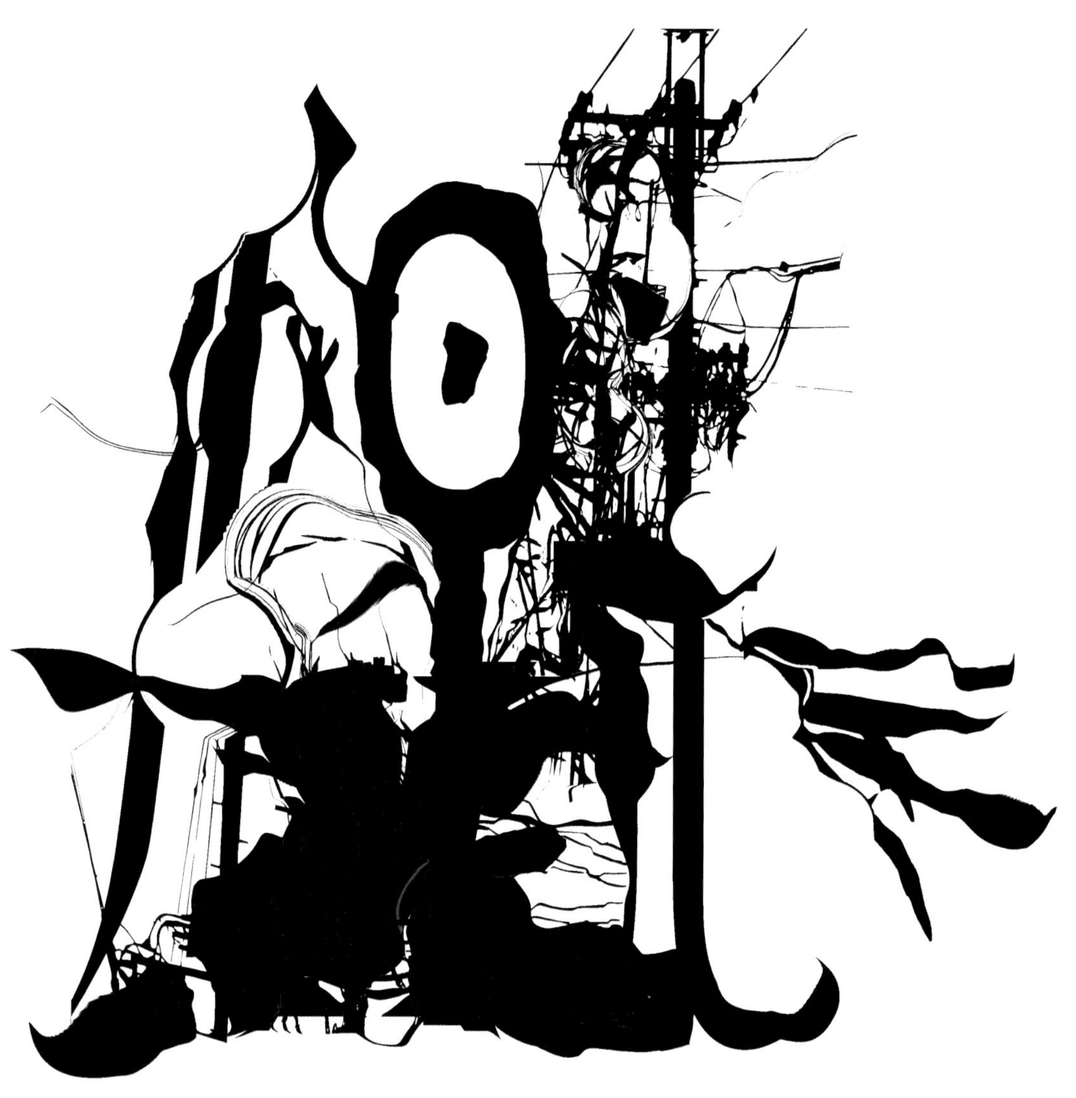

Note

The characters combined in this montage are from Chasanoff's FBT font, italics version.

Plate 137

No. 7515, 2006, digital montage. AC Fonts series.
Allan Chasanoff Archive, Yale University Art Gallery

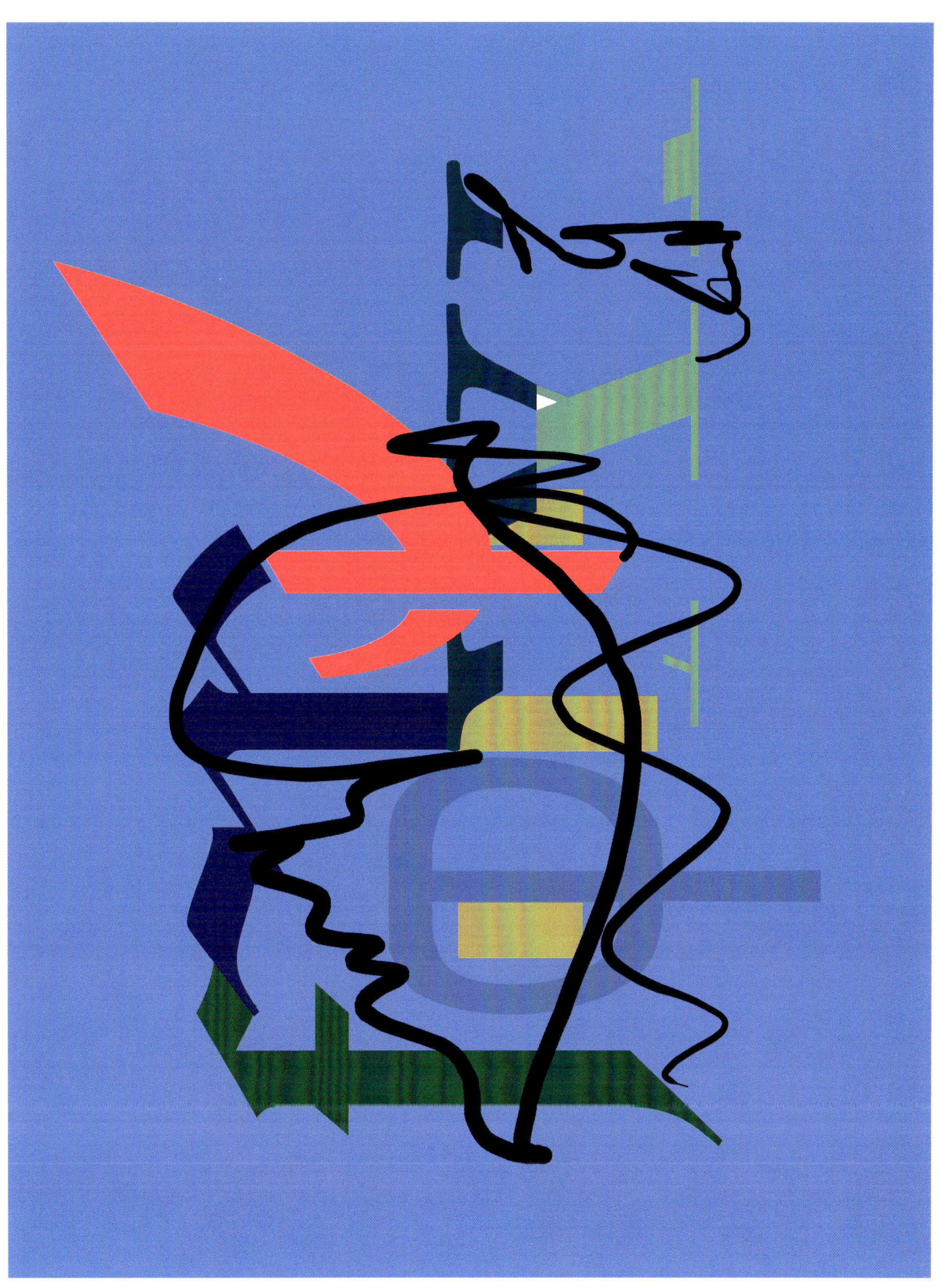

Note
Here characters from Chasanoff's Font 6, Half Bauhaus, Half Didot, and Half Notre Dame fonts are rotated and superimposed by drawn or scribbled lines.

Plate 138
No. 7506, 2006, digital montage. AC Fonts series.
Allan Chasanoff Archive, Yale University Art Gallery

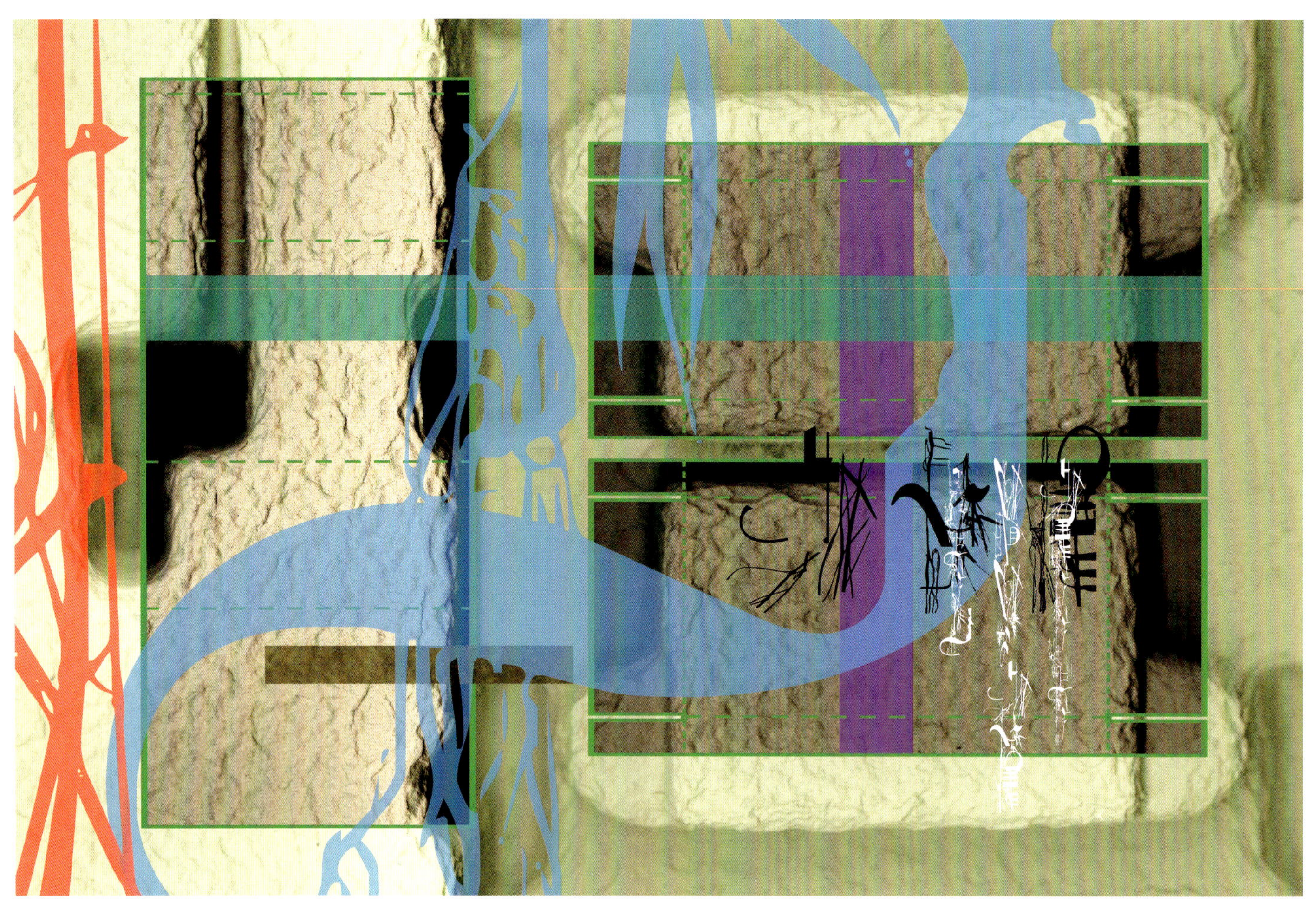

Note

The characters included here are all from Chasanoff's AMF font. He commented, "It's a war between the font and the box. We can almost say, Is it a war [of] consumer capitalism? Of product versus speech? If I can't speak, I'm gonna buy, which is a passive sort of a thing. . . . This [image] is definitely completely being dominated by speech."

Plate 139

No. 7405, 2006, digital montage. Box (outline) series.
Allan Chasanoff Archive, Yale University Art Gallery

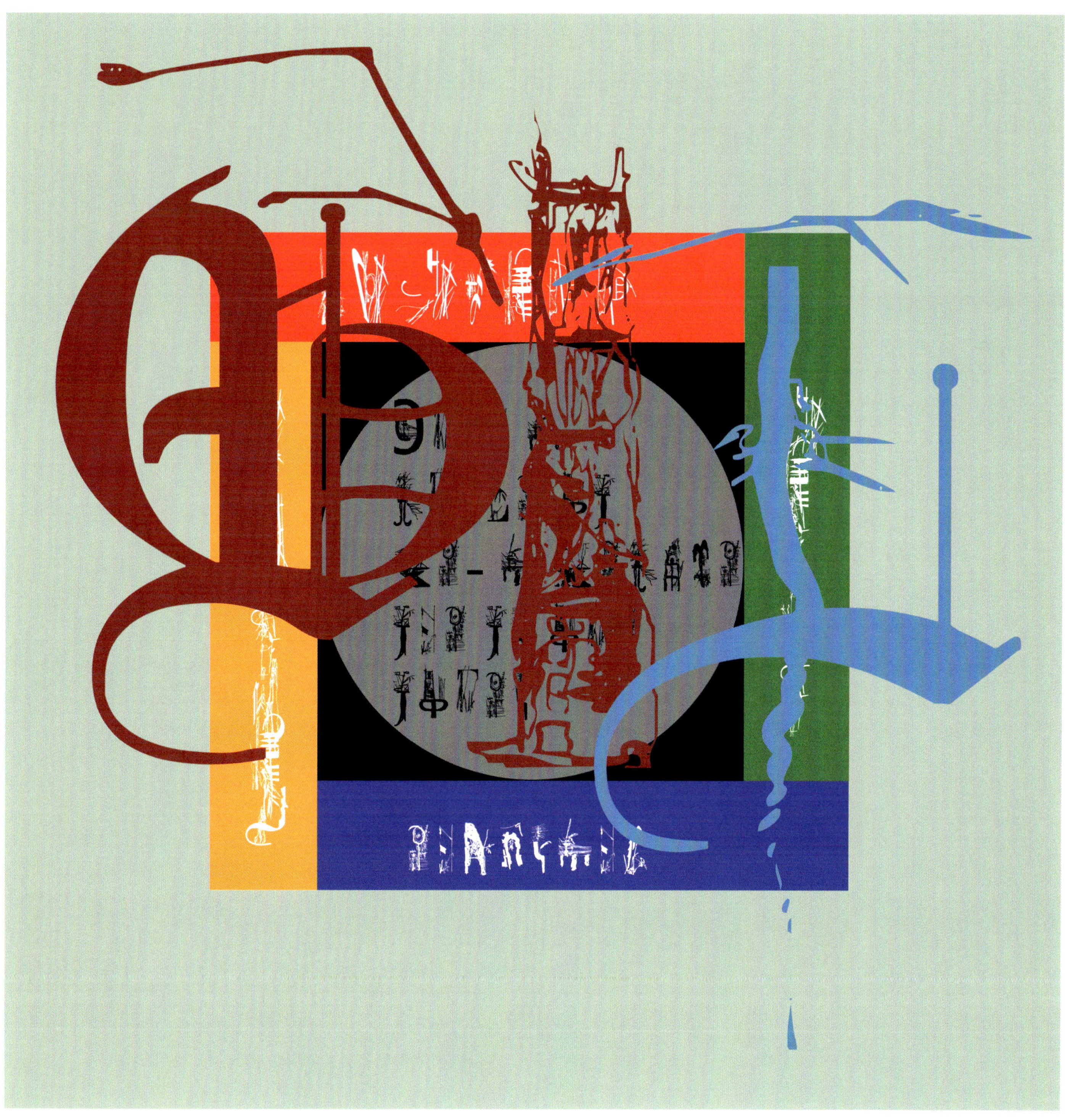

Note
The font used in the yellow, red, and green rectangles is AMF; in the blue rectangle and gray circle, FBT. The two large characters—A and C—in the top layer are also AMF.

Plate 140
No. 7915, 2007, digital montage. Barn Door series.
Allan Chasanoff Archive, Yale University Art Gallery

Looking Down:
Multi-Line

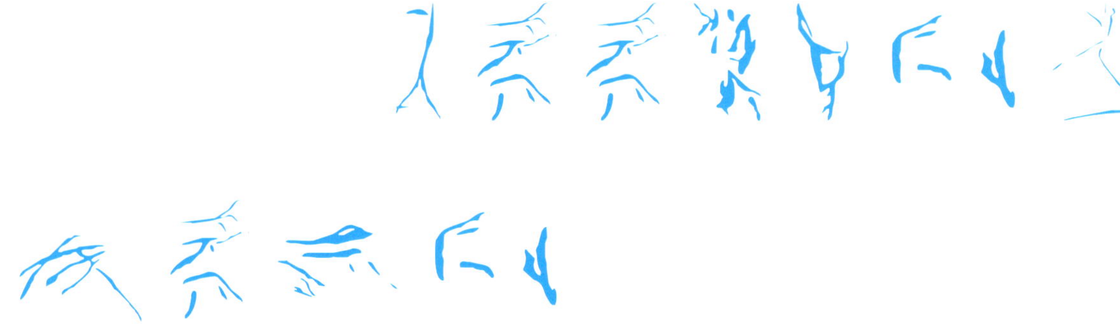

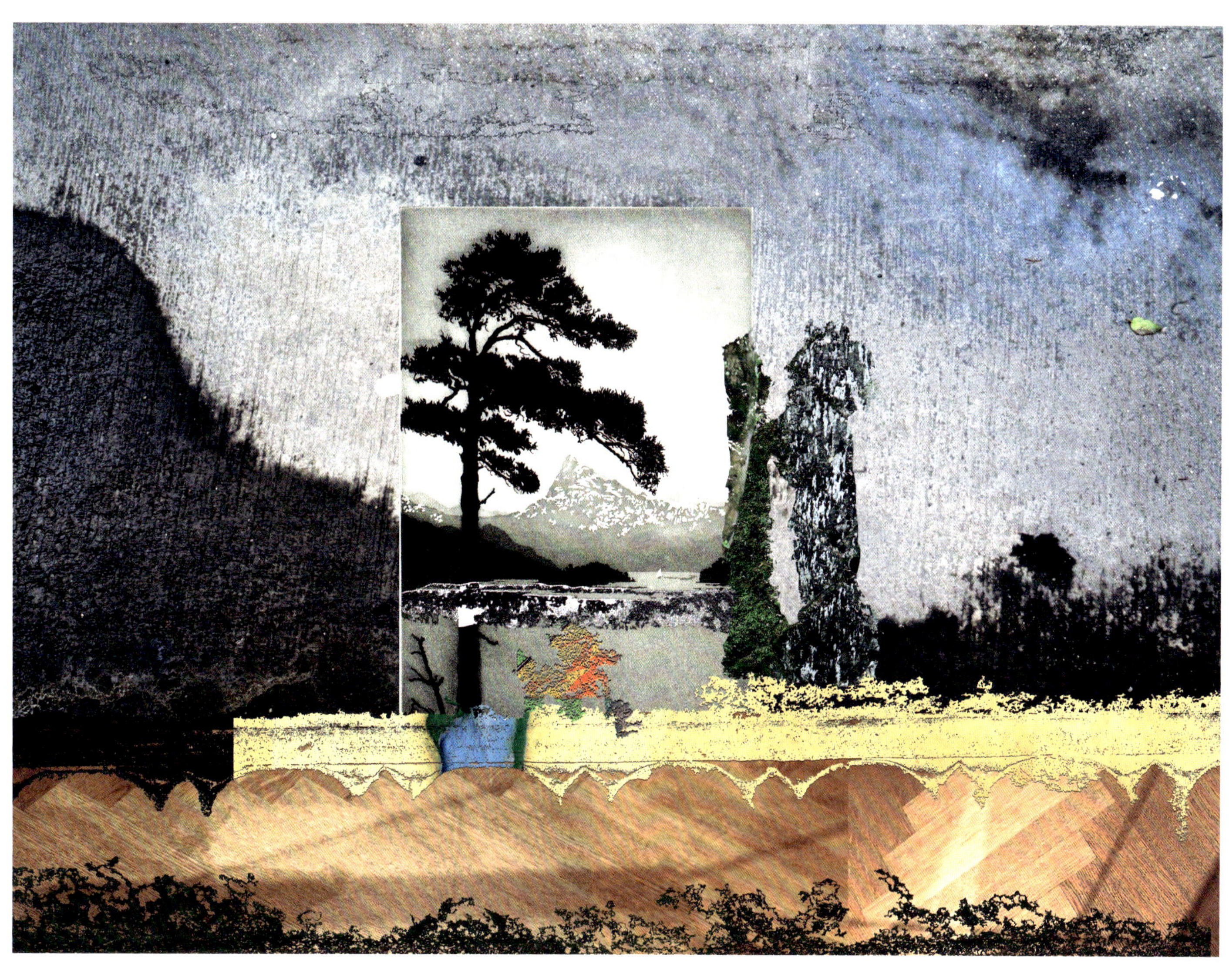

Note

The background here is one of Chasanoff's photographs of pavement that reminded him of Chinese landscape painting (see pl. 142). The details of flooring come from his photographs shot at the Metropolitan Museum of Art featuring shadows of artworks. The shape with arches is most likely extracted from one of his photographs of the fence around the Morgan Library and Museum.

Plate 141

No. 12489, 2018, digital montage. Multi-Line project.
Allan Chasanoff Archive, Yale University Art Gallery

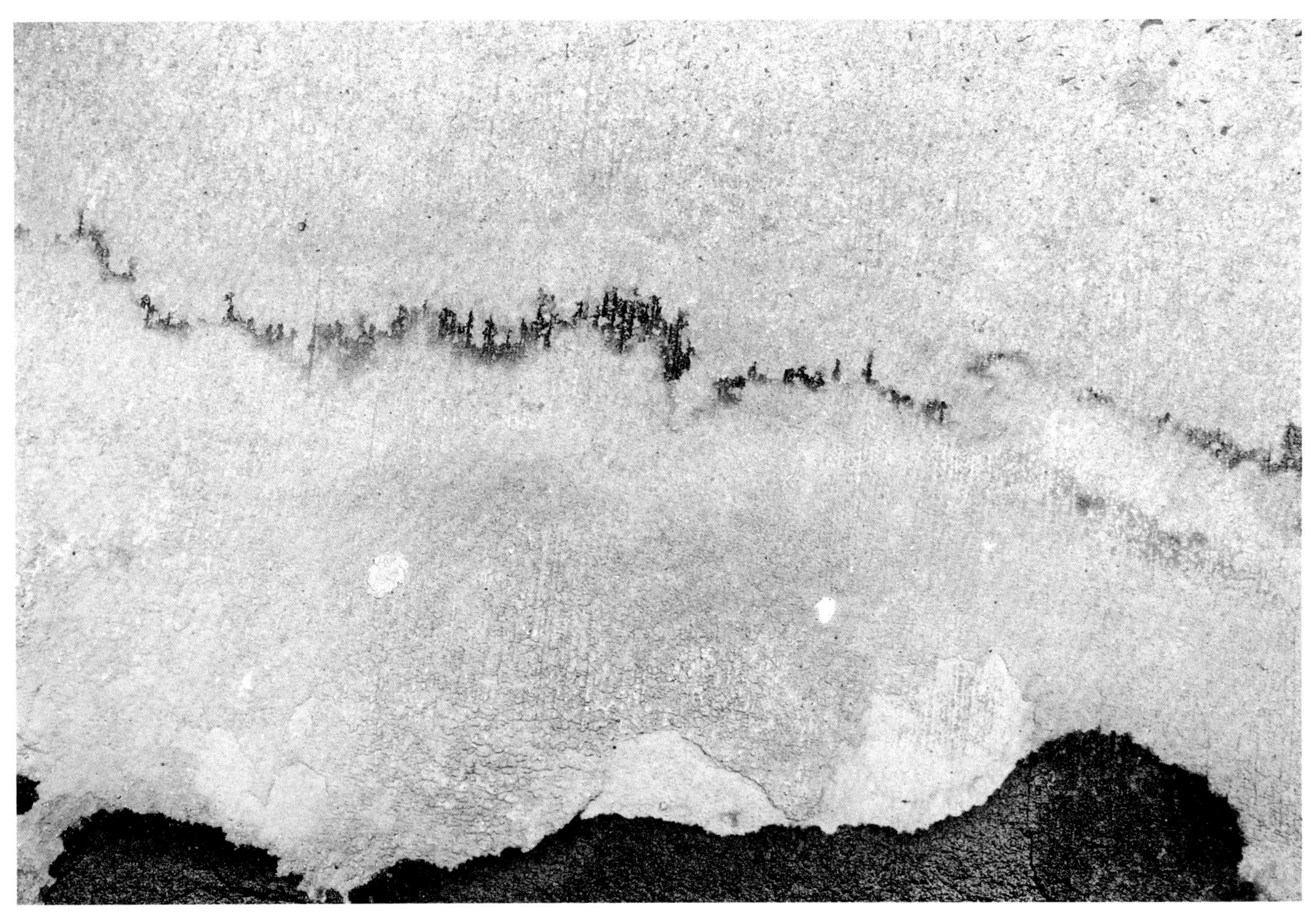

Note
Early in the Multi-Line project, Chasanoff photographed pavements that, for him, evoked Chinese landscape painting.

Plate 142
No. 12596, 2015, digital image file. Multi-Line project.
Allan Chasanoff Archive, Yale University Art Gallery

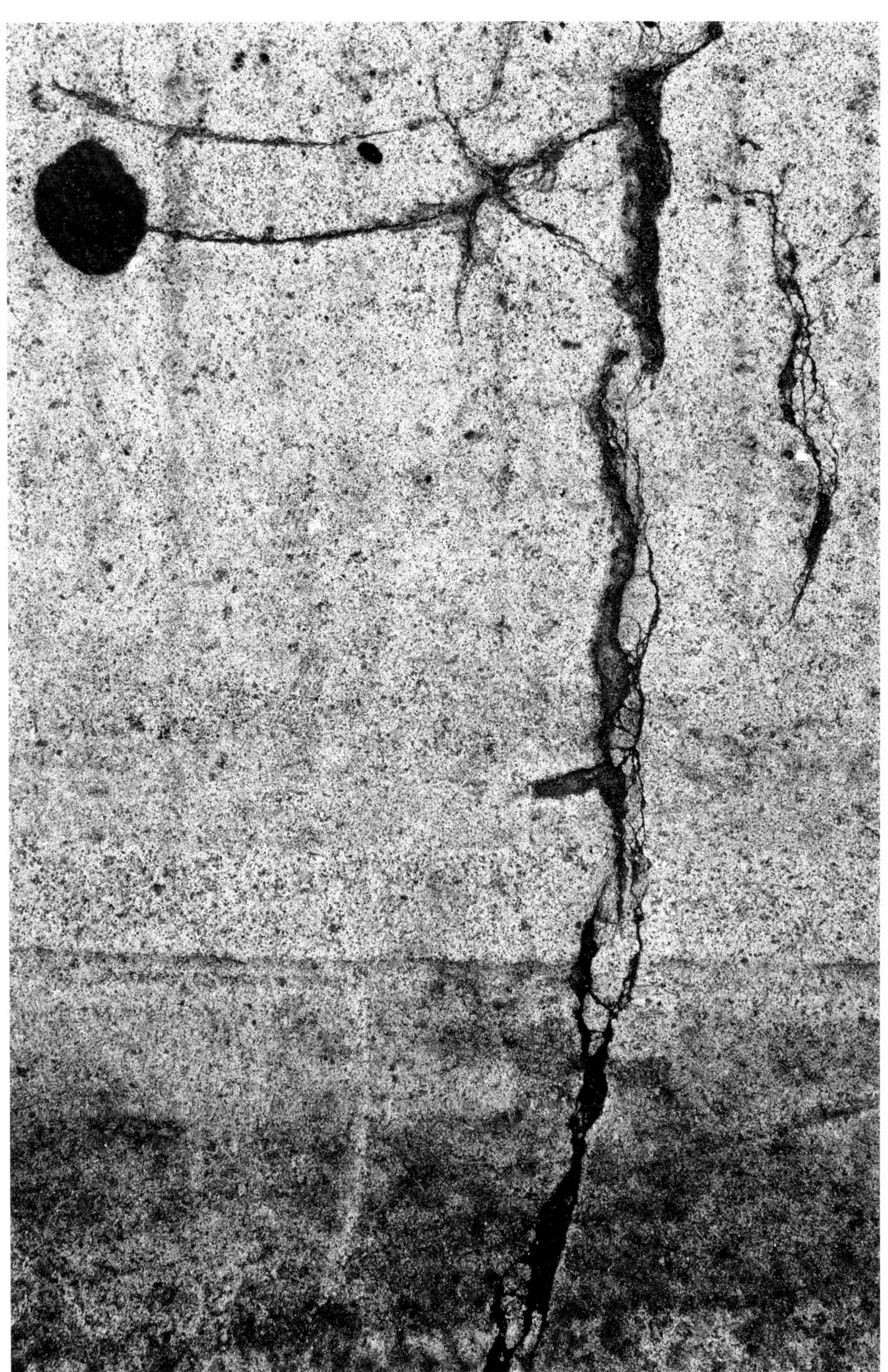

Note
In these pavement cracks, Chasanoff saw a thin human figure with a penis.

Plate 143
No. 12446, 2016, digital image file. Multi-Line project.
Allan Chasanoff Archive, Yale University Art Gallery

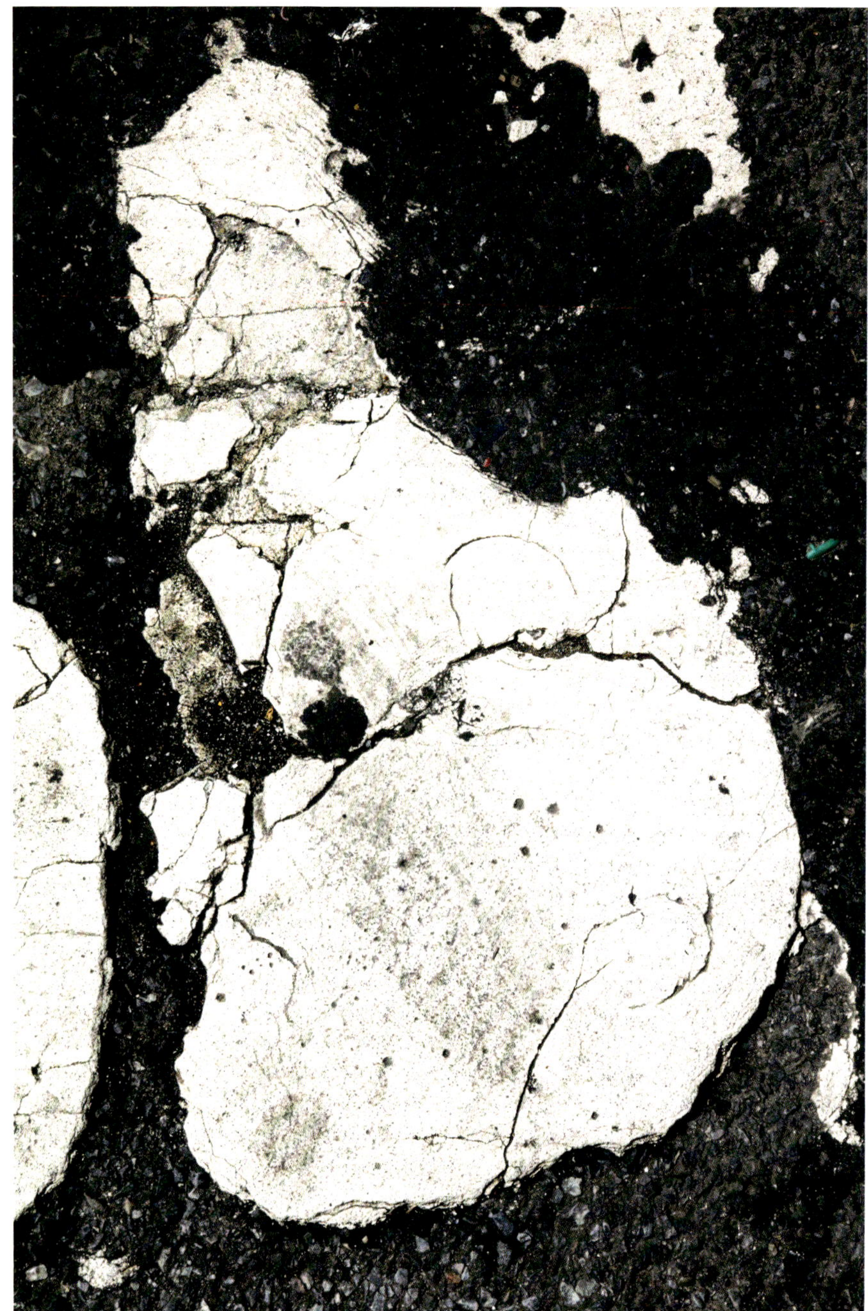

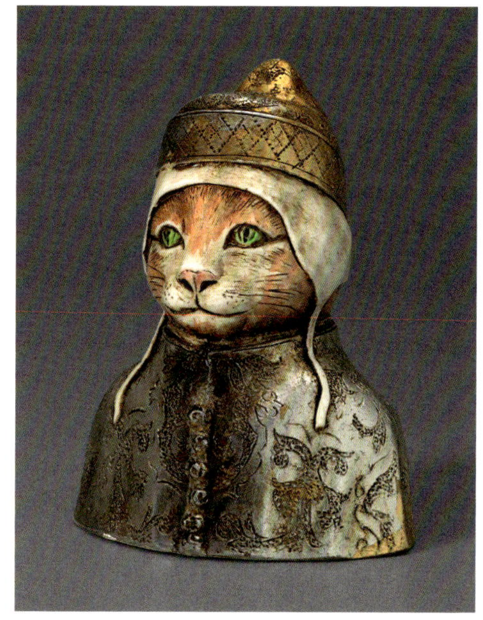

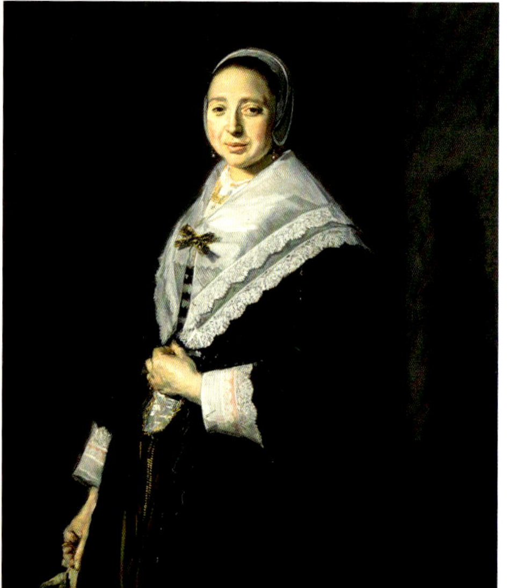

Note

Seen right-side-up, this pavement-paint formation recalls one of Chasanoff's props—a cat in a bonnet—and a painting by Frans Hals.

Plate 144

No. 12572, 2016, digital image file. Multi-Line project.
Allan Chasanoff Archive, Yale University Art Gallery

(top right) Cat with bonnet. Porcelain. Allan Chasanoff Archive, Yale University Art Gallery

(bottom right) Frans Hals, *Portrait of a Woman*, ca. 1650–52. Oil on canvas. Saint Louis Art Museum, Museum Purchase and funds given by the John M. Olin Charitable Trust, Friends Fund, Mr. and Mrs. Sydney M. Shoenberg Sr., Stella Kuhn and Effie C. Kuhn, Mrs. Clifford W. Gaylord, Mr. Joseph L. Werner, Mr. and Mrs. Daniel K. Catlin, Martha I. Love, Mr. and Mrs. Henry B. Pflager, The Steinberg Charitable Fund, Mr. and Mrs. Lansing W. Thoms, the Weil Charitable Foundation, Mrs. Arthur C. Drefs, and Mr. and Mrs. John P. Meyer, 272:1955

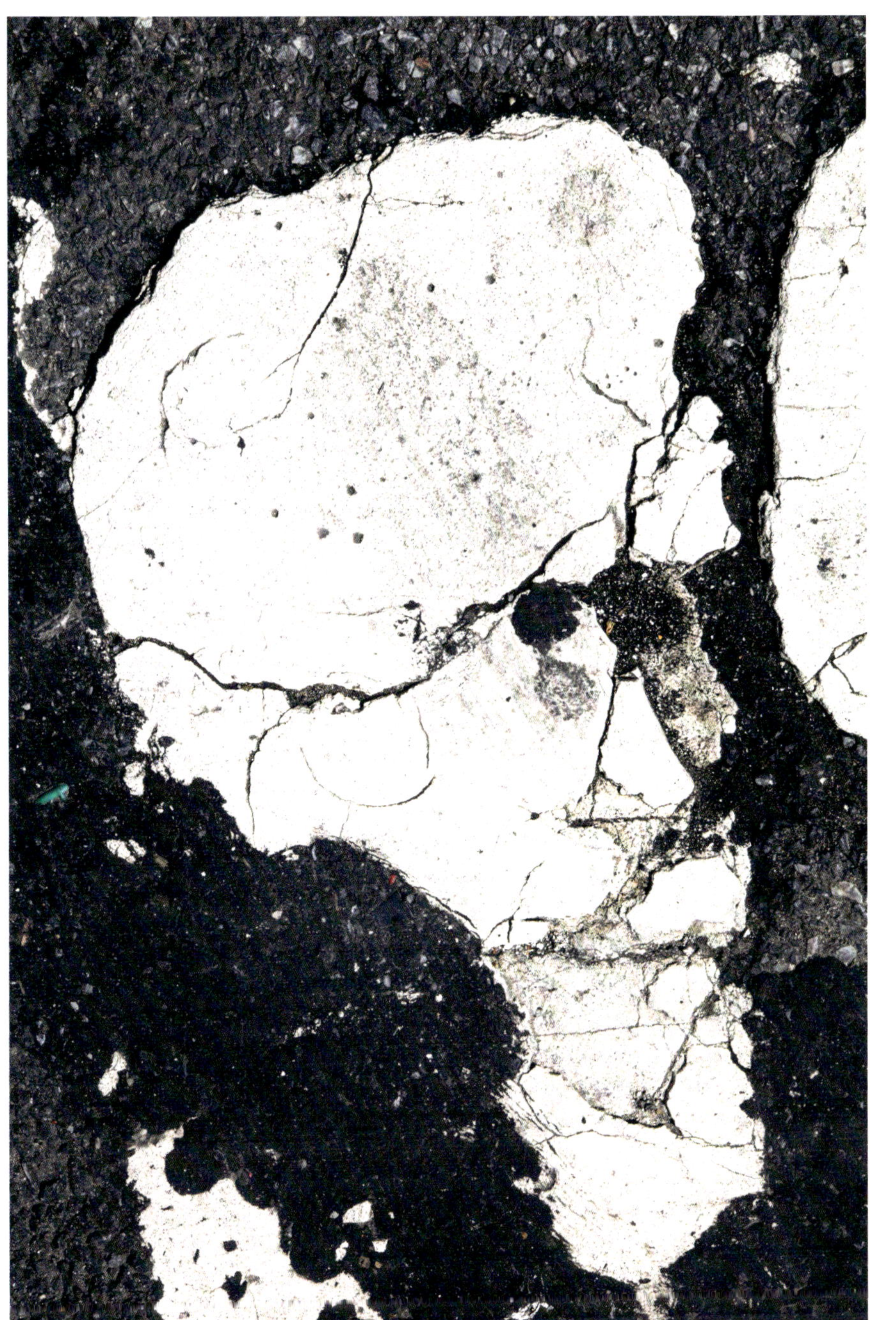

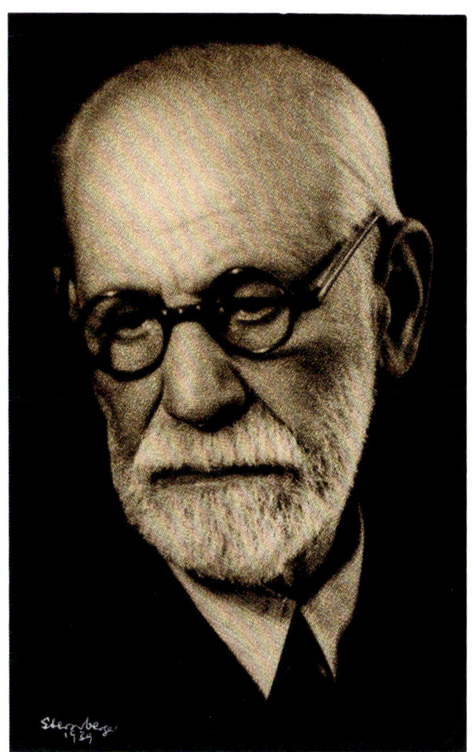

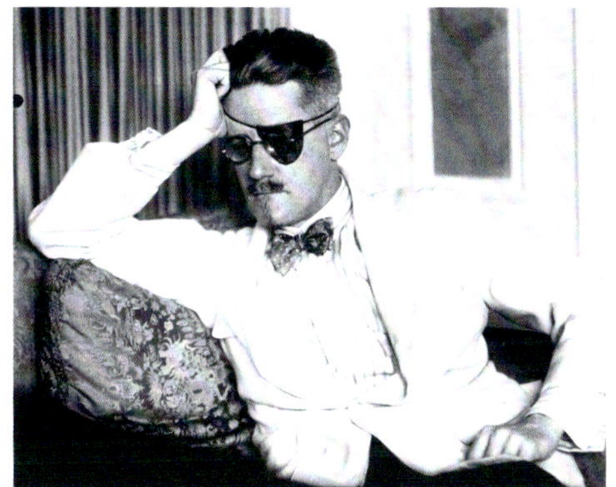

Note

Seen upside-down, the formation resembles a skull or recalls portraits of Sigmund Freud and James Joyce (the latter in Chasanoff's photography collection).

(top right) *Sigmund Freud*, 1939. Postcard reproduction of a photograph. Freud Museum, London, IN22

(bottom right) Berenice Abbott, *Portrait of James Joyce*, 1926. Gelatin silver print. Museum of Fine Arts, Houston, The Allan Chasanoff Photographic Collection, 91.336

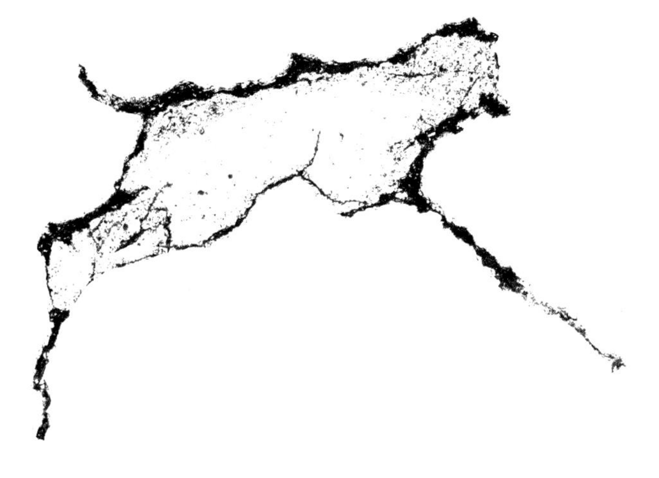

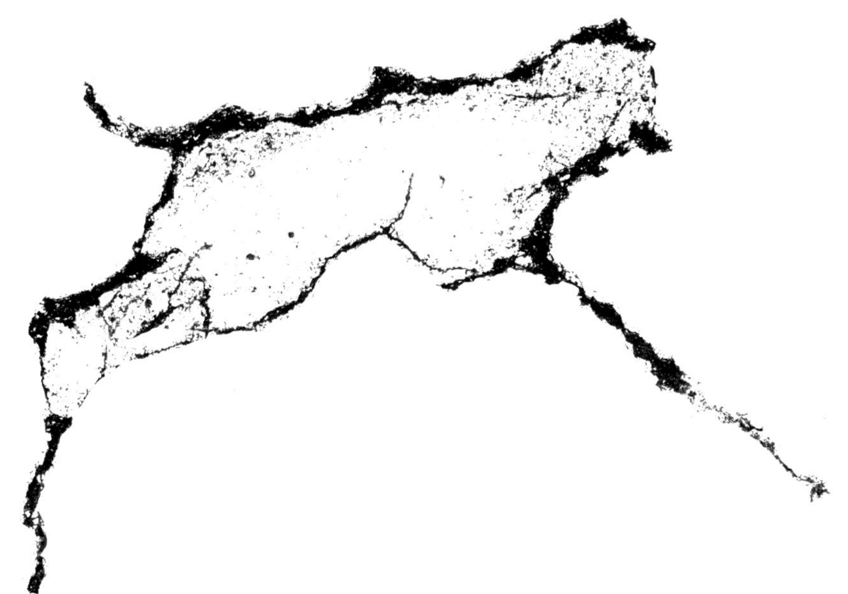

Note
The image extracted from the pavement cracks in plate 145 is one of many “crack drawings” generated by the Multi-Line project, the one in plate 146 resembling a dog or a horse. Chasanoff combined it with other imagery in plate 147.

Plate 145
No. 12497, 2016, digital image file. Multi-Line project.
Allan Chasanoff Archive, Yale University Art Gallery

Plate 146
No. 12496, 2016, extraction from digital photograph. Multi-Line project.
Allan Chasanoff Archive, Yale University Art Gallery

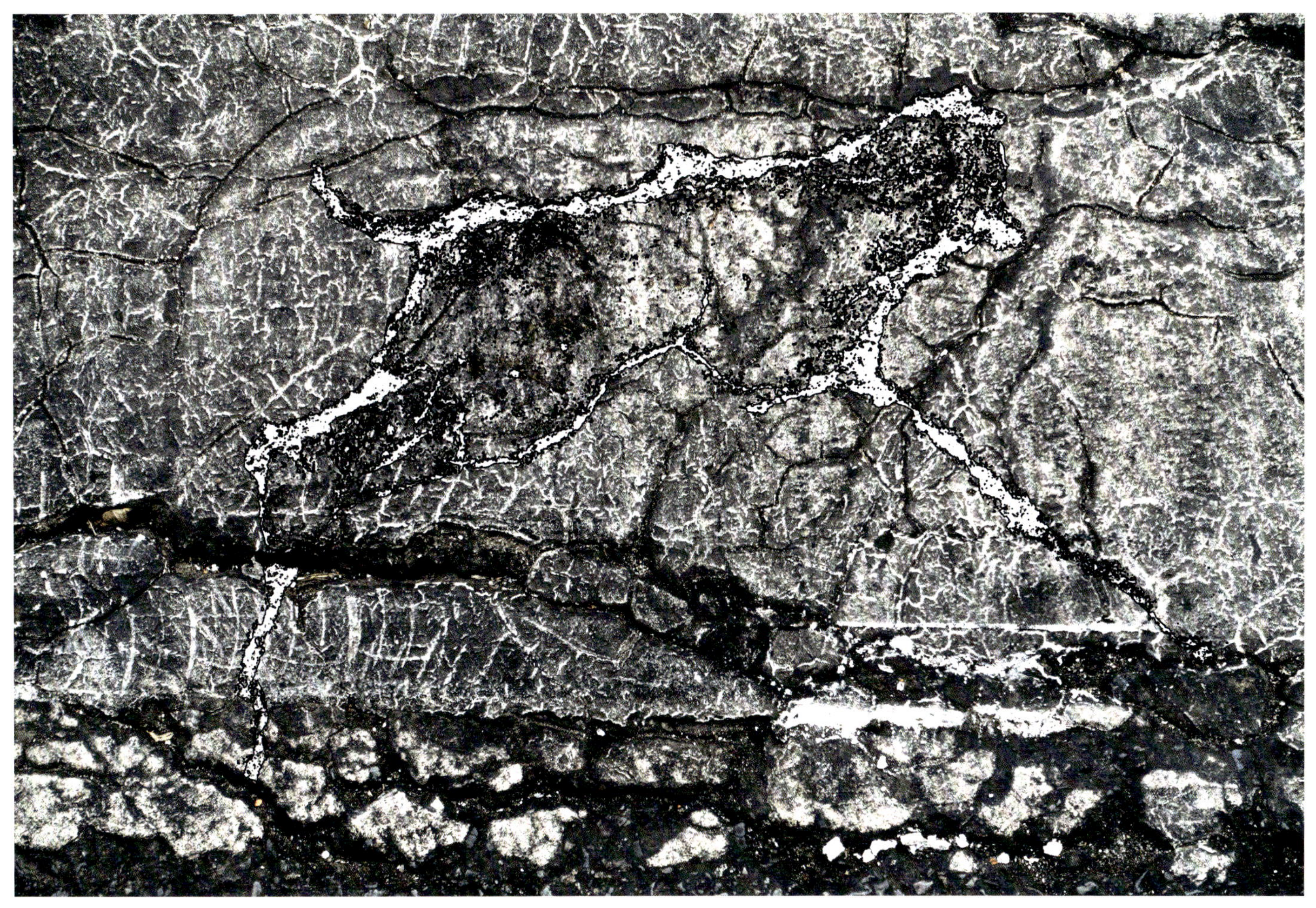

Plate 147
No. 12451, 2018, digital montage. Multi-Line project.
Allan Chasanoff Archive, Yale University Art Gallery

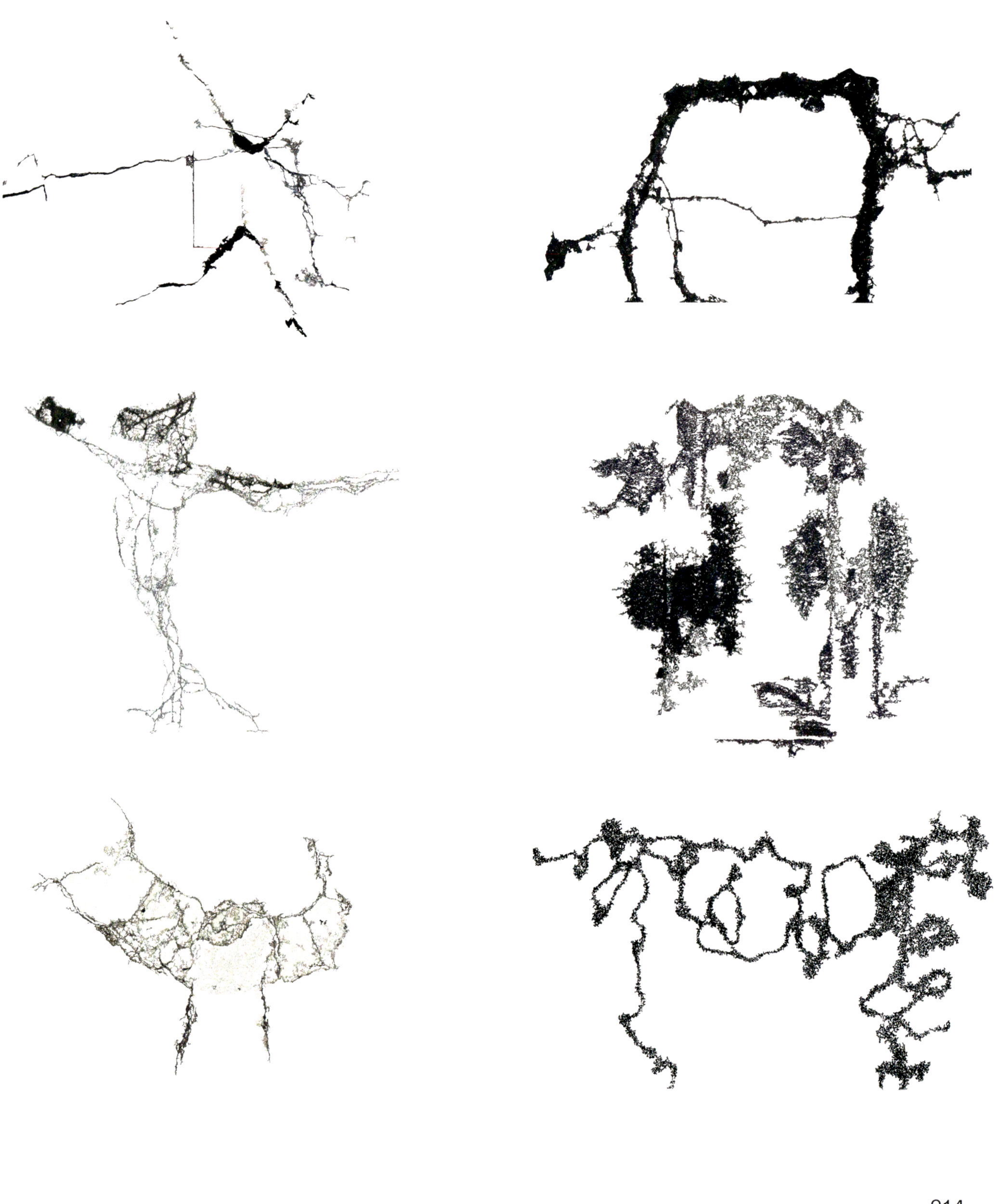

Note
These “crack drawings” were created by Chasanoff through selection and extraction for their resemblance to human or animal figures or organic forms. The drawings at center right and bottom right originated in photographs of the fence around the Morgan Library and Museum.

Plate 148
No. 12502 (2016), digital montage; nos. 12500 (2016), 12493 (2018), 12630 (2018), 12492 (2018), 12635 (2018), extractions from digital photographs. Multi-Line project.
Allan Chasanoff Archive, Yale University Art Gallery

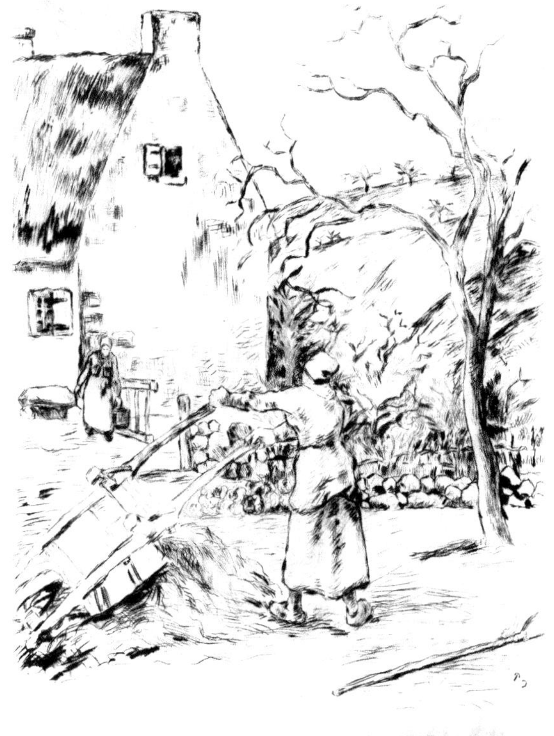

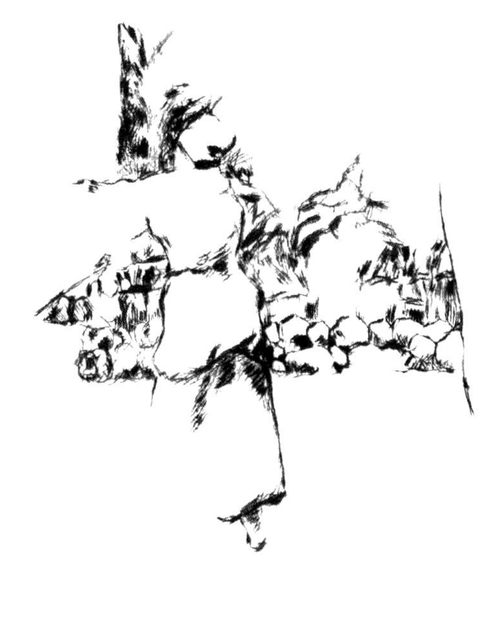

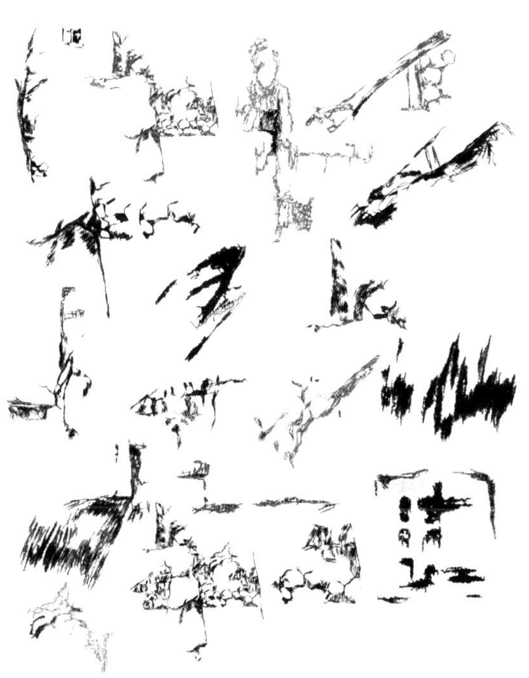

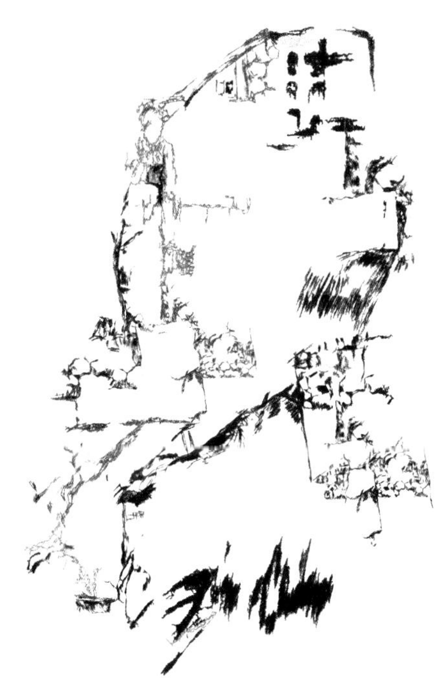

Note
After scanning a drawing by Camille Pissarro in an auction catalogue, Chasanoff extracted, separated, and recombined lines from it to create new drawings.

Plate 149
No. 12615, 2018, extraction from digital scan; nos. 12616, 12614, 2018, digital montage.
Multi-Line project.
Allan Chasanoff Archive, Yale University Art Gallery

(top left) Camille Pissaro, *Femme vidant une brouette* (No. 12617, 2018, digital scan. Allan Chasanoff Archive, Yale University Art Gallery), 1880. Etching and drypoint. Location unknown

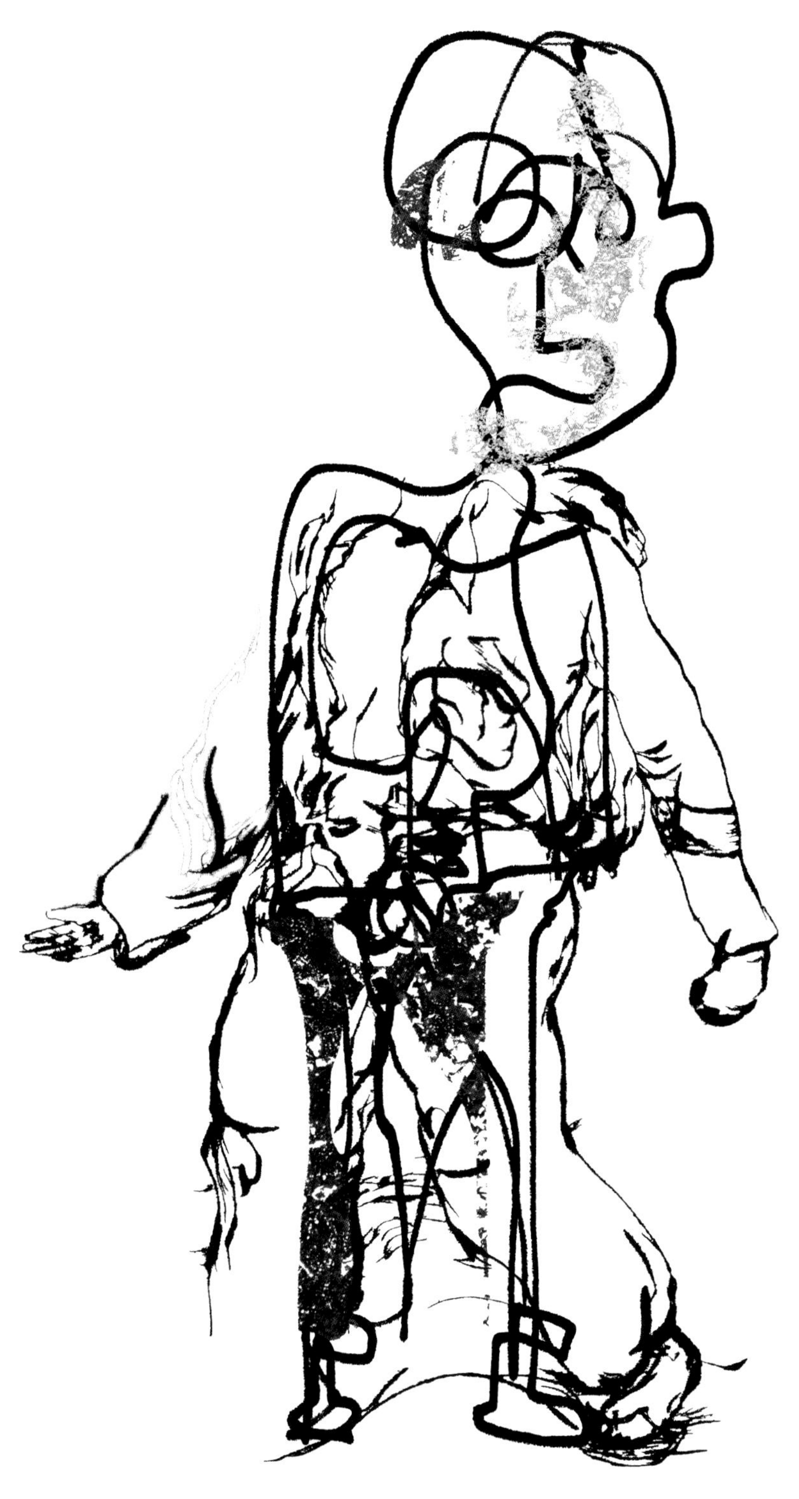

216

Note
To create this figure, Chasanoff combined lines selected from a work by Georg Baselitz with cracks from his own pavement photographs and a drawing he made with the Zen Brush application.

Plate 150
No. 12578, 2018, digital montage. Multi-Line project.
Allan Chasanoff Archive, Yale University Art Gallery

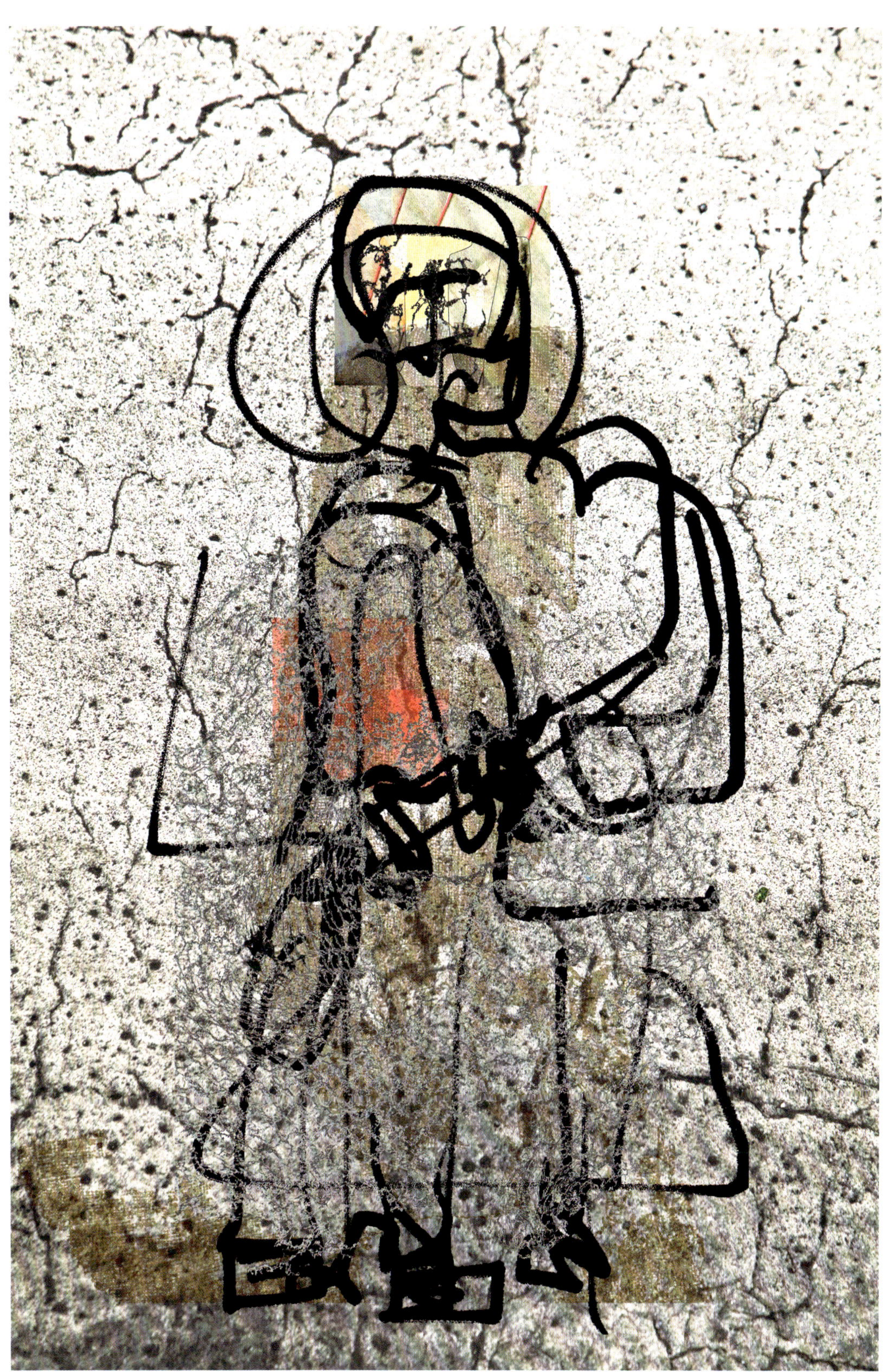

Note

Chasanoff combined two drawings he made with the Zen Brush application, lines from his pavement photographs, a detail from one of his Morandi (outline) images, and an extraction from a scan of a work by Alberto Burri and placed them on one of his pavement photographs, used as background. He felt the resulting image evoked an Eastern Orthodox icon, a musician with an instrument, or a soldier in a rain of bullets.

Plate 151

No. 12490, 2018, digital montage. Multi-Line project.
Allan Chasanoff Archive, Yale University Art Gallery

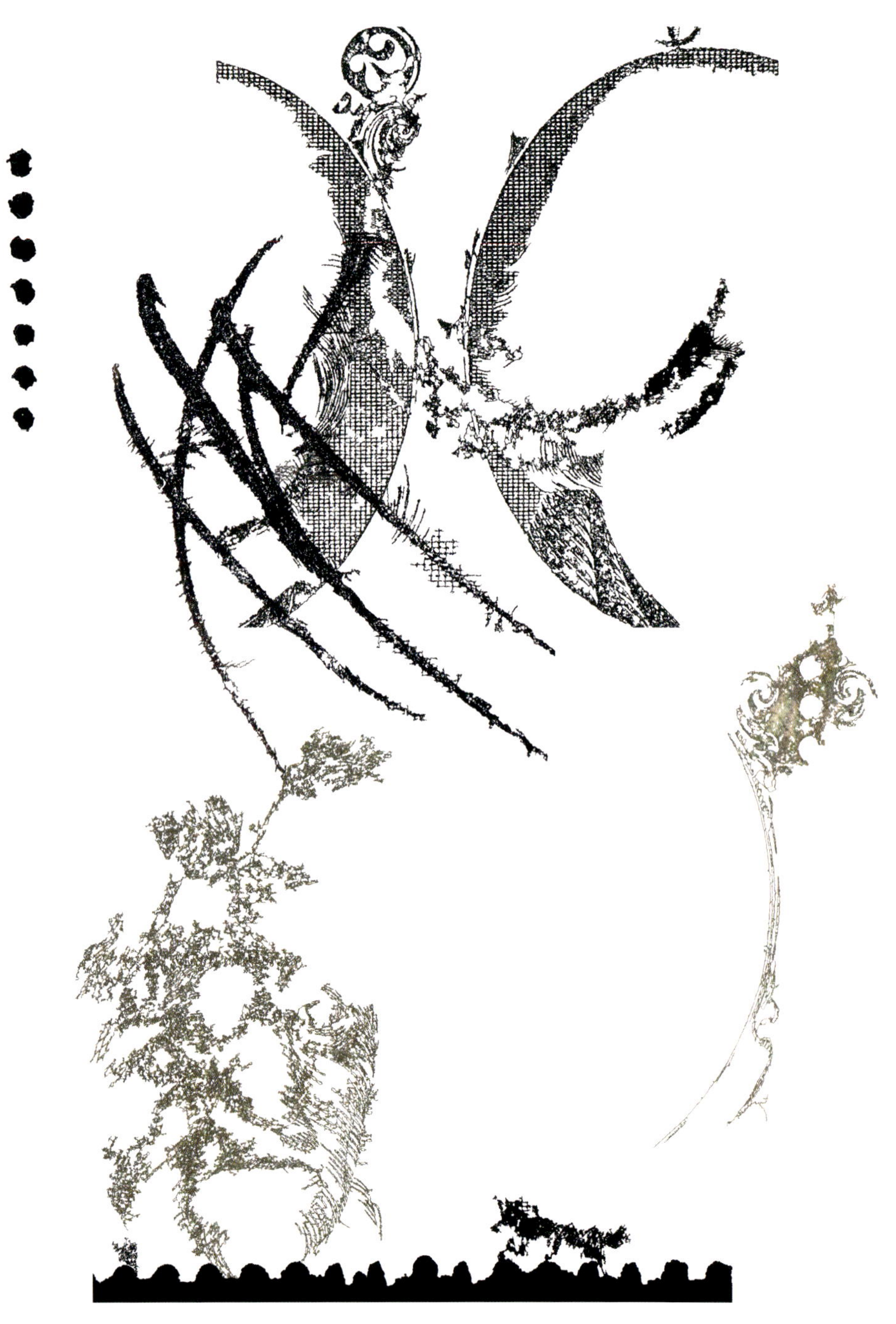

Note

Many of the lines and shapes here originate in the nineteenth-century U.S. postage stamp known as the "Black Jack," bearing the face of President Andrew Jackson, of which Chasanoff collected canceled examples.

Plate 152

No. 12467, 2018, digital montage. Multi-Line project.
Allan Chasanoff Archive, Yale University Art Gallery

Note
This image was selected from a single photograph of pavement. In it, Chasanoff saw a man with a protruding belly reclining under the moon.

Plate 153
No. 12472, 2017, extraction from digital photograph. Multi-Line project.
Allan Chasanoff Archive, Yale University Art Gallery

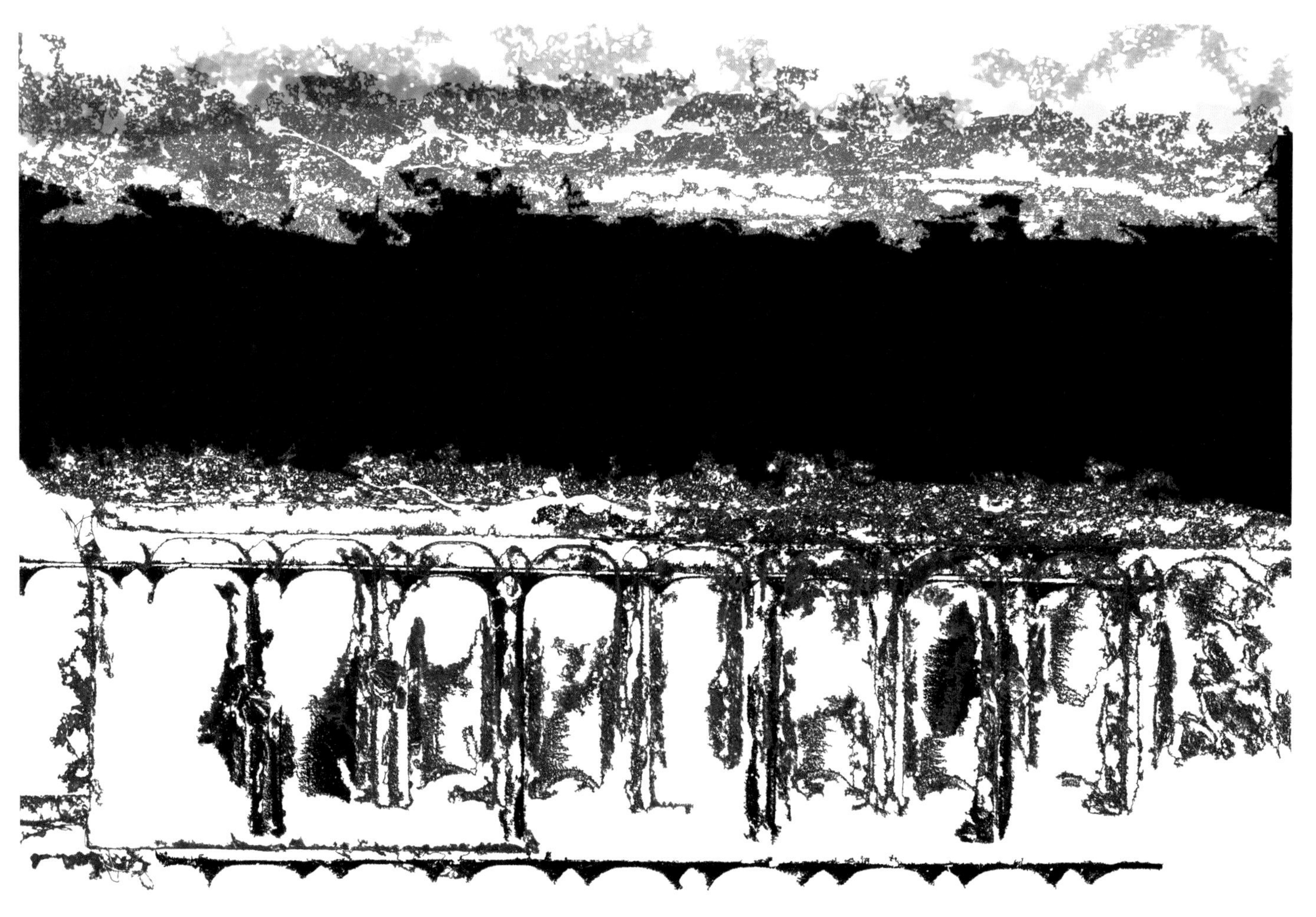

Note

The arches at bottom are selected from photographs of the fence around the Morgan Library and Museum.

Plate 154

No. 12476, 2018, digital montage. Multi-Line project.
Allan Chasanoff Archive, Yale University Art Gallery

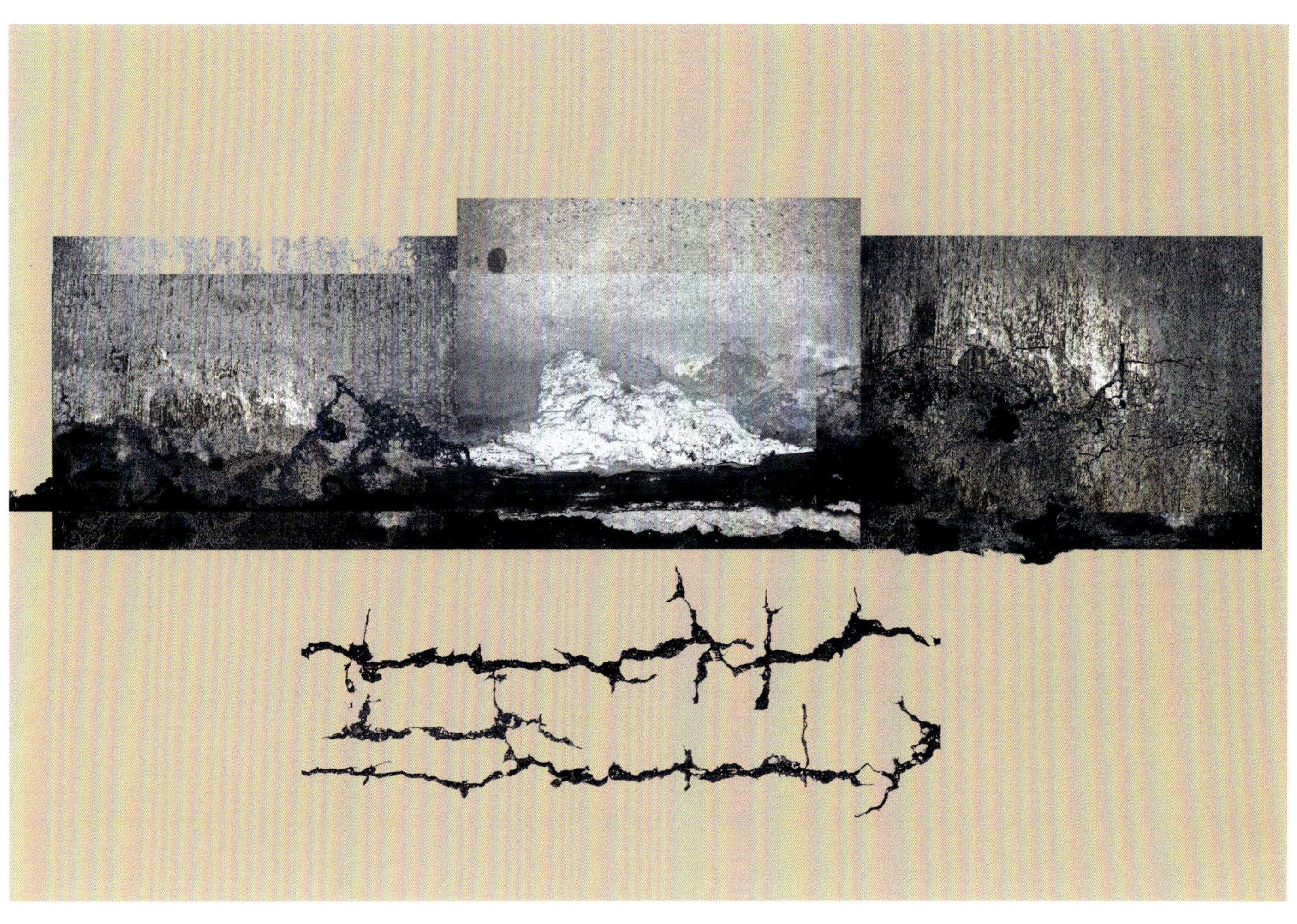

Note
The crack formations at bottom relate to Chasanoff's interest in asemic writing.

Plate 155
No. 12479, 2018, digital montage. Multi-Line project.
Allan Chasanoff Archive, Yale University Art Gallery

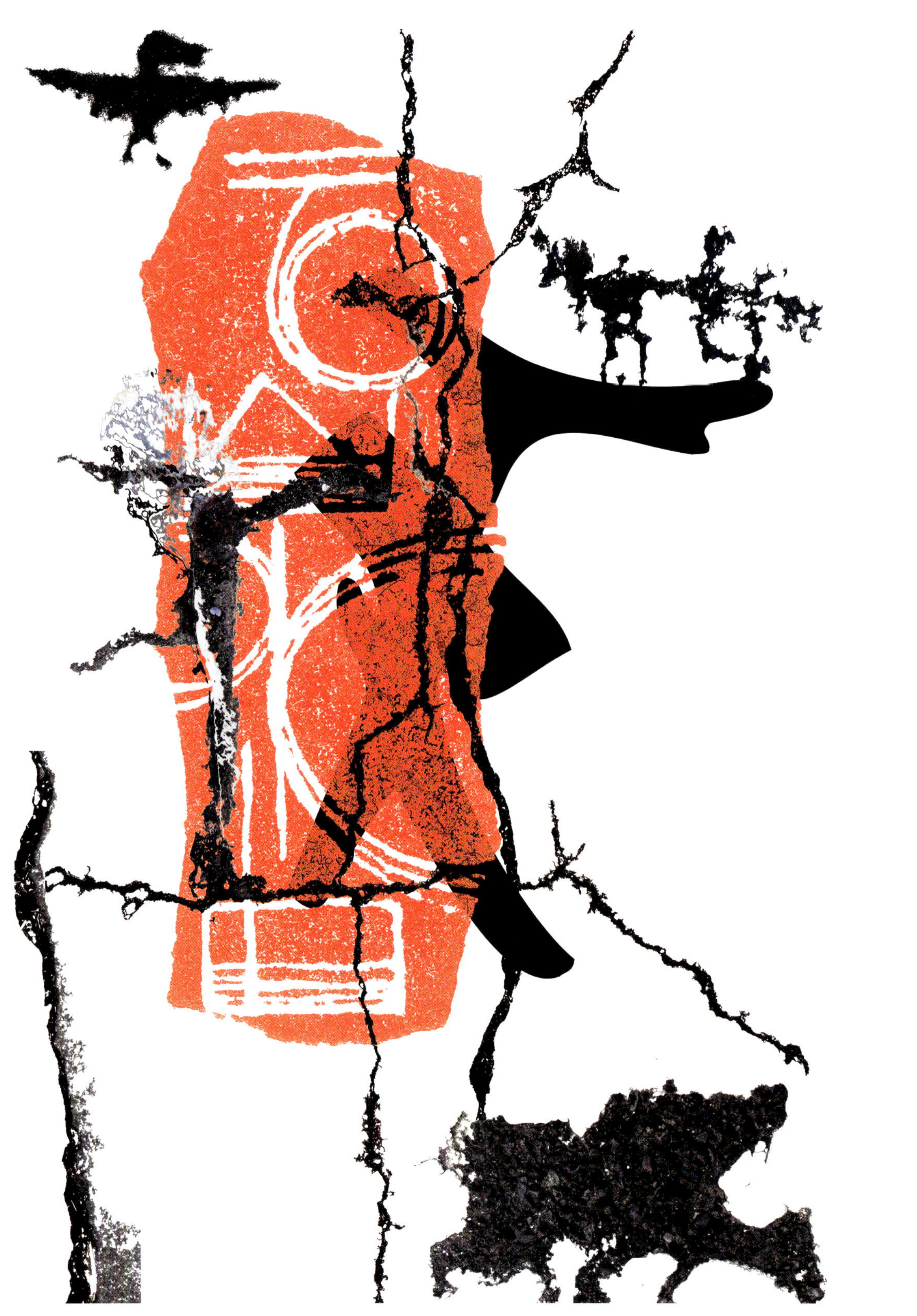

Note

This montage includes the character *X* from Chasanoff's Erasure font (bottom layer at center), selections from his pavement photographs, and the impression in red of a Mother's Tongue seal by Atsuko Segawa (see pl. 111).

Plate 156

No. 12484, 2018, digital montage. Multi-Line project.
Allan Chasanoff Archive, Yale University Art Gallery

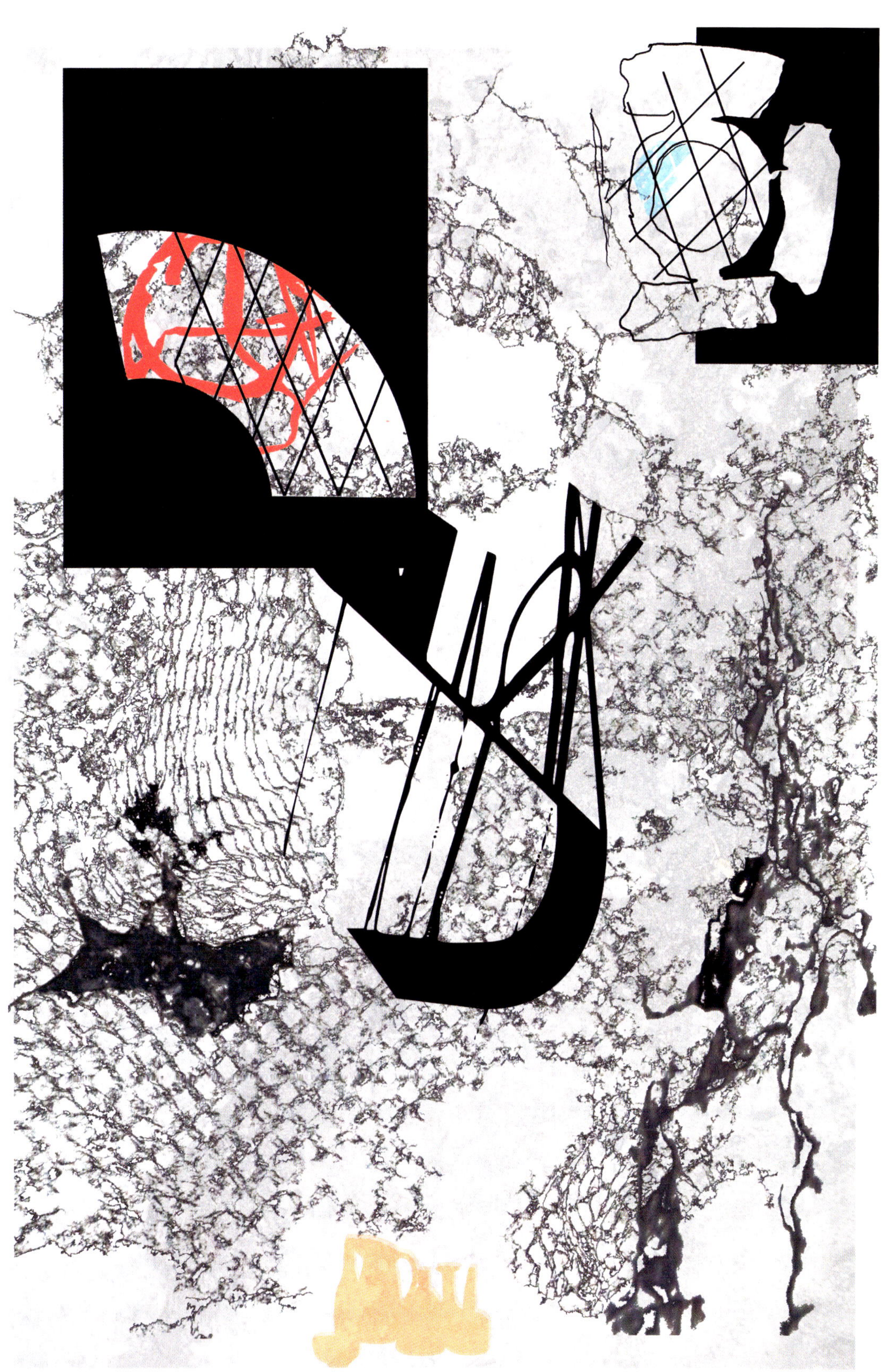

Note

Several elements of Chasanoff's vocabulary appear here: a character from his BAPHT font (upside-down and horizontally flipped *A*), a barn door, his favored Giorgio Morandi setup (see fig. 5), the diamond (or *X* or harlequin) pattern, a fan, and what is probably a scanned and distorted impression of a Mother's Tongue seal by Yuka Kera (in red; see pl. 111). In addition, there are selections from his pavement photographs.

Plate 157

No. 12485, 2018, digital montage. Multi-Line project.
Allan Chasanoff Archive, Yale University Art Gallery

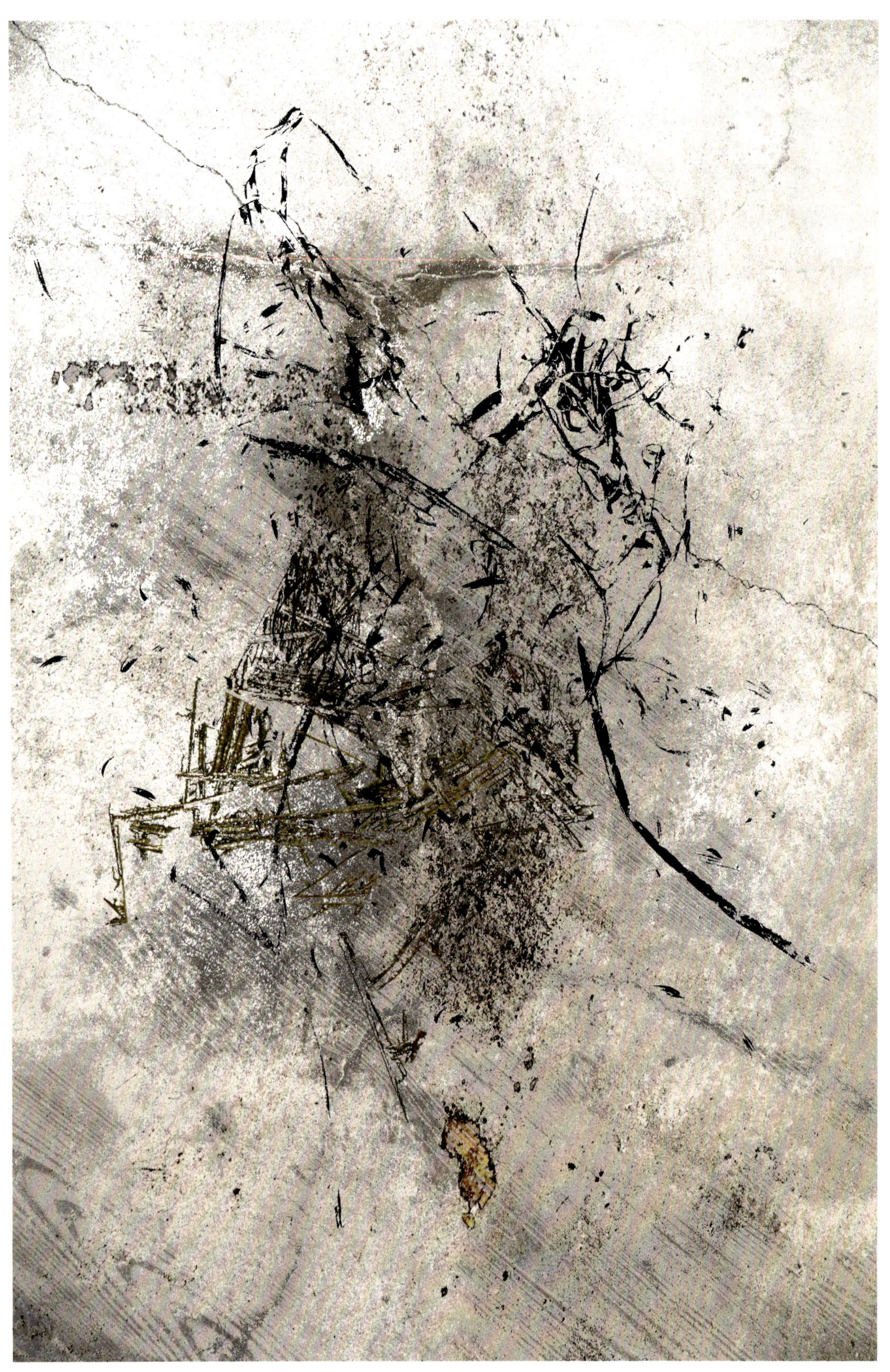

Note
This image includes scans of metal shavings given to Chasanoff by his close friend Richard Benson, photographer and dean of the Yale School of Art from 1996 to 2006. They came from Benson's studio and relate to Chasanoff's interest in erasure/erasings. The image was made two years after Benson's death.

Plate 158
No. 12470, 2019, digital montage. Multi-Line project.
Allan Chasanoff Archive, Yale University Art Gallery

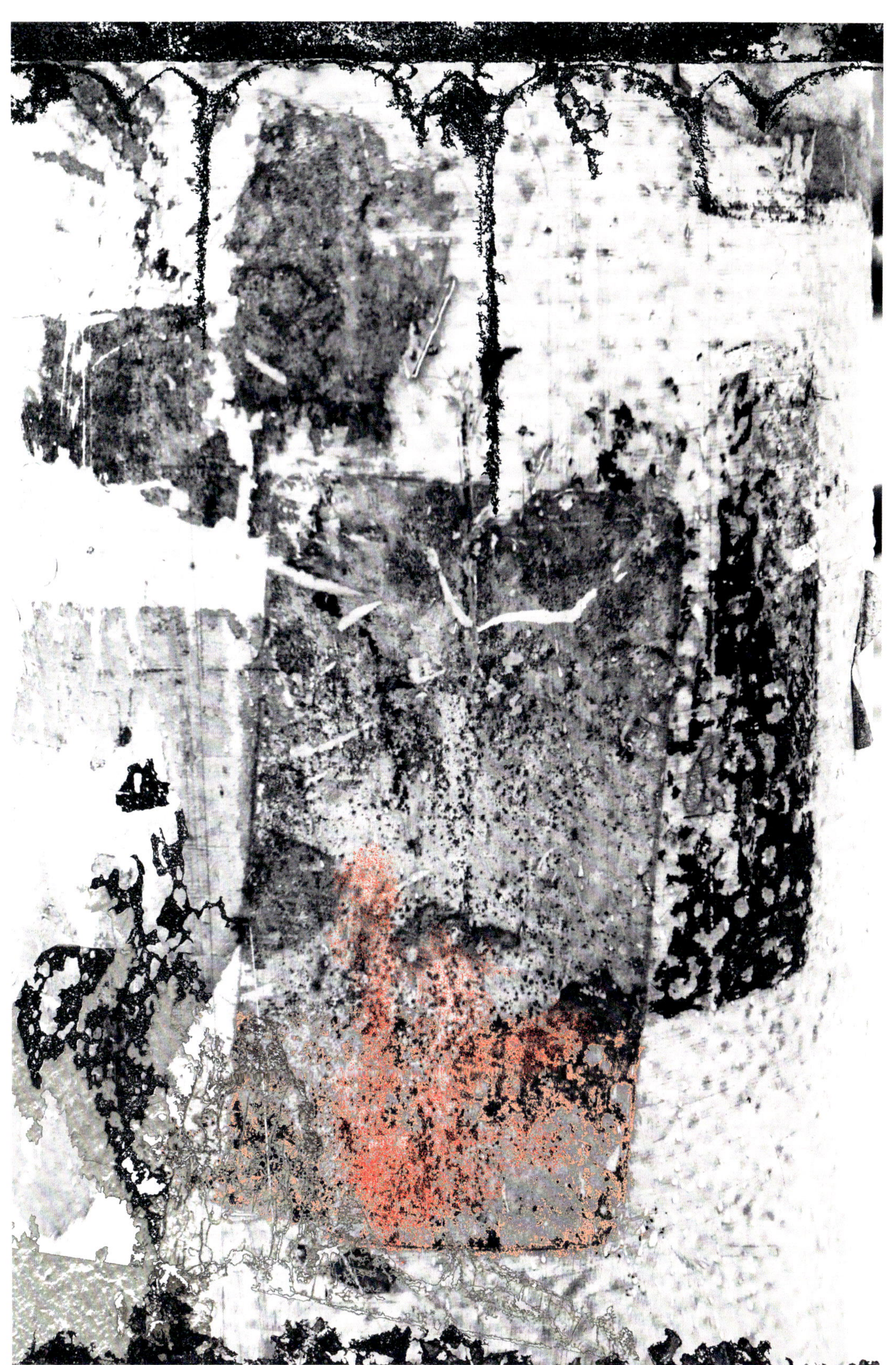

Note

The arches at top are selected from photography of the fence around the Morgan Library and Museum. The background likely derives from Chasanoff's photographs of utility poles in his Murray Hill neighborhood that bore torn paper announcements or posters (see posters in pls. 12, 14, 48).

Plate 159

No. 12445, 2019, digital montage. Multi-Line project.
Allan Chasanoff Archive, Yale University Art Gallery

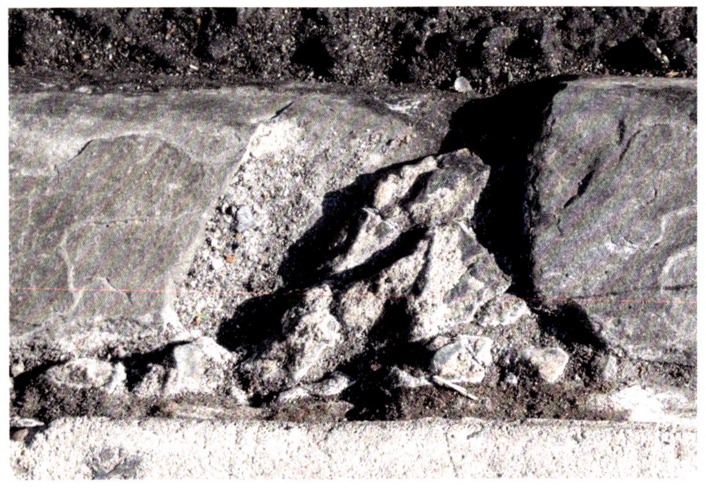

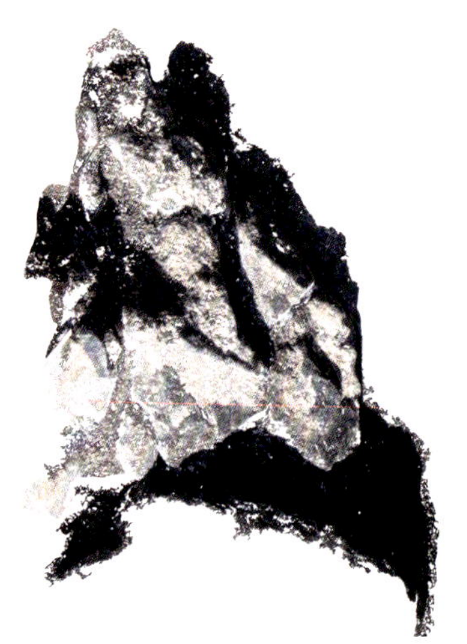

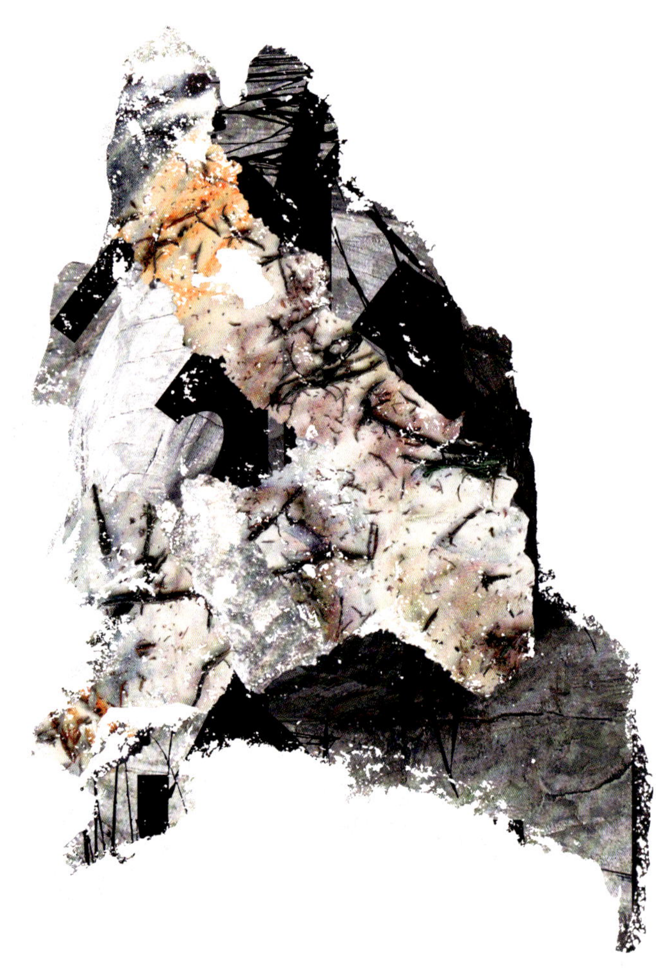

Note

A shape (top right) extracted from a pavement photograph (top left), then rotated, suggests two figures, perhaps male and female, with one abducting the other. To Chasanoff, it also suggested traditional images of the Pietá. He filled the shape's outline with content from a straight photograph (scanned erasings) and a montage, combining image and font (bottom).

Plate 160

No. 12600, 2019, digital image file; no. 12608 (detail), 2019, extraction from digital photograph; no. 12603, 2019, digital montage. Multi-Line project.
Allan Chasanoff Archive, Yale University Art Gallery

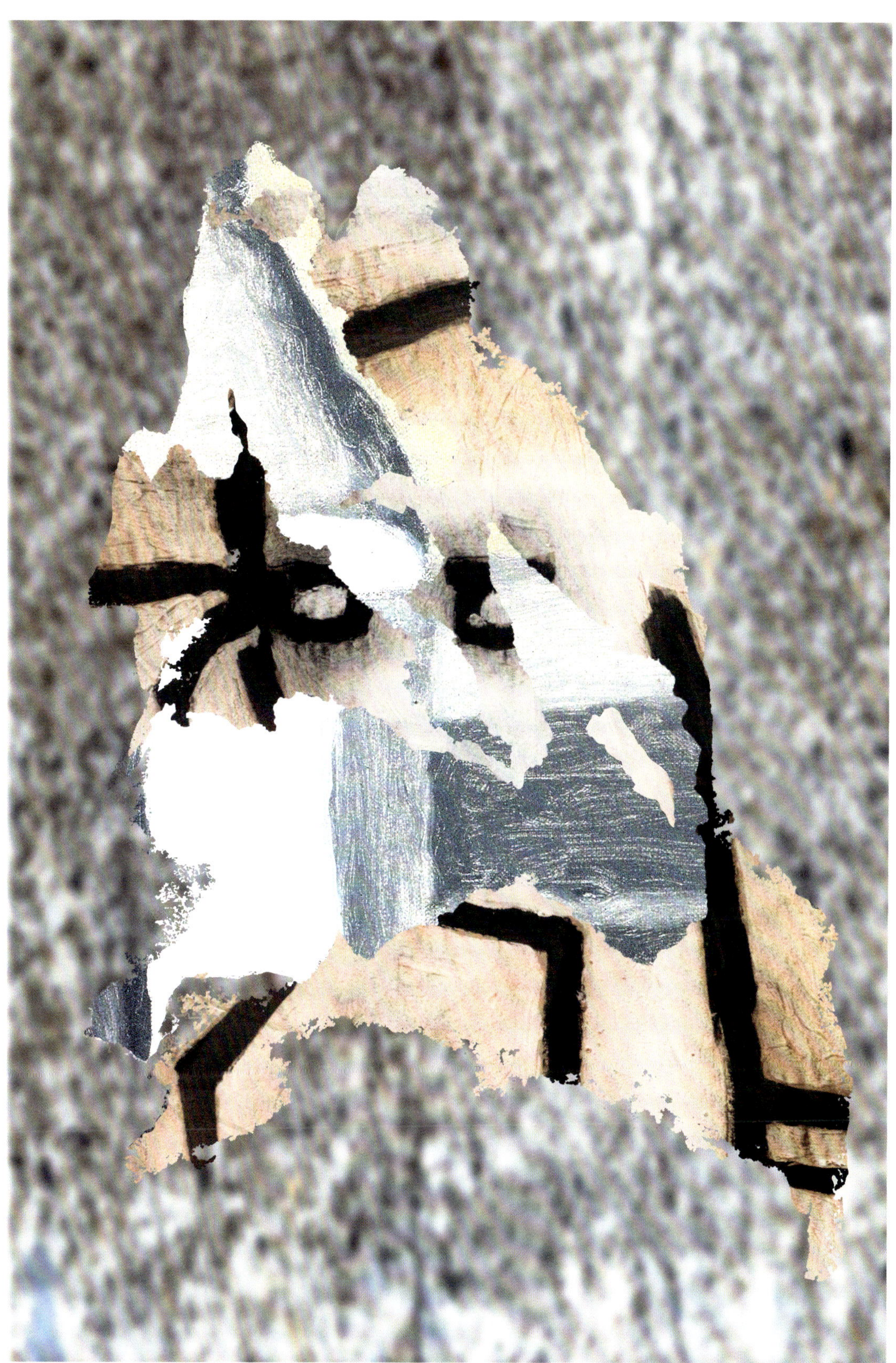

Note

In an example of appropriation, Chasanoff filled the abduction- or Pietá-like shape (pl. 160, top right) with extractions from paintings by Giorgio Morandi (*Still Life*, 1963; Vitali no. 1313) and Paul Klee (*Girl in Mourning*, 1939). This image was pinned on his office wall at the time of his passing, on October 18, 2020.

Plate 161

No. 12601, 2019, digital montage. Multi-Line project.
Allan Chasanoff Archive, Yale University Art Gallery

Back to the
Third Dimension

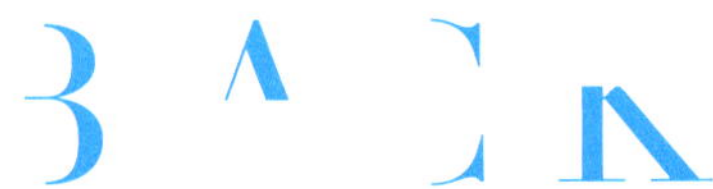

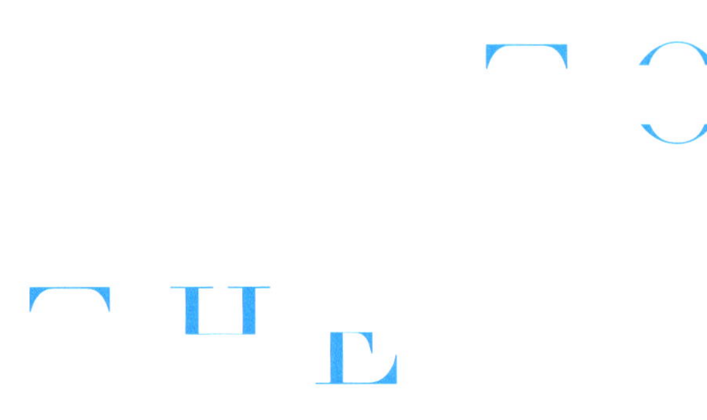

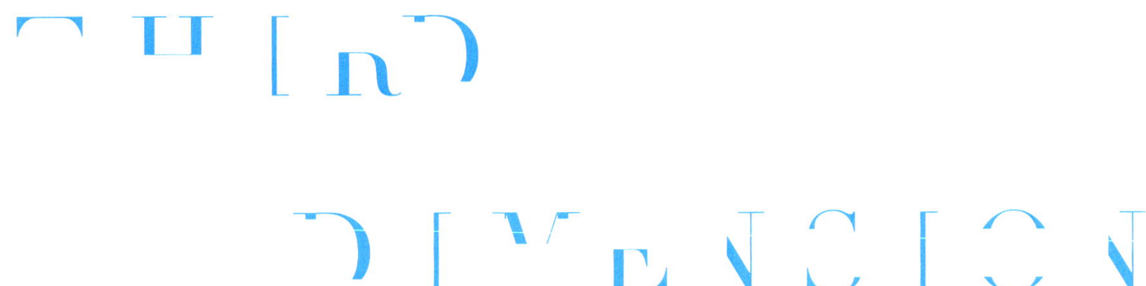

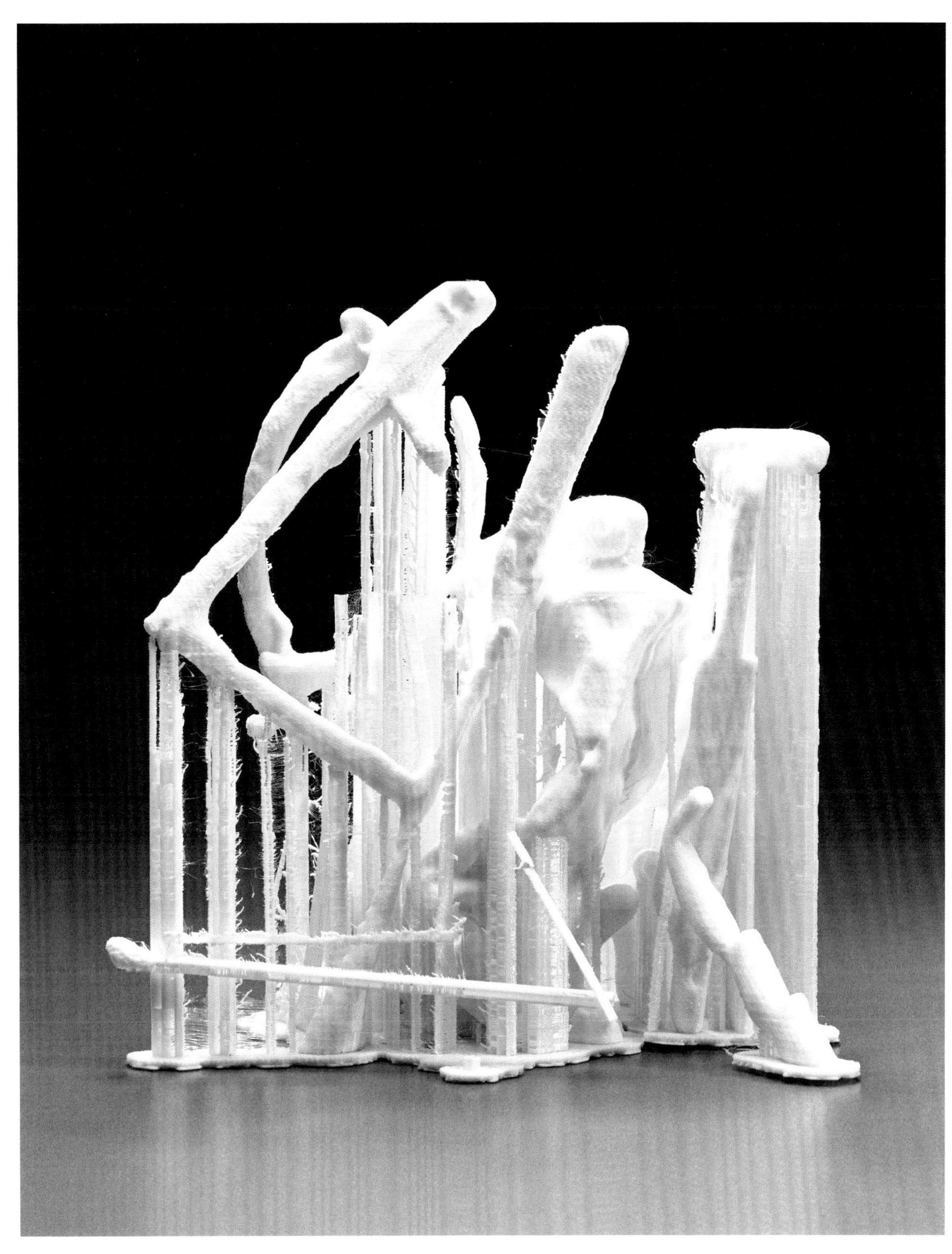

Plate 162
Untitled (with paint tube), ca. 2013–14, 3-D-printed polylactic acid,
5 ½ × 6 × 4 ½ in. (14 × 15.2 × 11.4 cm).
Allan Chasanoff Archive, Yale University Art Gallery

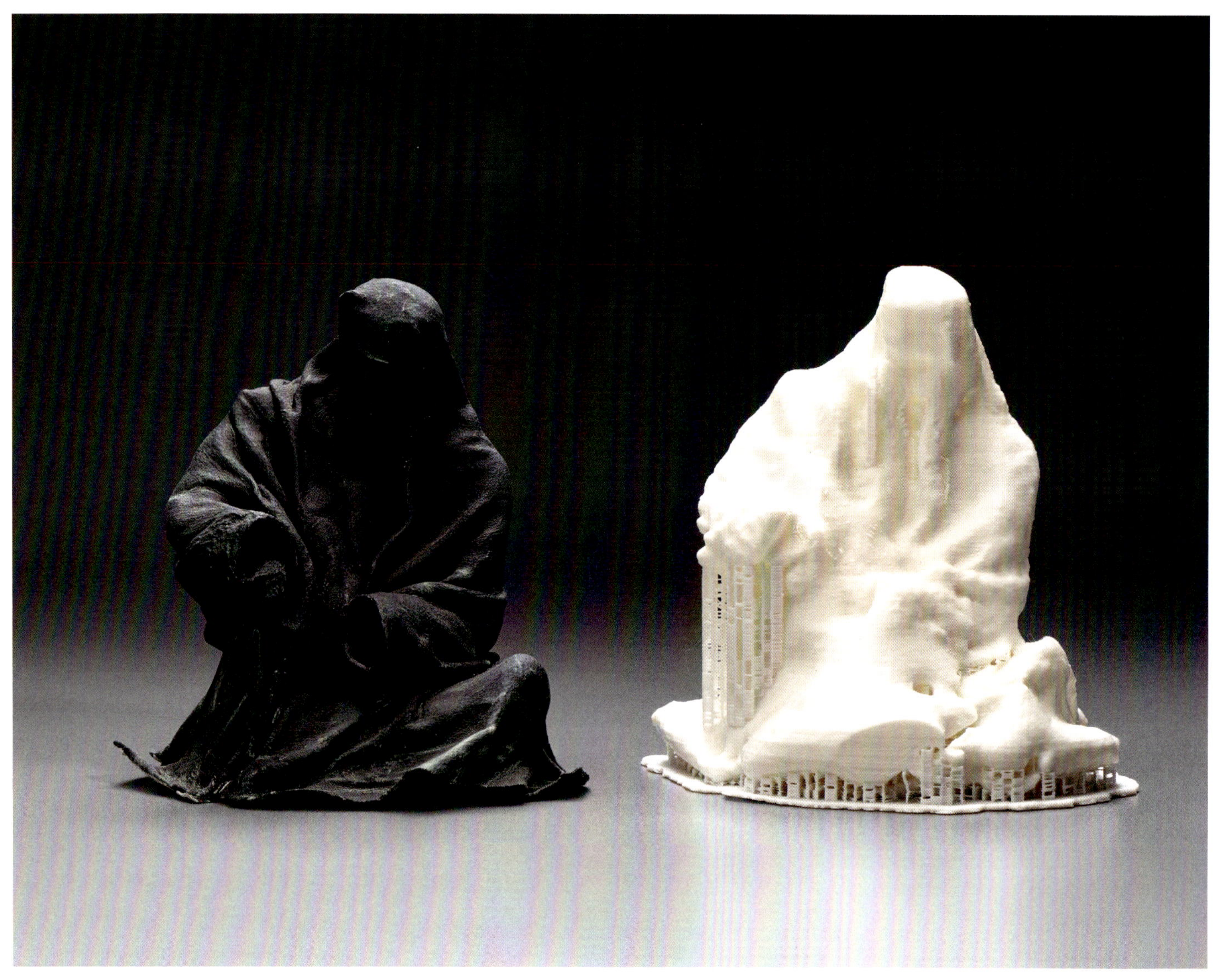

Note

The figurine at left, made from book-binding leather, reminded Chasanoff of the Pietá; the print at right was created from a 3-D scan of it.

Plate 163

(left) Leather figurine. (right) Untitled (Pietá), ca. 2014. 3-D-printed polylactic acid, 4 ¾ × 4 ¼ × 3 ¼ in. (12.1 × 10.8 × 8.3 cm).
Allan Chasanoff Archive, Yale University Art Gallery

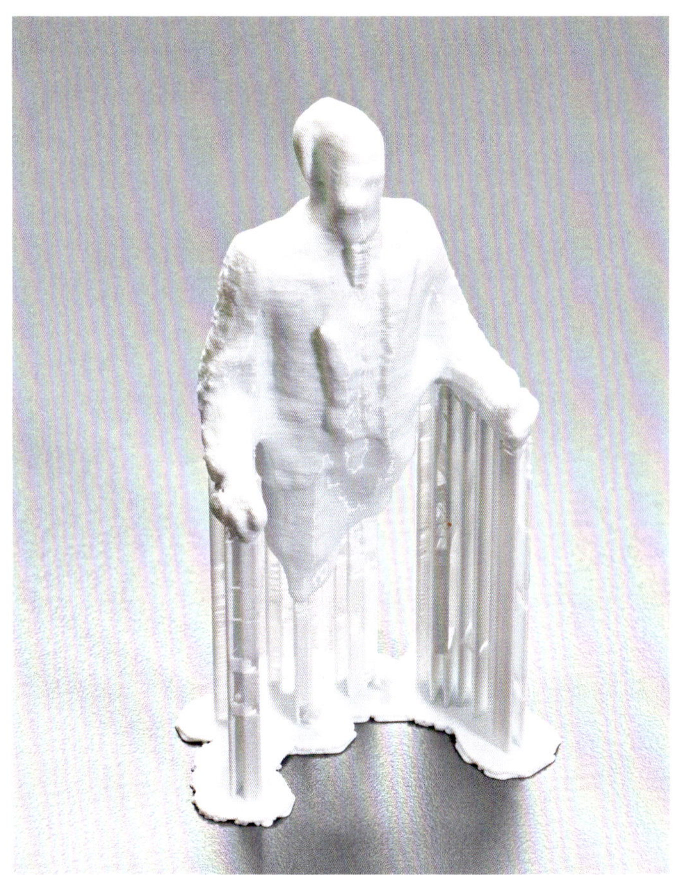

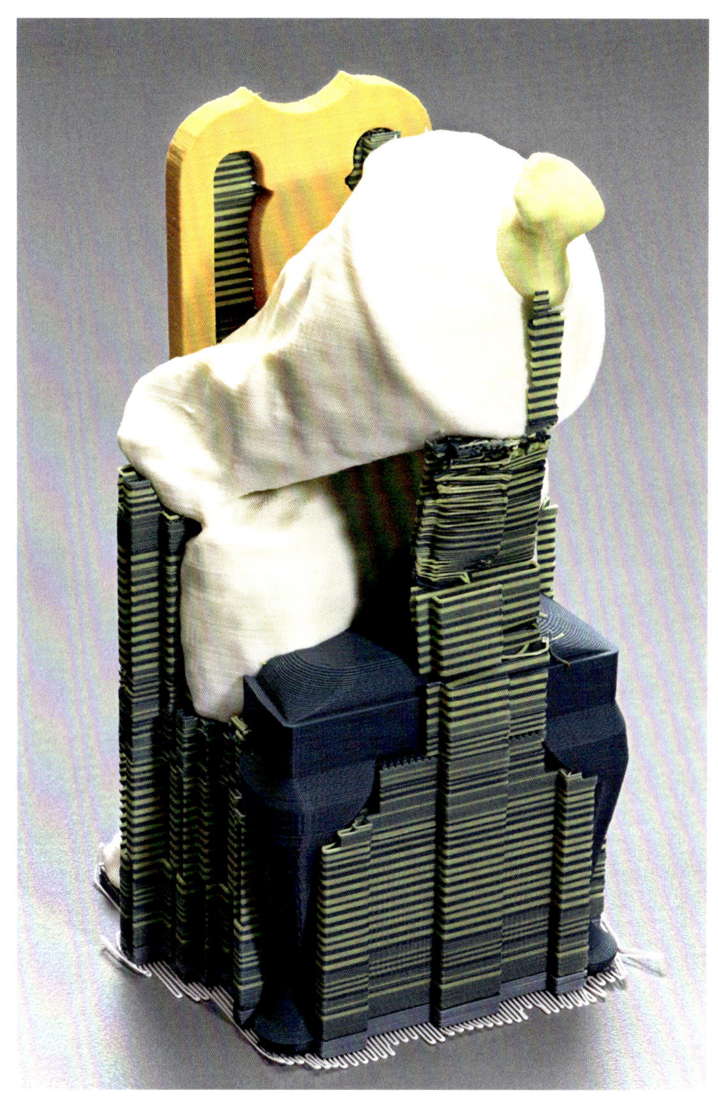

Note

The 3-D print in plate 164 was generated from a 3-D scan of a plastic figurine of Sigmund Freud.

Plate 164

Untitled (Freud), ca. 2013. 3-D-printed polylactic acid, 4 × 2 × 1½ in. (10.2 × 5.1 × 3.8 cm).
Allan Chasanoff Archive, Yale University Art Gallery

Plate 165

Untitled (chair with paint tube), ca. 2019–20. 3-D-printed polylactic acid,
4¾ × 2½ × 2½ in. (12.1 × 6.4 × 6.4 cm).
Allan Chasanoff Archive, Yale University Art Gallery

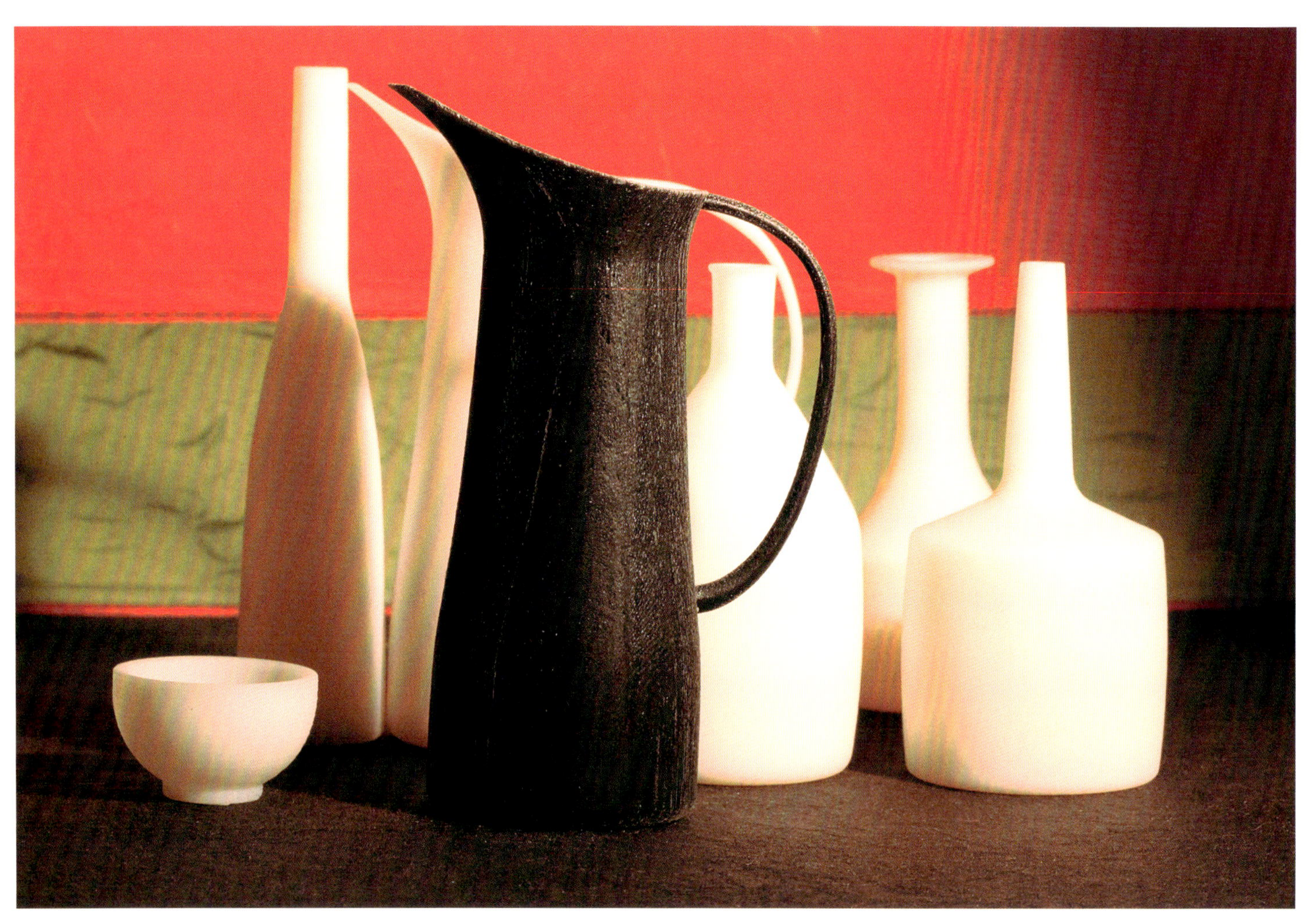

Note

This still life setup features 3-D prints inspired by the vessels in Chasanoff's preferred Giorgio Morandi work (see fig. 5). The prints were produced from files designed in the software Crystal in the 1990s.

Plate 166

No. 11347, 2009, pigmented inkjet print. Morandi series.
Allan Chasanoff Archive, Yale University Art Gallery

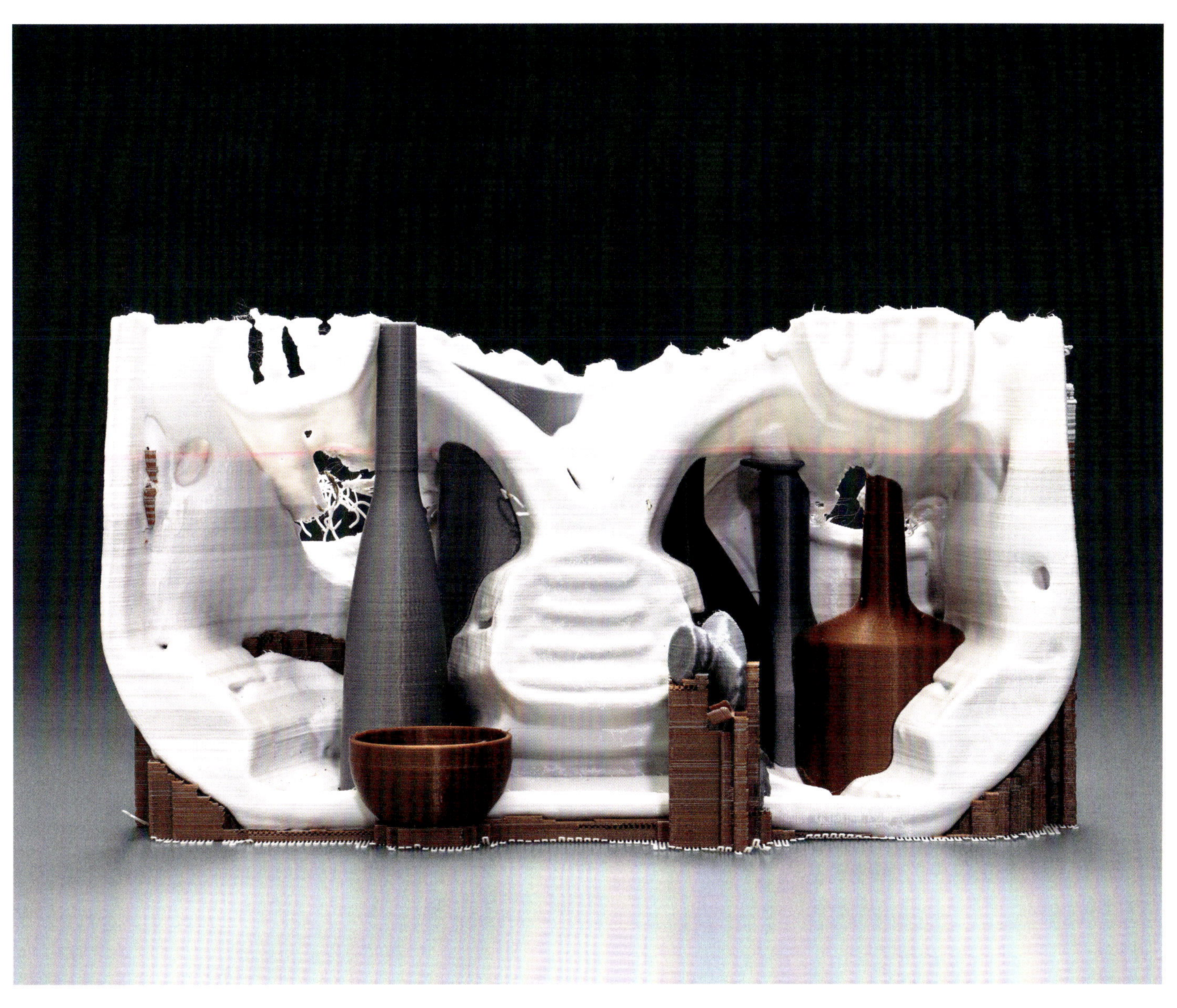

Plate 167

Untitled (cup carrier with Morandi vessels and paint tube), ca. 2019–20. 3-D-printed polylactic acid, 3 ¾ × 7 ¼ × 3 in. (9.5 × 18.4 × 7.6 cm). Morandi series. Allan Chasanoff Archive, Yale University Art Gallery

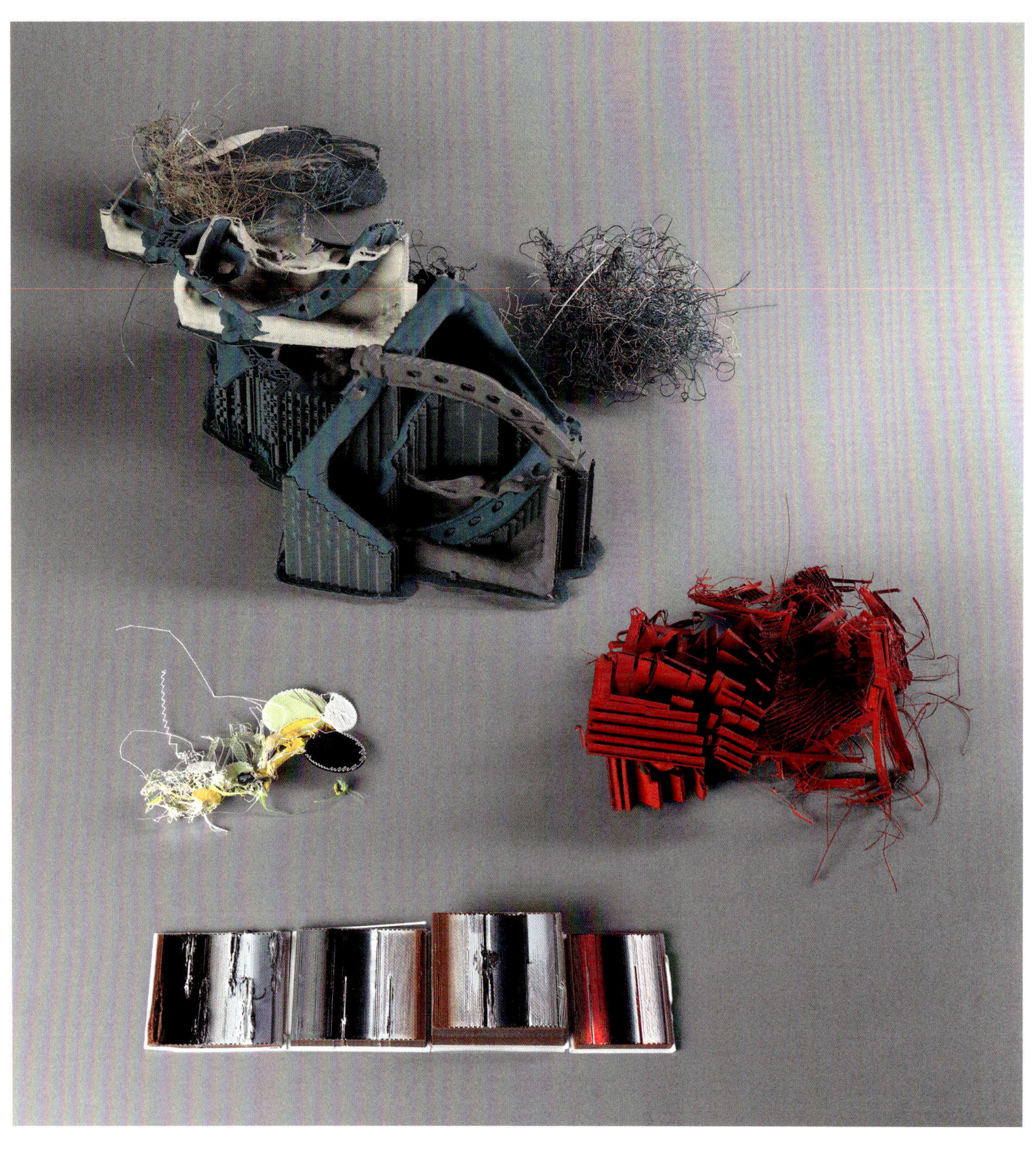

Note

At top, an untitled composition in blue and gray appears in a finished version (in front) and a version in which printing went wrong (behind). The pieces in the middle row are printer's errors; the four aligned striped pieces at bottom are printer's waste, or purge blocks. All appealed to Chasanoff as sculptures as well as props for still life setups.

Plate 168

Untitled, Untitled (printer's errors), Untitled (printer's waste or purge blocks), ca. 2019–20.
3-D-printed polylactic acid, overall 6 × 21 ½ × 25 in. (15.2 × 54.6 × 63.5 cm)
Allan Chasanoff Archive, Yale University Art Gallery

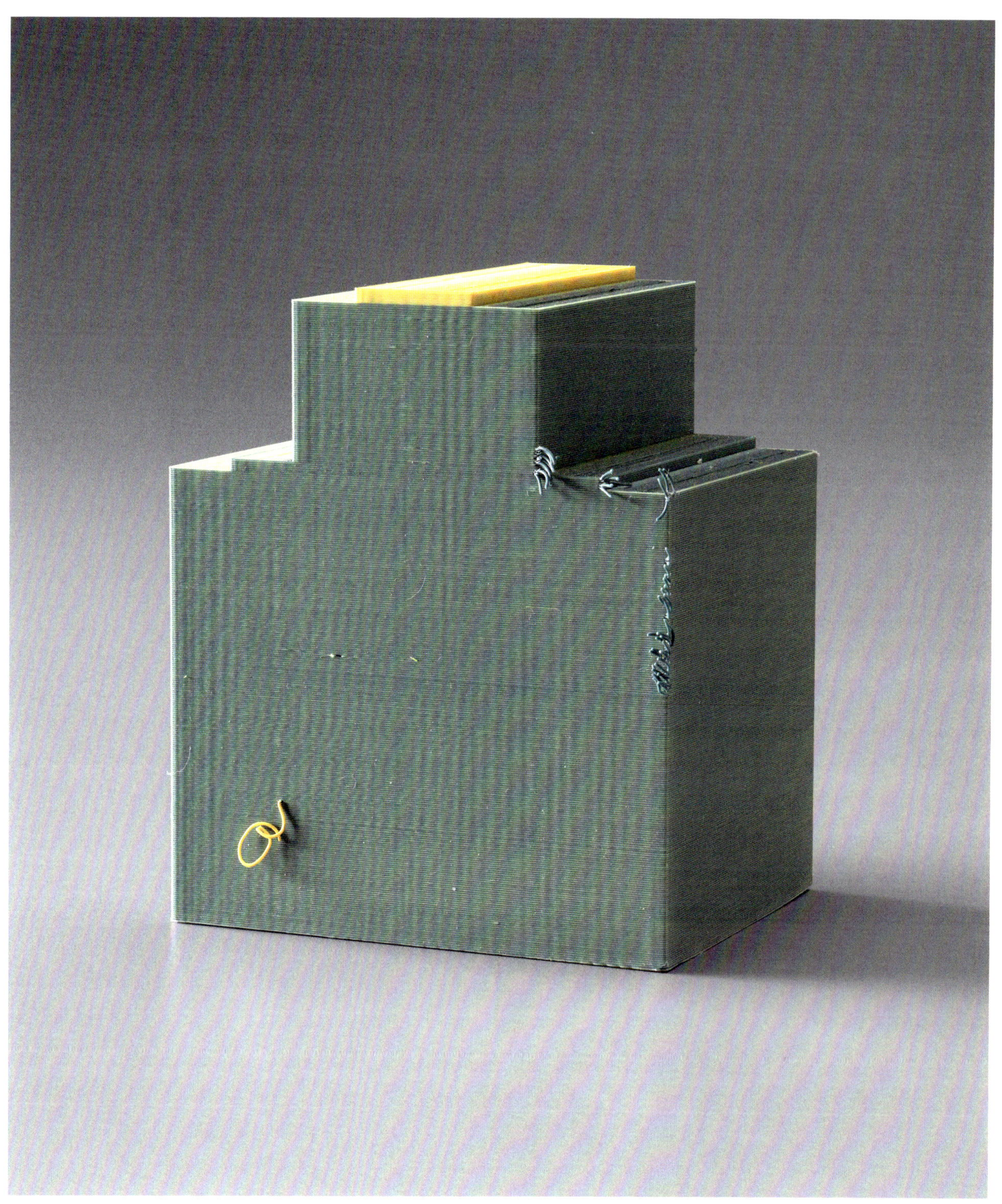

Plate 169
Untitled (printer's waste or purge block), ca. 2019–20. 3-D-printed polylactic acid, 3 ½ × 3 ½ × 2 ½ in. (8.9 × 8.9 × 6.4 cm)
Allan Chasanoff Archive, Yale University Art Gallery

Produced by the Yale University Art Gallery
Tiffany Sprague, Director of Publications and Editorial Services
Grace Zhou, Editorial and Production Assistant
Kathleen Mylen-Coulombe, Rights and Reproductions Coordinator

Project Editor: Livia Tenzer

Designed by Christopher Sleboda and Kathleen Sleboda
Typeset in 11 pt. ABC Diatype Semi-Mono
Printed by Meridian Printing in East Greenwich, R.I.

First printing

Yale University Art Gallery
1111 Chapel Street
P.O. Box 208271
New Haven, CT 06520-8271
artgallery.yale.edu/publications

Distributed by
Yale University Press
302 Temple Street
P.O. Box 209040
New Haven, CT 06520-9040
yalebooks.com/art

Library of Congress Control Number: 2023940479
ISBN 978-0-300-27339-7

Cover illustrations: (*front and back*) No. 11863, 2015, digital montage. Morandi (outline), Staircase (outline) series; half-title page: No. 7289, 2006, digital montage; p. 9: No. 3868, 1986, gelatin silver print; p. 10: No. 12407, 2012, pigmented inkjet print; p. 13: Nos. 6482, 6485, 6484, 2005, digital scans. Back of Photo series; p. 14: No. 1070, ca. 1996, digital montage; p. 17: Nos. 5655, 5599, 5602, 2002, digital scans. Cotton series; p. 18: No. 6545, 2004, digital scan. Erasure series; p. 21: No. 12632, 2018, extraction from digital photograph. Multi-Line project. All Allan Chasanoff Archive, Yale University Art Gallery

Photo credits: fig. 4: © Estate of Ray K. Metzker, Courtesy Howard Greenberg Gallery, New York. Photograph © The Museum of Fine Arts, Houston; fig. 5: © 2023 Artists Rights Society (ARS), New York/ SIAE, Rome; fig. 7: © Cy Twombly Foundation; p. 211, top right: © Freud Museum London; p. 211, bottom right: © Berenice Abbott/ Commerce Graphics Photo. Photograph © The Museum of Fine Arts, Houston; Jud Haggard; p. 215, top left: Courtesy Swann Auction Galleries